Conceiving Revolution:
Irish Nationalist Propaganda during the First World War

Conceiving Revolution

Irish Nationalist Propaganda during the First World War

Ben Novick

FOUR COURTS PRESS

This book was set in 10.5/12.5 pt Ehrhardt
by Mac Style Ltd, Scarborough, N. Yorkshire, England for
FOUR COURTS PRESS LTD
Fumbally Lane, Dublin 8, Ireland
Email: info@four-courts-press.ie
and in the United States for
FOUR COURTS PRESS
c/o ISBS, 5824 N.E. Hassalo Street, Portland, OR 97213.

© Ben Novick 2001

A catalogue record for this title is available from the British Library.

ISBN 1–85182–620–3

All rights reserved.
Without limiting the rights under copyright reserved above,
no part of this publication may be reproduced, stored in or introduced
into a retrieval system, or transmitted, in any form or by any means
(electronic, mechanical, photocopying, recording or otherwise),
without the prior written permission of both the
copyright owner and publisher of this book.

Printed in Great Britain by
MPG Books Ltd, Bodmin, Cornwall.

To Leo McNamara – friend and teacher

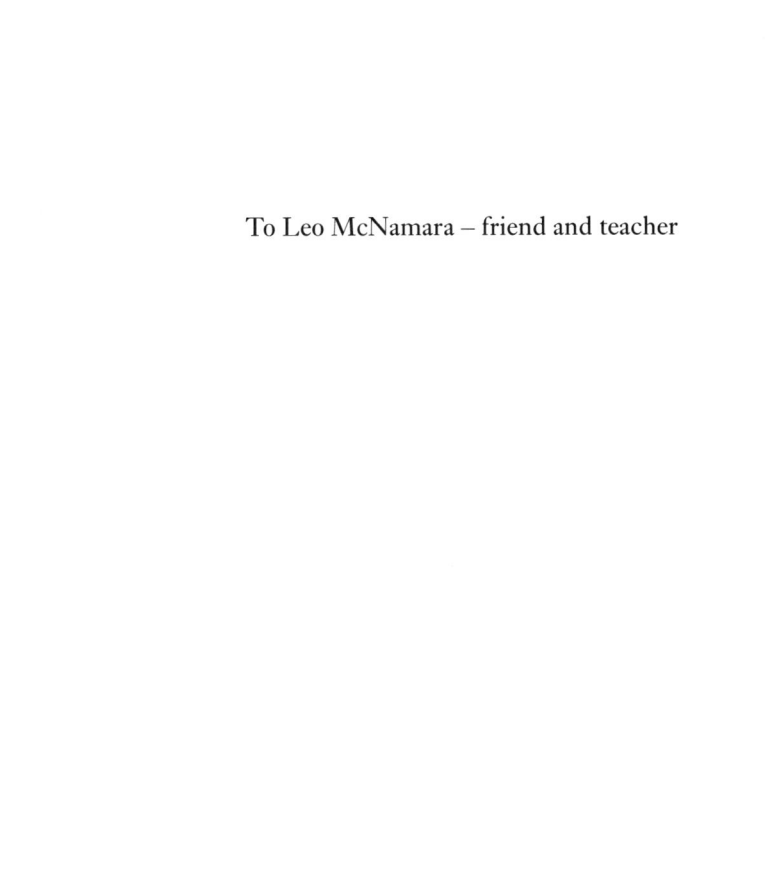

Contents

LIST OF ABBREVIATIONS	9
LIST OF ILLUSTRATIONS	11
ACKNOWLEDGMENTS	13
INTRODUCTION	15
1 Dupes, death and courage: advanced nationalist perceptions of the Great War and Irish soldiers in the British army	51
2 The Great War and the use of history in atrocity propaganda	72
3 Liars, savages, and the champion of Christianity: moral posturing and atrocity propaganda	103
4 Youth, sex, and Charlie Chaplin: 'moral tone' and the Irish revolution	132
5 Land agitation, famine, and the Great War, 1914–18	170
6 Humour in advanced nationalist propaganda	188
7 Aggression and the Irish revolution	222
CONCLUSION	246
SELECT BIBLIOGRAPHY	249
INDEX	263

Abbreviations

ACS	*An Claidheamh Soluis*
BNL	British Library Newspaper Library, Colindale
Bod	Bodleian Library, Oxford
CC	*Cork Celt*
CCORI	Central Council for the Organization of Recruiting in Ireland
CSORP	Chief Secretary's Office Registered Papers
CUL	Cambridge University Library
DRI	Department of Recruiting for Ireland
EHR	*English Historical Review*
EI	*Eire Ireland*
FF	*Fianna Fáil*
FJ	*Freeman's Journal*
Hib	*Hibernian*
Hon	*Honesty*
IC	*Irish Citizen*
IF	*Irish Freedom*
IHS	*Irish Historical Studies*
IRC	Irish Recruiting Council
IV	*Irish Volunteer*
IW	*Irish Worker*
IWI	*Irish Weekly Independent*
JCH	*Journal of Contemporary History*
JMH	*Journal of Modern History*
KSRL	Kenneth Spencer Research Library, University of Kansas, Lawrence, Kansas
NA	National Archives, Dublin
Nat	*Nationality*
NLI	National Library of Ireland, Dublin
Og	*Young Ireland (Eire Og)*
OH	P.S. O'Hegarty Collection, University of Kansas
PRO	Public Record Office, Kew
Samuels	Arthur Warren Samuels Collection, Trinity College, Dublin
SF	*Sinn Féin*

9

SFJ	*Sunday Freeman's Journal*
TCD	Trinity College, Dublin
UCD	University College, Dublin
WIT	*Weekly Irish Times*
WFJ	*Weekly Freeman's Journal*
WR	*Worker's Republic*

Illustrations

1.1	*Redmond's Advice!* (by-election poster, 1918, KSRL)	68
2.1	*Irishmen Avenge the Lusitania* (CCORI recruiting poster, 1915, TCD)	74
2.2	*Unconquerable!* (1916, Samuels Collection, TCD)	82
2.3	*Worse than Heppenstall, the Walking Gallows* (by-election leaflet, 1917, NLI)	95
3.1	*For the Glory of Ireland* (CCORI recruiting poster, 1914, TCD)	105
3.2	*Is Your Home Worth Fighting For?* (CCORI recruiting poster, 1915, TCD)	121
4.1	*The Coming of the Hun* (*Irish Worker*, 21 November 1914)	137
4.2	*The Last Hours of Padric Pearse* (propaganda poster, 1916, KSRL)	140
4.3	*Sean Healy* (propaganda leaflet, 1917, KSRL)	142
4.4	*Life among the Gaels of Old* (*Young Ireland (Eire Og)*, 2 June 1917)	145
4.5	*Irishmen – Why Don't You Join the Army?* (Sinn Féin leaflet, 1913 (?), KSRL)	155
4.6	*The Irish Party's Only Props in Longford* (by-election poster, 1917, KSRL)	159
4.7	*Imperial Theatre of Varieties* (*Spark*, 21 August 1915)	162
4.8	*Easter Week Commemoration Concert* (Sinn Féin advertisement, 1917, KSRL)	163
5.1	*Farmers of Ireland* (DRI recruiting poster, 1916 (?), TCD)	172
6.1	*When the 'T' Kettle Sings* (*Quiz*, October 1915)	191
6.2	*'Don't Larf, Chummies!'* (*Irish Fun*, Christmas and New Year, 1916)	199
6.3	*'On the Road'* (*Quiz*, October 1915)	200
6.4	*Dora* (Ballad cover sheet, 1918, Samuels Collection, TCD)	207
6.5	*Conscription* (anti-conscription cartoon, 1918, Samuels Collection, TCD)	209
6.6	*'Following in Father's Footsteps'* (Sinn Féin cartoon, 1918, Samuels Collection, TCD)	210
6.7	*'The Will of the People'* (Sinn Féin cartoon, 1918, Samuels Collection, TCD)	210
6.8	*De Valera's Handshake* (*Irish Fun*, January 1918)	214
6.9	*Gentle D.O.R.A.* (George Monks cartoon, 1918, Samuels Collection, TCD)	215

Illustrations

6.10 *The First Irish Conscript* (George Monks cartoon, 1918, Samuels Collection, TCD) 215
6.11 *The Conscripts' Chorus* (anti-conscription cartoon, 1918, Samuels Collection, TCD) 218
6.12 *Redmond & Co.* (cartoon, 1917, KSRL) 219
6.13 *The One Bright Spot!* (*Irish Worker*, 7 November 1914) 220
6.14 *In His Own Juice* (Sinn Féin cartoon, 1918, Samuels Collection, TCD) 221

CREDITS

Illustrations 4.1, 4.7, 6.3, 6.4, 6.16: British Library; 2.1, 3.1, 3.2, 5.1: Department of Early Printed Books, Trinity College, Dublin; 2.2, 6.7–10, 6.12–14, 6.17: Arthur Warren Samuels Collection, Trinity College, Dublin; 1.2, 4.2, 4.5–6, 4.8, 6.15: Department of Special Collections, Kenneth Spencer Library, University of Kansas; 6.1, 6.5–6: National Library of Ireland.

Acknowledgments

This book originated as a doctoral dissertation at Oxford University. As with the dissertation, I am grateful first and foremost to two people who have made all the difference to this book: Roy Foster and Senia Paseta. Roy was a model supervisor and an intellectual inspiration since my arrival in Oxford in the fall of 1996. Senia also worked closely with me while I was at Oxford, and went above and beyond the call of duty to read numerous drafts in my third year. These words can only acknowledge a debt to them that can never be repaid.

Working on this book, I have enjoyed the help and criticism of numerous scholars, both in Oxford and around the world. I am particularly grateful to my dissertation examiners, Charles Townshend and P.J. Waller, for their astute criticism and generous help. In Oxford, I wish to especially thank Adrian Gregory, Marc Mulholland, John Regan, and William Thomas for their friendship and advice. Roy Foster's bi-monthly seminar on Irish History provided me, as it has a generation of graduate students, regular inspiration and challenge. Elsewhere: Joost Augusteijn, Queen's University Belfast, and the attendees at his conference on the nature of the Irish Revolution; Joanna Bourke, Birkbeck College, University of London; Marie Coleman, University College Dublin; Richard English, Queen's University Belfast; David Fitzpatrick, Trinity College Dublin; Keith Jeffery, University of Ulster; and Patrick Maume, Queen's University Belfast, who has suffered gladly my numerous e-mails and letters regarding mysterious Irish nationalists, and always responded with a generous wealth of information.

In the United States, I was lucky to be able to present sections of the original dissertation at the annual meetings of the American Conference for Irish Studies, the largest professional association of Irish historians and literary scholars in the world. From the ACIS, I would like to especially thank Lawrence McBride, Illinois State University, for his trenchant editorial criticism; Sean Farrell Moran, Oakland University, for arranging a talk there on my research topic; Lucy McDiarmid, Villanova University, for her help and advice; and Gary Owens, University of Western Ontario, for reading an entire draft of my thesis. Joan Dean, University of Missouri-Kansas City, introduced me to the little-known P.S. O'Hegarty Collection at the University of Kansas, sending reams of photocopied material across the Atlantic, and then providing a lovely place to stay while I did my own research there in the summer of 1998. I am also grateful to the staff of the many archives in which I worked, especially James Helyar in the

Kenneth Spencer Research Library at the University of Kansas, who allowed me access to uncatalogued material in the P.S. O'Hegarty collection. I would like to acknowledge the generosity of Mrs Patricia Medley, for granting me access to the papers of Augustine Birrell deposited in the Bodleian Library, Oxford.

My numerous research trips to Ireland were made a delight by the generosity and friendship of John McBratney, who opened hearth and home to me, often on very short notice. I would also like to mention the friendship and hospitality of Colm Ó Cleirigh and Peter MacDermott, whose dinner parties still make my head hum.

Funding for the research that went into both my dissertation and this book was provided by a number of bodies, most significantly the British Marshall Aid Commemoration Commission, whose Marshall Scholarship allowed me to come to Oxford, and Merton College, whose Domus Senior Scholarship allowed me to complete this work on a generous cushion of funding. I am also grateful to the Governing Body of Christ Church, for support with research trips in 1997 and 1998; the Graduate Studies Board of the University of Oxford for financial support; the Faculty of Modern History for the A.M.P. Read Scholarship in 1998–1999; and the Beit Foundation for Commonwealth History, which funded a research trip to Kansas in 1998.

Throughout this process, my friends in England, Ireland and the United States have been ever supportive and helpful. Special mention must be made of three particular people who provided sharp insights during this time: Jeremy Dauber, Sarah Wilkinson, and Kate Heard.

I would like to thank my family, both here and abroad, for their constant love. Without them, this book, and far more, could never have happened.

Oxford – Ann Arbor
1996–2001

Introduction

'Ireland [is] in the care of a set of irresponsible fanatics', wrote Lily Yeats to John Quinn after the victory of Sinn Féin in the December 1918 General Election. 'They read nothing but their silly little papers written by their companions'.[1] The 'silly little papers' Yeats described were the newspapers of advanced nationalism.[2] These newspapers, together with broadsheets, ballads, speeches and poetry, formed the propaganda of the Irish revolution. In sum, this created what James C. Scott would later refer to as 'the first open statement of a hidden transcript, a declaration that breaches the etiquette of power relations'.[3] By speaking out in a co-ordinated fashion against British rule in Ireland, advanced nationalist propagandists made a 'symbolic declaration of war'.[4] The propaganda of 1914–18, however, occurred in the context of a literal declaration of war, and in the midst of Ireland's enthusiastic participation in and support for the war efforts of the United Kingdom. This book is the first full-length study of this propaganda during the Great War, exploring how the war influenced the discourse of revolutionary nationalism, and in turn, helped bring about the victory of Sinn Féin in December 1918.[5]

The irony of the early years of the Irish revolution lies in two sets of figures. Approximately 144,000 Irishmen joined the British armed forces as volunteers during the Great War, and another 58,000 reservists were mobilized immediately

1 New York Public Library, John Quinn Papers, Lily Yeats to John Quinn, 30.12.18. My thanks to Roy Foster for this citation. 2 'Advanced' nationalism or nationalist refers to Irish men and women who were interested in a greater degree of separation from the United Kingdom than that offered by Home Rule. This differentiates them from 'Constitutional' or 'Parliamentary' nationalists (also known as 'Redmondites'), who, for the most part, supported the war effort, believed in Home Rule, and followed the dictates of John Redmond's Irish Parliamentary Party. Using the term 'advanced' avoids the inaccurate and value-laden labelling of 'radical' or 'extreme', and allows one to cover all members of this area of the political spectrum – from the IRB to Sinn Féin, from conservative Catholics to political leftists such as Jim Larkin or James Connolly. 3 James C. Scott, *Domination and the Arts of Resistance: Hidden Transcripts* (New Haven, 1990), p. 8. 4 Ibid. 5 Even Michael Laffan's long-awaited study of Sinn Féin during this period (Michael Laffan, *The Resurrection of Ireland: The Sinn Féin Party, 1916–1923* [Cambridge, 1999]), while using pungent propaganda cartoons to illustrate its chapters, avoids any in-depth analysis of advanced nationalist propaganda during the Great War, save for a brief section that examines propaganda mainly to do with the Easter Rising. Patrick Maume's brilliant new book, *The Long Gestation: Irish Nationalist Life, 1891–1918* (Dublin, 1999), uses some advanced nationalist propaganda to demonstrate the ethos of radical nationalism during these 27 years, but his study is of a far larger subject than propaganda itself.

before the war began in August 1914.⁶ Balanced against these 202,000 were the 1,000 to 1,500 men and women who fought the British army in the streets of Dublin during the Easter Rising of 1916. Despite the more than hundred-fold difference in numbers, the experience of the Easter rebels has been constructed to hold a greater importance for the history of Ireland. The Easter Rising, not the Great War, has traditionally been acknowledged by historians of Ireland as the central political event of these years. To the victors go the spoils, including the construction of a national (and nationalist) history. In the Free State, Éire, and the Republic of Ireland, until very recently, political and commemorative constructions of the war years ignored the contribution of the men who fought in Ireland's name around the globe.

Even academic historians have fallen prey to this agenda. T.W. Moody and F.X. Martin's history textbook, *The Course of Irish History*, based on Radio Telefís Éireann presentations in the mid-1960s, and still used in its third edition by undergraduate courses around the world, makes no mention of the Great War.⁷ The flourishing of new historical work around the 1966 anniversary of the Rising, while producing excellent scholarship on nationalist movements, also virtually neglected the impact of the Great War.

The Great War reappeared in Irish historiography with the publication of F.S.L. Lyons' *Ireland since the Famine* (1971)⁸, but it was not until the 1980s that historians began detailed studies of Ireland's participation in the Great War. Led by David Fitzpatrick, historians such as Patrick Callan, Martin Staunton, Terence Denman, and Thomas Dooley⁹ saw Ireland as an integral part of the United Kingdom's war effort, its recruiting rates mirroring British trends, and its troops, Catholic and Protestant alike, facing the same odds as their British comrades. The second half of the 1990s has seen the re-invigoration of local studies. Historians such as Joost Augusteijn and Peter Hart, modelling their work on Fitzpatrick's ground-breaking *Politics and Irish Life* (1977), have begun to unravel the social, cultural, and economic backgrounds of the men and women who became revolutionaries, demonstrating that they shared many of the same characteristics as the men who joined the British army before and during the Great War.¹⁰

---

6 David Fitzpatrick, 'Militarism in Ireland, 1900–1922', in Thomas Bartlett and Keith Jeffery (eds.), *A Military History of Ireland* (Cambridge, 1996), pp. 386–8.   7 Donal McCartney, 'From Parnell to Pearse (1891–1921)', in T.W. Moody and F.X. Martin (eds.), *The Course of Irish History* (2nd ed, Cork, 1987), pp. 294–313.   8 F.S.L. Lyons, *Ireland since the Famine* (London, 1971).   9 Cf. Callan, 'Voluntary recruiting for the British army in Ireland during the First World War' (UCD, Ph.D., 1984); Staunton, 'The Royal Munster Fusiliers in the Great War, 1914–1919' (UCD, M.A., 1986); Denman, *Ireland's Unknown Soldiers: the 16th (Irish) Division in the Great War* (Dublin, 1992); Dooley, *Irishmen or English Soldiers?* (Liverpool, 1995).   10 Cf. Augusteijn, *From Public Defiance to Guerrilla Warfare: The Experience of Ordinary Volunteers in the Irish War of Independence, 1916–1921* (Dublin, 1996); Hart, *The I.R.A. and its Enemies: Violence and Community in Cork, 1916–1923* (Oxford, 1998).

This book is in large part an attempt to fill a hole in Irish historiography. From the work of Peter Hart and Joost Augusteijn, and David Fitzpatrick before them, the social structure of Irish republicanism has become far clearer. The more recent work of Thomas Hennessey[11] has explored the social structure of pro-war Ireland, but to this date no historian has adequately explored the connections between the Ireland that fought on the Somme and Gallipoli, and the Ireland that rose at Easter 1916. The two Irelands are inextricably linked.

Irish participation in the Great War reflected a European-wide pattern: an early surge of enthusiasm, both by civilians and volunteers; a long period of gradual decline in recruiting, marked first by boredom with the lack of action, and then frustration at the number of casualties; and finally, a general sense of war-weariness as the blood of young Irishmen kept flowing in the fields of France, Flanders, and Mesopotamia. This weariness and increasing horror of the impact of war was not alone enough to destroy support for the war, but its effects were noticeable. Dublin filled with wounded men, as did Cork and Belfast. In the worst days of 1915 and 1916, following offensives at Loos and the Somme, Dublin hospitals admitted 500 new cases a day.[12] Even staunch supporters of the war effort saw their faith crumbling following the destruction of the Irish Tenth Division at Gallipoli in the summer of 1915. Both Page Dickinson and Katharine Tynan saw Gallipoli, not the Easter Rising, as the moment their feelings towards the British began to turn. Dickinson, who had remarked on the absolute enthusiasm seen in Dublin upon the outbreak of war, could in later years barely write of Gallipoli,[13] while Katharine Tynan, recalling a visit to Dublin shortly after the disaster of Suvla Bay, wrote 'Dublin was full of mourning, and on the faces one met there was a hard brightness of pain as though the people's hearts burnt in the fire and were not consumed ... It was not easy to be happy'.[14]

The growing frustration in Ireland with the war helped turn the Great War from being a central event in the daily lives of Irish men and women into an integral factor in the revolutionary transformation of Irish society that took place during the war years and resulted in the victory of Sinn Féin in the December 1918 General Election. The propagandists of advanced nationalism, men and women experienced, for the most part, in the art of persuasive journalism, harnessed the general attitudes to the war and exploited them to create aggression against the age-old enemy of England. The war became the central theme of their propaganda, a propaganda that both influenced and reflected public opinion. Propagandists were able and willing to change classic tenets of nationalist faith in order to match public opinion and win votes.

11 Thomas Hennessey, *Dividing Ireland: World War I and Partition* (Dublin, 1998).   12 Neil O'Flanagan, *Dublin City in an Age of War and Revolution, 1914–1924* (UCD, M.A., 1985), pp. 41–3.   13 Page Dickinson, *The Dublin of Yesterday* (Dublin, 1929), pp. 71, 117–19.   14 Katharine Tynan, *The Years of the Shadow* (London, 1919), p. 178.

The Great War marked a watershed in Irish life, as it did elsewhere in Europe, and while hundreds of thousands of Irish men and women actively supported the war effort,[15] simultaneously a growing number of nationalists sent out the opposite message – a message of resistance to war, to conscription, and to British rule in Ireland. Opposition to war, and more specifically to the recruiting campaigns of the British government in Ireland, solidified support for the Sinn Féin party. The ground swell of popular sympathy that greeted the aftermath of the Easter Rising gave advanced nationalists an opening for practical success in Irish politics. The Easter Rising should be seen not as a transformative moment, but rather as a moment of intensification – a fulcrum upon which public opinion pivoted, and propaganda grew far more focused against the British and pro-war Irish. The war began to be used as a specific reason for joining Sinn Féin. By-election campaigns in the spring and summer of 1917 featured posters reminding voters that only Sinn Féin could save their sons from conscription. Military intelligence officers around Ireland after the Rising claimed that the rise in Sinn Féin membership was due to a fear of military service.[16] As Irish society grew weary with the long war, propagandists harnessed this frustration, converting it into anti-British views that could be channelled into support for advanced nationalism.

ORIGINS OF PROPAGANDA

The anti-war propaganda of advanced nationalists drew on a long tradition of anti-British writings. The most important influence on Arthur Griffith was the writing of Fenian activists, most especially John Mitchel's *Jail Journal*. Griffith wanted a copy of this book placed in every Sinn Féin club in Ireland. Fenian ideas permeated later propaganda. The glorification of prisoners stemmed from the memory of the rebellion of 1798, but even more from the journals of the Fenians and the commemoration of the Manchester Martyrs. Advanced nationalists saw no complication in seizing symbols and symbology used by Parliamentarians and Parnellites throughout the nineteenth century for their own.[17] For more extreme nationalists, men and women who planned the Easter Rising, the Fenian ideal of 'propaganda of deed' greatly influenced the strategy

---

15 If the numbers of active service recruits are not enough evidence for this statement, then one only need look at the reaction around Ireland to Armistice Day in 1918. Dublin was awash in Union Jacks, and soldiers were cheered throughout the countryside (cf. BNL, *IWI*, 16.11.18; *WIT*, 16.11.18). Even the advanced nationalist press admitted, albeit with disgust, that most people were thrilled the allies had won the war (cf. NLI, *An t-Oglach*, 30.11.18, pp. 3–4). While advanced nationalist propagandists, as will be demonstrated herein, were aware of the realities of the world in which they lived, nevertheless they did their best to deny the salient fact of Irish support for the war. 16 PRO, Colonial Office Papers, CO 904 157/1: Military Intelligence Reports, Midlands District, September 1916. 17 On this topic, see Lawrence McBride (ed.), *Images, Icons and the Irish Nationalist Imagination* (Dublin, 1999).

of the Rising itself. Rather than expecting a military victory, locations in Dublin were selected for their psychological and propagandistic impact on the population, instead of their defensive strength. Funerals, especially those of O'Donovan Rossa in 1915 and Thomas Ashe in 1917, were consciously modelled on the funeral procession of American Fenian Terence Bellew MacManus.[18]

The closest parallels between old and new propaganda can be found in the anti-recruiting propaganda of 1914. The Boer War, fought only fifteen years before, had been greeted with a great surge of anti-recruiting activity in Ireland. Despite the enthusiasm with which Irishmen joined the colours to fight in South Africa,[19] many others, including the majority of the Irish Parliamentary Party, were opposed to the war. The exploits of the Irish Brigade formed to fight alongside the Boers were avidly followed. The Irish Transvaal Committee, founded in 1899 by Arthur Griffith and Maud Gonne, made resistance to recruiting one of two planks in its platform. This committee in turn formed the nucleus of Cumann na nGaedhael. Griffith's new paper, the *United Irishman*, focused on stopping recruiting, arguing that resistance to the recruiting sergeant was part of a larger programme of self-reliance.[20]

With the formation of Sinn Féin and Bulmer Hobson's Belfast-based Dungannon Clubs in 1905, an anti-recruiting stance became central to an Irish advanced nationalist ethos. Hobson concentrated on producing and selling leaflets and handbills around Ireland by the thousands. Authorities, as during the Great War, were reluctant to prosecute, as these prosecutions were frequently unsuccessful and resulted in even greater publicity for advanced nationalists.[21] Many of the pamphlets produced by the Dungannon Clubs between 1905 and 1907 were reprinted in the early days of the Great War. Some were reproduced in their entirety, unchanged, such as the popular *Irishmen in the English Army*, written by Hobson, Alice Stopford Green, and Roger Casement, which appeared originally in 1906, and was reprinted in 1914.[22] Other leaflets were reproduced and changed only slightly, with Germany replacing South Africa as the target of English aggression.[23]

As with the Great War, the first decade of the twentieth century saw a multitude of advanced nationalist groups participating in the anti-recruiting movement. The IRB, Irish National Foresters, and the Board of Erin branch of the Ancient Order of the Hibernians (AOH) all participated, and British police thought that the Gaelic League, the Fianna, and the Gaelic Athletic Association (GAA) were especially active in the movement.[24] Of propagandists active during

---

18 See Chapter seven for a more detailed study of these two funerals. 19 O'Flanagan, 1985, p. 43. 20 Terence Denman, ' "The red livery of shame": the campaign against army recruitment in Ireland, 1899–1914', *IHS*, vol. 29, no. 114 (Nov. 1994), pp. 212–13, 218. 21 Ibid., pp. 220–1. 22 Ibid., p. 219. 23 PRO, Colonial Office Papers, CO 904/161/3: Distribution of Anti-Recruiting Leaflets, 1914–16, CO 904/162/2: Anti-Recruiting Notices seized, 1913–15. 24 Denman, 1994, pp. 222, 227–8.

the Great War (other than Griffith, James Connolly, and Hobson), Denis McCullough, P.T. Daly, Seamus MacManus, and Patrick O'Hourihan were all considered important anti-recruiting activists before 1910.[25]

The war years wrought great change on the style and focus of anti-recruiting propaganda,[26] and this book, especially chapter one, will explore this at greater length. The idea of being opposed to recruiting, and the idea that this was a necessary aspect of being an advanced nationalist did not begin with the Great War. The men and women who fought the recruiters of the British army during the war were walking a well-trodden path, and it would take some time before the unique nature of the war they resisted transformed their discourse into something original.

Advanced nationalist propaganda, the main focus of this book, formed only a small fraction of the total propaganda circulating in Ireland during the Great War. By far the largest amount of propaganda available to an Irish audience came from the British and pro-war Irish organizations tasked with creating and maintaining support for the allied war effort in Ireland. Pro-war propaganda is not what this book is about, but it does appear throughout for comparative purposes. It is therefore important to spend a little time discussing aspects of the pro-war propaganda campaign, focusing on the pattern of recruiting in Ireland, the sources of appeal in the propaganda, how propagandists actually worked, and the strength of large-scale circulation.

From Patrick Callan's 1984 UCD Ph.D. thesis, 'Voluntary Recruiting for the British Army in Ireland during the First World War', we learn that pro-war recruiting campaigns can be divided into five separate temporal periods. While the War Office and Irish Command had direct technical control over Irish recruiting until June 1918, in reality civilian agencies played a central role in the management and administration of the campaigns from 1915. During the first months of the war, until April 1915, recruiting propaganda in Ireland was organized on an *ad hoc* basis. Many of the surviving posters from this period are very similar to those issued by the Parliamentary Recruiting Committee (PRC) in Great Britain. Callan believes, and I agree, that this was because both the War Office and Irish Command 'shied away from introducing new material aimed specifically at nationalists. The soldiers feared what might spring out from that Pandora's box'.[27]

The Central Council for the Organization of Recruiting in Ireland (CCORI), which existed from April to October 1915, was not an especially effective organization. Hampered in its recruiting efforts by such factors as the introduction of a Coalition Government, including Sir Edward Carson, in the

---

25 Ibid., p. 223. 26 Although as D.G. Boyce correctly states, Éamon de Valera's rhetoric after the Easter Rising was quite close to a classic Parnellite style (D.G. Boyce, *Nationalism in Ireland* ([Baltimore, 1982]), pp. 316–19). 27 Callan, 1984, p. 270.

United Kingdom in May 1915, its tenure saw a drop in recruiting levels from just over 6,000 per month in March and April 1915 to less than 2,000 in September 1915.[28] The central problem with the CCORI was its traditional approach to recruiting. Propaganda campaigns under the aegis of the CCORI focused on poster campaigns, mass recruiting meetings at which political figures would speak, and regimental tours to promote recruiting for specific battalions. The posters created by the CCORI fall into two broad thematic categories: first, an appeal to 'team spirit' – the idea that Irishmen should join up so as not to let the side down; and second, a direct appeal to the men through the use of specific imagery of Irish women. Neither method seems to have been all that successful.[29]

The CCORI was replaced by the Department of Recruiting for Ireland (DRI) in October 1915. The head of the DRI was none other than the Viceroy, Lord Wimborne. This in itself was enough to set the DRI apart from most other recruiting organizations, few if any of which enjoyed such active support from a senior government official. The DRI had been set up at a recruiting conference held at the Viceregal Lodge in Dublin at the beginning of October. Representatives from the Irish Parliamentary Party (John Redmond and Maurice Moore), the Unionist Party (Sir John Lonsdale) and the Catholic Church all met with Lord Wimborne to discuss ways of improving recruiting. The primary task the conference set itself was the launching of a new recruiting campaign. This had been suggested by John Redmond, who wrote Wimborne early in the meeting to suggest that a letter encouraging enlistment be sent to every man in Ireland between the ages of 19 and 41. He felt that every recruitable man in Ireland could be best approached by receiving in the post a 'personal' letter signed by representatives of all parties urging him to enlist. While the postal campaign was in its first month, all other normal recruiting activities, such as platform speeches, posters, and press articles, would be suspended, so that they could be used later 'refreshed and with renewed grip on public attention'.[30] After a month, representative Irishmen from local Irish regiments would be sent on recruiting tours, and reminder letters would be sent, along with advertisements reminding men that if they joined under this scheme, they could choose the regiment they would serve with. Finally, in the sixth week of the campaign, all normal recruiting activities would resume.[31]

The postal campaign was launched on 10 October 1915. It started slowly. In the rural districts of Western Ireland, the sudden receipt of the letters caused a massive panic. In County Clare, the letters arrived at the end of October, creating 'much consternation at first, because it was looked on as compulsory, but when it became known that it was a voluntary matter, the uneasiness died down, and

28 Benjamin Novick, 'No Ordinary War: Ireland during the First World War' (University of Michigan, A.B. thesis, 1996), appendix I. 29 Ibid., pp. 31–2. 30 National Library of Ireland [NLI], MS 15259: John Redmond Papers, Memoranda on recruiting, 1914–18, Memo, Redmond to Wimborne, October 1915. 31 Ibid.

the people took very little notice of the request'.[32] The Unionist F.W. Pennefather wrote to Lord Tennyson in December:

> 'You have probably heard something about the recent stampede of Nationalists to America, though the English papers said as little as they could about it. The facts were there ... A new system of recruiting was started ... Throughout the West, where there has been hardly any recruiting, the Nationalists thought this was a certain prelude to Conscription, and resolved to be off. Every berth on every steamer out of Ireland was booked for weeks in advance.[33]

While Pennefather exaggerated the response of Irishmen in rural areas of the island, the timing of the new DRI campaign was such as to cause a particularly unpleasant incident in Liverpool during November. A group of male Irish emigrants boarding the *Saxonia*, a steamer bound for America, were attacked by a mob, who jeered at them for running from the war. Stokers on the ship in question refused to shovel coal, and the emigrants had to be offloaded and wait for a later voyage. Pro- and anti-war propagandists both exploited this unfortunate event. The *Weekly Irish Times*, claiming that the Irishmen's presence in Liverpool was a clear example of cowardice, declared in an editorial 'Everybody will applaud the action of the *Saxonia*'s crew. This is the first strike action which will have won complete approval'.[34] Seamus Upton, writing in the advanced nationalist *Honesty* had a different interpretation. He blamed the Royal Irish Constabulary for the entire incident, claiming:

> In at least one remote district in Ireland, far from daily newspapers and from authentic information as to happenings in the exterior world, the local members of the R.I.C. declared to the people of the countryside that Conscription was to be put into immediate operation. The result was that several young men of the district hastily gathered their little effects together, and, assisted by their relatives, booked their passages to America on the Cunard steamer, the *Saxonia*. We know the sequel. The guileless youths were amongst the Irish emigrants who received such a chivalrous reception at the hands of an English mob of 'eligibles' at Liverpool a few weeks back. Bully for the R.I.C.![35]

What is intriguing about the reportage surrounding this incident is that the advanced nationalists made no pretense of disagreeing with people leaving

---

32 Breandan Mac Giolla Choille, *Intelligence Notes of the Chief Secretary's Office, 1913–1916* (Dublin: Rialtas na hEireann, 1966), p. 146.   33 NLI MS 3249: F.W. Pennefather Letters, 1907–17, letter, Pennefather to Tennyson, 17 December 1915.   34 BNL, *WIT*, 15.4.16, p. 6.   35 BNL, *Hon*, 4.12.15, pp. 1–2.

Ireland when threatened with conscription at this early stage in the war. It is unlikely that the R.I.C. actually claimed conscription was being put into effect, but the sudden appearance of an official-looking letter from the Viceroy of Ireland, coupled with the transition in Great Britain from the Derby Scheme to conscription at the same time as the postal campaign was occurring, led many to believe that Ireland was close to conscription.

Despite these incidents, the new recruiting campaign of the DRI had gotten off to a relatively good start, although the possibility of getting the 10,000 men a month requested by Lord Wimborne seemed out of reach. Canon James Hannay pointed out that 'We have had no scenes in Ireland like those which took place in England during the last days of Lord Derby's campaign. But we have had a fairly steady supply of recruits. The flow of men, which had almost ceased when the Lord Lieutenant began his new effort, has started again'.[36] In the first month of the DRI's existence, 6,058 recruits joined, far below the goal of 10,000, but three times as many as had joined up in September, and well above the number necessary to support the Irish battalions then at the front.[37] By 18 December, seven weeks after the campaign commenced on 30 October, 7,444 recruits had joined, a weekly average of 1,063.[38] Wimborne excused the campaign's failure to achieve its unreasonable goal, stating 'It is certain that the holiday season and the temporary dislocation caused by the introduction of the Military Service Bill have had an adverse effect from which there are already signs of a definite recovery'.[39]

Part of the explanation for the relative success of the postal campaign lies in its novelty. By October 1915 the war had been dragging on for 14 months and the Irish people had already rejected the traditional methods of recruiting: bands, speeches, parades and posters. These methods had worked fairly well earlier in the war, most notably in the special recruiting drive organized by Hedley Le Bas in Waterford in February 1915. Le Bas, from the Channel Island of Jersey, was an advertising expert who worked for the War Office as a 'lay adviser' for recruiting. He believed that 'publicity will find or create anything',[40] and set out to prove this in Waterford, a city where he had served with the 15th Hussars in 1880.

Le Bas combined a canny set of recruiting methods: bands and musical performances were geared towards the recruiting drive, an action that echoed sympathetically with the Waterford working class.[41] Financial bonuses for enlisting were offered, and an absolute advertising blitz filled the windows of the

36 James Hannay, 'Recruiting in Ireland To-Day', *The Nineteenth Century and After*, vol. 79, no. 467 (Jan. 1916), p. 180. 37 NLI MS 15259: John Redmond Papers, Memoranda on Recruiting, 1914–18, Recruiting Returns, September to December 1915. 38 Ibid. 39 NLI MS 10557: Maurice Moore Papers, Documents concerning Irish Soldiers in the British Army, Viceroy's Report, January 1916. 40 Thomas Dooley, 'Politics, Bands, and Marketing: Army Recruiting in Waterford City for 1914–1915', *Irish Sword*, vol. xviii, no. 72 (Winter 1991), p. 211. 41 Ibid., p. 215.

city and the backs of hackney cabs with specially made posters. In March, a grand finale was held to the recruiting drive, a large meeting at which Belgian refugees played music and gave talks on German atrocities, local figures from the National Volunteers and the Irish Parliamentary Party spoke, and well-known Roman Catholic priests from the area gave sermons.[42] Thomas Dooley, who has analyzed this special effort by the War Office, remarks that the drive's success lay in two key factors: the neutralization of anti-British sentiment, and the tapping of the National Volunteers as a source for manpower through a strongly localized appeal.[43]

As we will see throughout this book, the neutralization of anti-British sentiment was one factor that rarely, if ever, occurred in Ireland. Waterford's recruiting drive succeeded so well because much time and effort was put into making it a special case, one in which the people targeted must have felt a personal level of appeal from the recruiters. On a national level, such methods met with little success, especially by the late fall of 1915 when the DRI was really getting under way. The DRI did attempt a few novel approaches. In Ballinasloe, in the early spring of 1916, airplanes dropped recruiting pamphlets on the town, and a large clock was erected that counted off the number of recruits from the town who had joined.[44] None of this appears to have worked. The efforts of the DRI simply encouraged increased resistance from Sinn Féin and other advanced nationalist groups. 'Sinn Feiners increased and multiplied in a most alarming way', wrote Canon Hannay. They carried on vigorous propaganda, interrupted meetings, hooted speeches ...'[45]

Another likely reason why the DRI met with little success after its initial surge is that many of the motivating factors in voluntary enlistment had disappeared by the second autumn of the Great War. Thomas Dooley, studying the rationale behind Irish volunteerism, has argued that:

> Mobilization, feverish military preparations and general 'manifestations of the martial spirit' were enough to inspire some men to enlist. The sight of uniforms, the pomp of military life and an infectious militarism touched the popular imagination and made a definite appeal. As in Cork, where soldiers acquired a new respectability and attracted admiring glances, the lure of war's glamour 'pulled susceptible young Irishmen'.[46]

By the autumn of 1915, the sight of military uniforms in Ireland was no longer a novelty, nor, after the heavy casualties suffered by Irish regiments at Gallipoli in the spring and summer of 1915, was the 'pomp' of military life enough to outweigh the fear and reluctance to enlist for a dangerous war. It was this fear that advanced nationalist anti-war propagandists so brilliantly exploited.

42 Ibid., p. 215.   43 Ibid., p. 216.   44 Denman, 1992, p. 136.   45 Hannay, 1916, p. 176.
46 Dooley, 1995, p. 128.

Anti-war propagandists were greatly aided by the Easter Rising of 1916. Not only did this rebellion help reinforce the advanced nationalist cause, it also forced the British and pro-war Irish to stop any active forms of recruiting. Tours, meetings, marches – all forms of recruiting propaganda save posters were abandoned for two years. Left with an open field, and with consistent British aggression to play off of, anti-war advanced nationalists made great strides with their propaganda in the 23 months between the Easter Rising and the Conscription Crisis of March 1918.

Pro-war propagandists responded to the failure of conscription by April of 1918 with the launching of the most curious of recruiting endeavors during the war: the Irish Recruiting Council (IRC). For the first time in the war, the British government allowed a recruiting organization to be run by elected officials, well-respected members of the Irish Parliamentary Party who had also served in the army during the war. Stephen Gwynn, A.M. Sullivan, Maurice Dockrell, and Henry McLaughlin together ran the Council, and based their recruiting style on the earlier postal campaign of the DRI. Sending a letter calling on Irishmen to 'restore the name of Ireland to its honoured place among nations of the world',[47] the parliamentary leaders waited to see if there would be any response. The recruitment levels in Ireland for the British army in these last months of the war have caused much controversy. Recruiting rates rose astronomically in the last three months of the war – 9,845 men joined between August and November 1918, against 5,812 in the preceding six months.[48] However, this number is deceptive. Desperate for men, the Royal Air Force (newly formed from the Royal Flying Corps) and the Tank Corps had both decreed that men who joined up for these branches of service would be trained in mechanical engineering and maintenance, services that would be greatly in demand once the war ended. Over thirty per cent of the Irish volunteers in the last three months of the war chose to enter these branches.[49]

Ironically, this final surge in recruiting rates helps prove the necessity of an active propaganda. If the IRC only got its campaign properly underway in August 1918, then the rise in recruiting must have had something to do with the novelty of proactive recruiting methods after a more than two-year lull. In the same way, advanced nationalist propaganda, which rarely saw a lull during the 1914–18 period, helped encourage enlistment in various radical independence movements.

What advantages did pro-war propaganda have over the anti-war propagandists that are the subject of this book? One clear advantage at the start of the war was the British army's traditional appeal to poor, urban Irishmen. Indeed, as Pauline Codd maintains in her pioneering article on recruiting in Wexford, '"Pull" factors such as patriotism or compassion for "poor little Belgium" provided far weaker incentives to enlist than did the "push" factor of

47 Novick, 1996, p. 96. 48 Callan, 1984, p. 42. 49 Ibid., p. 43.

poverty and insecurity. As before the war, servicemen were largely drawn from the urban working-class for whom soldiering provided an alternative to unemployment'.[50] In other words, until the high casualty figures of 1915 decimated Irish regiments, the British army continued to offer an appealing choice in contrast to stifling urban poverty. Pro-war propaganda had little to do with this factor, but in an indirect sense, was greatly aided in its task by this more traditional rationale for joining up.

More directly on the propaganda front, the pro-war forces in Ireland enjoyed the essential support, financially and legally, of the government, both in Britain and in the Irish Parliamentary Party. This factor can not be underestimated when one considers pro-war propaganda in Ireland. It meant that the *Freeman's Journal*, the enormously influential organ of the IPP, was 100 per cent behind the recruiting effort. It meant that nationally famous figures like the Redmond brothers, Tom Kettle, and Maurice Moore would lend their weight and influence to the recruiting campaigns. It meant, most of all, that propaganda posters, the most widespread form of recruiting propaganda, held three trump cards over their anti-war rivals:

1. Pro-war propagandists posted their recruiting messages across Ireland with the aid of the inimitable network of the Royal Irish Constabulary. Recruiting authorities sent their posters to local R.I.C. barracks across Ireland and expected the police to post them around towns and villages and to remove anti-war posters that might have been displayed as well. According to Henry Robinson, the R.I.C. were 'kept busy as recruiting posters, anti-recruiting posters, Sinn Fein and rebel manifests [sic] ... shouted at the people from the blank walls all over the country'.[51]
2. Pro-war propagandists could send their messages around the country without fear of legal censorship, and their newspapers published freely throughout the course of the war, voluntarily cooperating with the Press Censor, Lord Decies. In contrast, the British masterminded a large-scale postal censorship campaign against advanced nationalists during the war,[52] and, as is discussed elsewhere in this book, constantly harassed and shut down advanced nationalist newspapers.
3. The financial support of the British government allowed pro-war propagandists to produce far more colourful and better-made posters – in numbers, as discussed elsewhere, exponentially greater than the anti-war material studied in this book. Extrapolating from the known print runs for recruiting posters preserved at Trinity College (the most complete collection still in existence), Patrick Callan reaches a total number of 1,843,286 posters.[53] We cannot be certain of the exact numbers of the pro-war posters produced

50 Pauline Codd, 'Recruiting and Responses to the War in Wexford', in Fitzpatrick (ed.), 1988, pp. 25–6. 51 Cit. in Callan, 1984, p. 276. 52 Cf. Ben Novick, 'Postal Censorship in Ireland, 1914–1916', *IHS*, vol. 31, no. 123 (May 1999), pp. 343–56. 53 Callan, 1984, p. 304.

in Ireland during the Great War, or their total cost, but it is clear that the populace was swamped with pro-war and pro-recruiting imagery.

This section has served as a brief overview of the pro-war recruiting propaganda campaigns active in Ireland at the same time as the anti-war campaigns that are the subject of this book. It is impossible to study the one without being aware of the other. As this book is an effort to explain some of the factors in the shift of Irish public opinion from pro- to anti-war, and from Home Rule to independence, we must be aware that the walls of Irish cities and the backs of Irish cabs bore posters that extolled the British army, and posters that scorned it.

PROPAGANDA AND PROPAGANDISTS

Much propaganda produced during the Great War is lost, either through the wear and tear of time, or through the destruction of the Four Courts during the Irish Civil War. The ballads and broadsheets printed by advanced nationalists during the war were flimsy, and it is only in the past thirty years that archives and research libraries have acknowledged their potential importance, and turned their attention to preservation. For this book, collections of propaganda were examined at five major sites: Trinity College and University College, Dublin; the National Library of Ireland; the Kenneth Spencer Research Library at the University of Kansas, Lawrence, Kansas; and Cambridge University Library. Trinity College holds the private collection of Arthur Warren Samuels, Solicitor-General for Ireland between 1917 and 1919. Samuels ordered police to turn samples of seized material over to him. Thus, this collection, while strong on post-1916 material, nevertheless reflects a double bias – first, it only drew on seized material, and second, it only contains material that interested Samuels himself. The National Library holds a more extensive collection of ephemera, especially in the William O'Brien papers, and a virtually complete run of Sinn Féin election pamphlets from the General Election of 1918. At the University of Kansas, the Kenneth Spencer Research Library holds the P.S. O'Hegarty Collection, which includes uncatalogued material generously made available for this project. In the archives at University College, Dublin, private papers of important nationalists hold personal collections of propaganda, including many election leaflets and much poetry. The majority of propaganda used in this study, however, comes from the advanced nationalist press, much of which is preserved at the British Newspaper Library in Colindale, as well as some in the National Library of Ireland.

Ephemeral propaganda from 1917 was produced by an official Sinn Féin Department of Publicity, run by Robert Brennan, who was ably assisted by Desmond FitzGerald and Frank Gallagher.[54] A recent memoir by Michael Kevin

---

54 Cf. Robert Brennan, *Allegiance* (Dublin, 1950); Desmond FitzGerald, *Memoirs of Desmond FitzGerald, 1913–1916* (Dublin, 1968); Frank Gallagher ['David Hogan'], *The Four Glorious*

O'Doherty reveals that his father, Seamus O'Doherty, also helped Brennan, and O'Doherty even credits his mother with creating the well-used election slogan 'Put Him In to Get Him Out'.[55] Éamon de Valera also took an active role in editing election propaganda, in part because he disliked Arthur Griffith's influence as a propagandist.[56]

A large portion of the ephemeral material is drawn from ballad sheet manuscripts. This is a source that has rarely been used by past historians,[57] but is now being recognized as important in its own right.[58] To understand what James Cahalan calls 'the secular myth of the nation-state', cultural historians must 'piece it together from a thousand scattered sources and render it explicit'.[59] Gary Owens ranks songs as equal in importance with histories, poems, novels, and monuments in constructing and articulating the idea of an Irish nation.[60] The ballad style, and the production of ballad sheets, has always been a popular form of cultural dissemination in Ireland. However, these ballads were not always popular with advanced nationalist groups, especially in the nineteenth century. As David Lloyd points out, the vast majority of nineteenth- and early twentieth-century ballads were urban, and reflected not the idealized peasant culture promoted by nationalists, but rather the gritty milieu of the Dublin and Belfast streets from whence they came.[61] Ballad sheets remain important historical source, however, because they 'carried on a fugitive existence in the margins between the personal and the political, charging a personal event or memory with the impact of a political catastrophe – and vice versa'.[62] The prolific number of political ballads that remain from the war years leads one to believe that these formed an important part of the advanced nationalist propaganda campaign, although direct evidence for this is rare, and somewhat conflicting. In contrast to the careers of Sean O'Casey and Peadar Kearney, both of whom first became known as nationalist balladeers, other ballad writers at the time had less success at integrating their songs into the corpus of nationalist music. A programme for a November 1916 Manchester Martyrs' Commemoration Concert in Cork shows

---

Years (Dublin, 1953). Herbert Pim, in his unreliable 1920 memoir *Sinn Féin* (Belfast, 1920), claimed that 'hundreds of leaflets were distributed, all purporting to come from the 'National Council' but really the work of the writer' (Pim, 1920, p. 23).   55 Michael Kevin O'Doherty, *My Parents and Other Rebels* (Dublin, 1999), p. 24.   56 Brennan, 1950, p. 163.   57 C. Desmond Greaves' *The Easter Rising in Song and Ballad* (London, 1980) preserves the music and words for some of the ballads examined in the course of this research, but this collection is virtually unique among secondary works on the period.   58 The standard work still remains George-Denis Zimmerman's interesting yet incomplete work *Irish Street Ballads and Rebel Songs, 1798–1900* (Geneva, 1966).   59 James M. Cahalan, *Great Hatred, Little Room: The Irish Historical Novel* (Syracuse, NY, 1983), p. 18.   60 Gary Owens, 'Nationalist Monuments in Ireland *c*.1870–1914: Symbolism and Ritual', in Raymond Gillespie and Brian Kennedy (eds.), *Ireland: Art into History* (Dublin, 1994), p. 117.   61 David Lloyd, *Anomalous States: Irish Writing and the Post-Colonial Movement* (Dublin, 1993), pp. 92–3.   62 Luke Gibbon, *Transformations in Irish Culture* (Cork, 1996), pp. 145–6.

that only two current political songs, the 'Frongoch' version of *Alive, Alive, O!* and Eamonn Ceannt's *Ireland over All* were performed along with such old chestnuts as *Who Fears to Speak of '98* and *God Save Ireland.*[63]

Many of the ballads written during the war appeared first in the newspapers of the advanced nationalist press. The newspapers of advanced nationalism presented a far from monolithic political viewpoint during the war years, and a close textual study of the surviving papers highlights ideological fissures within the movements of advanced nationalism. Some subjectivity was involved in the choice of newspapers to examine. Experts differ on how many newspapers in Ireland can be classified as 'advanced nationalist' during the war. If one includes regional newspapers that published 'Sinn Féin Notes' sent out by Sinn Féin Headquarters in Dublin, then 24 newspapers could be counted.[64] However, only 12 of these newspapers had national circulation, and most that published 'Sinn Féin Notes' contained no other propaganda. Very few regional advanced nationalist newspapers survive, and this study focuses therefore on newspapers with national circulation that were written by activist propagandists.[65] Also eliminated from the study were newspapers that only came around to a 'Sinn Féin line' in the last six months of the war, and labour papers after 1916, as labour moved away from the nationalist line espoused by James Connolly and Jim Larkin before the Easter Rising. Papers with larger circulation that appealed to constitutional nationalists or unionists (*Freeman's Journal, Irish Independent* and *Irish Times*), along with D.P. Moran's *Leader*, which modified its anti-British tone as soon as the British authorities complained, were used solely for purposes of contextualization, as none of these papers was intended as advanced nationalist propaganda. *Scissors and Paste*, a newspaper begun by Arthur Griffith as a direct challenge to censorship regulations, was also left out of the study. While it caused great difficulties for British authorities, it included no new writing, consisting entirely of clippings pasted together from pre-war and pro-British newspapers.

The newspapers and journals studied can be divided into nine categories:

- **Arthur Griffith/Sinn Féin**: Arthur Griffith (ed.), *Sinn Féin* (1914); Arthur Griffith (ed.), *Eire Ireland* (1914); Arthur Griffith, Seamus O'Kelly (eds.), *Nationality* (1915–16, 1917–18); Herbert M. Pim ('A. Newman') (ed.), *Irishman* (1916–18).
- **Physical Force/IRB**: Sean MacDermott, Bulmer Hobson, P.S. O'Hegarty (eds.), *Irish Freedom* (1914); Terence MacSwiney (ed.), *Fianna Fáil* (1914);

63 KSRL, OH D590: 'Programme of 1916 Manchester Martyr's Commemoration Concert, Cork'. 64 Research list compiled from appendix in Virginia Glandon, *Arthur Griffith and the Advanced Nationalist Press* (New York, 1985), holdings in the British Newspaper Library, and the National Library of Ireland. My thanks to Dr Senia Paseta and Dr Ben Levitas for their help in producing this list. 65 A good summary of these major newspapers can be found in Maume, 1999, pp. 162–3, and in Glandon, 1985.

Sean Doyle ('Ed. Dalton') (ed.), *Spark* (1915-16); Seamus Upton ('Gilbert Galbraith') (ed.), *Honesty* (1915-16); Piaras Beaslai (ed.), *An t-Oglach* (1918).
- **Irish Volunteer – Official**: Laurence de Lacey, Eoin MacNeill, Bulmer Hobson (eds.), *Irish Volunteer* (1914-16); Anon. (ed.), *Cork Celt* (1914).
- **Catholic**: J.J. O'Kelly (ed.), *Catholic Bulletin* (1914-18); Reverend F.S. Pollard, John J. Scollan (eds.), *Hibernian* (1915-16).
- **Irish-Ireland**: The O'Rahilly (ed.), *An Claidheamh Soluis* (1914-16) Manus O'Donnell, J. Ford, Piaras Beaslai (eds.), (1916-18); Edward Dwyer (ed.), *Gael* (1916).
- **Labour**: Jim Larkin, James Connolly (eds.), *Irish Worker* (1914); James Connolly (ed.), *Irish Work* (1914); James Connolly (ed.), *Worker* (1915); James Connolly (ed.), *Worker's Republic* (1915-16).
- **Suffragist**: Francis and Hanna Sheehy-Skeffington (eds.), *Irish Citizen* (1914-18).
- **Youth**: Bulmer Hobson (ed.), *Fianna* (1915-16); Aodh de Blacam, M.S. O'Lonnain (eds.), *Young Ireland (Eire Og)* (1917-18); Brian O'Higgins (ed.), *St Enda's* (1918).
- **Humour**: Brian O'Higgins (ed.), *Quiz* (1915); Brian O'Higgins (ed.), *Irish Fun* (1915-16, 1917-18).

While not much is known of the backgrounds or subsequent life of some of these editors and propagandists, anecdotal information remains about how they produced advanced nationalist newspapers. With the exception of Griffith's short-lived daily *Eire Ireland* (1914), advanced nationalist papers were either weeklies or monthlies. Weekly papers were finished by Wednesday night or Thursday morning, and published on the Saturday of each week. Robert Brennan, who worked with Arthur Griffith in 1917 and 1918, recalled that Griffith himself wrote most of the leading articles for his newspapers, and this seems to be a consistent pattern with all editors, who set both the general tone and the actual text of these papers.[66]

These newspaper propagandists moved in a small world of nationalist Dublin. Of the editors whose backgrounds are known, only Herbert Pim, Laurence de Lacey and Terence MacSwiney consistently worked in cities other than Dublin.[67] Pim, a Belfast Quaker who converted to catholicism in 1912 and took the pseudonym A. Newman, based his work in Belfast and Dublin during the war. MacSwiney split his time between Cork and Dublin, organising for the IRB and Irish Volunteers, editing the Cork-based *Fianna Fáil* until its closure at the end of November 1914 and contributing vitriolic articles to the *Irish Volunteer*. De Lacey, editor of the *Irish Volunteer* until December 1914, had started his

---

[66] Brennan, 1950, pp. 207-8. [67] Arthur Griffith's first series of *Nationality* (1915-1916) was printed in Belfast, but its editorial department remained in Dublin. (R.M. Henry, *The Evolution of Sinn Féin*, Dublin, 1920, p. 188).

journalistic career on the *Enniscorthy Echo*, and printed the *Volunteer* on the presses in Enniscorthy. De Lacey was an active Volunteer and IRB member, who fled to America in February 1915 after police discovered two men in possession of gelignite and seditious leaflets hiding in his home.[68]

Two printers were used regularly by most of these newspapers: Patrick Mahon on Yarnhall Street, whose presses printed the *Irish Volunteer* after December 1914, *Eire Ireland*, *Sinn Féin*, *Scissors and Paste*, and the second series of *Nationality*; and the Gaelic Press, located on Liffey Street. Mahon was a thorn in the side of British officialdom. When his presses were seized in February 1915 following the closure of *Scissors and Paste*, Mahon successfully sued Dublin Castle and had his material returned after a month's delay.[69] The Gaelic Press, printer of the *Spark*, *Honesty*, and the *Gael*, was raided in March 1916 following a particularly violent editorial in the *Gael*. Its premises were smashed apart, but quickly rebuilt following a fund-raising campaign begun in the *Spark* and *Honesty*.[70]

The support of the editors of the *Spark* and *Honesty* for their fellow journalists in the *Gael* highlights an important element of journalistic propaganda during the Great War – the co-operation between editors of different papers. Newspapers frequently re-printed columns, poems, and editorials from different nationalist papers, and new papers on the scene were greeted as welcome additions rather than competition. This can be best seen in the close relationship between Pim, Griffith, and de Blacam. Pim agreed to turn the *Irishman* into a Sinn Féin paper after the Rising, as Griffith was still in prison and unable to resurrect *Nationality*. When de Blacam decided to found *Young Ireland* in April 1917 in order to help mould the nationalist ideals of Irish children, Pim became a prolific contributor of detective stories, gave *Young Ireland* free advertising space in the *Irishman*, and encouraged readers of the *Irishman* to subscribe to *Young Ireland*. Griffith in turn allowed *Young Ireland* to use Sinn Féin Headquarters on Harcourt Street as its editorial offices from the summer of 1917.

The funding for these newspapers reflected the spectrum of political views that they represented. Throughout the war the British government remained

---

68 PRO, Colonial Office Papers, CO 903/19: Chief Secretary's Office Judicial Division: Intelligence Notes, 1915, fols. 33–34; *IV*, February 1915 et fl. De Lacey ended up in San Francisco, where he married and began to edit a weekly paper, the *Leader*. In 1917 he was sentenced to 18 months in prison and fined $5000 for entering into a conspiracy to liberate Franz Bopp, the former German Consul-General, and E.H. Von Schack, the Vice-Consul, both of whom had been interned in April 1917. (Cf. BNL, *WIT*, 3.11.17, p. 2). **69** PRO, Colonial Office Papers, CO 904/160/2: Suppression of Newspapers: 'Scissors and Paste', 1914–1915, Letter, Corrigan & Corrigan to Chief Secretary's Office, Dublin Castle, 13 March 1915. Cf. also Ben Novick, 'DORA, Suppression, and Nationalist Propaganda in Ireland, 1914–1915', *New Hibernia Review*, vol. 1, no. 4 (Winter 1997) [1997a], pp. 41–57. **70** BNL, *Spark*, 2.4.16, 9.4.16; *Hon*, 8.4.16.

convinced that advanced nationalist papers were funded by 'German gold'. Parliamentary accusations of this nature drove Augustine Birrell to approve the first wave of official newspaper closures in late November 1914,[71] and Eoin MacNeill was dogged by accusations of taking German gold, often made by the parliamentarian Lord Mayor of Dublin, Lorcan Sherlock.[72] This accusation was never proven during the war, and research for this book has uncovered no evidence to further support such a claim. Newspapers were funded in a variety of ways. Official newspapers of various movements received support from their parent organizations. Thus, the *Irish Volunteer* received part of the dues paid into the central committee by Irish Volunteers,[73] and the IRB supported *Irish Freedom*. The IRB also sponsored Arthur Griffith's first series of *Nationality* (1915–16), but he had to rely on private contributions for the second series.[74] Griffith's earlier 1914 papers were supported in part by organizations (*Sinn Féin*), and in part through individual contributions (*Eire Ireland*). American organizations also gave money. The *Hibernian*, mouthpiece of the Ancient Order of Hibernians Irish-American Alliance wing, was supported by contributions from AOH branches in the United States. All newspapers supported by the IRB were, in reality, reliant on funds from Clan-na-Gael.[75] Labour papers were supported by subscriptions, charity, and occasional union dues. Most other newspapers not linked to an organization relied on advertisements, and the support of like-minded nationalists, as seen with the launch of *Young Ireland (Eire Og)* in 1917. Despite the variance of political and social beliefs expounded in the newspapers, a close web of support was drawn between advanced nationalists of all stripes.

Ironically, while we know a fair amount about production and funding of newspapers, very little is known about the men and women who produced these newspapers. Best known is Arthur Griffith, supreme propagandist of the Irish revolution. Editing four newspapers himself, his influence also extended to other propagandists. Herbert Pim's *Irishman* was converted to a Sinn Féin paper

---

71 Cf. Novick, 1997a, pp. 41–57.   72 Cf., among others, BNL, *EI*, 4.11.14, p. 2. Sherlock would later deny that he made these accusations. Cf. BNL, *IWI*, 19.12.14, p. 5.   73 The *Irish Volunteer* is unique. Founded by the proprietors of the *Enniscorthy Echo*, led by William Sears, in January 1914, it was to be both a private commercial venture and the mouthpiece of the organisation. Until the end of November 1914, it was edited and published by Laurence de Lacey in Enniscorthy. At the end of November, warned by the British government, the proprietors decided to stop printing, at which point £100 was advanced from Volunteer funds and it began to be written and published at Volunteer headquarters in Dublin. Eoin MacNeill was the titular editor, but wrote only the notes on the first page, leaving the actual editorial and managerial work to Bulmer Hobson (cf. Bulmer Hobson, *Ireland Yesterday and Tomorrow* (Dublin, 1968), pp. 68–9).   74 As part of the IRB's support for the first series of *Nationality*, Griffith had to accept Sean MacDermott as business manager of the newspaper (Padraic Colum, *Ourselves Alone! The Story of Arthur Griffith and the Origin of the Irish Free State* [New York, 1959], p. 137).   75 The Clan-na-Gael sent $98,297 to the IRB between August 1914 and April 1917 (Robert Kee, *The Green Flag* [London, 1972], p. 545).

following the Rising under strict instructions from Griffith.[76] Griffith was even given grudging respect by British officials. Augustine Birrell told Asquith's cabinet in 1914 that Griffith was 'extremely clever' and 'able to write an argumentative article at least as well as anybody else'.[77] To fellow advanced nationalists, Griffith was a hero. Readers of the *Spark* voted him 'The <u>MAN</u> for Dublin' in 1915,[78] and Eileen Prendergast won a prize from the *Catholic Bulletin* for her 1918 essay 'My Favourite Hero', which concluded:

> Arthur Griffith is among the greatest, the cleverest, the most far-seeing and least self-seeking man that ever held the destinies of a nation; he is among the simplest, the most refined, and the kindliest gentleman that ever Ireland sent forth to speak in her name. It must be real this hero-worship which I feel for him. It comes to me in my best moments, for, when kneeling I pray 'God save Ireland', and in the same breath I pray 'and God save Arthur Griffith, too'.[79]

Even Éamon de Valera's dislike of Griffith, attested to by the propagandist and memoir writer Robert Brennan,[80] was hidden in propaganda, since Sinn Féin chose to present a united front after October 1917.

Some basic information can also be found about other propagandists. Aodh de Blacam, first editor of *Young Ireland*, was born Hugh Blackham in London. Son of Ulster protestant home-rulers, he converted to catholicism and moved to Donegal around the beginning of the Great War. In later years he remained active in journalism, and served on Fianna Fáil executives in the 1930s and 1940s, continuing to attack emigration from Ireland in both his own columns and in governmental publications.[81] Herbert Pim, the most influential Sinn Féin propagandist after Arthur Griffith,[82] returned to Ireland from a brief internment

---

76 Despite Griffith's public support for Pim, he was frustrated with his leadership of Sinn Féin. Writing to Lily Williams from Reading Gaol in November 1916, Griffith moaned that 'my well-meaning but feather headed friend Herbert Pim seems to be muddling up Sinn Féin a bit. However, we must trust in God to take him in hand and show him how to unmuddle it'. (Cit. in Laffan, 1999, p. 72). **77** Bod., Augustine Birrell Papers, MS dep. c. 301: Cabinet Memoranda by Birrell on Ireland, 1911–1916, 'The State of Ireland', November 1914, fols. 365–7. The *New Statesman* also sardonically approved of Griffith, stating in 1914 that he has 'been preaching anti-Englishism in the pages of *Sinn Féin* (very well he does it too – Trietschke and those Teutons are dull dogs in comparison)'. (*New Statesman*, 5 December 1914, p. 215). **78** BNL, *Spark*, 7.3.15, p. 3. **79** Bod., *Catholic Bulletin*, August 1918, p. 401. **80** Brennan, 1950, p. 163. **81** My thanks to Dr Patrick Maume, Queen's University, Belfast, for this material. **82** Richard Davis cleverly refers to Sinn Féin doctrine immediately after the Easter Rising as 'Pim Féin'. (Cf. Richard Davis, 'The Advocacy of Passive Resistance in Ireland, 1916–1922', *Anglo-Irish Studies*, vol. III (1977), pp. 19–34). Pim himself exaggerated his influence. In 1920 he wrote that he resurrected the *Irish Volunteer* in mid-November 1914, helped start *Nationality* for Griffith in Belfast, and personally wrote an average of 20 columns per week for *Nationality*, including, on one memorable occasion, writing an entire 24 column

in August 1916 to resume editorial control of the *Irishman*, and led the Sinn Féin Party until Arthur Griffith came out of prison in December 1916. Michael Laffan judges Pim harshly, considering him an 'outlandish' figure, and maintaining that 'his brief prominence reflected the vacuum or lack of talent available to radical nationalists'.[83] Following Griffith's return, Pim remained an important voice in the nationalist press until 1918, when, sickened by the growing violence of advanced nationalism, he abandoned his support for nationalist Ireland, surrendered editorial control of the *Irishman*, and became a unionist once more. Soon after his return to unionism he left Ireland for London, where he ran an ultra-right anti-Sinn Féin weekly with his friend Lord Alfred Douglas, who had also been a contributor to *Young Ireland* in 1917.[84] Patrick Maume discusses the possibility, originally raised by Michael Judge, that Pim was a British agent, but dismisses this idea, remarking that if 'he had been a British agent, his handlers would have kept him in Sinn Féin while he could still be useful'.[85] Of the propagandists whose actual identities are known, and who were in Ireland in 1916,[86] two were executed as leaders of the Rising (MacDermott and Connolly), one died in action (The O'Rahilly), two tried to stop the Rising (Hobson and MacNeill), and four others fought (O'Higgins, Beaslai, Pim and MacSwiney). Arthur Griffith always claimed that he had appeared at the GPO to volunteer, and was told to leave, as his services as a propagandist were more important. Again, there is no hard evidence to support this self-aggrandising story.

Three of the propagandists have eluded virtually all effort to discover their identities. Sean Doyle, who edited the *Spark* under the pseudonym 'Ed. Dalton', was a Volunteer colleague of Robert Brennan's in Enniscorthy, but nothing else is known. A recent memoir has even put forth the possibility that the *Spark* was edited by Seamus Upton, who edited *Honesty* under the pseudonym of 'Gilbert Galbraith'.[87] Edward Dwyer, editor of the *Gael*, also remains a mystery as does M.S. O'Lonnain, whose name does not appear in any reference books or memoirs from the period.[88]

---

issue. (Pim, 1920, p. 17). Except for his help in getting *Nationality* printed in Belfast, these claims seem spurious at best. He was responsible after the Rising for the issue of the 'Sinn Féin in Tabloid Form' pamphlet series (ibid., p. 20), and had edited the earlier Sinn Féin 'Tracts for the Times' series (1915–16) (ibid., p. 18). 83 Laffan, 1999, pp. 70–1. 84 Maume, 1999, p. 240. 85 Ibid., pp. 187–8. 86 De Lacey had fled to the United States a year previously. 87 O'Doherty, 1999, p. 27. 88 There is a chance that O'Lonnain was actually Griffith. He took over the editorship of *Young Ireland* in December 1917, at which time the newspaper moved its editorial offices to No. 6 Harcourt Street (Sinn Féin Headquarters). O'Lonnain immediately produced a multi-part anti-Masonic story, written in a very similar style to Griffith's writing. Virignia Glandon credits de Blacam and Griffith with editing *Young Ireland*, mentioning also the possibility that J.J. Burke worked as acting editor. (Glandon, 1985, pp. 188 and 282). An anonymous addendum to the microfilm of *Young Ireland* held at the British Newspaper Library states that Griffith took over editorial control of the newspaper 'at some later date'. However, since Glandon and the British Newspaper

Introduction 35

Many propagandists at this time (and indeed throughout the Great War) used pseudonyms as a matter of course, leaving one with the intriguing question of just why there was this need or desire for anonymity. The need for security is a partial explanation, but not a very satisfactory one. The pseudonyms used by early propagandists writing in radical newspapers in 1914 were perhaps created for this reason, as they faced imprisonment and the loss of their business if the newspaper was closed down. Later propagandists, especially the writers of ballad sheets, did not face the same risks. It seems more likely that the creation of pseudonyms came about for two important reasons. First, it allowed the artist to show a further creativity. Lists of 'Sinn Féin nicknames and code words' compiled by British intelligence from the internees through the course of the war[89] show a highly developed sense of sardonic fun. Edward Carson was nicknamed 'The White Chief of Bigotry', and the Irish Parliamentary Party MP for West Galway, William O'Malley, was nicknamed 'Phospherine' after an incident in 1913 in which he invested public funds in a phosphate company in British Guyana that promptly folded.[90] The code words are topical to their era. Metaphors of illness abound, as most of these came from the summer and autumn of 1918 during the influenza pandemic. Being arrested was referred to as 'ill', while avoiding capture by the British was called 'escaping the flu'.[91] The fertile imaginations that dreamt up the nom-de-plumes 'Sliabh Ruadh' ('Red Mountain') and 'The Rajah of Frongoch' (Joseph Mulkearns) were showing off their wit. Secondly, the use of general anonymity was in keeping with a long tradition of radical anonymity, both in propaganda and in action. Many a dark night in rural Ireland during the late eighteenth and early nineteenth centuries was lit by burning barns set afire by mysterious 'Captain Midnights'. Journalists in United Irish journals in 1798, and in Thomas Davis' *Nation* fifty years later, frequently used pseudonyms as well. The furtherance of tradition in propaganda also sparked the use of anonymity. The use of general anonymity by propagandistic balladeers contributed to the acceptance of their new songs as part of the folk tradition. As Hugh Shields has pointed out, ballad sheets contained very little reference to their provenance, and the only reference to the music was the title of the air to which the new words were set.[92] A goal of the

Library are both dealing with *Young Ireland* through 1922, it can not be said with certainty that O'Lonnain and Griffith are one and the same. For good reference works on the nationalist characters of this period, see Maume, 1999, pp. 223–45, and Padraic O'Farrell, *Who's who in the Irish war of independence and civil war, 1916–1923* (Dublin, 1997).   89 PRO, Colonial Office Papers, CO 904/164/4: Postal Censorship, Irish Internees, 1918, 'Code words and nicknames used in Correspondence of Irish Internees'.   90 Another possible origin for this nickname is the health tonic 'Phoferine', which O'Malley advertised in 1917. (Cf. *IWI*, 1917).   91 PRO, Colonial Office Papers, CO 904/164/4: Postal Censorship, Irish Internees, 1918, 'Code words and nicknames used in Correspondence of Irish Internees'.   92 Hugh Shields, 'Printed Aids to Folk-Singing, 1700–1900', in Mary Daly and David Dickson (eds.), *The Origin of Popular Literacy in Ireland* (Dublin, 1990), p. 139.

revolutionary balladeers was the integration of their songs into the corpus of 'old' tunes from which both new songs and the general idea of the Irish nation were drawn. An example of the quick acceptance possible for these tunes is Sean O'Casey's 'The Grand Oul' Dame Britannia'. Published in 1916 before the Easter Rising, this jaunty melody became an instant best seller. From that point forward, O'Casey was identified in propaganda publications as 'the author of 'The Grand Oul' Dame Britannia'.[93] Within two years, 'Britannia', unaccredited, was being used as the basis for other revolutionary songs.[94] It had managed to achieve the iconic, and anonymous, status of a folk tune.

Despite the anonymity of many propagandists, the British government still did what it could to censor propaganda, and to stop the dissemination of newspapers, posters, and ballads around Ireland. Censorship efforts by the British were focused on two main areas of propaganda – the press, and ephemeral propaganda distributed through the postal system. Postal censorship was more effective than press censorship, allowing British intelligence to compile quite reliable lists of advanced nationalist suspects before the Rising, and often circumventing nationalist attempts to disseminate propaganda.[95] Press censorship managed to close newspapers, but propagandists always found a way to avoid regulations. Press censorship occurred in three distinct waves before the Easter Rising. In late November 1914, under pressure from conservative MPs and military officials in Dublin, Augustine Birrell ordered the seizure of the *Irish Worker* and *Irish Freedom*. *Sinn Féin* and *Eire Ireland* stopped of their own accord after this, and Eoin MacNeill, the new editor of the *Irish Volunteer*, promised to moderate his paper's tone. Griffith reappeared on the scene one month later with *Scissors and Paste*, a newspaper that managed to avoid Regulation 27 of the Defence of the Realm Act (DORA) by containing no original work by current propagandists. Following a modification of the regulations in late February 1915, the newspaper was closed down, and the presses seized. For the next year little was done against the advanced nationalist press beyond general harassment. In March 1916, however, following an inflammatory editorial in the *Gael*, the Gaelic Press, which printed the *Gael*, the *Spark*, and *Honesty*, was raided. The *Gael* ceased publication, but the *Spark* and *Honesty* switched printers and missed only one weekly issue.

The Easter Rising put an effective halt to newspaper propaganda for the next six months, as most propagandists were deported and imprisoned following the Rising. However, the imposition of official (as opposed to *ad hoc*) censorship after the Rising did little to stop the re-birth and growth of the advanced nationalist press.[96] By the autumn of 1916 Herbert Pim's the *Irishman* had returned as a Sinn Féin paper, and Arthur Griffith's second series of *Nationality* appeared in the winter of 1917.

93 Cf. TCD, Samuels 5/49. 94 Cf. TCD, Samuels 5/111. 95 Cf. Novick, 1999, pp. 343–56. 96 Maume, 1999, pp. 187–8.

If anything, such official censorship merely meant that propagandists were kept busy finding ways of avoiding the censor. Laffan remarks that Arthur Griffith, following the refounding of *Nationality* in 1917, 'was forced to devote much of his time and ingenuity to circumventing government controls'.[97] Frank Gallagher's memoirs inform us how Lord Decies', the official press censor, attention was distracted. According to Gallagher, propagandists regularly slipped 'dangerous proofs' past Lord Decies by speaking with him on subjects very dear to him: horse-racing and the evil of income tax.[98]

PROPAGANDA: THEORY AND LIMITATIONS

Leonard W. Doob, one of the deans of propaganda theory in the United States, wrote that 'a clear-cut definition of propaganda is neither possible nor desirable'.[99] Thus, in this section, rather than trying to find one single definition of propaganda, a series of working definitions will be presented to guide the reader around what propaganda actually means in this book, and how we can use theory to help see how successful Irish advanced nationalist propaganda actually was.

Starting at the most basic level, the *Oxford English Dictionary*'s second definition of propaganda is 'any association, systematic scheme, or concerted movement for the propagation of a particular doctrine or practice'.[100]

Harold Lasswell, one of the first scholars this century to attempt a systematic analysis of propaganda campaigns and the construction of a theory for how propaganda works, defined propaganda in 1934 as 'the technique of influencing human action by the manipulation of representations. These representations may take spoken, written, pictorial, or musical form'.[101] The Institute For Propaganda Analysis, created in the United States in 1937, supported this multiplicity of techniques, arguing that the main idea behind a propaganda campaign is that 'our emotion is the stuff with which propagandists work'.[102]

More recent scholarship, such as Garth Jowett and Victoria O'Donnell's illuminating study *Propaganda and Persuasion*,[103] emphasizes the controlling nature of propaganda. Jowett and O'Donnell argue that propaganda goes beyond other forms of persuasion. 'Sharing techniques with information and persuasion, propaganda does not seek mutual understanding or mutual fulfillment of needs.

---

[97] Laffan, 1999, p. 260. [98] Gallagher, 1953, pp. 40–1. Also cit. in Laffan, 1999, p. 260. [99] Leonard W. Doob, 'Propaganda', in E. Barnouw *et al.* (eds.), *International Encyclopedia of Communications*, vol. 3 (New York, Oxford University Press, 1989), p. 375. [100] 'Propaganda' in *Shorter Oxford English Dictionary* (Oxford, 1967), p. 1599. [101] Harold D. Lasswell, 'Propaganda', in Edwin Seligman (ed.), *Encyclopedia of the Social Sciences*, vol. xii (London, MacMillan, 1934), p. 13. [102] The Institute For Propaganda Analysis, 'How to Detect Propaganda', in Robert Jackall (ed.), *Propaganda* (London, MacMillan Press, 1995), p. 222. [103] Garth Jowett and Victoria O'Donnell, *Propaganda and Persuasion* (2nd edition) (London, Sage Publications, 1992).

Propaganda deliberately and systematically seeks to achieve a response that furthers the desired intent of the propagandist'.[104] Jowett and O'Donnell's standard definition relates to the current definition of propaganda used by NATO: 'Any information, ideas, doctrines, or special appeals disseminated to influence the opinion, emotions, attitudes or behaviour of any specified group in order to benefit the sponsor, either directly or indirectly'.[105]

Many theorists of propaganda, following Doob's dictum that began this section, have avoided finding a single definition for propaganda, and focused instead on what propaganda, or propaganda campaigns, must contain in order to be successful.

Most modern theorists agree that a successful propaganda campaign must have a sense of 'resonance' with its target audience. This idea grew from the success of Nazi propaganda. The Nazis, basing their propaganda campaigns on the ideas of both Adolf Hitler and Joseph Goebbels, demonstrated the power of propaganda based on a direct appeal to the emotions, with constant repetition of few ideas, an avoidance of objectivity, and the constant use of stereotyping.[106]

Terence H. Qualter was among the first post-World War II theorists to emphasize the necessity of 'audience adaptation', writing in 1962 that 'propaganda, to be effective, must be seen, remembered, understood, and acted upon ... adapted to particular needs of the situation and the audience to which it is aimed'.[107] The French theorist Jacques Ellul, who wrote in 1969, further developed this idea:

> Propaganda must be familiar with collective sociological presuppositions, spontaneous myths, and broad ideologies, not just of individuals or of particular groups, but those shared by all individuals in a society, including men of opposite political inclinations and class loyalties. A propaganda pitting itself against this fundamental ... structure would have no chance of success.[108]

A more individualistically psychological approach was taken by Paul Kesckemeti in 1973, defining a propagandist as 'someone giving expression to the recipient's own concerns, tensions, aspirations, and hopes ... the propaganda voices the propagandee's own feelings'.[109]

Since I believe that the idea of audience resonance is central both to defining material as propaganda and considering the relative success of a propaganda

---

104 Ibid., p. 35. 105 Cit. in Philip Taylor, *British Propaganda in the Twentieth Century* (Edinburgh, Edinburgh University Press, 1999), p. xii. 106 Jowett and O'Donnell, 1992, pp. 185–6. 107 Terence H. Qualter, *Propaganda and Psychological Warfare* (New York, Random House, 1962), p. xii. Cited in Jowett and O'Donnell, 1992, p. 4. 108 Jacques Ellul, *Propaganda* (tr. Konrad Keller and Jean Lerner) (New York, Alfred A. Knopf, 1969), pp. 38–9. 109 I.D. Pool et al., *Handbook of Communication* (Chicago, Rand McNally, 1973), p. 264.

campaign, readers will see throughout this book that I emphasize the connections between Irish nationalist traditions and advanced nationalist propaganda – the use of resonant imagery, resonant language, and older styles of political campaigning. There were breaks with these connections, as discussed in the first chapter of this book, but for the most part, advanced nationalists had the great advantage over British and pro-war propagandists that their use of Irish symbology, while calling for an independent Ireland, had a greater resonance than the concomitant usage of this material by those who wished for Ireland to remain in a subordinate relationship with Great Britain.

A seldom discussed aspect of propaganda is the question of how much difference a propaganda campaign makes on public opinion. This is extremely difficult to quantify, and theorists of propaganda are in much disagreement on this issue.[110] Early theorists, such as Harold Lasswell, viewed propaganda with fear and awe as a new sort of weapon. Basing his ideas on what he considered to be the 'effect' of First World War propaganda, Lasswell wrote in 1927:

> The fact remains that propaganda remains one of the most powerful instrumentalities in the modern world. It has arisen to its present eminence in response to a complex of changed circumstances which have altered the nature of society.... A new flame must burn out the canker of dissent and temper the steel of bellicose enthusiasm. The name of this new hammer and anvil of social solidarity is propaganda.[111]

The Nazification of Europe, coming as it did on the wings of massive international propaganda campaigns,[112] led many scholars in the post-World War

---

110 Indeed, the one large-scale effort at quantifying the influence of a propaganda campaign, Carl Hovland, Arthur Lumsdaine, and Fred Sheffield's analysis of the impact of the *Why We Fight* propaganda films on American enlisted men during World War II, concluded that the films had a mixed effect on its audience. Commissioned by the US Army to determine whether or not these films, shown to all recruits, 'shaped interpretations and opinions in ways necessary to developing an acceptance of military roles and related sacrifices', the researchers found that the films did not motivate the recruits to serve and fight. Nor did the films help deepen resentment toward the enemy or encourage the support of the allies' unconditional surrender policy. What the films did help shape were the recruits' beliefs about facts portrayed in the films: for example, many more recruits believed that the Battle of Britain had helped stop a German invasion of England after they saw these films. (Jowett and O'Donnell, 1992, pp. 129–30).   111 Harold D. Lasswell, *Propaganda Technique in the World War* (New York, Knopf, 1927), pp. 220–1.   112 Obviously, German military conquest was a key factor as well. However, the conversion of a sizeable minority (if not a majority) of citizens in occupied territories to Nazi doctrine came about through an astonishingly successful series of propaganda campaigns that used radio, film, mass demonstrations, the press, art, and public speaking in coordinated efforts the likes of which had not been seen before. The best analysis of this propaganda remains Robert Herzstein's *The War that Hitler Won* (New York, G.P. Putnam's Sons, 1978).

II era to lend even more weight to the idea that propaganda was an all-powerful weapon. The conduct of the United States in Vietnam, where the largest propaganda campaign ('Hearts and Minds') in history was launched, further encouraged writers in the late 1960s and early 1970s to consider the force of propaganda. Ellul, writing in 1969, made the stirring claim that:

> Propaganda will turn a normal feeling of patriotism into a raging nationalism. It not only reflects myths and pre-suppositions, it hardens them, sharpens them, invests them with the power of shock and action.[113]

Focusing on how propagandists manage public opinion, Malcolm Mitchell came to a similar conclusion, likening the propagandists' relationship to the public to that of 'a burning glass which collects and focuses the diffused warmth of popular emotions, concentrating them upon a specific issue on which the warmth becomes heat and may reach the firing-point of revivals, risings, revolts, revolutions'.[114]

In Ireland from 1914 to 1918, advanced nationalism saw all of these – a revival of nationalist spirit, a rising or revolt in 1916, and a democratic revolution in 1918. It might be fair to expect that, having written a book on the propaganda of this revolution, I agree wholeheartedly with Lasswell, Ellul and Mitchell's perception of propaganda as all-powerful in society. This, however, is not the case. These three scholars, and others as well, influenced perhaps by Gustave Le Bon's pioneering nineteenth-century work on mass psychology *The Crowd: A Study of the Popular Mind*, in which the prejudiced Le Bon declared that 'Men are ruled by ideas',[115] and that when in a crowd, the general lowering of intellect creates an atmosphere in which, under the influence of suggestion, man will undertake certain acts of with irresistible impetuosity,[116] neglect to address the effect public opinion has on propaganda. Driving this work, at the heart of my analysis of advanced nationalist propaganda, is a belief in the circular relationship of propaganda and public opinion: that propaganda influences the public's desires, but in turn is influenced by their needs. Much like advertising, propaganda must respond to external events and fluctuations in public opinion.[117]

Thus, throughout this book, I have drawn connections between events of 1914–18, primarily events of the Great War itself, and the propaganda of advanced nationalism. The main reason that I feel advanced nationalist

113 Ellul, 1969, pp. 40–1.   114 Malcolm Mitchell, *Propaganda, polls, and public opinion: Are the people manipulated?* (Englewood Cliffs, New Jersey, Prentice-Hall, 1970), p. 111. Cited in Jowett and O'Donnell, 1992, p. 33.   115 Gustave Le Bon, *The Crowd: A Study of the Popular Mind* (London, E. Benn Publishers, 1947), p. 7.   116 Ibid. pp. 33–6.   117 Few other propaganda theorists have used this idea. Jowett and O'Donnell come close when they remark that 'although it [propaganda] can be carried out independently of the physical environment, it can also under certain circumstances be shaped by that environment'. (Jowett and O'Donnell, 1992, p. 157).

propagandists ran a successful campaign was their ability to adapt their propaganda to match the mood of the Irish public. In the first year of the war, when enthusiasm was high for enlistment in the British army, propagandists ran a carefully managed campaign that discouraged enlistment without insulting the volunteers for British service. As public opinion turned against the slaughter of the war, propagandists linked resistance to the war, and to conscription, with support for advanced nationalism.

The question of effect is one that, at least in part, still must remain unanswered. This book does adhere to Jowett and O'Donnell's ten stages of propaganda analysis, discussing:

1. The ideology and purpose of the propaganda campaign
2. The context in which the propaganda occurs
3. Identification of the propagandist
4. The structure of the propaganda organization
5. The target audience
6. Media utilization techniques
7. Special various techniques
8. Audience reaction to various techniques
9. Counterpropaganda, if present
10. Effects and evaluation.[118]

However, some of these stages, especially numbers eight and ten, are impossible to explore fully given that the propaganda this book studies comes from a period before the use of opinion polls, and without access to the individual psychology of the men and women involved. Can we nevertheless make an attempt to answer the question of effectiveness for advanced nationalist propaganda?

The Institute for Propaganda Analysis, an American non-profit organization set up in 1937, published in that same year a series of requirements for effective propaganda campaigns. These have become known as the 'ABC's of Propaganda Analysis', and a brief look at these requirements supports an argument for advanced nationalist propaganda being very effective. According to the Institute, the necessary factors for success were:

A. *Name Calling*: Giving an idea a bad label, and thereby rejecting it and condemning it without examining the evidence.
B. *Glittering Generality*: Associating something with a 'virtue word' and creating acceptance and approval without examination of the evidence.
C. *Transfer*: Carries the respect and authority of something respected to something else to make the latter accepted. Also works with something that is disrespected to make the latter rejected.

118 Jowett and O'Donnell, 1992, p. 213.

D. *Testimonial*: Consists in having some respected or hated person say that a given idea or program or product is good or bad.
E. *Plain Folks*: The method by which a speaker attempts to convince the audience that he or she and his or her ideas are good because they are 'of the people', the 'plain folks'.
F. *Card Stacking*: Involves the selection and use of facts or falsehoods, illustrations or distractions, and logical or illogical statements in order to give the best or the worst possible case for an idea, program, person, or product.
G. *Band Wagon*: Has as it's theme 'everybody – at least all of us – is doing it!' and thereby tries to convince the members of a group that their peers are accepting the program, and that we should all jump on the band wagon rather than be left out.[119]

Advanced nationalist propagandists, as the reader shall see, followed all of these methods.

Determining the effect of propaganda is impossible to do in an exact manner, an idea that was first, and most comprehensively, argued by Jacques Ellul:

> Propaganda's effectiveness – or the absence thereof ... can be done only by observation of general phenomenon, by the best possible use of our general knowledge of man and his socio-political environment, by a mixture of judgements of approximation, and by the best possible use of reasons. This cannot lead to figures or to strict certainties, but it yields certain probabilities and, above all, precludes the massive errors into which the exact methods lead us.[120]

The field of communications and information theory add further warnings on this subject, cautioning researchers to 'avoid the tempting pitfall of assuming that messages 'mean' the dictionary definitions of their contents to those to whom they are addressed'.[121] In a detailed sense, no direct answer can be given to the question 'how effective was advanced nationalist propaganda during the Great War?' On a general level, however, effectiveness can be analyzed through a balancing of opinions prevalent at the time.

Advanced nationalists themselves thought their propaganda very effective. Memoirists remarked on the influence of these newspapers. Reflecting on Arthur Griffith's *Nationality*, Desmond FitzGerald wrote:

---

119 Institute for Propaganda Analysis, 'How to Detect Propaganda', in *Propaganda Analysis*, vol. 1 no. 2 (November 1937). Cited in Jowett and O'Donnell, pp. 182–3. 120 Ellul, 1969, p. 277. 121 Murray Edelman, *Politics as Symbolic Action: Mass Arousal and Quiescence* (New York, 1971), p. 32.

> The little paper he edited had a very restricted sale. The smallness of its circulation might well have led people to assume that it was not likely to have any effect in the country, for people always think that influence must be direct and visible. Whereas in the realm of ideas it is more frequently indirect and occult.
>
> ... If you went into a newsagent's in a small town and asked for Griffith's paper, the reply was they did not stock it, or that they only had a certain number for people who ordered it. But if you moved on from there to some place where people were gathered together to talk and argue you would find somebody giving voice to Griffith's teaching, or even quoting him by name.[122]

An Irish Volunteer and IRB organiser in Kerry and then in County Wicklow, FitzGerald also recalled that 'the sense of utter isolation that had oppressed us was modified by the articles in the little weekly papers that we received'.[123] Sympathetic early historians of the Sinn Féin movement agreed. R.M. Henry in 1920 wrote '*Eire* [Griffith's *Eire Ireland*] did not so much make, as voice, the opinions of a considerable section of Irish Nationalist opinion. The newspapers were scanned eagerly every morning all over Ireland'.[124] Constitutionalist newspapers reluctantly agreed that advanced nationalist propaganda, long before the Easter Rising, could be very effective. Thomas Dooley cites the case of the Waterford *Standard* in 1914:

> Newspapers which seditiously reported on behalf of the 'anti-British, anti-recruiting and pro-German campaigns' in Ireland had small circulations and little influence. But some of them were distributed for free and reinforced by leaflets and 'that personal propaganda which counts for so much in Nationalist Ireland'. Conceding that they had a 'pernicious effect on enlistment' in their efforts to 'vilify the British Army, poison Irish sentiment against England, and destroy Mr Redmond's position', the *Standard* accused the government of delay and irresolution and called for the suppression of identified newspapers.[125]

Although discussing pro-war propaganda, Patrick Callan's point about the effectiveness of newspaper propaganda in Ireland during this period is worth noting. 'The press', wrote Callan, 'had a potential impact on opinion, and persistently played a subliminal role in forwarding the aims of the recruiting campaign when they reported favourably on them. This was much along the lines later suggested by Joseph Goebbels for the press'.[126]

122 FitzGerald, 1968, pp. 2–3. 123 Ibid., p. 53. 124 Henry, 1920, pp. 180–1. 125 Cit. in Thomas Dooley, *Irishmen or English Soldiers?* (Liverpool: Liverpool University Press, 1995), p. 151. 126 Callan, 1984, p. 272.

Propaganda itself was highly valued by advanced nationalists. The *Irish Volunteer* called Sinn Féin's 1915 national pamphlet series 'The New Weapons' and considered them a 'formidable' part of the arsenal being deployed against British rule.[127] In the *Spark*, Sean Doyle extended the militaristic metaphors, likening the *Spark's* role on the Dublin scene to a 'man in the gap', fighting to maintain the 'right of Irish Nationalism to print and publish a paper in Dublin'.[128] The National Council of Sinn Féin continuously encouraged members around Ireland to publicize their activities, utilising both the advanced nationalist weeklies and the letter columns of daily newspapers. 'There is not a week passes', read a pamphlet produced for Cumainn in 1918, 'but some incident occurs in every county which could be turned to account in driving home the lesson that the country must look to Sinn Féin for its salvation'.[129]

Another argument for propaganda's effectiveness is the constant yet ineffectual censorship attempts made by the British government before the Rising.[130] While closing newspapers and fining proprietors may have had a slightly deleterious effect, the free publicity engendered in large-circulation papers by such actions more than made up for these losses. Trials of advanced nationalists for seditious activity or illegal possession of arms were widely covered in more standard newspapers, and advanced nationalists quickly turned Irish courts into their own bully pulpits.[131] British political opinion reinforced the idea of the importance of propaganda before the Rising. Enormous pressure was brought to bear on Asquith, Birrell, and Nathan by Tory MPs in the autumn of 1914 eager to close down Dublin's seditious press, and the London *Times* and *Morning Post* consistently complained about the widespread printed sedition found around Ireland.

How well did advanced nationalist propaganda reach England? British public opinion was crucial to the later efforts of Irish nationalists in the War of Independence, and the *Irish Bulletin*, under the direction of Desmond FitzGerald, would be specifically set up to promote the Irish nationalist line in Great Britain. The Great War saw no such equivalent, but nevertheless Irish propaganda reached newspapers and journals in Great Britain to an unprecedented degree, given its original level of circulation. The *New Statesman* even quoted Griffith's *Nationality* directly in 1918 to attack the trumped-up 'German plot'.[132] News and information reached papers through correspondents based in Ireland, most of whom were anonymous contributors,[133] and English

127 BNL, *IV*, 15.5.15, p. 6.   128 BNL, *Spark*, 1.8.15, p. 4.   129 KSRL, OH Q42:58, Sinn Féin Pamphlets, 'Propaganda', 1918.   130 Cf., as discussed earlier, Novick, 1997a; Novick, 1999.   131 The difficulties faced by the British administration in Dublin are well summarised in Lyons, 1971, p. 363. However, while the British government publicly declared their commitment to stamping out sedition, it is interesting to note that the propagandists who were not involved in other political activities do not appear in the Dublin Castle intelligence 'Personality files' recently released at the Public Record Office.   132 *New Statesman*, 25 May 1918, pp. 144–5.   133 Most of the Irish material in the *New Statesman* was written by J.M. Hone or James Hannay ('George Birmingham'). Before the war, Francis Sheehy-Skeffington

Introduction

journalists had private informants in Ireland as well.[134] Advanced nationalist journals themselves did occasionally reach England. Joe Good later recalled reading *Nationality* 'avidly' in London and Salisbury while attempting to organize Irish Volunteer branches on the English mainland.[135] However, major British papers rarely discussed Irish advanced nationalist propaganda itself, or its effectiveness. Rather, they used the existence of Irish propaganda as a crutch for their own political views. Conservative papers in 1914 promoted the censorship of Irish advanced nationalist newspapers in order to discredit Asquith's Liberal government. The *New Statesman* and the *Nation* displayed their liberal credentials by complimenting pre-war Sinn Féin doctrine, condemning government coercion in Ireland, and blaming Sir Edward Carson and the Orange Order for Irish problems – all common elements of wartime advanced nationalist propaganda.[136]

The best argument for pre-Rising effectiveness comes from a speech delivered by Justice Kenny at the opening of the Commission for the City of Dublin, two weeks before the Easter Rising. Kenny lashed out at the prevalent sedition in Ireland, claiming:

> It is difficult for any movement of that nature [army recruiting] to be a complete success if a propaganda of an openly seditious character, and one which seems to set all authority at defiance, be started in order to counteract it. We read in our daily papers of seditious literature ... and you have in the public thoroughfares of this city what I regard as the most serious attempt to paralyse the recruiting movement – namely, the display of large and attractive posters outside shop doors which must necessarily have a most mischievous and deterrent influence on certain classes of the population. I have seen these posters from time to time. No passer-by could fail to observe them. They purport to represent either the spirit or the contents of some weekly papers.[137]

also wrote regularly for the journal, but his pacifist stance caused him to lose his position as Irish correspondent upon the outbreak of war.   **134** Cf. Bod., Sir R.C.K. Ensor Papers, Memorandum on the State of Ireland, Thomas Naylor to Ensor, 19 December 1916, Box 86. Naylor blamed British policies for forcing people to support Sinn Féin.   **135** Joe Good, *Enchanted by Dreams: The Journal of a Revolutionary* (Maurice Good [ed.]) (Dublin, 1999), p. 12. W.B. Yeats claimed in 1924 that *Tomorrow* was printed at a labour press in Manchester or Birmingham, and had stated earlier that this same press [actually in Manchester] had printed Arthur Griffith's *Nationality* during the First World War. (Material from W.B. Yeats' unpublished correspondence, courtesy of Professor Roy Foster). There is no further evidence to support this claim, however Yeats was writing very soon after the First World War, and it is possible that a press in Manchester published occasional issues of *Nationality* without British knowledge.   **136** Cf. *Nation*, 15.6.15, 17.2.17, 18.8.17, 15.12.17; *New Statesman*, 5.12.14, 6.2.15, 6.5.16, 20.10.17, 2.3.18.   **137** BNL, *WIT*, 15.4.16, p. 4. The editor of the *Weekly Irish Times* agreed, complaining that 'there is no doubt that much of this expense and this labour is nullified by the speeches, demonstrations, and publications of the seditious minority. The

After the Rising, propaganda grew even more effective. Following on F.S.L. Lyons' earlier assertions,[138] Peter Hart has uncovered primary evidence to help prove that the 'patriotic cult' of the Rising depended in large part on the 'flood of rebel memorabilia, of postcards, mass cards, song sheets, pamphlets, flags, badges, pictures, photograph albums, calendars, and a host of other mass-produced items'.[139] Though self-serving, Major I.H. Price's remarks at the Royal Commission on the Easter Rebellion are worth noting as well. Price claimed that Sinn Féin propaganda cost the British army 50,000 recruits between 1914 and 1916, and focused on the *Irish Volunteer* and the *Gael* as having an especially 'bad influence'.[140]

A final measure that supports the effectiveness of war-linked propaganda comes from the results of a series of by-elections in 1917 and 1918 contested by Sinn Féin. Nine occurred during the war, eight contested by Sinn Féin. Of these eight, Sinn Féin won five (North Roscommon, Longford, East Clare, Kilkenny City, and Cavan). The other three (South Armagh, Tyrone, and Waterford) occurred either in the north, where the unionists and parliamentarians combined forces, or in John Redmond's old seat, which was won by his son. Unfortunately, the extant propaganda record is far from complete, and no figures survive which show the amount of propaganda circulated in counties during by-elections. Records of stump speeches, an important aspect of all Sinn Féin campaigns, are either non-existent or, appearing in opposition newspapers, extremely unreliable. Thus, a detailed study of the effectiveness of propaganda used in these elections is impossible. A close study of the remaining propaganda[141] shows that:

1. During the run-up to a by-election, Sinn Féin papers and the Sinn Féin Publicity Department concentrated almost entirely on the by-elections. Copies of *Nationality* were distributed for free in polling areas before the election.[142]
2. More speeches and rallies were held in the area, resulting in more arrests for political activity.
3. Violence increased, but mainly due to 'donnybrooks' and campaign riots rather than actions against the British government, or by the British government.

persistent stream of insults against the Army, and the unpunished reiteration of the lie that 'this is not Ireland's war', are bound to leave the worst possible impression on the minds of ignorant men'. (*WIT*, 15.4.16, p. 4. See also *IWI*, 15.4.16, p. 1). **138** F.S.L. Lyons, *Culture and Anarchy in Ireland* (Oxford, 1979), pp. 100–2. **139** Hart, 1998, p. 207. This evidence is further supported by R.M. Henry, who recalled: 'Sinn Féin pamphlets began to be in demand: a month after the Rising it was hardly possible to procure a single one of them. But if they could not be bought, thumbed and tattered copies were passed from hand to hand: their teachings and the doctrines of Sinn Féin were discussed all over Ireland'. (Henry, 1920, p. 224). **140** BNL, *WIT*, 3.6.16, p. 1. **141** I estimate that, disregarding records of public speeches, approximately 65% of by-election material survives. **142** Laffan, 1999, p. 101.

4. Similar if not exact propaganda was used for many campaigns, with the names of candidates and counties being changed.[143]

Michael Laffan's work on by-elections in this period supports their centrality to the Irish revolution. To the arguments mentioned above for the effectiveness of propaganda, he adds the high level of organization among Sinn Féin campaigners, citing the *Irish Independent*'s 1917 report of 'pamphlets ... being handed out by the thousand ... posters ... displayed at every cross-road and village in the constituency'.[144]

The constitutional nationalist response to Sinn Féin's propagandizing saw a gradual shift from ignoring the role of propaganda in the earliest by-elections[145] to blaming the British censorship for people being duped by advanced nationalist propaganda. According to the *Freeman*, if the British would only permit the free circulation of Sinn Féin material, then voters would realize the full horror of giving their votes to an insurrectionist movement.[146]

This shift highlights the fact that constitutionalists continually downplayed the effectiveness of Sinn Féin propaganda. In part this was because Sinn Féin was seen even in the early days of the war as an opponent of the Redmondite regime, and partly because advanced nationalist propaganda can not be seen as a completely effective form of protest during the war. What arguments are there for its relative ineffectiveness? A classic argument is to look at the low membership in the Irish Volunteers before the Easter Rising. In April 1916, police estimated that Eoin MacNeill's volunteers had only 4,000 men in the ranks.[147] Distribution of anti-recruiting propaganda before the Rising was also uneven. Oliver Brein, head of the Detective Department in the Dublin Metropolitan Police (DMP), reported to Birrell in March 1915 that very few anti-recruiting posters had been found posted or otherwise distributed in Dublin. The distribution of anti-recruiting leaflets throughout 1915 was concentrated in the south and west of Ireland, with counties Limerick, Galway, Cork, Tipperary, Wexford and Waterford appearing most frequently on lists prepared by Dublin Castle. No direct correlation can be found between a rise in anti-recruiting posters and a consequent fall in recruiting figures. The lowest level of

---

143 While not focusing on propaganda, Marie Coleman's 1998 UCD Ph.D. dissertation, 'County Longford, 1910–1923: A Regional Study of the Irish Revolution', is an excellent study of local politics and by-elections in the years of the Irish revolution. 144 Cit. Laffan, 1999, p. 100. 145 Cf. BNL, *WFJ*, 3.2.17; 5.5.17; 12–26 May 1917; 23.6.17; 14.7.17. See also pre-Rising and early 1917 *Irish Weekly Independent* for similar views. 146 BNL, *WFJ*, 18.8.17, p. 4. 147 Breandan Mac Giolla Choille, *Intelligence Notes from Dublin Castle, 1914–1916* (Dublin, 1966), p. 176. Kee uses this low figure to claim that 1914 Sinn Féin papers were ineffectual (Kee, 1972, p. 533). Tim Bowman makes a similar claim for ineffectiveness of anti-recruiting propaganda in his recent essay 'The Irish Recruiting and Anti-Recruiting Campaigns, 1914–1918', in Bertrand Taithe and Tim Thornton (eds.), *Propaganda* (Stroud, 1999), pp. 223–39.

recruitment for the British army in 1915 occurred between June and August. Except for a small rise in the number of 'seditious' posters seized in July, due solely to the display of the Irish Volunteer manifesto, there was no significant increase in the number of propaganda posters circulated in Ireland.[148]

Another method for approaching the question of effectiveness is to examine circulation figures, or degree of penetration. British and Irish Parliamentary Party officials contemptuously referred to advanced nationalist papers as the 'mosquito press',[149] and indeed, circulation of the papers was extremely low. Dublin Castle figures for circulation in February 1916 show that only the *Irish Volunteer* and *Nationality* had circulations of more than 4,500. The *Spark* sent approximately 2,400 copies around Ireland every week, and the remaining papers all sold between 1,000 and 1,500 copies per week.[150] Even factoring in approximately three readers per copy, this is still a relatively insignificant level of national penetration, especially when compared to the readership levels of pro-war material. The *Irish Weekly Independent* sold an average of 50-72,000 copies per week in 1914-15, and 50-69,000 copies per week in 1915-16.[151] Tierney, Bowen, and Fitzpatrick's research on recruiting posters for the British army preserved at Trinity College showed that the print-run for a poster ranged from 250 to 40,000 copies, with about one-third having a circulation of 5,000 copies.[152] Tom Dooley cites a pamphlet reprinting a speech delivered by John Redmond on the Western Front in 1915 that had a print run of 240,000 copies.[153] In contrast, the anti-war poster with the largest known print run was an anti-conscription leaflet, 15,000 copies of which were seized on a train in 1915.[154]

However, circulation figures for all newspapers were growing during 1916, and the British government became more and more nervous about the impact of these papers. Speaking at the Royal Commission on the Easter Rebellion, Major I.H. Price declared that in fact *Nationality* had a circulation of over 8,000 copies, and greatly influenced nationalist opinion around Ireland.[155] Newspapers, with the exception of *An t-Oglach*, were sold openly at newsagents around Ireland, and propagandists exploited both the efficient postal service and rail system to

---

148 Cf. Novick, 1996, p. 43. **149** Although, as Dr Marc Mulholland (St Catherine's College, Oxford) has pointed out, mosquitoes also carry malaria, so this reference may have been somewhat ironic. **150** PRO, Colonial Office Papers, CO 903/19/1: Chief Secretary's Office, Judicial Division, Intelligence Notes, 1915, 'Table on Circulation of Seditious Newspapers', fol. 40. **151** BNL, *IWI*, 30.10.16, p. 4. **152** Mark Tierney, Paul Bowen and David Fitzpatrick, 'Recruiting Posters', in David Fitzpatrick (ed.), *Ireland and the First World War* (Dublin: Trinity College History Workshop, 1988), p. 54. **153** Dooley, 1995, p. 139. **154** PRO, Colonial Office Papers, CO 904/192: Dublin Castle Police and Crimes Division: Index to Correspondence Relating to Illegal Activities, November 1915 to March 1916. See also Novick, 1997a, p. 54. **155** BNL, *WIT*, 3.6.16, p. 1. Herbert Pim cites an even higher figure for the second series of *Nationality*, claiming a circulation of 60,000 copies per week (Pim, 1920, p. 27).

help disseminate their publications. After the Easter Rising advanced nationalist papers re-appeared in Dublin, and Sinn Féin also began to create 'Sinn Féin Notes', written by propagandists (usually Brennan or Griffith) at Sinn Féin Headquarters in Dublin, and sent to newspapers around the island.

With the anecdotal evidence of the importance of propaganda, we come as close as possible to answering the question of propaganda's effectiveness. This is not a question that can empirically be answered, but seeing that nationalists actively acknowledged the centrality of propaganda, closely followed a theoretical framework for successful propaganda campaigns, and that the weight of arguments for or against effectiveness tends to show that propaganda had an influential effect on public opinion, we can conclude that advanced nationalist propaganda certainly aided the rise of Sinn Féin. By linking their propaganda to the central public concern of the day – the Great War – and by being willing to change basic principles of their argument in order to better reflect public opinion, propagandists helped to bring about the creation of a revolutionary government in Ireland.

OUTLINE OF THE BOOK

The links between the war and propaganda are explored in this book through a series of thematic studies, demonstrating the consistent use of the Great War in all areas of propagandistic discourse. While the chapters are divided thematically, each chapter covers the Great War chronologically, so that readers may see the development of each style of propaganda through the four years of war. The book begins with three areas that appeared only because of the war. Chapter one examines advanced nationalist attitudes to Irish soldiers in the British army. Previous historians who have explored this question conclude that enlistment was viewed consistently as a sin and a shame. This research, using a greater corpus of material, demonstrates that in fact propagandists showed great sympathy for Irishmen in khaki, and even took pride in some of their exploits once Irish regiments began to see action and take casualties. Chapters two and three turn to Irish reactions to atrocity propaganda, one of the more prevalent styles of propaganda on all sides during the war. Chapter two looks at the response to specific German atrocities during the Great War, and then explores the use of history and current events by Irish propagandists in their battle against atrocity propaganda. Chapter three examines the moral posturing behind atrocity propaganda, and shows how advanced nationalist propagandists – especially Arthur Griffith – used British atrocity propaganda to brand the British government as a collection of liars and hypocrites. Both chapters reveal an intriguing mixture of attitudes among Irish propagandists, as in their writing they demonstrate both an extreme insular xenophobic racism and an awareness and ability to exploit specific events of the war for their own propagandistic purposes.

The next section of the book explores two areas of propaganda which at first glance appear to have nothing to do with the Great War, and yet which propagandists consciously chose to link to events of the war itself. The book's fourth chapter explores a topic which, more than any other studied here, has continuities with pre-war advanced nationalist propaganda: the 'moral tone' of the revolution. In this chapter, the model of the ideal Irish nationalist man and woman is discussed, as well as the role of youth in the Irish revolution and the fight against immorality, be it in the saloon, the music hall, or the whorehouse. This chapter shows that advanced nationalist encouragement of these moral crusades led to clerical support for their cause long before the Conscription Crisis of 1918. Chapter five looks at agrarian propaganda, an area that, it is argued, was first exploited in detail after the 1916 Rising. Following the Easter Rising, propagandists, especially those working for Sinn Féin, had to find a way to prove that Sinn Féin could effectively govern a free nation. They achieved this by demonstrating that British food policy during the war greatly harmed the Irish farmer, and by linking traditional Sinn Féin support for agrarian radicalism with a new anti-war stance.

In a final section, we look at two more generalized themes in Irish propaganda: the use of humour, and the encouragement of aggression. These two chapters explore my concept of the 'brutalization of discourse', the idea that as casualties grew in the Great War, and the Easter Rising visited war-time devastation on Dublin, propaganda grew angrier and angrier, transforming both the style of humour and the way in which aggression was encouraged. Arguments in these chapters suggest a plausible alternative to long-held assumptions about the Irish revolution. Concepts of blood sacrifice, it is argued, were far from universally important before the Easter Rising. Arthur Griffith remained of central importance to advanced nationalism after the Rising, and finally, post-1916 Sinn Féin should be seen as a product of conflicting ideologies of aggression, not as a conflict between pacifist and activist branches.

Throughout the period of the Great War, certain events and moments are marked by surges in propaganda output and shifts in public opinion: the losses at Gallipoli, the immediate aftermath of the Easter Rising, the death of Thomas Ashe, and the Conscription Crisis. Yet the Irish Revolution did not occur simply because of these events. The democratic election of a revolutionary government was made possible by the slow accumulation of public opinion. Just as a stone gathers momentum as it rolls down a hill, so too the Irish public coalesced behind the men and women of advanced nationalist movements. Propaganda helped to gather and focus this public opinion.

I

Dupes, death, and courage: advanced nationalist perceptions of the Great War and Irish soldiers in the British army

Previous research into advanced nationalist perceptions of recruits into the British army has concentrated either on pre-war attitudes[1] or, due possibly to a lack of sources, ignored the subtleties of attitudes during the war.[2] This chapter argues that the war was viewed with horror, and that the scorn and mockery found in propagandists' descriptions of recruits before and in the first months of the war disappeared as Irish troops began to see action. In place of this scorn, propagandists began to pity and mourn the loss of young Irishmen, reserving a growing sense of rage for the recruiters who lured them into service. The growing frustration and agony with the war felt by the population at large was easily exploited by advanced nationalist propagandists, as their press was the only arena in which truthful accounts of trench life could reach the general public without being obscured by sacrificial recruiting propaganda. The Easter Rising had little effect on the advanced nationalist attitude to Irish soldiers, although it brutalized the opinions held toward British soldiers. General attitudes to the war turned gradually from passive shock and astonishment to a more effective set of reactions, in which propagandists used and encouraged anti-war attitudes in the general populace to help Sinn Féin in its electoral campaigns from 1917 through the post-war General Election of December 1918.[3]

I

The overwhelming response by advanced nationalist propagandists to the outbreak of a pan-European war was one of passive astonishment and shock. Stunned first by the potential of slaughter, and then as the war progressed on its bloody track by the even harsher realities of Flanders, Gallipoli, and the Balkans, writers responded with a catalogue of war's horrors. To propagandists, service in

---

1 Denman, 1994, pp. 208-33.   2 Cf. John Ellis, '"Unity in Diversity": Ethnicity and British National Identity, 1899-1918' (Boston College, Ph.D., 1997).   3 The *Weekly Freeman's Journal* admitted that 'no cry was raised louder on Sinn Féin platforms than that extremism had killed Conscription ... that a vote for the policy of the Irish Party was a vote to put every able-bodied man of military age into khaki' (BNL, *WFJ*, 21.7.17, p. 4).

the British army during the war meant death. This fact, repeated throughout the organs of advanced nationalist propaganda circulating around Ireland before the Easter Rising, was used in different ways. To some propagandists, notably James Connolly, the killing fields emblematized class warfare and the hegemony of international capitalism. Others used vivid descriptions of the battlefields specifically to attack recruiting rhetoric or the perceived stupidity of the British officer corps leading regiments to their death. Unlike advanced nationalist perception of the soldiers themselves, however, the perception of the war did not change before the Easter Rising, remaining one of passive shock at the terrible wastage of so many lives. Unbridled by censorship, wishing in fact to challenge the censorship policies of the British government under the Defence of the Realm Act (DORA), editors of the advanced nationalist 'mosquito press' gave free rein to their pens, and produced a catalogue of horrors unique in the wartime United Kingdom.

Propagandists drew on familiar imagery to emphasize the terror of the war. Images of mothers played an important role. In Dora B. Montefiore's 1914 screed, 'Pass Along!', the author spoke directly to the figure of a mother in her tale, forced off a bus by soldiers travelling for free:

> You are the giver and the nurturer of life, therefore must you starve, and sorrow and tramp weary miles, carrying in your trembling arms the babe who, if he grows to manhood, the War Lords will also claim. Learn your real place, mother, in the present scheme of things, and ... pass along.[4]

Once this infant grew, and was claimed by the 'War Lords', only one outcome was possible for the mother. In *An Claidheamh Soluis*, the newspaper of the Gaelic League, a front-page cartoon in October 1914 showed an endless group of women and children huddled together on a beach.[5] All were dressed in rags, weeping, some praying, and some shaking their fists at an uncaring sky. The caption, to further accentuate the obvious implications of the picture, reads 'An Cogadh – Na Maithreaca'.[6]

To Jim Larkin and James Connolly, revolutionary socialists whose organizations were only loosely allied with other advanced nationalist movements in 1914, the war was seen first and foremost as a class issue. They were not alone in this view, but they were the main proponents. Arthur Griffith reprinted an editorial from the *Irish World*, the largest Irish-American newspaper of its day, which asked 'is Irish blood likely to be poured out lavishly that profits of English manufactures may mount up?'[7] Griffith, opposed to socialism despite his support for economic autarky, likely reprinted this editorial both to attack the spread of

---

4 BNL, *IW*, 19.9.1914, p. 1.   5 BNL, *ACS*, 24.10.14, p. 7.   6 'The War – of Mothers'.
7 BNL, *EI*, 9.11.14, p. 2.

British manufacture and to avoid censorship by using an excerpt from an American paper.

Unsurprisingly, Larkin and Connolly were more consistent in their use of class. They attacked the British and the rich with equal vigour, calling on the international working class to unite.[8] Connolly's close friend William Partridge, a member of the Dublin Corporation, attacked the idle rich, mentioning that at the Dublin theatres '[c]rowds were collected outside the shilling doors, an equal number was gathered outside the ninepenny doors, but the fourpenny doors were deserted'.[9] This distribution of audience had nothing to do with taste, or the play being performed. 'The fourpenny people', maintained Partridge, 'were seeing their relatives off to the front. It is ever thus, no matter what happens; it is the poor who will always pay'.[10]

Connolly himself had mixed feelings about the war. A week after he asked his readers to have nothing to do with the thieves of England, he admitted that he had cheered the departure of working-class reservists to the front, feeling that fighting perhaps would be the only way to truly overthrow the *ancien regime*.[11] The war itself, however, would be a nightmare. The direct economic consequences of conflict would kill poor people far from the front lines. 'In every bite of food you eat you will be compelled to pay for the war ... the war will mean hunger and misery to thousands'.[12] In Connolly's opinion, the poor would not just starve, they would become the agents, indirectly and directly, of their own destruction. Dora Montefiore warned the poor that they would be the men and women who 'forge the bullet, the shell, and the hidden mine, which shall rip, disembowel, and blast the bodies of your kindred and comrades'.[13]

One interesting facet of wartime advanced nationalist propaganda in Ireland is the lack of a strong pacifist voice.[14] Before the Rising, Francis Sheehy-Skeffington's public speeches and the activities of the Irish Neutrality League created some impact, but, despite having a natural outlet in the *Irish Citizen*, pacifist propaganda rarely appeared in the advanced nationalist press. Patrick Pearse and Thomas MacDonagh gave begrudging support for the protests of Hanna Sheehy-Skeffington against the British government when permission was refused for an Irish delegation to travel to the International Women's Conference

---

8 BNL, *IW*, 8.8.14, p. 2.   9 Ibid., p. 3.   10 Ibid.   11 Ibid., 15.8.14, p. 1.   12 Ibid., 'WAR! What it Means to You', p. 1 [Reprinted as a pamphlet and distributed in Belfast].   13 Ibid., 19.9.14, p. 1.   14 Richard Harrison briefly discusses the work of the Quaker Irish Peace Society in 1914 and 1915, which had sixteen members, and the creation of a Dublin branch of the Fellowship of Reconciliation, a 'radical' Christian pacifist movement, which concentrated on the distribution of anti-conscription and proselytising literature. The Fellowship sent a message of sympathy to Hanna Sheehy-Skeffington after the murder of her husband. However the events of the Easter Rising virtually precluded any alliance between Quaker and advanced nationalist groups (cf. Richard Harrison, *Irish Anti-War Movements, 1824-1974* [Dublin, 1986], pp. 47-8).

at the Hague in 1915, but this was an isolated incident.[15] The papers of Francis Sheehy-Skeffington reveal a partial explanation for this disappearance of organized pacifism. Writing to Mrs George Bernard Shaw in December 1914, Sheehy-Skeffington stated that personally 'I want Peace, first of all, no matter who wins; I cannot conceive of any result more disastrous than the continuance of the present barbarism'.[16] However, while he consistently maintained this stance in public appearances, Sheehy-Skeffington acknowledged that little appeared in print. 'I don't put these views into the IRISH CITIZEN', he wrote, 'which approaches the war solely from the feminist standpoint, and for which I personally write very little, merely keeping it going as a medium of expression for Irish women suffragists'.[17]

Other propagandists felt that peace might come once Irish leaders saw the true horrors of the front. Shortly before Redmond did visit the Western Front, *Honesty* suggested that he, Joseph Devlin, 'and the seventy other paid members of Parliament should see life in the trenches, and spend a week in a base hospital'.[18] If by doing this they became aware of the soldiers' suffering, then *Honesty* was certain that 'it would be hardly possible for them to continue on their career of mad Imperialism which has caused such misery'.[19] While Redmond and his recruiters encouraged men to place themselves at risk, the bungling of officers allegedly caused the actual deaths of recruits. Edward Dwyer compared the landings at Gallipoli to the failed end-run landings of the Walcheren Expedition in 1809.[20] He followed this attack on the British generals a month later with a quotation from Sydney Smith. Under 'The Dardanelles' in his regular column 'Quotations of the Moment', Dwyer wrote 'Nothing so expensive as glory'.[21]

The rising toll of the war was relentlessly catalogued by advanced nationalist propagandists, erring on the side of blood rather than caution. In late November 1914, Arthur Griffith reported that a Sergeant Donaghey, of the Second Battalion, Royal Irish Regiment, claimed that only 53 of the 1,400-man regiment had returned from France. Many of the others, he thought, might be prisoners of the Germans.[22] Inaccurate numbers such as these, inflated either by the Germans or by Griffith, might have discouraged men from enlisting. By the following spring, with a genuinely gruesome casualty count to report, advanced nationalist propagandists were themselves disheartened and discouraged. The

---

15 Cf. Margaret Ward, 'Nationalism, Pacifism, Internationalism: Louie Bennett, Hanna Sheehy-Skeffington, and the Problems of "Defining Feminism"', in Anthony Bradley and Maryann Gialanella Valiulis (eds.), *Gender and Sexuality in Modern Ireland* (Amherst, 1997), pp. 60-85. 16 NLI, Francis Sheehy-Skeffington Papers, NLI MS 22259 (iii): Letters by Sheehy-Skeffington, October 1914 to December 1914. Sheehy-Skeffington to Mrs Bernard Shaw, 14 December 1914. 17 Ibid. 18 BNL, *Hon*, 13.11.15, pp. 2-3. 19 Ibid. 20 BNL, *Gael*, 5.2.16, p. 7. 21 Ibid., 4.3.16, p. 6. 22 BNL, *EI*, 21.11.14, p. 1; also 24.11.14, '15,000 British Troops Reported Drowned', p. 1.

Reverend F.S. Pollard reported that the total number of British casualties through May 1915 had reached 280,000 men,[23] prompting him to ask ironically two months later '"Turkey Sick and Tired of War" says an evening paper's placard. No other country sick and tired? – What!!'[24]

Sick of war, disgusted by the rank slaughter of the battlefields, propagandists soon turned depictions of these horrors into powerful anti-recruiting messages. As the war began to take its toll of volunteers, word filtered back, sometimes through returning soldiers, and sometimes through the neutral press, of the realities of war. By the summer of 1915, the advanced nationalist press, unafraid of censorship restrictions, was the only mass published forum available for the dissemination of these reports.[25]

James Connolly reprinted an extract from a Canadian paper that had printed a letter it had received from a man in Loughinisland, County Down. The letter was published because 'it sounds very different to the highly coloured optimistic news you get in the capitalistic press, which is faking news daily to feed a gullible public on'.[26] A soldier, returning to Downpatrick from Mons, called the front line 'a regular hell'. 'Men's arms, legs, heads, and intestines were mixed with rock and clay and were blown skywards, and the rain of human blood which came down was indescribable'.[27]

The issue of wounded Irish soldiers was a complicated one for advanced nationalist propagandists. Traditional anti-recruiting propaganda made much of the failure of the British government to provide for its veterans,[28] yet a close reading of the wartime sources reveals that propagandists treated wounded veterans with a greater degree of care than before the war. The shock of seeing wounded men, however, was enough to justify some horror propaganda about their fate. In the *Spark*, Sean Doyle sarcastically remarked:

> A poem from Katherine [sic] Tynan appears in *New Ireland*; it is entitled 'A Prayer – For those who shall return', presumably from the war. A correspondent informs me that he has seen many who have returned and

23 BNL, *Hib*, 26.6.15, p. 2.   24 Ibid., 21.8.15, p. 8.   25 Cf. Eric Schneider, 'What Britons were told about the war in the trenches, 1914-1918' (Oxford, D.Phil, 1997), who maintains that knowledge about the 'realities of trench warfare' easily passed back to non-combatants via private correspondence, soldiers wounded and on leave, and the Red Cross. The mainstream wartime press, however, told civilians nothing about the harsher aspects of trench life. Regular Irish papers were no exception. Occasional eye-witness accounts, especially in the *Sunday Freeman's Journal*, showed the horrific side of trench life (cf. BNL, *SFJ*, 13.9.14, 1.11.14, 29.11.14) but these articles were accompanied by editorials that encouraged further enlistment to show respect for such gallant sacrifice. For further evidence on the failure of the regular press in Ireland, and consequent gap for the advanced nationalists, see R.M. Henry, who remarks that 'it may have been necessary to refrain from telling the whole truth in official reports, but ... this had the result of arousing suspicion and distrust'. (Henry, 1920, pp. 180-1).   26 NLI, *WR*, 17.7.15, p. 1.   27 Ibid.   28 The best example of this is probably the

he thinks God is more merciful to the ones who meet death in Flanders than to the unfortunate mental and physical wrecks he has seen.[29]

While propagandists' response to the horror may have largely been passive before 1916, with few suggestions made of how people could stop this killing, journalists were nevertheless able to use the slaughter of the war to their own advantage, deploying its horrors as strategic weapons of words and images which discouraged volunteers from taking the King's Shilling.

II

A chronological survey of propaganda reveals a complete switch during 1915 in the attitudes held by advanced nationalist propagandists toward Irish soldiers in the British army. Virtually all examples of mockery are found in the first calendar year of the war, and almost all instances of pity or sorrow are seen in the press from the summer of 1915 to the Easter Rising. This shift in attitude demonstrates not only the importance to advanced nationalist propagandists of external events, especially the destruction at Gallipoli in August 1915 of the volunteer Tenth Division,[30] but also the way in which propagandists adjusted their own opinions to fit public desire. When war began, advanced nationalist attitudes to soldiers reflected the scorn prevalent in pre-war anti-recruiting propaganda.[31] As Irish casualties mounted through 1915, especially after the Suvla Bay assault at Gallipoli in August 1915, public opinion began to turn against the war, but sympathy and support for Irish soldiers remained.[32] Advanced nationalist propaganda reflected and encouraged this change, linking resistance to the war with support for advanced nationalism, and avoiding the pitfall of scorning the male friends and relatives of potential voters.

The en-masse enlistment of approximately 40,000 Irishmen, 16,000 of them National Volunteers, in the British army in the first four months of the Great

'Sinn Féin Recruiting Car', a cart pulled by a donkey in 1913 which bore on its side placards reading 'Before Joining the British Army – Enquire – ... Why So Many Ex-Soldiers Die in the Workhouse?' 29 BNL, *Spark*, 23.5.15, p. 3. 30 Cf. Bryan Cooper, *The Tenth (Irish) Division in Gallipoli* (London, 1918) [reprinted Dublin, 1993]. 31 Denman, 1994. 32 A survey of mass-circulation newspapers in Ireland clearly shows this trend. The *Weekly Freeman's Journal* ran biographies of 'Dublin Heroes who Fell Fighting' at Gallipoli on its front page in September 1915, and blamed the casualties at Gallipoli on British generals, publishing a poem that claimed 'By dullard generals thus was lost/The gorgeous East, won at such cost/By the Irish at Gallipoli'. (BNL, *WFJ*, 11.9.15, 26.8.16). The *Irish Weekly Independent* attacked the 'blundering and indecision' of the British at Gallipoli (BNL, *IWI*, 15.1.16, p. 4). Even the Unionist *Weekly Irish Times* changed during 1915. Before the attack at Gallipoli, the Irish Roll of Honour was on an inside page – while from August 1915 it appeared on the front page every week, and included photos of 'Irish Heroes Killed and Wounded' (BNL, *WIT*, 21.8.15, p. 1, et fl.).

War was seen by advanced nationalists as more than a betrayal of the nationalist cause. The loss of so many potential volunteers ('soldiers of Ireland') meant the possible loss of any chance for Irish liberty.[33] Herbert Pim, writing as A. Newman, published his poem 'The Charmer' in the October 1914 *Irish Freedom*. Hearkening back to the show of force by the Volunteers at the Howth gun-running in July 1914, Pim reacted with dismay to the subsequent outbreak of war:

> Surely our day of destiny has come?
> For as one man our Nation stood to arms:
> And Ireland's soil caressed her children's feet,
> Marching behind no idiot fife and drum!
> But lo! a charmer cometh with his charms;
> And we must wrap us in our winding sheet.[34]

Sean O Concubair was brutal, instructing his readers to 'forget all you've suffered' promising 'A holocaust to you I'll offer/The blood of my own Volunteers'.[35] For Griffith, and even more Eoin MacNeill, the men who stayed with Redmond in the National Volunteers, and enlisted in the new Sixteenth (Irish) Division were sorely missed. Alice Ffrench viewed the war as a form of brutal birth control, claiming in 'Too Many Irish Again' that English war-lords used recruiting to destroy a young generation of Irishmen:

> But the statesmen of England are wiser to-day!
> They are killing two birds with one stone;
> To death and to glory! for England – away!
> And your place they'll fill up with one of their own.[36]

Angered by the rush of young men to imperial colours, poets of the nationalist movement unleashed dramatic attacks on their enlistment. It was not enough merely for their fellow Irishmen to condemn these men – poets called on the spirits of the Irish nation, and of the martyred dead of Ireland's past to assault anyone who dared to join. In 'Ireland's Malediction', published in October 1914, Arthur Harvey raged:

> Great God! – Are ye fool or a knave that ye dare
> Come to me for a blessing instead of my scorn;
> ...

---

33 The IRB's almost immediate planning of a Rising to take place during the war leads one to think that perhaps MacDermott was exaggerating his dismay in *Irish Freedom*. Griffith's attitude, however, seems to be genuine.   34 BNL, *IF*, October 1914, p. 6.   35 BNL, *SF*, 22.8.14, p. 1.   36 Ibid., p. 11.

> When England has done with thee Satan comes on;
> Dare not say thou wert mine! – lest I gain his contempt.[37]

Brian O'Higgins placed the curse of 'Ireland's Dead': 'On every man who fights to-day for England in her need'.[38]

The crucial fact to note with both these examples, the only ones found which so explicitly condemn recruits, is that they were written and published before any volunteers had seen significant action. This is a central difference that seems to have escaped other historians examining this period.[39] The hatred in Harvey's and O'Higgins' writing is obvious, but volunteers had yet to be killed in the war when these were written. Once Irish troops began to participate in violent combat, harsh mockery and derision virtually disappeared.

Once Irish volunteers in the British army began to suffer casualties, the worst that was said of them was that they were misguided fools who had been tricked into volunteering for certain death by recruiters. Connolly in particular was careful to differentiate between his attitude to the war and volunteers, and to the actual fact of casualties. Early in the war, again before significant numbers of Irish troops had fallen in action, he headlined an article 'Recruiting – Let the Wastrels Go', and declared 'let the dupes go – Ireland is well rid of them. There will be more room for the good men who remain behind'.[40] Brian O'Higgins' 1914 poem 'A Call to Arms' begged the 'strong young men of Erin' to 'Be tools and fools no more/Reserve your strength and daring/For her who needs them sore'.[41]

These attitudes were modified by the following year. In his essay, 'The Slums and the Trenches', published in the *Worker's Republic* in February 1916, and later re-issued as a pamphlet, Connolly called the Irish soldiers 'these poor misguided brothers of ours', poor men of the Dublin slums who had been 'tricked and deluded into giving battle for England'.[42] Connolly himself never rejoiced at the death of soldiers in battle. As early as September 1914, he wrote 'I am not writing this because I glory in the tales of the British dead. Those poor rank and file were, and are, no enemies of mine, of my class, nor of my nation'.[43]

Connolly's guarded respect and pity for these men is a far cry from the curses that greeted recruits in the first days of the Great War. As Irish troops began to prove their commitment in blood, scorn for them virtually disappeared in the advanced nationalist press.[44] A holocaust of blood wiped out the shame of

---

37 BNL, *IW*, 17.10.14, p. 4. 38 BNL, *IF*, October 1914, p. 7. 39 Cf. Ellis, 1997, pp. 342-61. 40 BNL, *WR*, 5.9.14, p. 1. 41 KSRL, OH B3542: Brian O'Higgins, *Sentinel Songs* (Dublin, 1918), 'A Call to Arms' (1915). 42 NLI, *WR*, 26.2.16, pp. 1-2; and NLI MS 1428: MS essay, *The Slums and the Trenches*. 43 BNL, *IW*, 5.9.14, p. 1. 44 One concrete example of scorn after 1915 was found, an editorial in the *Spark* in January 1916, condemning Irish 'mercenaries' who joined the British army, and were forced to 'serve as cock-shots for German,

enlistment by Irish soldiers. Just as the vast majority of scornful examples came from the first months of the war, most sympathetic examples come from 1915 and 1916, continuing right up to the last issues of newspapers before the Easter Rising briefly silenced the propaganda of nationalist Ireland. This pattern reinforces the contention that external events on the front lines contributed to the change in attitude, and that indeed there was a measurable change of attitude. The Great War transformed advanced nationalist beliefs about Irish troops in the British army. It is difficult to say exactly why this change occurred. Perhaps advanced nationalist propagandists were themselves overcome by the pity of war – or, to take a more cynical view, perhaps all this reveals is a clever manipulation of public opinion. For advanced nationalism to succeed politically, its publicity organs had to appeal to public sentiment – and from 1915 on, this sentiment was more and more in favour of a party which allowed people to oppose the war without disrespecting the men who fought.

Two examples from a single newspaper will suffice to show the general attitude of advanced nationalists after 1915. In the first number of the *Gael* in January 1916, 'The Typical Soldier' explained to readers how an ordinary man who enlists is 'hectored, brow-beaten, repressed, sworn at, made into a machine to obey all orders'.[45] The writer asked the readers 'How would you like to be him. Do you not pity him'.[46] Two months later 'M.A.E.V'. (Maeve Cavanagh) wrote a story entitled 'The One Way Out', which demonstrates perfectly how courage in action, even suicidal courage, served as a form of redemption. Kate Smith's son, Ned, joined the British army while drunk, whereupon Kate threw him out of the house, forbade him the rosary beads of his 'Fenian Father', and begged God to never let him return. In order to be forgiven, Ned kills himself charging against German guns. When Kate learns the news, 'a great sorrowful cry rent the air: "My son, my son!"'[47] Ned Smith, a fictional representation of Irish soldiery, had overcome the disgrace of enlistment through suicidal courage, and in so doing, had reawakened his mother's love.

Propagandists even displayed pride at the warring exploits of Irishmen, both fictionalized and real.[48] John B. Kennedy's poem 'Tipperary' celebrated the life

---

Austrian, Turkish, and Bulgarian snipers'. (BNL, *Spark*, 30.1.16, pp. 1–2). Dr John Ellis uses two other examples from the Samuels' Collection, but one of these ballads was written before 1914 (references to the 'Red of England'), and the other refers only to *basic* training, and has nothing to do with action seen by Irish troops. (Cf. Ellis, 1997, p. 343. Material cited in Ellis under TCD, Samuels 5/26. Also found in CUL HIB.5.916.21). Patrick Maume cites an editorial in *Honesty* from April 1916 in which the editor implied that those who fought for the allies were condemned to Hell, but Maume fails to draw a distinction between allied and specifically Irish troops. (Cf. Maume, 1999, p. 166, discussing *Honesty*, 15 April 1916).   45 BNL, *Gael*, 29.1.16, p. 16.   46 Ibid.   47 Ibid., 18.3.16, p. 7.   48 Michael O'Leary, V.C., perhaps the first Irish 'Hero' of the war, was a consistent source of mockery in propagandistic

and death of Mickey O'Fay, killed fighting for the British. O'Fay is a source of pride for his creator, and not someone destined for eternal fire:

> He's singing the psalm of the fighting race
> And his soul soars wide o'erhead.
>
> He killed three foemen before he fell
> (Och, the toll he'd take, and the skulls he'd break!)[49]

A more gruesome pride was felt by an anonymous author who penned a tribute to Cork soldiers, 'Dedicated to the Irish Brigade, Morrison's Island'. Following the British stand on the Marne which turned back the first German offensive of the war, the author proudly reported on the conduct of local Irishmen in the affray, remarking that 'The river Aisne has ceased to flow, 'tis choked with German dead,/And the bodies cannot float, because they're filled with British lead'.[50]

Advanced nationalist leaders publicly declared their respect for Irish front-line veterans. MacNeill stated in February 1916:

> Let me say plainly that if any Irishman is convinced that he will serve Ireland by becoming a British soldier, and if he acts on that conviction, he is a patriotic and a brave man. If any Irishman thinks sincerely that Mr Redmond is entitled to be the keeper of his political conscience, and that he serves Ireland by following Mr Redmond's advice without reserve, and if for that reason he becomes a British soldier, he is a brave man.[51]

J.J. Burke, a frequent columnist in the *Worker's Republic*, attacked the reluctance of Irishmen who refused to enlist or help the nationalist struggle, remarking 'the Irishmen in the British army have at least the courage of their convictions – and they die for them'.[52]

While propagandists might consider the deaths of Irish recruits to be a waste, the actual deaths were used in propaganda to advance the nationalist cause. The deaths of volunteers, indeed even the deaths of regular army men and reservists who were suffering casualties from the very first days of war, convinced propagandists that the war was a betrayal of Home Rule promises. If the enlistment of men marked the possible end of any chance of full independence, then the deaths (and potential deaths) of so many marked the end of Home

---

writings. However, this mockery was directed at O'Leary's participation in recruiting drives, not his actual actions in battle. **49** BNL, *IV*, 28.11.14, p. 2. **50** KSRL, OH G26, *CC*, 3.10.14, p. 1. It is interesting to note that while the author is writing about a local unit from Cork, it still refers to the Germans being full of 'British lead'. **51** BNL, *IV*, 12.2.16, p. 1. **52** NLI, *WR*, 29.1.16, p. 8.

Rule's guarantees. *An Claidheamh Soluis* asked 'What of all the promises of Asquith and of his Irish satellites? ... These promises are as shattered as the ranks of the brave Irishmen who fell in front of the English at Suvla Bay and in the English rear in Serbia'.[53]

The courage of the Irishmen seeing action stood in sharp contrast to the perceived cowardice and hypocrisy of the recruiters who had convinced them to join.[54] From the very start of the war, recruiters were held responsible for the deaths of men in the army. 'Recruiting Sergeant John Redmond', a cartoon from the *Irish Worker* by Ernest Kavanagh, shows John Redmond dressed as a recruiting sergeant, luring a young man towards a British trench where the grim figure of Death stalks over piled corpses.[55] Recruiters were murderers, not just cowards. Connolly cried that 'from the blood-soaked graves of the Belgian frontiers the spirits of murdered Irish soldiers of England call to Heaven for vengeance upon the Parliamentarian tricksters who seduced them into the armies of the oppressor of their country'.[56]

Rather than curse the soldiers braving shellfire to eternal damnation, propagandists began to turn this malediction on to recruiters, threatening them with what one historian has called 'vengeance ... of Biblical proportions'.[57] 'A Veteran' writing in the *Irish Volunteer* declared that 'to barter away the lives of 40,000 young Irishmen as part and parcel of a Parliamentary bargain is an offence crying to Heaven for vengeance'.[58] Maurice Healy[59] came in for an especially vitriolic attack in the *Spark*. Calling Healy a 'prostitute' and a 'youth with evil venomed tongue', Tadg Barry cursed him, praying that 'may every vile thought in your head,/Begetting lies of Ireland's dead/Be heard yet – where they echo well/In the congenial pits of Hell'.[60]

Press coverage of the Gallipoli campaign was universally disliked. James Connolly called the Dardanelles a 'fiasco', and wrote a bitter article in December 1915 attacking the War Office's complacent announcement of the peninsula's evacuation:[61]

> The Irish families who have lost sons, brothers and fathers in the Dardanelles ... will not derive much comfort from the statement ... we ask

---

53 BNL, *ACS*, 18.12.15, p. 8.   **54** Three titles from Maeve Cavanagh further illustrate this point. 'England's Recruiting Jackals', 'The Coming of the Irish Judas and his Paymaster' and 'To Ireland's Betrayers' were all published in the *Irish Worker* in the first two months of the war.   **55** BNL, *IW*, 5.9.14, p. 1.   **56** BNL, ibid., 29.8.14, p. 1.   **57** Ellis, 1997, p. 358.   **58** BNL, *IV*, 31.10.14, p. 15.   **59** Subaltern in the Royal Dublin Fusiliers, and son of Irish Parliamentary Party MP T.M. Healy.   **60** BNL, *Spark*, 2.1.16, p. 4.   **61** This sentiment was shared to a certain degree by constitutionalist newspapers. The *Irish Weekly Independent* blamed the failure of Gallipoli on the 'blundering and indecision' of British generals (BNL, *IWI*, 15.1.16, p. 4), and the *Weekly Freeman* ran a poem claiming that 'By dullard generals thus was lost/The gorgeous East, won at such cost/By the Irish at Gallipoli'. (BNL, *WFJ*, 26.8.16, p. 4).

them to remember all the funny stories and cartoons about the panic at Constantinople ... and all the other products of a diseased imagination with which the Capitalist press lured thousands of Irishmen to their destruction.[62]

Anger at differing casualty rates between Irish and British regiments appeared almost immediately in the advanced nationalist press. Griffith reminded his readers in August 1914 that the Irish had suffered disproportionate casualties in Buller's campaign during the Boer War,[63] and the Irish Neutrality League later passed a resolution proposed by Griffith condemning similar happenings in the Great War.[64] The disaster of Gallipoli spread this rage further. *Honesty* remarked that most of the troops at Gallipoli were Irish, and that 'the whitening bones of the Colonial and Irish troops on the Gallipoli Peninsula constitute perhaps the most colossal monument ever raised to Murder by Muddling'.[65] Casualties at Gallipoli did come predominantly from Irish and ANZAC forces. The Twenty-Ninth Division, where the Royal Dublin Fusiliers and the Royal Munster Fusiliers held pride of place, lost over 9,000 men killed in action, or about one in five of the total killed in the entire campaign.[66]

The anger felt by advanced nationalists at these inequitable casualties, and the belief that Irish regiments were being ignored in dispatches, is one of the few issues upon which Irishmen across the political spectrum of constitutional and advanced nationalism agreed before the Conscription Crisis of spring 1918. John Dillon complained in Parliament, and Denis Gwynn, a Home Ruler and stout supporter of John Redmond, declared that the perception of unfair casualties was widespread in Ireland.[67] Canon James Hannay ('George Birmingham') believed that the failure of the British to publicize heroic deeds harmed recruiting:

> We read long casualty lists and mark in them the names of friends. But what do we know about the way they fell? ... We are a people not ... blind to the glory of great deeds. It stirs the dullest of us to find the names of those we know blown backwards to us from the lips of fame ... The management of a democracy at war is not the same thing as the drilling of a squad of recruits ... Theirs, no doubt, but to do and die? But ours? We must know what we are to do and how our sons are to die.[68]

---

62 NLI, *WR*, 25.12.15, p. 7. See also *Hib*, 27.11.15; *Hon*, 30.10.15, 1.1.16. 63 BNL, *SF*, 29.8.14, p. 3. 64 Ibid., 17.10.14, p. 1. 65 BNL, *Hon*, 27.11.15, pp. 3-4. 66 Cf. Robert Rhodes James, *Gallipoli* (London, 1965) for more details. 67 Cf. Hennessey, 1998, pp. 109-10. 68 Hannay, 1916, p. 180.

Some advanced nationalists expressed the notion that if they were in power such wanton bloodshed would be avoided. Maeve Cavanagh informed her young readers that 'if the past generation had had the advantages which are held out to us to-day Ireland might not now be sending out Irishmen to manure the battlefields of Europe'.[69] The majority of writings[70] showed true pity for the men suffering on the front lines. Before the Rising, this pity, and a form of respect as well, even extended to British soldiers. In January 1916, the *Hibernian* featured a front-page editorial remarking 'to give the English their due, they have furnished – including the Colonies – an enormous quota of men to swell the ranks of their country's fighting forces'.[71] A month earlier *Honesty* had published gruesome statistics showing that the casualties around Loos had reached 95,000 in the previous three months, and wondered whether it was really 'worth while beating the Germans if the cost of the victory is to be commensurate with that paid for the triumph at Loos'.[72]

Part of the sorrow and anger felt by propagandists at so many men being killed and wounded was that these were young, healthy men. Young men were a commodity already in short supply in Ireland before the war, due mainly, it was felt, to high rates of emigration and the after-effects of the Great Famine. Rather than seeing the recruits as moral and physical degenerates, the *Cork Celt* called the Dublin Fusiliers 'fine types of Irish manhood ... in the bloom of their youth they were going forth to fight'.[73] The *Celt* regretted the deaths of many of these men, with only 42 remaining of the original 600.[74] *Nationality*, in a poem that was a far cry from the derision of the first year of war, combined sympathy for Irish soldiers with some xenophobia, remembering that many of the men who were now suffering in the army had once been Irish Volunteers:

> And some far away in Flanders,
> Or out at the Dardanelles,
> Are targets for German cannon
> Or mangled by Moslem shells[75]

The horrific loss of so many Irishmen was a cause for anger, disgust, and sorrow among advanced nationalist propagandists. As with the fact of the war itself, propagandists were able to use the suffering of these men to their own

---

69 BNL, *Fianna*, December 1915, p. 3.   70 Even the *Hibernian*'s stern 'The Curse and its Cause' article from October 1915 (erroneously cited by Patrick Maume as appearing in the *Spark*, and used by him as an example of advanced nationalist condemnation of Irish recruits) ([Maume, 1999, p. 166]), in which a Father McHugh declared that those soldiers who were burned to death by German flame-throwers were suffering a 'swift and terrible punishment' for volunteering, showed pity for the actual deaths witnessed on the Western Front and at Gallipoli.   71 BNL, *Hib*, 15.1.16, p. 1.   72 BNL, *Hon*, 11.12.15, p. 4.   73 KSRL, OH G26: *CC*, 17.10.14, p. 1.   74 Ibid.   75 BNL, *Nat*, 2.10.15, p. 2.

advantage. Crucially, however, they were able to do this without mocking the men themselves. Above all, the men who died were Irishmen, and brave ones at that. The tragedy for nationalists was that their deaths happened in the wrong country. As 'The Wounded Irishman' wrote in the *Worker's Republic*, 'Full many a noble Irish lad has bravely fought and fell, chum:/And oh! it makes my heart feel sad, to think 'twas all for Belgium'.[76]

III

Easter Week of 1916 could be seen as Ireland's first civil war of the twentieth century. Irish insurgents and soldiers in Irish regiments, some actually related, fought each other in the streets of Dublin. In a truly literal sense, the Rising brought the war home to Dubliners, who saw trenches dug in St Stephen's Green and the centre of their city destroyed by the modern weapons of war. Did this event change Irish nationalists' attitudes to the men in the firing lines of France and Flanders?

We know from the research of Jane Leonard and Terence Denman that the Rising had little effect on the Irishmen serving on the Western Front. According to Leonard, most Irish officers in the British army at the time saw it either as 'a stab in the back', or, if less experienced and in Ireland at the time, as a source of excitement.[77] Terence Denman, studying the Sixteenth (Irish) Division, which first came under German attack at Hulluch during the week of the Rising, describes how regiments of the division were informed of the Rising by German troops, and responded by playing patriotic airs, singing *God Save the King*, capturing the German propaganda placards, and even hanging an effigy of Sir Roger Casement in no-man's-land.[78]

An anonymous poet in 1916 attempted to express the emotions felt by an Irish soldier fighting against the rebels during the Rising. A soldier whose father went out with the Fenians, and whose grandfather fought in '48, hears of the Rising, and immediately thinks 'I heard the Sinn Féiners had risen/... My heart gave a jump at the thought/I would join with the boys in the Rising/And fight as my Forefathers fought'.[79] Quickly, he realizes the impossibility of this, as 'the Rising brought joy to the Germans/To Irishmen sorrow & shame'.[80]

If the majority of serving officers (and men, as far as can be known) reacted with disgust and anger to the treacherous behaviour of sections of the Irish

---

76 NLI, *WR*, 6.11.15, p. 8.   77 Jane Leonard, 'The Reaction of Irish Officers in the British Army to the Easter Rising of 1916', in Hugh Cecil and Peter Liddle (eds.), *Facing Armageddon: The First World War Experienced* (London, 1996), pp. 256-68.   78 Denman, 1992, pp. 129-30.   79 NLI MS 15317: 'Verses as if by an Irishman who fought in the British Army against the Irish in Easter Week', 'Easter Monday'. Cit. also in Hennessy, 1998, pp. 143-4.   80 Ibid.

population, how did the population react to British and Irish soldiers, once the soldiers had actively participated in the bloody suppression of the Easter Rising? From research into post-Rising propaganda, it becomes clear that the Rising, by demonstrating the possibility of practical resistance to the British, changed, and indeed brutalized the discourse of propagandists dealing with war. This alone, however, was not enough to change the general tone in propaganda of exhaustion with and hatred of the war, nor indeed to change the overall respect and pity felt for Irish soldiers in the army by propagandists.

As will be seen with humorous propaganda, aggressive propaganda directed against British soldiers became more marked after the Rising, and propagandists began to take a conscious glee in the suffering of British soldiers. Propagandists quickly sought written revenge against Englishmen, soldier and civilian alike. Calling on German zeppelin pilots who could actually reach London, the Irish-American newspaper the *Irish World* wrote in mid-May 1916:

> In Dublin Town they murdered them,
> Like dogs they shot them down;
> God's curse be on you England, now,
> God strike your London town.[81]

Nationalist poets greeted with glee actual battles in which British forces met with heavy casualties, so long as few Irish troops were involved. The June 1916 battle of Jutland, which originally appeared inconclusive, and only later came to be seen as an important British naval victory, was discussed in poems by internees at Knutsford Prison. *The Day of the Scagger Wreck*,[82] written at Knutsford Prison when news of Jutland arrived, rejoiced at the allies' misfortunes, both in the North Sea and at Verdun.[83] The 'Sean Bhean Bhocht' told what would happen when the rebels heard the news of the allied powers' various defeats. The rebels would 'get right down and pray,/That the Huns may shoot away,/Every scrap of England's sway, says the Sean Bhean Bhocht'.[84] In contrast, the Somme battles during the summer and autumn of 1916 passed without a mention, as Irish regiments, north and south, participated in some of the worst fighting, and paid a terrible price.[85]

81 CUL, HIB.5.916.27: *Irish World*, 13 May 1916, 'Vengeance'.   82 The author probably meant 'Skaggerak', the German name for the battle.   83 Despite the lack of any British troops there.   84 UCD, The O'Rahilly Papers, P102/495: *Songs and Poems: The REBELS who Fought and Died for IRELAND in Easter Week, 1916*, 'The Day of the Scagger Wreck'. 85 An interesting support for this contention is that the official British film *Battle of the Somme*, which was seen by a record 10,000 people in Dublin during the first half week of its opening in September 1916, was completely ignored in the advanced nationalist press. (Cf. Nicholas Reeves, 'Through the Eye of the Camera: Contemporary Cinema Audiences and their 'Experience' of War in the film, *Battle of the Somme*', in Cecil and Liddle [eds]., 1996, p. 783).

When only British troops were involved, propagandists freely scorned their suffering. The sight of the Union Jack being flown at half-mast over St Patrick's Cathedral on Empire Day in 1917 caused Arthur Griffith to wonder if Archbishop Bernard believed that 'England was up the pole', and remarked that nevertheless 'no proceedings under the Defence of the Realm Act have been instituted against the Dean of St Patrick's'.[86] Indeed, generous and practical responses to the sufferings of Irish Volunteers and their dependants after the Rising were often clouded by gratuitous cruelty towards British wounded who were recuperating in Dublin. A Cumann na mBan member, suggesting that convalescent Volunteers be given places in the countryside to recuperate for a few weeks, complained that 'there are Irish men and women devoting all their time and attention to English wounded soldiers, and are we going to neglect our own?'[87] Even the Kerry Branch of the Irish Creamery Managers' Association was not immune to such mixed reactions. At a May 1917 meeting, a Mr J. Byrne of Ballymacelligot proposed to send a gift of butter from each creamery to the dependants of the Volunteers who 'sacrificed their lives and liberties on behalf of their country', arguing that 'there was much if not more reason why assistance should be given to the dependants of these men than to the victims of the present war, who some time ago received parcels of butter from almost all creameries'.[88]

As with propaganda before the Rising, writers blamed the recruiters of the Redmondite Irish Parliamentary Party for the deaths of so many Irish recruits. Unlike the writings from 1914 to Easter 1916, the aggression directed against recruiters was far more focused, and writers began to find a way to effectively attack the men who had led the youth of Ireland to premature death. *Young Ireland* went so far as to suggest that a Home Rule parliament would have placed the Irish in a far more dangerous position. If Redmond had been ruling Ireland in 1914, it maintained, 'the poor, the weak, and the factionist would have been drafted to Flanders, whilst the sterling, uncompromising Redmondite would have had his reward in an immunity from anything martial'.[89] Advanced nationalists greeted with mixed emotion the untimely death of John Redmond himself in March 1918. Redmond was disliked – Seamus O'Sullivan called him an 'Apostate Leader, England's Tool'[90] – but this opinion was mainly expressed before his death.[91] Some moderate propagandists

---

86 BNL, *Nat*, 2.6.17, p. 2.   87 Ibid., p. 5.   88 Ibid., p. 2.   89 BNL, *Og*, 23.2.18, p. 5.   90 BNL, *Fianna*, November 1915, p. 9, and UCD, O'Rahilly Papers, P102/500, Poems on the Easter Rising, 'To J.E.R'.   91 John Ellis argues that Redmond was considered one of the worst villains in Ireland, generalising from the most extreme commemorative pamphlet, one written by 'M. Ni. G' [possibly Maire Nic Chearbhaill] which remarked viciously 'England indeed has lost a friend. She has lost no greater since the death of Diarmuid McMurragh'. (Cf. NLI ILB 300 Series, ILB 300 P6, fol. 97, 'John Redmond is Dead', and Ellis, 1997, p. 349).

of advanced nationalism saw his death as a tragedy. Griffith acknowledged that Redmond had become a pawn of the empire, noting that Parnell died 'the most hated and feared man of his century by England', while the 'armed forces of England' marched in Redmond's funeral procession to muffled drums.[92] Nevertheless, Redmond had led the Irish nation at Westminster, and his death was still 'a tragedy utterly different and entirely pitiful – a tragedy of the poor human nature which impels us to pray that the Lord may have mercy on John Redmond's soul'.[93] The *Catholic Bulletin* criticized some of Redmond's more recent actions, but laid the blame for these decisions at the feet of 'degenerate elements' which had infiltrated the Irish Parliamentary Party, and made sure to state that they desired 'in no way to asperse the memory or the motives of the late leader'.[94]

The most important difference in rhetoric directed against recruiters before and after the Rising is the way in which post-Rising propagandists used their anger to encourage people to vote for Sinn Féin, and by electing a party opposed to the war, remove the chance of their having to serve in the British army. The Easter Rising created a set of electoral opportunities for Sinn Féin, but it was the Great War that was used in propaganda to promote the advantages of voting the advanced nationalist line. The death of recruits was no longer merely wastage or a cause of sorrow, but rather also a potent new weapon in the electoral arsenal of Sinn Féin. Michael O'Flanagan, the 'Sinn Féin Priest', summed-up the differences between Sinn Féin and Parliamentarianism in September 1918, pointing out that Irish Parliamentary Party policy was 'to send 167,000 men to shed their blood for our friend England and die bitterly repenting their foolishness, like Tom Kettle ... To be conscripted to fight in a war because John Dillon held and still holds, that it is Ireland's war'.[95]

Older anti-recruiting posters were re-used in by-elections leading up the general election of December 1918. Dr Patrick McCartan's unsuccessful by-election campaign in South Armagh saw the graphics from a brutal 1915[96] anti-war poster (figure 1.1) placed above a text that explicitly spelled out the difference between the Sinn Féin and Parliamentary policies. 'Fathers of Armagh', the poster asks, 'Do you want your boys to Live in Ireland instead of Dying in France, Flanders, Egypt &c.?'[97] Election propaganda turned the rhetoric of the Parliamentarians back on themselves. After John Dillon and

---

92 BNL, *Nat*, 16.3.18, p. 1.   93 Ibid.   94 Bod., *Catholic Bulletin*, April 1918, pp. 158–9.   95 CUL, HIB.7.918.12: 'The Two Policies: Sinn Féin or ... Parliamentarianism'.   96 The date is clear from the old-fashioned ('Kitchener Blue') uniforms worn by the skeletons, and by Redmond's reference to 'an Irish regiment', something which he did not begin doing with regularity until 1915.   97 NLI, ILB 300 Series, ILB 300 P9, fol. 44. Illustration from KSRL, OH Q42:14 (Sinn Féin Propaganda). Original anti-recruiting poster cited in Ellis, 1997, p. 358.

1.1 *Redmond's Advice!* (by-election poster, 1918, KSRL)

Joseph Devlin reaffirmed that they had done their best to recruit men into the army, Sinn Féin asked 'On their very own showing, was not the Irish Party the Party which shed seas of Irish blood? No less than 60,000 Irishmen have been mutilated and slaughtered in this war – FOR WHAT? Who are Dillon and Devlin, to traduce the Sixty-Eight Men who died in Easter Week?'[98] Despite the domestic violence of Easter Week, Sinn Féin was able to advertize itself as a party of peace, attracting war-weary voters.

The Easter Rising itself did not seem to affect the attitude that propagandists held towards Irish troops. The vast majority of advanced nationalist journalists evinced strong displays of sympathy and even pride and respect for the Irish volunteers in the British army. The dilemmas underpinning the conflict of the Rising, the actual battle between men who knew each other, or were related to each other, highlighted the idea that recruits were also men acting according to the conscience of their wills, and following what they considered to be their duty. Close friends and relatives of some of the most important leaders of the Rising fought in the British army, or even were involved in the suppression of the Rising.[99] Some propagandists even encouraged the idea that all men, in the army and the Volunteers, loved and would die for Ireland. Having shot a young rebel who was shooting at him, the narrator of 'Easter Monday' cursed that 'a ball that was meant for a German/Went home in an Irish boy's breast', yet rested secure that 'He in the heaven above/Will fight hard & pray hard/For the Land that both of us love'.[100]

While individual soldiers later recalled abuse from civilians after the Rising,[101] advanced nationalist leaders encouraged a policy of forgiveness and understanding. In his last message to the Irish people, a piece of writing which would be highly publicized and distributed as propaganda around the island, Casement noted the courage of soldiers on the Western Front, remarking 'I cast no stone at the millions of brave dead throughout Europe – God rest their souls in peace'.[102] The deaths in action of some of the very men who had worked hardest as recruiters, especially Tom Kettle and Willie Redmond, went a long

---

98 NLI, ILB 300 Series, ILB 300 P1, fol. 58.   99 Leonard cites the case of Captain Eugene Sheehy, 4th Royal Dublin Fusiliers; an un-named officer commanding the firing squad for Joseph Plunkett, who was excused on revealing that he was a childhood friend of Plunkett's; and William Kent, brother of Eamonn Ceannt, who was killed in action with the Royal Dublin Fusiliers in 1917. (Cf. Leonard, 1996, pp. 260-3). The *Catholic Bulletin* of September 1916, writing the obituary of the rebel Richard Reilly, mentioned that two of his brothers had joined the British army, and one of them had been killed in France. 'So varied', wrote the author, 'are our conceptions of duty'. (*Catholic Bulletin*, September 1916, p. 523).   100 NLI MS 15317: 'Verses as if by an Irishman who fought in the British Army against the Irish in Easter Week', 'Easter Monday'. Also cit. in Hennessey, 1998, pp. 143-4.   101 Cf. Jane Leonard, 'Facing "the Finger of Scorn": Veterans' Memories of Ireland after the Great War', in Martin Evans and Ken Lunn (eds.), *War and Memory in the Twentieth Century* (Oxford, 1997), pp. 59-72.   102 NLI, ILB 300 Series, ILB 300 P1, fol. 63; and CUL, HIB Series, HIB.7.916.9.

way towards erasing the considered hypocrisy and cowardice of the Redmondites.

Herbert Pim's the *Irishman* went so far as to apologize for a 'light-hearted reference to Professor Kettle'[103] that had gone to press in its last issue before news of Kettle's death on the Somme had reached the editor. 'Those who knew Professor Kettle recognized in him a good soul and brilliant wit', wrote Pim. 'He was far too good for the Party with whom he was unfortunately associated. We record our sorrow at his untimely death. May he rest in peace'.[104] M.S. O'Lonnain used Kettle's courage to mock Joseph Devlin in April 1918, writing 'we have little reason to expect from Devlin the same fighting instinct of a Tom Kettle. Idealism, however inconsequent, is not to be expected from a bodach [churl]'.[105] The sacrifice of Willie Redmond was also used to attack other recruiters. However, even though advanced nationalists used his death for propagandistic purposes, they still grew angry with Redmondite attempts to exploit the death of their leader's younger brother. Aodh de Blacam responded to 'Mystified's' query in July 1917 immediately after Redmond's death at Messines Ridge: 'No, I cannot tell you anything about Major Redmond. Like you, never heard of him till he died'.[106] A year later, having taken the editor's job at *Young Ireland*, M.S. O'Lonnain was far more sympathetic. Attacking the 'Masonic Valour' of Sir Edward Carson, he wrote:

> Speaking at the Man-Power debate gude Sir Yadward [Carson] remembered when he rode at the head of some hundreds of Carson's army to the recruiting offices one morning, and he was more proud of this act than anything he had done in his life. Well, God rest his soul Willy [*sic*] Redmond rode a little further. But Willy [*sic*] was a Catholic, not a Freemason.[107]

Propaganda that showed sympathy to Irish soldiers was not isolated to a few examples. Sympathy for Irish recruits was prevalent in propaganda both before and after the Easter Rising. When war first came to Ireland in August 1914, propagandists reacted to the surge in enlistment with disgust and anger. The tone and style of their anti-recruiting propaganda reflected the mockery and scorn of much pre-war material. Quickly, however, as Irish casualties grew and the war stretched on, attitudes shifted. The war was viewed with increasing horror, and by the summer of 1915 pity, sympathy, and pride in Irish soldiers had

---

103 From 'The Fruits of Compromize', an article on the Irish Parliamentary Party and Home Rule (*Irishman*, 23.9.16, p. 2): 'One might picture Captain Kettle in one of his brighter moments making a midnight call upon the two Johns and a Joe, and awakening those astonished persons to assure them that "Home Rule is on the Statute Book"'. 104 BNL, *Irishman*, 30.9.16, p. 2. 105 BNL, *Og*, 13.4.18, p. 1. 106 Ibid., 7.7.17, p. 7. 107 Ibid., 20.4.18, p. 2.

replaced scorn. By presenting an anti-war platform that respected the combatants involved, advanced nationalist movements were able to attract recruits and eventual votes from the population of an increasingly war-weary Ireland.

2

The Great War and the use of history in atrocity propaganda

'To persuade the masses to fight', wrote James Morgan Read in 1941, 'they must be led to hate'.[1] One way in which the masses were taught to hate during the Great War was through atrocity propaganda. This chapter examines the advanced nationalist response to atrocity propaganda used in Ireland. Atrocity counter-propaganda served a set of crucial functions in war-time Ireland: it acted as a buffer against the lurid tales of pro-war propagandists; it created a novel way of attacking British activities throughout the war; and showed the importance of history and folk-tradition to the construction of an Irish identity. These traditional folk-tales of British evil far outweighed new atrocity propaganda, and by using current events, advanced nationalist propagandists demonstrated their skill at using the war to their own advantage.[2]

I

The sinking of the *Lusitania* in May 1915 and the German execution of British nurse Edith Cavell are two of many specific atrocities from the Great War that were widely used in propaganda. How did advanced nationalist propagandists react to such reports? With these particular atrocities, no attempt could be made to deny their occurrence. Neither, despite the perceived immorality, hypocrisy, and barbarism of the British, could it be claimed that they were fabrications. However, with each of these cases, anti-war propagandists found a way to attack the British, and especially what they felt to be the criminal cowardice of British officials.

The *Lusitania*, pride of the British Cunard Line, was torpedoed off the south coast of Ireland on 7 May 1915 as she neared the end of a journey from New York to Liverpool. In calm seas and bright sunlight, she went down quickly, sinking in under twenty minutes. Of the passengers and crew, 1,198 drowned. British propagandists made much of this action. Not only was the *Lusitania* the

---

1 James Morgan Read, *Atrocity Propaganda, 1914–1919* (New Haven, 1941), p. 2. 2 Other historians studying this issue have ignored the centrality of atrocity counter-propaganda to the use of history. Cf. Donal McCartney, 'The Political Use of History in the Work of Arthur Griffith', *JCH*, vol. 8, no. 1 (January 1973), pp. 3–20.

largest ship yet sunk by a U-boat, there was hope that the horror felt by many Americans at the loss of fellow countrymen[3] would hasten America's entry into the war. The disaster also had particular significance in Ireland. Sunk almost within sight of Kinsale Head, the *Lusitania* carried many Irishmen on board, from passengers in steerage to more well-known figures, such as Sir Hugh Lane, modern art dealer, collector, and director of Ireland's National Gallery. Survivors and corpses were landed at Queenstown, and Under-Secretary Sir Matthew Nathan's office at Dublin Castle had to handle both providing for the survivors and communicating with the Home and War Offices in London.

Recruiting propagandists quickly seized the incident. *Irishmen Avenge the Lusitania*[4] (figure 2.1), 7,500 copies of which were printed in Dublin by John Shuley & Co. for the Central Council for the Organization of Recruiting in Ireland (CCORI), attempted to appeal to Irish sensibilities about the affair. The green sea in the foreground is dotted with drowning figures, including two women and a child. The faces of the father and young girl in the immediate foreground are intentionally Irish, with dark hair and dark eyes. The father, swimming for driftwood with an unusually large toddler on his back, is exhausted, and will not reach the flotsam. The overall effect of this poster, however, combining the drowning Irish and the sinking ship, is somewhat bathetic. Dominating the picture-plane from the background third, the out-of-scale ship rears out of the water. Funnels ablaze, and ringed in the smoke of roiling explosions, the *Lusitania* begins her swift descent to the bottom of the Irish Sea. Clearly visible is the Union Jack, still proudly waving. While the artist was correct to place a Union Jack on this British-registered ship, it was still perhaps a slight error of judgement on an Irish poster. This remains one of the few extant graphic posters specifically designed for Ireland that makes use of British colours.[5]

The *Spark* took the lead in enunciating the anti-war, and, in this case especially, anti-British reaction to the event. In a long article on 16 May entitled 'The *Lusitania* Martyrs', Sean Doyle savaged the British version of the sinking. He reminded his readers that the German Embassy in London had warned neutral travellers two weeks before the sailing that crossing on British ships put their lives in danger. 'The dictionary has been burst to fragments', wrote Doyle, 'in applying epithets to the Germans for not proving themselves liars'.[6] Doyle attacked British negligence in not providing a destroyer escort for the ship, 'although the Germans had by official advertisement, by letter, and by word of mouth at the wharf in New York, announced their determination, although German submarines were known to be off the south-west coast of Ireland, obviously watching for the *Lusitania*'.[7] Doyle felt that the 1,200 passengers [*sic*] had been 'induced' to embark by promises from the British manager of the Cunard Line that the *Lusitania* was too fast for any German submarine.

3 128 American citizens drowned.   4 TCD, Irish Recruiting Posters, Case 55a/9.   5 The background of the sinking *Lusitania* is actually taken directly from a drawing in the *Irish*

2.1 *Irishmen Avenge the Lusitania* (CCORI recruiting poster, 1915, TCD)

Doyle stated that any concern shown in the 'corrupt and cowardly' press for the passengers was completely fictitious. If the press was actually concerned about the passengers, he wrote, 'it is not "the Huns" they would demand vengeance on'. The entire incident was being used simply to promote recruiting for the very 'forces of the Power upon which the travellers on the *Lusitania* were induced to rely for protection'. The worst fabrication came from the *Irish Independent*, which had claimed that women had been landed at Queenstown wearing clothes loaned to them by sailors. The inference, Doyle maintained, was that the sinking had been so sudden that the women had to run from their beds into the lifeboats. There was just one problem with this tale. 'The super-liar who concocted this yarn forgot that women are generally clothed by two o'clock in the afternoon'.[8]

Long before the *Lusitania* sank the German press claimed that the ship was being used to transport munitions from New York. It was open knowledge that the *Lusitania* and her sister ship the *Mauretania* were auxiliary cruisers in the Royal Navy in time of war. This fact, published yearly in the Naval List since 1903, was conveniently left out of most accounts of the disaster. Doyle made sure to feature a reprint of the pertinent page in a prominent place. The final proof for Doyle that the *Lusitania* had carried guns and ammunition was a stock report from New York. The moment news of her sinking reached Wall Street, Bethlehem Steel lost all its profits and then dropped a further ten points. '"Bethlehem Steel" manufacture cannons. – *Verb. Sap'*. wrote Doyle bluntly.[9]

There was in fact ammunition on board, more than eleven tons of gunpowder and 1,250 cases of shrapnel. This nullified the time-honoured rule that merchantmen should never be fired on without warning.[10] Griffith's new IRB-funded weekly, *Nationality*, mocked Edward Carson's claims during the investigation that the shells and munitions on board were useless, and were not 'intended for some warlike purpose'.[11] Griffith claimed to have investigated the matter himself, and discovered that 'this ammunition, which could not be utilized, was bought by England from America as a matter of benevolence, and that the empty shells were needed to put eggs in'.[12]

Pro-war Irish reacted angrily to the 'Sinn Féin' support for Germany's sinking of the *Lusitania*. A Christmastide recruiting meeting in Dingle featured Sergeant-Major O'Rahilly of the Connaught Rangers. Claiming that the 'Sinn Féiners' were 'on the side of the Dark Demon',[13] he went on to remind his listeners that the '"Sinn Féiners passed a resolution congratulating Germany on what they called a glorious achievement", the sinking of the *Lusitania*'.[14] There is, in fact, no evidence that this occurred, certainly not at the level of the Sinn Féin National

Weekly Independent (cf. BNL, *IWI*, 15.5.15, p. 8). 6 BNL, *Spark*, 16.5.15, pp. 1–2. 7 Ibid. 8 Ibid. 9 Ibid. 10 Read, 1941, p. 200. 11 BNL, *Nat*, 26.6.15, p. 1. 12 Ibid. 13 BNL, *IV*, 25.12.15, p. 2. 14 Ibid.

Committee, as this would have been reported in Griffith's *Nationality*. Pro-war councils, on the other hand, did pass resolutions condemning the German act. Kinsale Corporation brought in a verdict of wilful murder against the Kaiser, and publicly apologized to the 'Huns' for comparing them to the Germans.[15]

By the autumn of 1915, advanced nationalist newspapers maintained that the *Lusitania* incident was 'worked out as a means of getting recruits'.[16] The *Hibernian* noted that even the 'bitterly anti-German' *Irish Catholic* now admitted that the Germans were within their rights to sink the ship, as it was carrying ammunition sufficient to kill 'at least 500,000 Germans'.[17] Journalists were now clear about where the fault lay: 'The blame for the loss of life rests chiefly with the British Cunard Company, that induced unsuspecting passengers to travel on a floating British arsenal'.[18] The use of the *Lusitania* in propaganda did diminish with time, and more importantly, as British propagandists realized that the United States would not enter the war because of this isolated incident. But the destruction of that vessel retained its iconic power for all sides throughout the war. To the British and pro-war Irish, it was a symbol of German treachery. To the advanced nationalists, it remained a symbol of British duplicity. In 1918, police raided Sinn Féin headquarters in Dublin, and came away with more than 2,000 documents. One seized leaflet, written in 1917, was entitled *Irishmen: Remember! Be on Your Guard!*[19] It catalogued the ills of Ireland, and the corrupting influence of the British 'Spider' in recent years. The author scorned Englishmen who were horrified at the sinking of the *Lusitania*, and yet forbade commerce between Holland and Belgium:

> The *Lusitania* with cases of munitions from America to England was torpedoed and sunk. This crime was so black, so inhuman, – though timely notice had been given to neutrals – that self-righteous Englishmen held up their hands in horror, and yet it is against neutrality to run a waggon [*sic*] of gravel from Holland into Belgium.[20]

The immorality and cowardice of the British went hand in hand, and propagandists were enraged when perceived cowardice resulted in the deaths or suffering of Irishmen. The crowded waters of the Irish Sea and the English Channel remained happy hunting grounds for the U-boats throughout the war. Specific shipping losses caused by German actions were turned in advanced nationalist press reports into anti-British diatribes. Accusations of cowardice, culpability, and the prevarication of the pro-war press climaxed with the sinking of a Dublin mail boat, the *Leinster*, in October 1918. This was a great and specifically Irish tragedy, with over 600 Irish men, women, and children drowned

15 BNL, *Hib*, 18.9.15, pp. 2–3. See also Dermot J. Lucey, 'Cork Public Opinion and the First World War' (University College Cork, M.A., 1972), p. 64. 16 Ibid. 17 Ibid. 18 Ibid. 19 NLI, MS 10494: Documents Seized in Raid on Sinn Féin HQ, March 1918: *Irishmen: Remember! Be On Your Guard!* 20 Ibid.

in St George's Channel. Pro-war propaganda, organized at this point by the Irish Recruiting Council, issued far starker recruiting appeals than after the sinking of the *Lusitania* in 1915. Rather than creating a poster showing the death throes of ship and man, posters instead were printed which carried only the bold and grim message 'Irishmen: Remember the 'Leinster' – And Avenge Your OWN DEAD'.[21]

An examination of the advanced nationalist response shows the great confusion that could arise in a time of censorship and conflicting eye-witness reports. However, despite the differences between the three main accounts that remain of this tragedy, certain common elements are found in all of them. The British government was blamed for the occurrence of the disaster, the British soldiers on board behaved in a cowardly and murderous fashion, rescue efforts did not happen (again because of a high-level British decision), and the Dublin press covered-up the truth of the event.

Propagandists disagreed on how the *Leinster* was sunk. The pamphlet *Who Sunk the Leinster?* maintained that since the ship was hit simultaneously on both sides, a mine 'of the duplex kind', used by the Royal Navy, was responsible. The English Admiralty knew the answer, but was keeping silent.[22] Both a general election leaflet entitled *The Leinster Outrage*[23] and *An t-Oglach*, the clandestine organ of the Irish Volunteers,[24] believed that the ship had been sunk by a German torpedo. All three sources, however, agreed that British soldiers had been on board, either 900,[25] 500,[26] or 600 of them.[27] The private company that ran the *Leinster* had already been warned about carrying soldiers on board a non-combatant ship, a warning recently reinforced by a German submarine, which surfaced and told the captain his ship would be sunk if it carried any more troops. To avoid difficulties, the company changed the sailing time to the middle of the day, when submarines were less active.[28] Despite the threat from U-boats, the government ordered the *Leinster* to continue carrying soldiers. Five hundred places on each trip were to be kept open for their transport.[29]

Although it now carried troops, the ship was still not escorted by the Royal Navy, nor by 'a single seaplane'.[30] When Dr MacNamara in the House of Commons claimed that the Navy did not possess ships fast enough to accompany the *Leinster*, propagandists responded:

> Where, oh where are the fast destroyers of 40 miles an hour speed? Where are all the newly built submarine chasers? Have we not been told the submarine is well in hand? Where is the silent navy? The navy that has put the Germans in a ringed fence, or is it a paper one? The navy that has orders to run away from its own drowning sailors?[31]

21 TCD, Irish Recruiting Posters, Case 55c/76. 22 CUL, Hib.918.10: *Who Sunk the Leinster?* (Henceforth L1). 23 NLI MS 18388: Manuscripts Relating to Sinn Féin Election Propaganda, 1918–1929: *The Leinster Outrage* (henceforth L2). 24 NLI, *An t-Oglach*, 29.10.18, p. 4 (henceforth L3). 25 L1. 26 L2. 27 L3. 28 L2. 29 L3. 30 L1. 31 L1.

All reports agreed that when the ship was attacked, the soldiers on board panicked. According to the pamphlet *Who Sunk the Leinster?*, the 900 English soldiers on the ship drove women and children back from the lifeboats, swinging their rifles and shouting 'To 'ell with the bloody Hirish [sic], save yourselves!'[32] Election propaganda claimed that the soldiers went 'mad with panic', and charged a lifeboat that was being launched full of women and children. The soldiers overturned the boat, and all the occupants drowned.[33] *An t-Oglach* was the most extreme of all. Two American naval officers who had been on board the *Leinster* told 'people in Dublin' that the English soldiers had 'behaved with incredible cowardice and brutality when the ship was struck by the torpedo, trampling down women and children in the rush for the boats'.[34] Reporters for the newspaper 'confirmed' this story by maintaining that one female survivor was badly bruised by blows from the soldiers, and the body of a woman was recovered with a bullet hole in it.[35] Mayhem and violence on deck were praised when Irishmen were responsible. *Who Sunk the Leinster?* reported that 'a steward of the *Leinster* got to a boat by knocking down with a hatchet a soldier who barred his way – Good man steward'.[36] The American officers featured in *An t-Oglach* also took time to pay tribute to the 'fine behaviour' of the crew. All, the paper proudly pointed out, 'without exception Irishmen or Welshmen'.[37]

British conduct only grew worse after the *Leinster* sank. Survivors floated amidst the wreckage in broad daylight, just ten miles out of Kingstown Harbour. Despite the close distance, and the fact that Dublin Bay was full of shipping, no rescue efforts were made for two hours. While Chief Secretary Edward Shortt 'looked on', two other mail boats steamed directly through the wreckage without stopping.[38] After much procrastination, a belated rescue effort was made, and ships reached the area in less than twenty minutes.[39] Identities of officers and men were hidden during the inquest, with names appearing in casualty lists bearing the prefix 'Mr'.[40] Police were sent to the houses of the survivors, ostensibly to take them to hospitals, but actually, according to propagandists, to keep interviewers away.[41]

The answers offered by the author of *Who Sunk the Leinster?* grew more hyperbolic in their desire to answer its title question. The author suspected that the British had sunk the mail boat themselves: 'Does it suit her vampire existence better to have Irish women and children unnecessarily killed so that she can make capital out of the catastrophe?'[42] The timing of the disaster was suspect: 'the act filled the pause between Germany's Peace Note and America's reply'.[43] It is highly unlikely that the British would sink a passenger ship simply to encourage

32 L1.   33 L2.   34 L3.   35 L3.   36 L1.   37 L3.   38 L2.   39 According to the *Weekly Irish Times*, 19.10.18, boats set out immediately from Kingstown, but passengers were in the water for almost an hour and a half. The Viceroy, Lord French, in a telegram to the King, excused this by blaming 'very heavy seas' which made rescue efforts difficult.   40 L1.   41 L1.   42 L1.   43 L1.

recruiting and demonize Germany, especially after four years of warfare.[44] Both pro- and anti-British propagandists reacted to an event that was honestly out of their control, and made 'capital out of catastrophe'. Pro-war recruiters were given the perfect opportunity to inject a note of personal revenge into their propaganda, while advanced nationalists saw these incidents as examples of criminal stupidity and cowardice by the British government.

With the *Lusitania*, the *Leinster*, and other shipping 'atrocities', the dichotomy of reaction was extremely clear-cut. Both sides could mourn the innocent victims, and reports only truly differed in where the finger of blame should be pointed. The division between pro-British and anti-British reaction was hazier in another iconic infamy perpetrated by the Germans during the Great War: the execution in October 1915 of Edith Cavell. Here again, propagandists used foreign current affairs to denigrate the British.

Cavell, the daughter of an Anglican clergyman, had stayed in Belgium following the German occupation. She was in charge of a nursing order in Brussels, and remained there helping tend to wounded soldiers, both allied and German. She became involved with local resistance groups, helping smuggle out messages, and finally, soldiers as well. In late August 1915, German authorities broke the back of the resistance movement, capturing Cavell and 34 others. After being held for more than two months, they were all brought to trial in October. Cavell freely confessed to having helped allied soldiers cross the frontier, and acknowledged that some of them had rejoined their units in England, going so far as to read a thank-you note she had received from one of the men she helped.[45] Her confession even implicated eight other people who had not been arrested. She was found guilty, sentenced to death, and executed with two men on 15 October 1915.[46]

The first serious problem with turning this case into an atrocity was that Cavell had confessed to a capital crime. Under German military law, helping enemy soldiers to rejoin their units was punishable by death, and, as James Read wrote, 'military law made no differentiation between sexes'.[47] Read argued further that despite the use of the phrase 'judicial murder' in the English press, what the English thought to be lacking was mercy. By refusing clemency to a woman who was English, a nurse, and the deeply religious daughter of a clergyman, Germany had managed to create the perfect atrocity story for the British.[48]

The Irish advanced nationalist press reaction mainly focused on the hypocrisy of the British and French reaction to Cavell's execution:

---

44 A recent piece of nationalist history, Roy Stokes' *Death in the Irish Sea: The Sinking of the RMS Leinster* (Dublin, 1998) unconvincingly advances an accusation similar to *Who Sunk the Leinster?* 45 Read, 1941, p. 212. 46 Ibid. 47 Ibid., p. 216. 48 Ibid.

England should not grumble. *She* is not showing very much compassion for spies, and alien offenders, of whom ten have been shot in London since the outbreak of war. So far, the meagre details published in the Press have given no sex distinctions.[49]

Griffith was 'no less sorry for Miss Cavell than for the two German women ... whom the French shot this year on similar charges; and we await the declaration of Chivalrous England that henceforth the Allies will cease to shoot women convicted by their courts-martial'.[50] Two years later, he returned to the same subject, claiming to be 'nauseated' by 'the hypocrisy of a Press which made the welkin ring with shrieks about the execution of one woman by the Germans, while it approves the execution of several women by the Allies'.[51] He admitted that 'women-spies' could be more dangerous than 'men-spies', but adamantly professed that 'civilization, which England and her allies profess to be fighting for, will not be promoted by the execution of women'.[52]

The execution of a woman did disgust these men. Griffith felt that the shooting of any woman, even when justified by the 'Laws of War', 'excited repugnance in the hearts of most men'.[53] He personally was 'sorry to read of any woman being shot'.[54] *Honesty* acknowledged her admission of guilt, but said, 'we cannot see why some little clemency could not have been shewn her'.[55] Cavell's actual actions were viewed with mixed respect. Propagandists remarked on her use of a nurse's uniform as a 'cloak for treachery', but acknowledged that 'by her acts she was helping her country to victory. It was this feeling helped her to die bravely. All honour to her'.[56]

Sean Doyle was infuriated by the Protestant City of Dublin Hospital's attempt to raise money for a memorial to Cavell in the hospital. Pointing out that 'England is the only nation which honours her spies',[57] he attacked the idea of Cavell being honoured in a medical setting:

> An Irish hospital – or an hospital of any kind – is the last place for her commemoration. By her action in using the uniform of the nurse to cover her political conspiracies, she has rendered that once universally respected uniform suspect now in every belligerent nation, and consequently, has hampered the humane work of those women of all nations who sincerely wish to alleviate the sufferings of war. Certainly, above all classes, nurses and doctors have little reason to wish for a commemoration of Miss Cavell.[58]

---

49 BNL, *Hon*, 6.11.15, p. 2. In fact, the United Kingdom did not execute any female spies during the Great War. **50** BNL, *Nat*, 30.10.15, p. 3 **51** BNL, *Nat*, 20.10.17, p. 1. **52** Ibid. **53** Ibid. **54** Ibid., 30.10.15, p. 3. **55** BNL, *Hon*, 6.11.15, p. 2. **56** Ibid. **57** BNL, *Spark*, 16.1.16, pp. 1–2. **58** Ibid.

One article on Cavell was outrageous enough to warrant the rare distinction of a mention in Under-Secretary Sir Matthew Nathan's correspondence. In *Nationality*, Griffith hoped that England might, in future, only employ men in her 'Secret Service'. This, however, would have its disadvantages:

> If an English female S.S. Agent be convicted, and the Huns execute her, England can extract some profit from her death by lifting up the voice in indignation and calling on Neutral Nations to witness how the Huns murder women. Obviously this could not be done in the case of a man S.S. agent – once shot he has no further market value.[59]

The Foreign Office got wind of this article, and sent it along to Augustine Birrell's office in London, ordering them to find out more about the source. A.P. Magill, Birrell's private-secretary, passed the information on to Nathan with the suggestion that *Nationality* should be suppressed. Nathan was reluctant to take action. He felt that the article was 'beastly', but did not want to move against the paper unless a wholesale suppression of the advanced nationalist press was in the offing.[60] Griffith and his compatriots were free for the time being to continue their attacks on Great Britain.

Throughout the Great War, advanced nationalist propagandists were quick to use current events to their own advantage. Even in the case of atrocities that then and now stand as prime examples of German brutality, propagandists managed to twist reports until it appeared that the British were equally to blame. In the haze of censorship during the war, advanced nationalist versions of events appeared equally plausible to the constructions of pro-war propagandists.

II

It is one of the central moments of the Irish Revolution. Patrick Pearse, having held off the British army for almost a week, surrenders his sword to his foe in a rubble-strewn Dublin street. The poster *Unconquerable!* (figure 2.2) presents an allegorical version of this important event. Pearse, proud and defiant in his Irish Volunteers' uniform, stands tall before a caricatured John Bull, who leans on a bloody sword. Beneath Bull's feet is a paper with 'Small Nationalities' upon it, and in his pocket he carries a bill to conscript Irishmen. In the background, shadowy figures of Irish prisoners cross the wrecked shell of the GPO. Wearing his manacles with dignity, Pearse refuses the recruiting entreaties of John Bull. Hanging on another ruined building nearby is a poster crying 'Remember

---

59 BNL, *Nat*, 30.10.15, p. 3.   60 Bod., Sir Matthew Nathan Papers, MS 465, Nathan to Magill, 9 November, 1915, fols. 261–2.

2.2 *Unconquerable!* (1916, Samuels Collection, TCD)

Belgium!' The poster is a direct imitation of a 1914 British pro-war poster that showed King Albert of Belgium defying the Kaiser in the ruins of his country. The artist has turned around a British figure of hatred, linking John Bull and the destruction of Dublin during the Rising to the depredations of the Kaiser's forces in occupied Belgium.[61]

Anti-war propagandists countered the use of German atrocities by contrasting them with old and new images of British brutality in Ireland. Changing only the subject, Irish atrocity propaganda imitated a pro-war style: it taught the people to hate, demonized the enemy, and uniquely, turned pro-war British discourse back on itself and spread a message of hatred to England and all she stood for.

The shooting of a crowd by the King's Own Scottish Borderers (KOSB) at Bachelor's Walk less than ten days before the start of the war was a boon to advanced nationalist propagandists. As news of German conduct in Belgium filtered back to the United Kingdom, anti-war journalists could respond with an 'atrocity' that had happened in the centre of Ireland's 'capital' city. The events of 26 July 1914 remained an insoluble counterpoint to any claims of German atrocities or murders on the European continent.

Arthur Griffith savaged the hypocrisy of atrocity propagandists in a long essay in September 1914, showing that the only documented case of women and children being murdered by soldiers recently was in Dublin. He concluded with an anecdote about the arrival of the first German POWs in London:

> The brave Britons who did not go to the front received them – so the English press admiringly tells us, with cries of 'Who killed the women and children?' A German might have replied – 'The King's Own Scottish Borderers' ... The only **proved** case of a woman or child being murdered by soldiers is the case in Bachelor's Walk – performed in Dublin in a time of peace under the protection of British law, and the perpetrators of which were sent to teach the Germans civilization.[62]

In a similar anecdote, James Connolly claimed that a German POW arriving in Dublin had responded (in perfect English!) to a woman who had accused him of murdering women and children, 'My dear lady, you are mistaken. We are not the Scottish Borderers. We are German soldiers'.[63]

Propagandists were gleeful at the fate of the officers and men of the KOSB. Called to active service when the war began, battalions of the Borderers left for France with the original British Expeditionary Force, and saw action in some of the first battles of the Great War. Major Haig, the officer who was commanding the detachment that fired on the crowd in July, was captured by the Germans and

---

61 TCD, Samuels 4/110. 62 BNL, *SF*, 12.9.14, p. 1. 63 BNL, *IW*, 3.10.14, p. 3.

spent the entire war in a POW camp.⁶⁴ The *Irish Worker* ran the news of the capture of two KOSB officers under the heading 'This Week's Joke', asking 'Funny, is it not?' that names of officers who were involved in the Dublin butchery should appear on their 'Nation's Roll of Honour'.⁶⁵

Bachelor's Walk, in the unfortunate person of Sylvester Pidgeon, even managed to disrupt Prime Minister Asquith's recruiting visit to Dublin in September 1914. By clinging to life for two months after being wounded in the affray, and finally dying on the same day that Asquith and John Redmond were speaking to a recruiting meeting at the Mansion House, Pidgeon did a great service to advanced nationalist propagandists. On the evening of 25 September, while Asquith and others⁶⁶ were unsuccessfully working the crowd at the Mansion House, Irish Volunteers gathered in groups around the city.⁶⁷ Some carried Pidgeon's body in procession past the AOH and DMP guards standing outside the Mansion House, while others clustered around the Bank of Ireland to hear Jim Larkin swear 'Hatred to the Empire'.⁶⁸ Francis Sheehy-Skeffington attempted to speak to the crowd, but was quickly arrested. The crowd carried patriotic banners, including some reading 'Don't Join the Army – Remember Bachelor's Walk!'⁶⁹ The crowd was threatening, but no actual violence broke out. At one point a British officer in a motor car attempted to drive through College Green. Greeted by shouts of 'Hired Assassin!' he had to reverse and find a different route.⁷⁰ At Pidgeon's funeral mass the following Sunday, leaflets were distributed starkly warning nationalists that 'Our murdered brother calls upon you from the grave to remember that his blood lies upon the head of the British Army; an army whose records are foul with unnameable atrocities committed upon the Irish people'.⁷¹ Joining the British army would mean 'comradeship with those who at Bachelor's Walk murdered unarmed men, women and children'.⁷²

Pidgeon's co-incidental death simply encouraged the use of Bachelor's Walk against recruiting. Long before Pidgeon left the life that Griffith thought emblematized 'the modern history of Ireland',⁷³ Bachelor's Walk was a potent weapon for those opposed to Irishmen enlisting in the British army. The pacifist Sheehy-Skeffingtons had their disapproval of Bachelor's Walk heightened by a public letter of support sent by Sylvia Pankhurst to Hanna in the week after the incident. Pankhurst felt that the 'horrible shooting outrage' highlighted the 'extraordinarily mean cowardice' of the British government.⁷⁴

64 BNL, *Nat*, 30.10.15, p. 3. 65 BNL, *IW*, 24.10.14, p. 4. 66 See chapter six for an analysis of Ernest Kavanagh's cartoon of this meeting. 67 Ernie O'Malley's *On Another Man's Wound* (Dublin, 1936), contains an exciting account of Dublin on the evening in question (cf. O'Malley, 1936, pp. 25–6). In contrast, the *Sunday Freeman's Journal* called the advanced nationalist response a 'damp squib' (BNL, *SFJ*, 4.10.14, p. 3). 68 BNL, *IF*, October 1914, p. 5. 69 Ibid. 70 Ibid. 71 Ibid. 72 Ibid. 73 BNL, *SF*, 3.10.14, p. 3. 74 NLI MS 24135: Sheehy-Skeffington Papers: Letters from the Irish Women's Franchise League, 1912–15: Pankhurst to Hanna Sheehy-Skeffington.

'Stoneyballer's' popular song *It's a Wrong Thing to Fight for England* first appeared in the *Irish Worker* on 12 September. Sung to the tune of *Tipperary*,[75] it scoffed at the idea of Irishmen enlisting after what had happened in Dublin:

> Here in Dublin City a little time ago,
> The way that England loves us
> Her troops did truly show;
> They shot down helpless women
> And children in the streets,
> And now they ask us to forget
> And with loving arms her greet.[76]

One week later, 'Puachail Beag's' stern front-page letter printed under the title 'Our Duty to the Empire', warned readers 'if you really believe in murdering women and children (Scottish Borderer style) join Kitchener's Army'.[77]

Right up until the Easter Rising, propagandists used a variety of British actions to contrast with Germanic behaviour. At times the actions were non-specific, such as in the odd story 'Eirig! Eirig!' ['Arise! Arise!'] written for the children's newspaper *Fianna* in August and September 1915. Possibly written by Bulmer Hobson, the story concerns a dream in the classic *Aisling* style that the editor had when he fell asleep in the Irish countryside. He found himself standing on the shore of a prosperous nation, which was once clearly beautiful, but was now full of 'smoking roofs, numerous ruins, frightened half-starved, half-naked people maddened by some cruel tyrannical excesses, fleeing, fleeing, fleeing whither they knew not. Oh!'[78] They are hunted and killed by a 'villainous and hell-emitted soldiery' that the narrator is certain are Huns. He stares aghast at 'their swords wet with that defenceless blood – the blood of the tender babe, the gentle mother, the weakly aged, and light-limbed youth!'[79] At this point, in classic fashion, the first instalment of the story ends. A month later, our nationalist hero unsurprisingly beholds the figure of a beautiful woman, wearing a habit of white and green silk. His 'heart captured and mind enthralled', he wonders whether he has ever seen such a pretty sight before. He murmurs the first words that come into his head 'O, Queen of the Murdered Belgians!'[80] The woman however, is none other than Eire, 'queen of this sore-afflicted land'. She quickly reprimands the narrator, saying 'This land thou behold is not Belgium,

75 Although Larkin has it as sung to the tune of *It's a Wrong Thing to Crush the Worker* – a more appropriate version, perhaps, but one that is also coincidentally sung to the tune of the ubiquitous *Tipperary*. 76 BNL, *IW*, 12.9.14, p. 2. 77 Ibid., 19.9.14, p. 1. A popular 1914 anti-recruiting poster recalled Bachelor's Walk as well, reminding viewers to 'Remember Howth Sunday, July 26th, 1914, when "OUR" Army deliberately fired on unarmed citizens in revenge for the beating they got from unarmed Volunteers and Boy Scouts' (NLI MS 5637: Robert Barton Scrapbook, Vol. I, fol. 33). 78 BNL, *Fianna*, August 1915, p. 10. 79 Ibid. 80 Ibid., September 1915, p. 11.

nor the tyrants who oppress it, as thou seest, are not Germans!' The Queen of Ireland continues with a catalogue of the woes of her land, and concludes:

> 'O Ireland! Ireland! is it thus with thee that thine own children know thee not! THIS IS Ireland and there are thy foes, the cruel and cowardly murdering, slaying, robbing, ruining, destroying! Ah, Death is ever with them! Yes, my God, Death! But death to the helpless and defenceless children of my bosom'.[81]

The narrator, 'stunned', resolves to help set his queen 'upon a throne of gold', and kneeling at her feet, swears eternal loyalty. She cries the magic words, 'Eirig! Eirig!', and as enemy soldiers approach waving their swords, he finds a 'useful pike' to protect his queen. Brandishing his weapon, he beats off the 'onslaught of demons'. Suddenly, the dream ends, and he awakes resolving to help his nation to freedom.[82]

Atrocities that actually had a place in the real world appeared at times in other journals. In August 1915, an Orange mob attacked a group of monks out walking in County Antrim. Possibly because the Orangemen were all enlisted in the army, sentences were light. Only three men of the 30 involved were arraigned, and two went to prison for two months while the third was fined one pound. The *Spark* was glad to see that most of the press around Ireland was condemning this affray, but noted that 'the details of the outrage bear comparison with any of the "German Atrocities" concocted by frenzied London fictionists'.[83]

The seizure of printing presses and newspaper supplies at the Dublin-based Gaelic Press in March 1916 was greeted with cries of 'Prussianism' by surviving newspapers. Seamus Upton, editor of *Honesty*, scoffed at yet more British hypocrisy. How could the British papers raise cries of 'holy horror' at the Prussian 'smothering of truth' in occupied countries, while in Ireland:

> At the same time British Ministers, with a ruthlessness [sic] unexampled in any country, sends down its forces of armed military and police to destroy the property of an inoffensive and enterprising Dublin citizen, because he prints papers containing truths which neither the British authorities nor their West-British supporters are able to refute or contradict.[84]

The Easter Rising and executions immediately following hardly ever appeared in current atrocity propaganda used by the advanced nationalist press. The poster illustrating this section is an almost unique example of a direct comparison between the British in Dublin and the Germans in Belgium. This is not so much because there was a stricter censorship on writing about the Easter

81 Ibid.   82 Ibid.   83 BNL, *Spark*, 22.8.15, p. 2.   84 BNL, *Hon*, 8.4.16, pp. 1–2.

Rising.[85] The solution is even simpler – most of the leading propagandists either died in the Rising or were interned immediately after, and every advanced nationalist newspaper in Ireland was either suppressed or closed of its own accord (often because its editorial staff had vanished) in the week after the rebellion. The men and women involved in journalism had returned to their jobs within eighteen months, but by then, with Sinn Féin beginning to politically challenge the Irish Parliamentary Party, there were other things to think about. Atrocity propaganda that focuses on the Easter Rising did appear, however, in some post-Rising poetry.[86] *The Rebels* concluded with the threatening stanza:

> It's printed in the paper
> Of the Hun's atrocity,
> But think about the English,
> Who spared no property.
> They shot down our brave fellows,
> All of whom we know so well,
> But those who did the dirty work,
> Will be punished down in hell.[87]

Specific mention of the Rising also appeared in foreign propaganda used by Sinn Féin in the General Election campaign. An election leaflet entitled 'What the Unpurchased Press in America Thinks of Easter Week'[88] reprinted an article from the *New York American* of 16 May 1916. Having just received conclusive word of the executions, the pro-nationalist journal raged:

> We should think that even one of these boot-lickers to say nothing of decent Englishmen would blush to pronounce the name of Belgium again, would never open his mouth to talk of 'Atrocities' or 'Humanities' again. With the blackened walls and tumbled ruins of Dublin echoing the volleys of firing squads, shooting down surrendered prisoners, whose crime was to love their native land and yearn for its independence and liberty.
>
> We hope for decency [sic] sake we shall hear no more snivelling in America over broken stained-glass or shattered statues at Rheims and Louvain.[89]

Some German propaganda intended for Ireland but seized en-route by Scotland Yard included a message to 'Irish Soldiers' from an Irishwoman named Mrs

85 Cf. NA CSORP 1916 13187 for permission to sell Sinn Féin stamps, NLI MS 26154 (Joseph Brennan Papers) for discussion of the suppression of seditious literature following the Easter Rising. 86 Cf. Ellis, 1997, chapter 6, for some examples. 87 UCD P102/495: O'Rahilly Papers: 'The Rebels', in *Songs and Poems of THE REBELS Who Fought And Died FOR IRELAND In Easter Week, 1916*. 88 NLI ILB 300 Series, ILB 300 P5 fol. 92. 89 Ibid.

Leonard Marshall who claimed to have accompanied Casement in his Irish Brigade recruiting visits to Lemberg.[90] Still trying to recruit soldiers for an Irish Brigade, she recalled to their minds the (exaggerated) horrors of both Bachelor's Walk and Easter Week:

> Have they seen the Murders of Batchelor's [sic] Walk – the horrors of Easter Week when a Nurse was shot in cold blood by the Red Coats – When O'Rahilly lay dying and they would not allow a woman to moisten his dying lips with the cup of water he prayed for! Our poets, our writers shot down like Sheehy Skeffington the Pacifist!!!
> ... Revive the Glories of our past – An Irish Brigade, Boys! And if an Irish woman is wanted to lead it, my father's daughter is here![91]

In the main, however, current atrocity propaganda dealt with just that – the day-to-day 'atrocities' committed by the British, both towards the Irish and the Germans, in the final two years of the war. The deportation of 28 leading nationalists in late February 1917[92] was greeted with anger by *Nationality*, with Griffith noting another example of British press hypocrisy. In the *Daily Mail* of 23 February, there was an approving story on the deportation of Irishmen to England on page three, and an atrocity story about Germans deporting Frenchmen to POW camps on page six.[93]

While Griffith's propaganda became more aggressive after the Rising, journalists who used their newspapers to incite physical violence still enraged him. The jingo press of Great Britain was notorious in his eyes for supporting men like this. His least favourite newspaper proprietors and editors were the Harmsworth brothers and Horatio Bottomley (editor of *John Bull* and self-styled British recruiting supremo), but in late 1917 he took the opportunity to attack the Mancunian millionaire Sir William Hulton, the second-largest proprietor of newspapers and magazines in the United Kingdom (after Lord Northcliffe). Hulton's most profitable enterprises were the *Daily Sketch* and the *Daily Dispatch*, and it was a leading article in the latter with which Griffith took umbrage. In a 7 December note on the capture of two German airmen shot down during a raid on England, Hulton advised 'They should be **quietly** hanged. Their fall might have killed them, and **we could say it did**'.[94] 'Here is England!' wrote Griffith in disgust.[95]

90 No evidence can be found to support this claim.   91 TCD, Samuels 3/82.   92 The 28 were sent to Oxford, where they resided until late March, when they were moved to the village of Fairford, in Gloucestershire. Lawrence Ginnell, long-time Sinn Féin supporter in the House of Commons, accused the government of moving the men as soon as the Irish had made arrangements to 'pursue their studies in the Bodleian Library'. The British government denied this charge (*Hansard*, xcii, 1917, 1316).   93 BNL, *Daily Mail*, 23.2.17, pp. 3 and 6; *Nat*, 3.3.17, p. 1.   94 BNL, *Daily Dispatch*, 7.12.17, p. 4.   95 BNL, *Nat*, 22.12.17, p. 1.

The brutal treatment of Irish prisoners became an important element of anti-British atrocity propaganda after the Rising. Thomas Ashe died following a forced feeding during a hunger strike in September 1917. His death, and the determination of other republican prisoners to follow his example and also refuse food and water, raised a chorus of protest. Michael Fogarty, the nationalist bishop of Killaloe, wrote a public letter entitled 'Done to Death Behind the Walls of Mountjoy', which Sinn Féin re-printed and used as a propaganda leaflet through the General Election. Fogarty thought it horrible that Ireland had to stand by while 'decent, young Irish boys' were slowly starved behind prison walls, or thrown 'in their last gasp out to die like dogs in the street'.[96] This sort of atrocity might be expected 'in the ancient Bastille, or the dungeons of Naples, or the black prisons of Russia; but as altogether impossible under English rule'.[97] The world, stated Fogarty, had no need to wait for the future to see 'in these hideous atrocities what the triumph of English culture means for small nationalities'.[98]

Religious leaders began more and more often to add their voices to the chorus of complaints. Ten months after Ashe's death, Dr Hallinan, bishop of Limerick, shocked catholics when he revealed that 'in some prisons in England our Irish catholic prisoners have got no opportunity of hearing Mass on Sundays since their incarceration'.[99] This, the Bishop reminded his readers, 'is happening not in Belgium under the Germans, but in England, that boasts that she is fighting for the reign of right and justice and the freedom of small nations all the world over'.[100] That same month, republican prisoners in Belfast jail protested for political status. Their resistance was quickly broken, and the prisoners were kept in handcuffs for more than a week. Many of them were beaten by warders, stripped, and forced to sleep in cells after being sprayed with fire hoses. Worse than the physical brutality was the inability of these men to receive Holy Communion. *English Horrors in Irish Jails* was printed in August 1918, and used as a campaign leaflet by Sinn Féin in the General Election. It savaged the terrible conditions forced on the catholic prisoners, and acknowledged that any sympathy Ireland had left for the Belgians was because they too suffered under similar oppression.[101]

The actions of the British in Ireland during the Great War, filtered through the biased lens of advanced nationalist propagandists, produced a series of 'atrocities' as brutal as anything that occurred on the continent. The atrocities in Ireland had all the more potential impact on an audience as they happened in a familiar setting, before the eyes of civilian population. Whatever the Germans might do, advanced nationalists believed the English were doing far worse. Nevertheless, in comparing domestic events to the horrors of war, propagandists entered into an arena of discourse created by their opponents. German atrocities,

96 NLI MS 5637: Robert Barton Papers: Scrapbook, vol. I, fol. 17. 97 Ibid. 98 Ibid. 99 BNL, *Nat*, 24.6.18, p. 1. 100 Ibid. 101 NLI ILB Series 300, ILB 300 P4, fol. 32.

mostly in Belgium, became the model to which other atrocities were compared and contrasted, demonstrating that even if their existence were doubted, their presence was dangerous enough to the advanced nationalist cause to be constantly addressed. Germany inadvertently created a situation in which events of the war changed advanced nationalist discourse.

III

> It's a long road through Irish history,
> It's a wade through a bloody sea,
> Every milestone marks the gravestone,
> Of a nation once prosperous, free.
> (From *A Scrap of Paper*, 1914)[102]

'England is the only enemy Ireland ever had', read a German propaganda leaflet which was dropped over Irish troops in the allied lines in 1917.[103] This was a central credo of advanced nationalist thought, and in turning to the more than seven centuries of English rule in Ireland, anti-British atrocity propagandists were able to find much grist for their mill. Ireland's history was marked with brutal incidents and images that resonated powerfully with both nationalist and catholic audiences. By drawing on constructed traditions and history, advanced nationalists were able to perform two important functions: first, they counteracted a prevalent form of recruiting propaganda; second, and more importantly, they equated support for the wartime policies of the Irish Parliamentary Party with support for the historic evils of British rule. Advanced nationalists co-opted signs and symbols traditionally used by the Parliamentarians, thus displaying themselves as the guardians of a nationalist heritage, and the avatars of a nationalist dawn. By linking current events of the war to a collective memory[104] of exploitation, propagandists created a viable political culture that could be led by advanced nationalists.

What events in Irish history did historical propagandists use? Most major instances of British action against the Irish appeared during the war. Some propagandists focused on comparisons between British atrocities in Ireland and German atrocities on the continent, while others used British atrocities in Ireland to discourage recruiting.[105]

102 BNL, *EI*, 13.11.14, p. 2. 103 TCD, Samuels 2/61. 104 Following Robert Gildea's definition of collective memory as 'the collective construction of the past by a given community' (Robert Gildea, *The Past in French History* [New Haven, 1994], p. 10). 105 Research uncovered forty-four instances of non-humorous historical atrocity propaganda. Of this number, twenty-five mentions dealt specifically with comparisons between British and German atrocities, and nineteen used atrocities to discourage recruiting.

To analyze these figures, pre-war Irish history was divided into six categories: pre-1798; the 1798 Rebellion; the 19th century, including the Famine, but before the Land War; the Land War; the Boer War; and finally, sequential atrocities, in which propagandists would cite major atrocities from 1172 to the present. These 'sequential' atrocity comparisons show the highest incidence in both categories, appearing in six direct comparisons to German atrocities and seven anti-recruiting messages.[106] After the sequential propaganda, the two categories diverge. The 1798 Rebellion appears most frequently in direct atrocity comparisons because it had entered folk memory as a horribly bloody affair, one in which an inordinate number of atrocities *had* been perpetrated by all sides. This folk memory had been reinforced less than twenty years before the First World War when many advanced nationalist propagandists had participated in the 1898 centenary commemorations of the Rebellion.[107]

Taking the nineteenth century as a whole, we see an equal number of mentions (six) in both categories. Events of the latter half of the nineteenth century were within living memory at the outbreak of the Great War. Young people would know stories of the famine days from their parents, and emigration had only increased greatly in the second half of the century. To Griffith and other economic nationalists, this loss of a viable working population, sparked by a famine allegedly caused by government policy, was in itself a great atrocity. The Manchester Martyrs, who feature only in more general anti-recruiting atrocity-propaganda, were an important unifying symbol for nationalists in the pre-war years. *God Save Ireland*, the ballad commemorating their final words, was often featured at Irish Parliamentary Party and UIL gatherings, and the death of these men before a jeering crowd became an obvious choice for propagandists interested in showing simultaneously the courage of the Irish and the immorality of the British.

The Boer War is the final event that saw a significant number of mentions. Eighty per cent of the anecdotes occurred in the category of atrocity comparisons, and again, this is due to the nature of the Boer War itself. Fighting a tenacious guerrilla force, British troops had been forced to turn to reprisals and the imprisonment of non-combatants in their attempt to break the will of the Boer fighters. Griffith himself felt a kinship with the Boers. He had spent time in South Africa at the turn of the century, and his earlier paper the *United Irishman* had supported the Boers during the war. Leading separatist and

---

106 This is possibly due to the psychological weight of presenting a string of atrocities stretching back through the ages. This acted as a catch-all, ensuring that each recipient could relate to some aspect of the atrocities discussed. 107 Cf. Timothy J. O'Keefe, 'The 1898 Efforts to Celebrate the United Irishmen: The '98 Centennial', *Eire-Ireland*, Vol. xxiii, no. 2 (Summer 1988), pp. 51–73; and '"Who Fears to Speak of '98?" The Rhetoric and Rituals of the United Irishmen Centennial, 1898', *Eire-Ireland*, vol. xxvii, no. 3 (Fall 1992), pp. 67–91; also Senia Paseta, '1798 in 1898: The Politics of Commemoration', *Irish Review*, vol. 22 (1998), pp. 46–53.

constitutional nationalists, such as John MacBride and Arthur Lynch, had fought in the Irish Brigade with the Boers. Most importantly to atrocity propagandists, many of the same officers and politicians involved with the British war effort had participated in the Boer War and its attendant brutalities.

References to atrocities before 1798 were at times inexact mentions of the general brutality of British rule in Ireland. In his sarcastic column in the *Irish Worker*, 'Facts and Fancies from the Front', J.J. Burke ['J.J.B'.] paid tribute to the sheer scale of British terror in Ireland. 'The German people are a clever race', he wrote, 'but they will never devise such exquisite torture as England specially prepared for those she NOW loves'.[108] Each German soldier in Belgium, he claimed, was given a copy of the book 'English Rule in Ireland', bound in human flesh and written in blood. Close study of this book was the main reason for the 'unmentionable savagery alleged to have been committed by the German Butchers on the Sanctified Allies'.[109]

Cromwell was the great hate figure of early-modern Irish history, the man held responsible for the destruction of the old Gaelic way of life and expulsion of the great Catholic families into the wastes of Connaught. In 1916, the retired British General Sir Evelyn Wood wrote a book in which he stated that the Kaiser was worse than Cromwell, because Cromwell had never murdered women and children. Furious, Griffith responded:

> This great truth, disseminated in Drogheda and Wexford, where the story is still believed that Cromwell's Englishmen murdered in cold blood the women and children of the two towns, should inspire the young men of Drogheda and Wexford to go forth and die for Cromwell's England.[110]

F.S. Pollard used the memory of Cromwell to publish a bitter recruiting appeal in 1915. 'Humanity's fragrant essence, Cromwell her dearest son', he wrote, 'has bound you to his mother with bonds of enduring love'.[111] Now England, 'Cromwell's Queen mother' was ringed with foes, and her own children were afraid to leave her. Patriotic Irishmen, inspired by the memory of Cromwell's 'low wistful voice' saying 'To Hell or Connacht', should volunteer to help the 'patroness of every virtue'. If the Irish did not volunteer to fight, then England would surely 'totter agonized to the grave'.[112]

The depredations of Cromwell paled in comparison with the more recent atrocities perpetrated by the British during and after the 1798 Rebellion. Six weeks after the war had begun, Griffith discovered an easy way for the British to create German atrocities. 'A history of the insurrection of 1798 will supply similar material for a thousand more "German atrocities"', he remarked, 'by the easy process of changing "English" into "German", and alleging that these

108 BNL, *IW*, 5.9.14, p. 2. 109 Ibid. 110 BNL, *Nat*, 12.2.16, p. 1. 111 BNL, *Hib*, 14.8.15, p. 1. 112 Ibid.

things are happening to-day in France and Belgium'.[113] Some atrocities, however, had yet to be discovered by the Germans, namely blowing men from the mouths of cannon, cannibalism, and pitch-capping.

Ballads and folk-tradition were used in darkly sarcastic comparisons to alleged German atrocities. A clipping from the *West Australian Record*, in which a nineteenth-century ballad on 1798, *Shamus O'Brien*, had appeared, was reprinted in the *Gael*:

> 'Twas the custom, whenever a peasant was caught,
> To hang him by trial, barring such as were shot.
> There was trial by jury going on by daylight,
> An' the martial law hanging the lavings by night.

'To what Belgian or Polish atrocity', asked the editors, 'does it refer?'[114]

The simple mention of 1798 was enough to break up a recruiting meeting. At Christmas of 1915, Lieutenant Eugene Sheehy[115] was condemning German atrocities when a voice from the crowd cried 'What About '98?' A debate then ensued between people in the audience, and Sheehy left the platform amidst general laughter and declarations of men refusing to enlist.[116] Enlistment was considered an absolute betrayal of the principles of 1798, as 'M.W. of Killosanty' wrote in 1914:

> We're singing now God Save the King, we're loyal to the core;
>   We've forgotten '98, we're English evermore.
> And Emmet, Tone, Lord Edward, who gave their heart's red tide
> From Heaven look with scorn on the race for whom they died.[117]

Following the execution of Edith Cavell in October 1915, *Honesty* wondered whether the Germans had learned to abuse women in that way from the English officers who commanded Hessian regiments in Ireland between 1798 and 1803.[118] Pro-war propagandists jumped at the chance to equate the atrocities of 1798 with the presence of Hessians in Ireland. A recruiting poster from the summer of 1918 that focused on the deaths of Irish fishermen from submarine attacks asked its audience:

> Do you wonder that the Germans treat Irishmen like this? Have you forgotten what the Germans did in Ireland once before – the Hessians in Wexford in '98, whose deeds were condemned by the British Viceroy of the

---

113 BNL, *SF*, 26.9.14, p. 1.   114 BNL, *Gael*, 5.2.16, p. 16.   115 First Lieutenant in the Royal Dublin Fusiliers. Son of David Sheehy, MP, and brother-in-law of Tom Kettle and Francis Sheehy-Skeffington.   116 BNL, *Nat*, 25.12.15, p. 7.   117 BNL, *IV*, 24.10.14, p. 10.   118 BNL, *Hon*, 6.11.15, p. 2.

day? We had a saying in Ireland then that every true Irishman should 'kill a Hessian for himself'. The Germans are the same in 1918 as in 1798 ... Isn't the saying of '98 good enough now? If you cannot 'kill a Hessian for yourself' the least you can do is to support those who are fighting against the German murderers of 300 Irishmen.[119]

This relatively weak defence, shifting the blame for 1798 on to what was hoped to be a common enemy, was countered by propaganda like J.J. Burke's article 'Out of the Past', published in the *Hibernian* one week before the Easter Rising.[120] Burke acknowledged that Hessian troops committed atrocities in Ireland, but maintained that the procurers of mercenaries were as guilty as the mercenaries themselves. In fact, he stated, Hessians were brought over by the British specifically to remove 'the last barrier of compassion' and ensure that the ultimate infamy, the last 'weapon in the vast enginery of Hell' could be committed.[121] This atrocity, according to Burke, was mass rape of Irish peasant women. 'All other means had failed; but Rape would not fail. So Rape it was decided it should be'.[122] The rape of Irish women was covered under the rubric of 'Free Quarters', in which Irish peasants were forced to house strangers in a cramped, public space. 'Free Quarters', declared J.J.B., 'meant thrusting armed licentious men into the bedroom and bed of the peasant women. Free Quarters thus of necessity meant not only free board and free lodgings, it meant Free Rape'.[123]

A campaign leaflet from the May 1917 South Longford by-election in which Joseph McGuinness beat Patrick McKenna, the Irish Parliamentary Party candidate, is illustrated in figure 2.3. Crudely drawn, it depicts a caricature of John Dillon as a gallows. He stands in a cross-filled field marked 'Flanders' with carrion birds wheeling overhead. His left arm ends in a noose, the noose that 'sent Sir Roger Casement to his doom'. The destruction of South Longford's young men is savaged by the text, but what is interesting is the metaphor used to describe Dillon. He is 'Worse than Heppenstall, the Walking Gallows'. Heppenstall, who, as the text reads, 'Longford with good reason since Ninety-Eight remembers',[124] was a great brute of a British officer. Active mainly in the midlands and especially in County Longford after the 1798 Rebellion, he received his nickname because he was so large that he would torture suspects by half-hanging them, pulling them off the ground over his back and walking around until they answered questions. By the turn of the twentieth century, Heppenstall had become a figure of folk-lore and horror, a British bogeyman to frighten nationalist children. Constitutional nationalists had reinforced a collective memory of Heppenstall by featuring him in their commemorative

119 TCD, Irish Recruiting Posters, Case 55B/50. 120 BNL, *Hib*, 15.4.16, p. 5. 121 Ibid.
122 Ibid. 123 Ibid. 124 NLI ILB Series 300, ILB 300 P10, fol. 74.

The Great War and the use of history in atrocity propaganda 95

Worse Than Heppenstall, The Walking Gallows.

Longford with good reason since Ninety-Eight remembers Heppenstall, the Walking Gallows. Here is a picture of Dillon, who is worse than the Walking Gallows. You see his cruel left hand as the noose on the hangman's rope that sent Sir Roger Casement to his doom. Dillon or Redmond would not move one finger to save him. You see the graves in Flanders where the youth and manhood of South Longford will lie if McKenna wins, and Redmond and Dillon can help the Government to pass Conscription for Ireland, as they are publicly pledged to do by their speeches in Parliament.

Mr. John Dillon, M.P., in the House of Commons on 29th March last offered England one hundred thousand Young Irishmen in exchange for the rotten, sham Home Rule Act.

A vote for Dillon's nominee, McKenna, is a Vote for Conscription—is a vote to send your Sons, your own flesh and blood, to nameless graves in Flanders, where their corpses will be torn in pieces by vultures and carrion crows!

McKenna will get his £400 a-year from the Government. The relations of Dillon and the rest of the Irish Party will get every Government job that is going. But your sons will be under the clay in Flanders or Mesopotamia!

It was the Men of Easter Week who kept off Conscription last year from Ireland. Another Secret Session of Parliament is to be Held in Two Weeks' Time. If Longford Elects McKenna, England Will Surely Apply Conscription to Ireland.

Voters of Longford, the only way to keep your Boys at Home on your own Hearthstones, is

VOTE FOR MACGUINNESS.

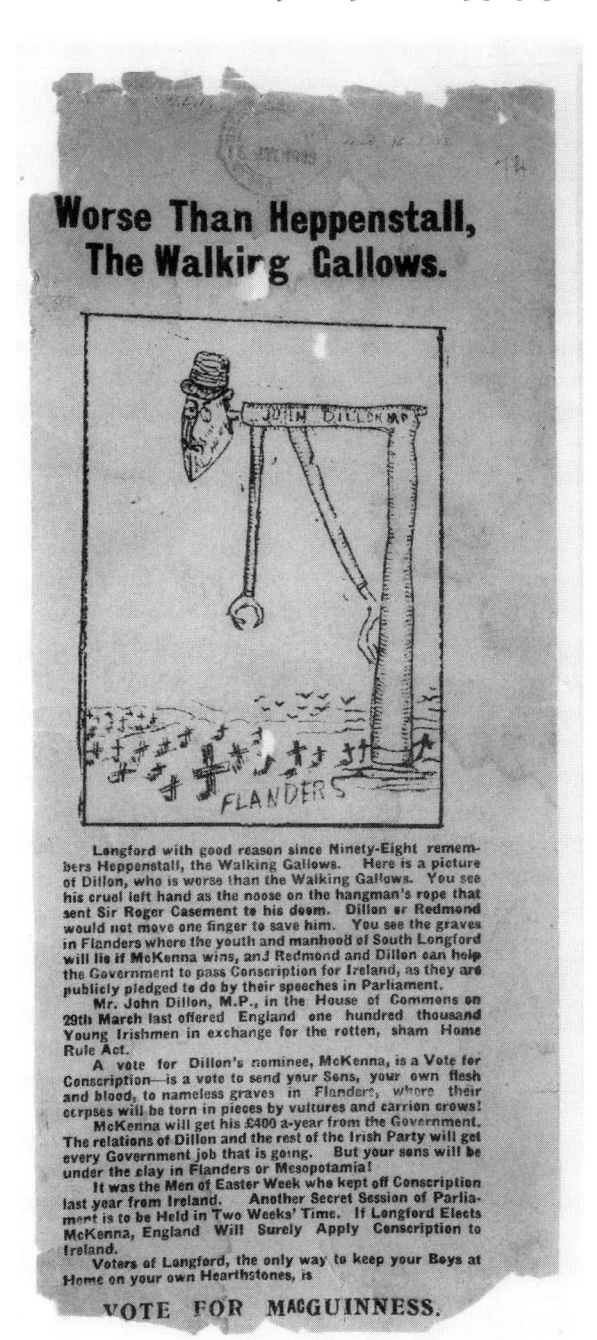

2.3 *Worse than Heppenstall, the Walking Gallows*
(by-election leaflet, 1917, NLI)

propaganda for 1798 centenary celebrations in 1898.[125] Once again, advanced nationalists were co-opting earlier figures of constitutional hatred.

This leaflet combined past and future, memory and anticipation. Dillon is shown on a First World War battlefield, and the text of the poster begs voters not to vote for his nominee, who would then receive £400 a year while the voters' sons, conscripted into the British army, will lie in 'nameless graves in Flanders, where their corpses will be torn in pieces by vultures and carrion crows!'[126] Yet the image chosen by the propagandist to represent a figure of terror, and the title, which is much larger than any of the text, both refer to an iconic atrocity from 1798. The propagandist has brilliantly combined a potent local symbol of horror, drawn in a crude, folk style with the general fear of current events, the fear that Ireland would face conscription if the Irish continued to support Redmond and Dillon's party.

During the nineteenth century, Ireland lost nearly half its population to emigration or death. This was an indisputable fact, proved by census returns, and was not denied by British propagandists. The reasons for the loss of population, however, were disputed. If the Great Famine was an act of God, then the British could hardly be blamed for the deaths and forced emigration. But if, as many advanced nationalists believed, and which held great weight in Irish folk traditions then and now, the Great Famine had been instead a calculated act of genocide by the British, then the loss of population during the nineteenth century was the most terrible atrocity the world had ever seen. Griffith believed this. Almost all of the instances in which nineteenth century British policies were compared to German atrocities come from the pages of his newspapers. He considered the war to be an excuse for the British government to complete the task they had begun in the nineteenth century when they had killed 'in days of peace two out of three [sic] of a nation's men'.[127] England's recruiters were now coming to Ireland, speaking to the 'remnant' and 'coaxing them off to her battlefields where she designs them to slay her enemies and get slain themselves – thus by the one stroke ridding herself of the "German menace" and the Irish question'.[128] He used this same theme to his own advantage in his successful campaign for the East Cavan parliamentary seat in May 1918. Turning *Nationality* into his own bully pulpit, he proclaimed dramatically:

> The world is staggering through its bloodiest war; but the casualties of the belligerent nations bear as yet no proportion to the casualties of Cavan. Where there should be 500,000 men and women there are 90,000. Where there were actually three men there is but one left. Where there were six women there are two. And God slew none.[129]

125 My thanks to Prof. Lawrence McBride, Illinois State University, for this information. 126 NLI ILB Series 300, ILB 300 P10, fol. 74. 127 BNL, *SF*, 10.10.14, p. 2. 128 Ibid. 129 BNL, *Nat*, 4.5.18, p. 2.

Re-iterating a favourite complaint, he continued that 'if this were true of Belgium, what a sustained cry of horror would ring round the world from the British Press'.[130]

While Griffith was virtually unique in likening the Great Famine to German atrocities, the losses suffered by Ireland during the nineteenth century were a frequently used weapon against general recruiting for the British army. Eoin MacNeill lashed out against the idea that Irishmen should enlist to fight Prussian militarism. 'In one century of British militarist supremacy', he wrote, 'Ireland has lost more in men, in trade, and in industries than Belgium, the cockpit of Continental militarism, has lost in all the wars of modern times'.[131] If the Irish did want to fight militarism, then they had no need to go to France. Anti-recruiting posters recalled the 'Famine of '47' when 'England deliberately starved nearly two millions of Irishmen and drove another million and a half in exile'.[132] The courage of the Fenian prisoners of 1867, dying in British prisons, was also used to spark nationalist fervour.[133]

No action of the British in the nineteenth century was as important to anti-recruiting propaganda as the executions of Allen, Larkin, and O'Brien, the Manchester Martyrs. The indisputable courage of these men who were executed for shooting a policeman during the bungled rescue of two Fenian leaders from Manchester's jail was a constant reminder to nationalists to stick to their cause and not betray their memory.[134] The annual commemoration of their death was always an opportunity for propagandists to force readers to search their consciences, or, as the more extreme would have it, 'a time for the renewal of our allegiance to the cause for which these martyrs died, a reiteration of our hate of the power which murdered them'.[135]

In 1914 *Eire Ireland* used an entire page to discuss two events, the Manchester Martyrs' Commemoration Day and the All-Ireland Football Final at Croke Park between Wexford and Kerry. The newspaper interviewed a Father Condon for an article entitled 'What would the Martyrs Think of the Recruiting Campaign?'[136] Father Condon recalled that while walking in the memorial procession he had wondered what would happen if the souls of the murdered men left their 'Felons' Graves' and returned to Ireland. What would they say faced with a campaign that asked Irishmen to support the Empire that had killed them? He finished with the easily answered question, 'would Allen, Larkin, and O'Brien approve of the sending of our manhood to lay down their lives on the battlefields of Belgium and France?'[137]

The commemoration in Manchester that same year highlighted the gulf

130 Ibid.   131 BNL, *IV*, 10.10.14, p. 12.   132 NLI MS 5637: Robert Barton Papers: Barton Scrapbook, vol. I, fol. 33.   133 Ibid.   134 See Gary Owens, 'Constructing the martyrs: the Manchester executions and the nationalist imagination', in McBride (ed.), 1999, pp. 18–36, for a brilliant study of the 'construction' of the martyrs' cult in nineteenth-century Ireland.   135 BNL, *IF*, December 1914, p. 8.   136 BNL, *EI*, 1.12.14, p. 4.   137 Ibid.

between advanced and constitutional nationalists who used the same historical figures as icons of their faith. The day's events were organized by Charles Egan and T.P. O'Connor of the Irish Parliamentary Party, and were used by both men as an opportunity to recruit men for the British army. The memory of the martyrs, in advanced nationalist eyes, was even further insulted by the presence of a band that played the national anthems of the allies and *Tipperary*. *Irish Freedom* was 'sickened' with the 'spectacle of the three loved names being coupled with the national anthem of England and the music hall jargon beloved of the descendants of those whose ribald songs and blasphemies contributed to the torture of the last hours of three of the best beloved of our patriots'.[138] Griffith produced a more violent account of this constitutional/advanced dichotomy. Quoting the Belfast *Evening Telegraph*, he reported that at a National Volunteer meeting in Toomebridge, near Belfast, a Mr Joseph Davidson had claimed that 'if Allen, Larkin, and O'Brien had been here to-day, they would be heart and soul with Mr John Redmond'. This statement, said Griffith, was greeted with shouts of 'It's a lie! They would shoot him!'[139]

Herbert Pim's pamphlet *Why the Martyrs of Manchester Died*, ninth in the Sinn Féin 'Tracts for Our Times' series,[140] was given a favourable review in the *Irish Volunteer* by Patrick Pearse. Taking a sarcastic tone, Pearse declared that the martyrs 'died, like the millions that died in the Famine, for the good of the English Empire. They died, in a word, because it was necessary to Defend the Realm'.[141] Ireland, Pearse felt, was perverse not to see these men as the 'necessary victims of Empire – the eggs that make up the English omelette'.[142] He concluded his review with a glowing recommendation. 'Mr Newman's[143] pamphlet is carefully calculated to foster Irish prejudices against England. It is therefore a dangerous pamphlet. Mr Newman's pamphlet is a glorification of Three Murderers. It is therefore an immoral pamphlet. Obviously, no Irish Volunteer will buy it'.[144]

Propagandists did not use the contra-example to recruits supplied by the Manchester Martyrs as an example of British atrocities. As with the case of Edith Cavell, matters were complicated by the fact that, regardless of the men's courage, they were judicially executed for a crime for which they had been convicted in an open court. It was far easier to use more egregious examples of British atrocities, atrocities that crucially, as they reached the turn of the century, fell into the living memory of advanced nationalists.

The Boer War was an ideal source for Irish atrocity propagandists. Many of the same generals and politicians currently active had seen action in South

138 BNL, *IF*, December 1914, p. 8. 139 BNL, *EI*, 26.11.14, p. 1. 140 Pim claimed a circulation of 5,000 copies for this pamphlet (cf. Herbert Pim, *Adventures in the Land of Sinn Féin*, unpublished MS, 1920). My thanks to Dr Patrick Maume, Queen's University, Belfast, for this source. 141 BNL, *IV*, 1.1.15, p. 5. 142 Ibid. 143 'A. Newman' being the pseudonym of Herbert Pim. 144 BNL, *IV*, 1.1.15, p. 5.

Africa, and advanced nationalists delighted in catching hypocrites and barbarians among the current heroes of civilisation praised daily in the pro-war press. Posters recalled Lord Roberts' order in the final year of the war 'that where the railway lines were tampered with by the Boers, the houses for a radius of ten miles were to be burnt'.[145] Journalists warned readers not to think that atrocities were a monopoly of the Germans, as the British had starved 20,000 Boer women and children to death in South Africa, and only won the war by convincing the Boers that their families would be exterminated if they did not surrender.[146] Reporters discovered that Lloyd George had protested against the actions of General Bruce Hamilton at Ventersburg, where the British had burned houses, captured supplies, and forced the Boers to feed the women and children. Lloyd George in 1901 declared this to be 'the most fiendish act any ruffian could commit'.[147] Now of course he sang a different tune, explicable because 'the Empire was not then fighting for civilization, which at that time was in no danger! Circumstances alter cases and Lloyd George with them'.[148]

Griffith maintained that even more women and children had died in concentration camps at Ventersburg – 26,000 by his count, or fully one-fourth of the Boer women and children in pre-war South Africa.[149] When Edith Cavell was shot in October 1915, Griffith admitted that the British had not shot any women in their war against the Boers. Instead they had simply burned down their houses, removed their supplies, and ordered them to 'get food from their embattled countrymen or, if they could not, starve to death'.[150] Almost every one of the daily papers in England voiced their approval of General Hamilton's actions at Ventersburg. Now, these same papers were 'in hysterics over the fate of Miss Cavell'. 'Somewhere on the veldt near Ventersburg', concluded Griffith, 'the ghosts of famished women and children must shriek to hear'.[151]

With the atrocities of the Boer War, advanced nationalist propagandists had once again reached current events, coming full circle from propaganda that attacked the British because of their activities in the middle ages or early modern era. Historical propaganda, drawing on familiar imagery, was used for different reasons. 1798 and its attendant atrocities outweighed German conduct in Europe, while the alleged economic destruction of Ireland during the nineteenth century was also considered atrocious by Griffith. Recent atrocities, within living memory, reinforced the idea of Britain as an oppressive force in the lives of Irishmen. But what of atrocity propaganda which used a sequence of events to attack the British? This was the most numerous style, appearing in thirteen of the fourteen anecdotes discovered. Its use, however, was relatively simple, overwhelming the reader with the accumulated weight of evil. A few examples

---

145 NLI MS 5637: Robert Barton Papers: Barton Scrapbook, vol. I, fol. 31. 146 BNL, *Hib*, 18.9.15, pp. 2–3. 147 Ibid., p. 6. 148 Ibid. 149 BNL, *Nat*, 18.9.15, p. 1. 150 Ibid., 30.10.15, p. 8. 151 Ibid.

will suffice to explore the style of this final form of atrocity propaganda in Ireland.

In the *Irish Worker*, J.J. Burke asked why England was creating German atrocities. Noting that 'all along the Germans have been saddled with crimes which England has been committing for centuries in Ireland',[152] he wondered if England was, 'through her Press Bureau, confessing to the world her awful crimes against God and man'.[153] German propagandists certainly would have hoped for this rationale to be true. In their propaganda directed at Ireland, they seemed unable to understand why the Irish would not support the Germans. In a propaganda leaflet for Irish troops, the pseudonymous author 'Hugh O'Neill' asked:

> Why should Ireland identify herself with England, the enemy of liberty, the destroyer of nations, the only enemy Ireland ever had? Had she not been a ruthless oppressor of the Irish from the landing of Strongbow in 1172 to the present time under George V? ... Did she not put twenty thousand Irish patriots to death by the rack, the pitchcap, or the gibbet, in 1796 [sic]?[154]

Mrs Leonard Marshall, also writing for the Germans, brought together a classic litany of atrocities, and even managed to include reference to British activities elsewhere:

> We have been England's eternal Victims for seven hundred years, that [sic] our Priests were pitch-capped and hanged, our women shot down round the Cross in Wexford. Our children murdered as the British soldier bayonetted [sic] the poor Indian babies during the Mutiny. That our industries were strangled, that they robbed us of our language, of all, all but our Catholic Faith for which we fought starved and bled![155]

Sean Doyle felt that Ireland might be able to forgive the wrongs done her in the past, but that she could never forget them. He wondered whether the 'Irish brain has developed senility', and if when remembering the German actions in 'Belgium, Rheims, and Scarboro', it had forgotten all of the past woes of Ireland. He dismissed the thought that 'crime, like wine, improves with age, and if the treaty breakings and the massacres in Ireland must, because of their antiquity, be regarded as nebulous traditions, or cloaked in the mantle of Imperial virtue'.[156]

Advanced nationalist public speakers also hammered home the message of England's brutality to Ireland outweighing anything that happened in Belgium.

---

152 BNL, *IW*, 28.11.14, p. 4. 153 Ibid. 154 TCD, Samuels 2/61. 155 TCD, Samuels 3/84. 156 BNL, *Spark*, 14.3.15, p. 1.

The Rev Dr Mannix, a leading Irish-Australian nationalist, addressing a monster meeting of 100,000 Australian Irish gathered in 1917 to show their support for Sinn Féin, cried:

> We have been asked – young men and even old men – to rush to Europe to avenge the wrongs of Belgium and the other small nations, and the call has not gone unheeded. (Cheers). But there is a small nation whose wrongs are older. (Cheers). (A voice – 'Ireland'). (Cheers). There is a nation whose scars are deeper than Belgium's scars. (Cheers). Her daughters have been ill-treated and her shrines and churches laid in ruins – and that not by Turks, or Austrians, or Germans. (Cheers).[157]

The piece of propaganda which best sums up the arguments used by advanced nationalist 'atrocity-mongers' to attack recruiting is a 1914 poem by Brian O'Higgins entitled *Who Is Ireland's Enemy?* The poem clearly illustrates one of the central problems faced by recruiters in Ireland at the beginning of the war – however much they demonized Germany, the fact remained that Germany had done very little to Ireland. England, however, especially when reflected in the cracked mirror of advanced nationalist propaganda, was evil incarnate:

> Who is Ireland's enemy?
> Not Germany nor Spain,
> Not Russia, France, nor Austria —
> They forged for her no chain;
> Nor quenched her hearths, nor razed her homes,
> Nor laid her altars low,
> Nor sent her sons to tramp the hills
> Amid the winter snow!
>
> Who murdered kingly Shane O'Neill?
> Who poisoned Owen Roe?
> Who struck Red Hugh O'Donnell down?
> Who filled our land with woe
> By night and day – a thousand times,
> In twice four hundred years —
> Till every blade of Irish grass
> Was wet with blood and tears?
>
> Who spiked the heads of Irish priests
> On Dublin Castle Gate?
> Who butchered helpless Irish babes,

[157] TCD, Samuels 2/103.

The lust for blood to sate?
Who outraged Irish maidenhood,
And tortured aged sires,
And spread from Clare to Donegal
The glare of midnight fires?

Who sent in thousands o'er the waves
To slavery and to shame
The children of the Irish land,
To end the race and name?
Who sold them like a herd of sheep,
And laughed with hellish glee
When Irish mothers, mad with grief,
Sought death beneath the sea?

Who scourged the land in '98
Spread torture far and wide,
Till Ireland shrieked in woe and pain,
And hell seemed fair beside?
Who plied the pitch cap and the sword
The gibbet and the rack?
O God! that we should ever fail
To pay those devils back!

Who robbed our land in '47
Of all her stores of food,
When at her gates with poisoned breath
Gaunt Famine grimly stood?
Who filled her fields with whitened bones?
Who sent across the sea
The kindliest hearts in all the world –
The kin of you and me?

Not Germany, nor Austria,
Nor Russia, France, nor Spain
That robbed and rieved this land of ours,
That forged her rusty chain:
But ENGLAND of the wily words –
The crafty, treacherous foe –
'Twas ENGLAND scourged our Motherland,
'Twas ENGLAND laid her low![158]

[158] BNL, *IF*, September 1914, p. 2.

3

Liars, savages, and the champion of Christianity: moral posturing and the use of atrocity propaganda

The widespread use of atrocity propaganda by the British press throughout the United Kingdom gave advanced nationalists an opening to attack the morality of the British conduct of the war. Led by Arthur Griffith's hatred of the Irish daily press that supported the war, propagandists savaged the perceived immorality and dishonesty of press reports about German atrocities in Belgium and France. Refusing to believe that the Germans could be capable of such offences, propagandists quickly responded to British claims by attacking the racial and ethnic make-up of the *entente cordiale*. These attacks on the native troops that served in the British and French armies both highlight a strain of racist and insular xenophobia that underlay advanced nationalist rhetoric during the war, and served to further demonize the British army and government. The native troops and their irreligious and brutal allies in France and Russia were ranged against Germany and Austria-Hungary, empires that were considered the last bastions of catholic power in Europe. Since Germany could be seen as a white and catholic champion, advanced nationalist propagandists eagerly anticipated the conquest of Ireland, and looked to Germany to save their religion and their race. Moralistic responses to atrocity propaganda, as with historical and specific responses studied earlier, served to counter-act the circulation of atrocity stories. More importantly, they show the importance of a sense of moral superiority to advanced nationalist discourse, and created an image of a decadent, immoral Britain, a national embodiment of the pornographer, wallowing in the sadism of atrocities. This specific kind of attack formed a unique and original part of a larger moral crusade undertaken by advanced nationalists during the war, and yet in creating this image of England, propagandists revealed their own biases and prejudices.[1]

I

The German invasion of Belgium in August 1914 was, in an ironic sense, a godsend to pro-war propagandists in Ireland. Here was not only a small nation

---

[1] Historians have long denied such racism. One exception is Dermot Keogh, *Jews in Twentieth-Century Ireland: Refugees, Anti-Semitism, and the Holocaust* (Cork, 1998), who acknowledges the anti-Semitism of Arthur Griffith and D.P. Moran, as well as the consistent anti-Semitic imagery in the *Irish Worker*.

for the British to defend, but also more importantly, a small catholic nation. Images of Belgium, accentuating the destruction of religious institutions, featured prominently in early atrocity propaganda. 'For the Glory of Ireland' (figure 3.1) was produced in 1914 by the Dublin printing firm of Hely's for the CCORI. It would be difficult to find another poster that combines more classic elements of propaganda – the appeal of a young and sexually powerful woman to a man's sense of traditional masculine duty, the Irish images of the shillelagh and traditional clothing, and of course, the representation of Belgium.[2] Burning religious buildings represent 'Belgium', which is visible here across a stretch of water from Ireland. The shell of a cathedral, referring most likely to Rheims, can be seen in the right of the background.

How did the Irish receive pro-Belgian atrocity propaganda? Canon James Hannay ('George Birmingham') declared in 1915 that 'the shelling of cathedrals by Germans, the stories of their treatment of priests and nuns and the imprisonment of Cardinal Mercier produced some, but not very much, effect on Irish opinion'.[3] A.P. Magill, Private Secretary to Chief Secretary Augustine Birrell, was even more negative about the effect of these posters. He recalled Sir Henry Robinson telling him during the war 'You think you are doing a great deal by your posters about the horrors of the war at the front and the brutalities of the Germans, but I can assure you they are having just the contrary effect to what you hope'.[4] R.M. Henry maintained that the 'invincible scepticism' that led Irish readers to mistrust English and Redmondite journalists' accounts of atrocities 'proved an unexpected obstacle to the recruiting campaign'.[5] If atrocity propaganda was in fact poorly received by the general population, it was savaged by the anti-war propagandists of advanced nationalism.

The first major atrocity of Germany's invasion of Belgium came at the end of August 1914, when the Germans burned a portion of the ancient university town of Louvain, and executed a number of its civilians. The French and British publics were outraged, and *The Times* called Germans 'Huns' for the first time.[6] There was no immediate response in the advanced nationalist press to the German action. It was only when this German atrocity began to be used by Irish Parliamentary Party recruiters as a central plank for their pro-war recruiting platforms that counter-propaganda efforts in the Dublin 'Irish' weeklies and monthlies became visible.

Arthur Griffith led the way, demolishing what he called the 'Great Louvain Lie' – that Louvain was 'wantonly destroyed' by the German army. Griffith did not claim that the Germans had spared Louvain, simply that they had responded to aggressive action by the civilian population of the city. 'A plan was laid out to

2 TCD, Irish Recruiting Posters, Case 55c/94.   3 James Hannay, 'Ireland and the War', *The Nineteenth Century and After*, vol. 78, no. 462 (Aug. 1915), p. 398.   4 Bod., MS Eng. c. 2803: Magill Papers, 'Memoirs of Andrew Phillip Magill', fol. 286.   5 Henry, 1920, p. 181.   6 Read, 1941, p. 58.

3.1 *For the Glory of Ireland* (CCORI recruiting poster, 1914, TCD)

draw the bulk of the German garrison out of Louvain by a sortie from Antwerp', he wrote, 'when the Louvainese, under the command of Belgian officers, were to rise, wipe out the remainder of the garrison, and recapture the city'.[7] The first part of the plan was successful. Once two-thirds of the German garrison left for Antwerp, 'machine-guns and rifles opened fire from hundreds of houses and the church of St Pierre upon the German troops left in the streets'.[8] It took twenty-four hours of heavy fighting for the Germans to regain the town, and during this period 'part' of Louvain was burned. 'This', claimed Griffith, 'was the alleged infamy'.[9]

Louvain, a centre of catholic learning since the Middle Ages, had possessed some Irish manuscripts, and was, with Salamanca, a continental focus for Irish religious education and scholarship. Pro-war propagandists immediately exploited these 'Irish connections'. In response, Eoin MacNeill, a medieval historian, pointed out that 'the truthful indignation mongers tell us about "the priceless Irish manuscripts of Louvain", suggesting, without an item of evidence, that these treasures have been destroyed by the barbarous Germans. Louvain lost its Irish manuscripts during an invasion of Belgium by the French, more than a century ago'.[10] Other propagandists complained in October 1914 that '[t]he Louvain bogey has been conveniently worked in with a subtle appeal to Irish catholics to rally to the British arms on behalf of catholic Belgium'.[11] More than a year later, writing under the pseudonym Theobald Keane, Francis Sheehy-Skeffington explained that while the use of Belgian atrocities was disappearing in English propaganda, in Ireland, 'Belgium is still the trump card – catholic Belgium, the "small nation", the victim of "breach of treaties" and of "German atrocities". It is continually to the front in the recruiting appeals; and it must be continually out-trumped'.[12]

In the immediate aftermath of Louvain, what appears to have angered advanced nationalist journalists most was the idea that the English and 'West-British' press had lied to further recruiting. When news came of Louvain's destruction, wrote *Irish Freedom*, 'our "Irish" pressmen looked up Louvain in the gazeteer to find out what country it was in, and reading with surprise that it had Irish associations, went into hysterics of well-simulated indignation'.[13] Recent research has shown that the Germans were not fired upon by a sizeable body of *franc-tireurs* in Louvain, but rather fired on their own men following a night action against a Belgian column advancing from Antwerp. The city, including the university library, burned not because of a defensive military action by the Germans or from an accidental kindling; the Germans fired it in revenge for their own military ineptitude.[14]

7 BNL, *SF*, 19.9.14, p. 1.   8 Ibid.   9 Ibid.   10 BNL, *IV*, 10.10.14, p. 12.   11 BNL, *IF*, October 1914, p. 1.   12 NLI MS 22275: Sheehy-Skeffington Papers: Copies of articles and speeches by Francis Sheehy-Skeffington, 1914–15, 'Ireland and Belgium'.   13 BNL, *IF*, October 1914, p. 1.   14 Mark Derez, 'The Flames of Louvain: The War Experience of an Academic Community', in Cecil and Liddle (eds)., 1996, pp. 617–30.

The truth was completely obscured at the time. The Germans, quite naturally, denied any atrocious acts in Louvain, and the advanced nationalist propagandists were simply following the German explanation in their accounts of what occurred. And while Louvain is a rather clear-cut example of extreme behaviour by the Germans, the hysterical accounts by pro-war newspapers easily led other incidents to be disbelieved. This aura of doubt that surrounded atrocity accounts would further harm pro-war recruiting attempts that used less obvious examples of German atrocities in Belgium.

Griffith assumed that all atrocity stories were not exaggerated, but made up by 'cowardly' journalists. Responding to stories about German soldiers driving women and children before them in Belgium, he claimed that the 'factory for the manufacture of German atrocities' was located in the back of a Fleet Street pub.[15] People who believed these wild atrocity tales were beneath his contempt. A story circulated at the beginning of the war in Dublin that German agents had connived to plant poison in the Roundwood Reservoir that supplied Dublin with drinking water. Griffith claimed that this story was planted by the RIC and spread by the bought press in order to give Dublin Castle the excuse of placing sentries over the reservoir. 'None of the idiots who swallowed the story', he acidly remarked, 'stopped to ask how, assuming a German was devilish enough to desire to poison the reservoir, he could manage to poison it, and what he would gain poisoning it'.[16] Griffith calculated that it would take 450 tons of 'poison' to make the water undrinkable – 'you might as well attempt to poison the Atlantic Ocean'.[17]

Advanced nationalist journalists did not believe that propagandistic lies would be limited to German atrocities. Following the Ottoman Empire's alliance with the Central Powers and entry into the war in October 1914, 'Carbery' opined in the *Irish Worker* that 'the sword of the Turk again rings through South Eastern Europe ... Presently, we shall hear blood-curdling stories of Turkish atrocities which will be just as reliable as those which are now being circulated about the Germans'.[18] Making up atrocities was an easy task. 'Willie Nelson', who had written the 'Na Fianna Eireann' column in the *Irish Volunteer*, mocked the atrocity mongers in the first issue of Bulmer Hobson's youth paper, *Fianna*. 'I am going to talk about the war', he wrote, 'because everyone talks about the war when they have nothing to say. It is as easy to manufacture a German atrocity as it is to sharpen your pencil'.[19]

Atrocity propaganda enjoyed a renaissance in the spring of 1915 following the publication of the Bryce Report in late May.[20] Seven Englishmen, led by the distinguished historian and quondam Chief Secretary of Ireland, James Bryce,

---

15 BNL, *SF*, 19.9.14, p. 3. 16 BNL, Ibid., 29.8.14, p. 1. 17 Ibid. 18 BNL, ibid., 7.11.14, p. 3. 19 BNL, *Fianna*, February 1915, p. 12. 20 The publication came coincidentally the week after the sinking of the *Lusitania*.

met to constitute an 'impartial' jury to hear reports from barristers and investigators who had interviewed scores of Belgian refugees and veterans. The Bryce Report seemed to confirm a number of stories that had been in wide circulation since the beginning of the war. Incidents of children having their hands chopped off appeared a number of times, as did lurid accounts of women with amputated breasts, an action which a priest claimed had been done by 'syphilitic German soldiers' as a warning to their comrades.[21] Later investigations, including one by the anti-German Lord Northcliffe, could find no evidence of any such mutilations.[22] Indeed, the Bryce Report must stand as an egregious example of wartime hysteria and gullibility in the United Kingdom, and a sad footnote to the distinguished and otherwise admirable career of Sir James Bryce.[23]

The Bryce Report disgusted anti-war propagandists in Ireland. Sean Doyle felt that its publication contributed greatly to the gross immorality of the British public:

> The details of some of these atrocities are, says the virtuous English press, of such a nature that a respectable newspaper cannot reproduce. This the Government is recommended to obviate by reducing the Atrocity Book to one penny – a price which will place the salacious stories within the reach of every boy and girl and grown up degenerate.[24]

The Germans indignantly denied the atrocity claims in the Bryce Report. Stories about children being mutilated were clearly made up by the Belgians, stated the German government, as the Belgians had frequently amputated natives' hands in the Belgian Congo before the war.[25] This argument received support from Doyle,[26] who reminded readers that the English recruiter H. de

21 Read, 1941, p. 37. 22 Ibid., p. 36. 23 Trevor Wilson puts it well in *The Myriad Faces of War*: 'The Bryce Committee did not produce a dishonest or fraudulent report in the sense that it reached conclusions shown by the evidence to be unsound. What it did do was carefully to avoid verifying the evidence ... Having carefully disqualified itself from reaching final conclusions either way, the Committee proclaimed Germany guilty in the most sweeping terms'. (Trevor Wilson, *The Myriad Faces of War* (Cambridge, 1986), p. 188). In an earlier *JCH* article (1979), Wilson used the Bryce Report 'as an example of the manner in which the pressures of war could affect the standards of conduct of honourable, enlightened, fastidious Englishmen'. (Wilson, 'Lord Bryce's Investigation into Alleged German Atrocities in Belgium, 1914–1915', *JCH*, vol. 14, no. 3 [July 1979], p. 370). This does not downgrade the actual horror of Germany's occupation of Belgium. As Wilson again writes, 'German authorities had prepared, and when it suited them had put into effect, a deliberate policy of terrorism against Belgian civilians, including the cold-blooded execution of civilian hostages and the destruction of towns and buildings of great historic and emotional significance'. (Ibid., p. 380). And yet, 'by a strange perversion of values, these things paled into insignificance once tales became current of raped women and mutilated children'. (Ibid). 24 BNL, *Spark*, 23.5.15, p. 4. 25 Read, 1941, p. 36. 26 No mention was made in advanced nationalist newspapers about Roger Casement's pre-war humanitarian efforts on behalf of Congolese natives.

Vere Stacpoole had written a novel about the Belgian Congo entitled *Pools of Silence*. Published by T. Fisher Unwin in 1910, the novel went through five editions in the first eleven months after its original publication. Doyle found it 'curious' and 'disgusting' to re-read this novel in 1915:

> Herein we find all the German atrocities of to-day – the wanton and inhuman slaying of inoffensive men and women, the brutal ravishing of women, the torture of children, the cutting off of hands, and so forth – all described in detail as being performed by the Belgians on the hapless Congolese.[27]

Advanced nationalist journalists were sympathetic to the German perspective, but this sympathy was extended more because supporting Germany's righteous indignation at the publication of the Bryce Report allowed them to strike at the British in their newspaper columns and editorials. When Arthur Griffith addressed the German response to the report in August 1915, he was more concerned with mocking the British attempts to distribute the Bryce Report than the actual complaints of the Germans. He re-printed a translation from the *Koelnische Zeitung* which claimed that German atrocities were made up in newspaper offices in London and Paris. 'That is all the 'proof' the world shall ever see of the German atrocities', wrote the *Zeitung*, 'for the simple reason that there never were any German atrocities, except those manufactured for overseas consumption by the Anglo-French brotherhood of saints'.[28] Griffith waxed sardonic about British indignation at this German denial. 'Imagine the audacity of the Huns in denying that there were any German atrocities, when the British Government is spending a hundred thousand pounds in their Free Distribution'.[29]

James Read states that there was a curious lull in atrocity propaganda between the sinking of the *Lusitania* and the Bryce Report in May 1915, and the German execution of Edith Cavell the following October. He explains this lull with a variety of reasons, including a decrease in the German air bombardment of England, and the improved treatment of POWs in German camps.[30] Most, though not all, of the specific atrocity counter-propaganda in Ireland was produced in reaction to some atrocity report in a British journal or recruiting speech. Therefore, it is not surprising to discover that responses to atrocity propaganda in Irish nationalist newspapers mirror the more general trend found by Read in the continental and British newspapers he studied.

By the autumn of 1915, newspapers were claiming that Horatio Bottomley had ordered his recruiting agents to stop using atrocities in their speeches. Belgian atrocities, along with 'The Scrap of Paper' and 'German Kultur' were

27 BNL, *Spark*, 30.5.15, pp. 3–4. 28 BNL, *Nat*, 21.8.15, p. 1. 29 Ibid. 30 Read, 1941, pp. 201–2.

now 'played out' and had been withdrawn by the central office.[31] In the *Hibernian*, Rev. F.S. Pollard took the time to lecture his audience on the catholic view of atrocities. Catholics, he stated, are forbidden by their religion to make false statements intended to injure the character of their neighbours. Irish catholics had been innocent of this transgression until August 1914, when atrocity propaganda began to circulate. According to Pollard, the war had heightened the deadly influence of the foreign press:

> Having ... taken the revue, the immoral paper, the seductive novel and other Anglo-French products to our bosoms, some of us have gone a step further, and seem to consider that we are justified in using calumny as a weapon of offence against the enemies of the British Empire.[32]

Even after the resurgence of atrocity propaganda following Cavell's execution in October 1915, atrocity promoters were still widely mocked in the nationalist press. In February 1916, the editor of the *Gael* highlighted 'The pro-Britishers who didn't improve on the telling of the atrocity yarn he was told', in his weekly 'We Want to Find' column.[33] A month later, Congreve was brought into play, describing the 'Atrocity Inventor' with his quote 'Thou liar of the first magnitude'.[34]

Editors also began to present practical responses to atrocity propaganda. Seamus Upton wondered in December 1915 why neutral countries did not attack Germany if the evidence of such atrocities really was overwhelming.[35] The British were busy attempting to convince neutral countries, especially the United States, of the rectitude of their cause. 'C.C'., writing in *Nationality*, took this distracted state as an excuse to call advanced nationalists into action:

> Anyway, John Bull is in a pious mood ... John's eyes are cast upwards towards heaven ... Let us work hard while we have still time. John cannot see us with the whites of his eyes.[36]

Propagandists also frequently used muddled reports from the allied press to serve their own purposes. In September 1915, Sean Doyle re-printed an excerpt from *An Claidheamh Soluis*, which purported to show how the 'All-lies' press twisted the facts to create an atrocity. The item was brief, and charted the progress of a November 1914 column in the *Koelnische Zeitung*, which had stated that church bells in Cologne had been rung when the Germans captured Antwerp. By the time the story had reached the Italian *Corriere de la Serra*, which had received the news from the London *Times* via Paris, the story had become transformed so that it now claimed that priests in Antwerp had been ordered to

31 BNL, *Nat*, 23.10.15, p. 4.   32 BNL, *Hib*, 18.9.15, pp. 2–3.   33 BNL, *Gael*, 5.2.16, p. 14.
34 BNL, Ibid., 4.3.16, p. 6.   35 BNL, *Hon*, 18.12.15, pp. 2–3.   36 BNL, *Nat*, 22.1.16, p. 6.

ring their own bells when Antwerp had been captured. When they refused, they were sentenced to penal servitude. The Parisian *Le Matin* ran the story again, this time claiming that *de la Serra* had reported that the recalcitrant priests were hanged head down, inside their own bells, while clad in their sacred vestments.[37] Lord Ponsonby used this exact account in his 1924 volume *Truth and Falsehood in Wartime*, which was written as an attack on the lies created under the rubric of 'propaganda' during the Great War.

James Morgan Read investigated Ponsonby's account, and quickly discovered that *The Times* and *Le Matin* had no mention of the story in November 1914. He concluded that Ponsonby had seen a translation of this piece, which appeared originally as a spoof in the *Norddeutsche Allgemeine Zeitung* in July 1915 under the title 'What Can be Made Out of a News Item'.[38] But where did Ponsonby see a translation? Read did not know that this item had appeared in two English-language papers two months later, one of which (the *Spark*) was considered enough of a threat by authorities that copies were sent to London to be read by Parliamentary leaders and government officials.[39] It is quite possible that Ponsonby had seen the version presented in either *Soluis* or the *Spark*. Thus, Doyle's failure to spot a German joke in 1915 may have contributed to Ponsonby's more public failure a decade later.

Advanced nationalists had to deal with more than newspaper accounts of set-piece German atrocities. First-hand accounts of atrocities by 'eye-witnesses' were frequently used in newspapers, and recruiters on the platform used atrocities to bolster their own arguments. How did anti-war journalists combat these tales? Scorn was a popular weapon. In *Eire Ireland*, Arthur Griffith published a clipping from the *Daily Mail* which he claimed had been sent him by the unimpeachable source, an 'Irish Priest'. In the letter, a 'Constant Reader' stated that he had recently spent a week in an Essex village where the main topic of conversation was a Belgian boy whose hands had been chopped off to prevent him from ever holding a rifle. Rather than swallow this common and horrific tale, the man went to the orphanage where this boy was supposed to be, and confronted the mistress. She swore that all her charges were fit, and that she had never had any such boy in her care. Griffith had no need to add to the comments of this reader, who declared indignantly, 'do you not think it high time such absurd atrocity stories, which are springing up from all quarters, should be excluded by the Press, with a reminder that "Seeing is believing", etc'.[40]

Scorn extended to Irish war heroes who helped in recruiting. Lieutenant Michael O'Leary, the first surviving Irish V.C. of the war,[41] was a favourite target

37 BNL., *Spark*, 5.9.15, p. 3. 38 Read, 1941, pp. 24–5. 39 See Matthew Nathan's papers in the Bodleian Library, Oxford, for further evidence, especially letters from Sir Nugent Everard in Nathan MS 452 and Walter Long, MP in Nathan MS 455. 40 BNL, *EI*, 1.12.14, p. 2. No record of this letter can be found in the *Daily Mail*. 41 O'Leary won the medal in 1915 while a corporal with the Irish Guards. He single-handedly charged a German machine-gun nest on

of advanced nationalist counter-propaganda. In January 1916, to cries of outrage, he declared at a recruiting meeting that he had seen a German soldier bayonet an innocent child after the battle of Ypres. *Honesty* responded angrily, asking, 'What was Lieutenant O'Leary doing when the German soldier was bayonetting [*sic*] the child at Ypres? Did he regard the matter in the light of a theatrical exhibition in which he had only a spectator's interest and could not actively interfere?'[42]

The greatest level of aggression in the propaganda was reserved for John Redmond, an acclaimed orator who often used atrocity accounts in his recruiting speeches. To Griffith and the others, he was nothing more than a liar. At Wexford in October 1914, Redmond asked his audience to consider 'how Ireland would stand if to-morrow Germany, having completed her task of murdering the Bishops and Archbishops and Priests of Belgium ... were to come and seize upon this country'. Griffith responded that Redmond knew this was false. No Bishop or Archbishop had been harmed by the Germans, and no church had been fired upon which had not first been seized by the French or British for use as a military stronghold.[43]

In 1916, Redmond was still harping on Belgian atrocities, although by now he had descended into the realm of immorality, at least as far as the nationalist press was concerned. In an editorial attacking the bad character of Belgian refugees in Ireland and England, J.J. Scollan savaged Redmond's recent speech at the Mansion House Recruiting Conference, where Redmond had mentioned the cruel treatment of Belgian nuns by Prussian soldiers.[44] While Scollan could not bring himself to repeat exactly what Redmond had said, Griffith had less compunction. Condemning it as an 'infamous lie', Griffith managed to recount Redmond's example. According to Redmond, German soldiers had broken into a convent, stripped all the nuns, and forced them to run naked through the streets. Griffith solemnly reminded his readers that this tale was the sort 'which Cardinal Hartmann and the catholic Bishops of Germany have solemnly denounced as the horrible "inventions of evil and degenerate men"'.[45]

The wide-spread use of atrocities by the British and pro-war Irish recruiters was viewed with disgust and anger by the editors and journalists of the separatist press who led the advanced nationalist propaganda campaign for most of the war. This use, however, allowed propagandists to attack a particularly prevalent form of moral abuse. Response to atrocity stories varied from scorn to anger and disbelief. Always, however, the reactions sought to differentiate between the intelligent and morally pure Gaelic Irish, who had the wit to disbelieve such monstrous tales, and the idiotic, degenerate 'West Britons', who obtained cheap, sadistic thrills from the lurid literature produced by British and Irish recruiting

the Western Front, killing 8 soldiers and capturing the rest of the gun's crew. For more information on advanced nationalists' attitudes to O'Leary, see chapter six.   **42** BNL, *Hon*, 22.1.16, pp. 1–2.   **43** BNL, *SF*, 10.10.14, p. 2.   **44** BNL, *Hib*, 26.2.16, p. 6.   **45** BNL, *Nat*, 19.2.16, p. 2.

agencies. This first type of posturing response to atrocity propaganda was strictly reactive, appearing only in response to British writing and speech making. In this next section, we turn to a more active form of advanced nationalist propaganda, an attack against Britain and her allies for their war against Christianity. Anti-British propagandists created an image of Britain as a sink of immorality. This image was abetted by the exigencies of a war that forced the United Kingdom to call on the many peoples of her Empire for aid in the time of peril, regardless of their race, colour, or creed.

II

The sheer scale of the Great War necessitated the recruitment of native auxiliaries into the armies of the British and the French. Both powers had a long history of using indigenous troops in their armies, the British most notably in India, and the French throughout North Africa. The Great War, however, was the first time that these troops were used in combat in Europe. The Germans, notwithstanding their own use of black troops in campaigns throughout German East Africa, bitterly complained in their atrocity propaganda about the presence of these men in the European theatre. Accentuating racial prejudices of their own soldiers and civilians, the Germans accused the Gurkhas and Sikhs who fought in Indian regiments of cannibalism and using poisoned knives, and laid similar charges at the door of French North African auxiliaries, known by both sides as 'Turcos'.[46]

Racist and racialist remarks were a central feature of Irish nationalist propaganda in general at this time. Jewish profiteers were blamed for the war,[47] Aodh de Blacam and M.S. O'Lonnain campaigned in *Young Ireland* to capture the rag trade from Polish Jewish traders,[48] and anti-Semitic caricatures of John Bull and John Redmond even appeared near the end of the war.[49] African nationalist desires were insulted in cartoons,[50] and cartoons and ballads mocked the conglomeration of nations and races all claiming to be 'fighting for Christianity'.[51] Atrocity propaganda that exploited the polyglot and polychrome make-up of the allied forces was therefore part and parcel of the general racism

---

46 Read, 1941, p. 137. **47** Cf. 'Oration delivered by Commandant Thomas Ashe at Casement's Fort, Adfert, County Kerry, on Sunday, 5th August, 1917' (TCD, Samuels 2/37). This attitude is inherited directly from Griffithite rhetoric during the Boer War, which he believed had been caused by Jewish merchants in Johannesburg. For more information see Louis Hyman, *The Jews of Ireland* (Dublin, 1972); Keogh, op. cit.; and Ben Novick, 'No Anti-Semitism in Ireland?: The Limerick 'Pogrom' and Radical Nationalist Stereotypes', in *The Jewish Quarterly*, vol. 44, no. 4, Winter 1997/8, pp. 35–41 [1997b]. **48** Cf. BNL, *Og*, 8.9.17, p. 6; 2.3.18, pp. 5–6. **49** Novick, 1997b. **50** TCD, Samuels 4/10. **51** Cf. esp. 'Sliabh Ruadh's' *We're Fighting Now For Christianity*, TCD, Samuels 5/17; Sean O'Casey's *We Welcome the Aid of Japan*, CUL Hib.4.918.3; and BNL, *IW*, 14.11.14, 'Crusaders', p. 1.

that imbued Irish nationalist thought at the time. The Irish, however, outdid the Germans in the breadth of their racism. According to Read, German atrocity propagandists accentuated the 'black peril', and minimized the threat to civilization from the Japanese, who joined the war on the allied side in 1915.[52] Not so the Irish. The Japanese, the Gurkhas, the Turcos, the Senegalese, and the irreligious French and Russians were attacked with equal vehemence and frequency. What was the purpose of such virulent discourse? Another historian who briefly mentions this form of propaganda dismisses it as a device used by advanced nationalists to prove the hypocrisy of England's war effort.[53] While an emphasis on British hypocrisy played a large role in most advanced nationalist propaganda, there are more important and complex reasons for racialist language. Primarily, stories about 'pagan' troops shocked the mainly catholic readers of this propaganda, and managed effectively to dehumanize the British forces. It was probably not co-incidental that British recruiting propaganda in Ireland made little use of the contributions of non-Christian troops to the war effort.[54] Advanced nationalist propaganda also presented Germany as a morally pure and catholic country, the last bastion of the Caucasian race in Europe. Here is seen the development of an important link in atrocity counter-propaganda. Germany fought England, the age-old enemy of Ireland, and Ireland, like Germany, strove to be a moral nation. The only way that England could crush Germany was to seek the aid of pagans and barbarians. This proved Germany's strength, and by extension, proved as well Ireland's rectitude and moral strength in the fight against the criminal Empire of the British.

Indigenous tribes from North America played a marginal role at best in the British and American armies. Even the suggestion, however, that a Canadian contingent was to include a detachment of 'Red Indians' was enough to set Griffith off in November 1914. Reporting this news, he assured his readers that 'these enlightened people may be trusted to co-operate with the cultured Turcos and Senegalese in the great war of "Civilization" against the savage Germans'.[55] The entry of the United States into the war in April 1917 complicated matters for those who would denigrate Native Americans. The American decision to enter into alliance with the *entente cordiale* against the Germans was met, for the most part, with a disappointed silence by advanced nationalist propagandists. *Young Ireland*, however, produced a rare example of anti-American atrocity propaganda in its Christmas issue for 1917, using the massacre at Wounded Knee in December 1890 to attack the barbarism of the United States government. The Red Indian was suddenly transformed from a savage into 'a simple, clean-living man, if not following the law of God, at least abiding by natural law'. By a clever

---

52 Read, 1941, p. 137.　53 Ellis, 1997, pp. 322–4.　54 In Britain itself, stories of Indian and especially Gurkha troops were a regular feature in the popular and children's press.　55 BNL, *EI*, 4.11.14, p. 4.

twisting of facts, M.S. O'Lonnain subtly likened the American Indian policy and the military's actions at Wounded Knee to the British treatment of the Irish. The Americans 'coveted his [the Indian's] rich lands, and exterminated him with ruthless ferocity'. The description of Wounded Knee ignored the Ghost Dance Ritual that the American military had arrested Indian leaders to suppress, and claimed instead that firing had broken out when a 'young brave', 'maddened by the indignities', fired his rifle into the air, drawing a 'point-blank volley' in return.[56]

The massacre itself was an act of barbarism by the Americans, far surpassing anything done in living memory by the British in Ireland, and *Young Ireland* did not shy away from the gruesome details:

> A volley was fired point-blank into the Indians. The latter were unarmed, save for a few rifles, and in a few moments half the men present had been killed. A minute later, to complete the job scientifically, four Hotchkiss machine guns were turned on the defenceless mass; 120 men and 250 helpless women and children were massacred in broad daylight ... a few little boys hiding behind a ridge ... were promised safety if they left their place of concealment. But on their doing so, the American troops butchered every one of them.[57]

The metaphorical congruence between Americans and British was made explicit in the editorial's conclusion. 'Nothing in the way of punishment', wrote the author, 'was done by the American Government to these Defenders of the Realm of America'.[58] Instead of the Natives being savages, it was now the American officials who were presented as irreligious barbarians. 'This', concluded O'Lonnain, 'is how some American troops, just twenty-seven years ago, celebrated the anniversary of Christ's coming on earth'.[59]

As in German racist propaganda, the central complaint of the Irish was the introduction of 'savage' races into white Europe. In an astonishing passage from *Nationality*, Griffith explicitly clarified this point. The English may have paid Indians for American scalps during the Revolutionary War, but North America was the Indians' 'native heath'.[60] 'Europe, not America, is the white man's land', wrote Griffith, and the 'introduction of savage Asiatics and Africans into Europe in war between civilized Powers is unparalleled in European history since anno domini. It is a betrayal of the white race, and an infamy pregnant with a grim and horrible danger and woe in the future'.[61] Propagandists carefully differentiated between the offending races. Gurkhas, members of Nepalese hill tribes who formed the elite corp of Britain's Indian Army, were not to be mistaken for

---

56 BNL, *Og*, 15.12.17, p. 4. 57 Ibid. 58 Ibid. 59 Ibid. 60 BNL, *Nat*, 30.10.15, p. 2.
61 Ibid.

representatives of the 'great Hindustani people', who 'look upon these nomadic and treacherous tribesmen with contempt'.[62] Parts of the Hindustani (as well as other Indian peoples) were working for independence from Britain at this time, and Griffith and other separatist leaders strove to find common cause with their fellow revolutionaries. Gurkhas, however, were completely treacherous. Griffith was disgusted that 'great, civilized England' would accept their services against a 'great white nation', and was shocked that the English appeared not to be ashamed to 'publish pictures about and gloat over methods which are akin to those of the coward and assassin'.[63]

Such 'civilizing methods' were not limited to the English. French Turcos, whose supposed atrocities were immortalized in Robert Graves' fictionalized memoirs *Goodbye to All That*, were accused by Griffith of decapitating Germans and carrying their heads in knapsacks,[64] of murdering German wounded in the hospital, and of burning unarmed Germans alive in a forest after their surrender.[65] Even worse were the depredations of the 'black' troops of the French and English. The very use of these troops, whose conduct in Europe was 'appalling',[66] was considered by Griffith to be the 'worst act ever committed by white men against the white race'.[67] African tribal soldiers, especially the Senegalese, were thought to be cannibals.[68] In a sardonic article on the religious morals of the allies, Griffith lauded 'the Senegalese, who, bating an ancestral weakness for cooked human flesh, are a most pious people'.[69] James Connolly fought pro-war propaganda that praised the courage of African troops by reprinting a letter from one Mr Tietze, the German-American Parks' Commissioner of Yonkers, New York. Mr Tietze had heard a report about a Bavarian regiment in action against a group of Senegalese:

> For more than an hour the Bavarians had been under a hot fire, [said Tietze] when they were told by their officers that they were facing black men. The men immediately went wild with anger. They threw off their knapsacks and even their coats, rolled up their sleeves and charged the Senegals with the bayonet. Within a few minutes the blacks were fleeing in a disordered rout.[70]

Read has argued that German racist propaganda used many of these same categories against the British, but avoided any mention of the 'Yellow Peril', except to downplay it. In Ireland, however, Japan, the 'one great non-Christian power'[71] in the war, came in for a fair share of the abuse. Before Japan even entered the war, English support for Japanese expansionist policy was questioned

---

62 BNL, *EI*, 12.11.14, p. 2. 63 Ibid. 64 BNL, *EI*, 16.11.14, p. 1; *SF*, 24.10.14, p. 2. 65 BNL, *SF*, 26.9.14, p. 1. 66 BNL, *Nat*, 30.10.15, p. 2. 67 Ibid. 68 Cf. Ibid., and *SF*, 26.9.14, p. 1. 69 BNL, *SF*, 24.10.14, p. 2. 70 BNL, *Worker*, 30.1.15, p. 1. 71 BNL, *SF*, 24.10.14, p. 2.

in Irish nationalist journals. Writing to *Sinn Féin* from Genoa, a Professor McHale claimed in October 1914 that England would land 'half-a-million Japanese on the coast of France to fall upon the backs of the Germans' if they were not held back by pressure from the United States. 'Is it a credible action of humane England', asked the professor, 'to bring the yellow barbarians of the Far East into the field against the Christian and catholic races of Europe?'[72] Once Japan did enter the war on the side of the allies, a flood of books began to appear in England praising aspects of Japanese life. 'Oriel' perused these books, and came to a conclusion 'in no degree creditable to the Japanese'.[73] Focusing on their imitation of western culture, he concluded that the Japanese were a 'race slowly emerging from barbarism, and whose only hope of salvation appears to be in aping the manners of European nations, even in their most vicious aspects'.[74] 'Oriel' agreed with the Chinese description of the Japanese as 'lie-Europeans', a phrase supposedly created 'in scornful allusion to their shoddy imitations of foreigners'. The clearest evidence of their backwardness was their treatment of women. 'It is only a barbarous race who could treat womanhood as the Japanese do their women', he wrote. 'It is really a perpetual state of abject slavery. At present the greatest Duchess or Marchioness in the land is her husband's drudge'. 'Oriel' sarcastically concluded that 'our' allies were 'very enlightened indeed'.[75]

While the participation of native troops in the allied force gave anti-war propagandists the chance to produce horrific tales of barbaric atrocities, these troops were not considered a serious threat to Germany, and by extension, to Christianity. Their use in the front lines lowered the image of the allies in Irish eyes, but the central concern of Griffith and others remained with the main foreign allies of Great Britain – the 'oppressive' Russians, and the 'irreligious' French, led until October 1915 by René Viviani, head of the French Grand Orient Chapter of the Freemasons. The war was fought for the creation of a future Utopia, in which the Germans and Austrians would have been exterminated, 'and above which waves the blended flags of Muscovy and Britain'.[76] An editorial by Griffith made clear that native troops were merely 'auxiliaries' in 'The War of Religion Against Irreligion'.[77] The major powers, all 'champions of Religion', included:

> England (where according to the authorities of the Established Church, only one man in six attends Divine Service on Sundays) ... France, governed by the Grand Orient, Belgium, whose people are all nominally

72 BNL, *SF*, 3.10.14, p. 1. 73 BNL, *Hon*, 29.1.16, p. 4. 74 Oriel would agree with the fears expressed by Douglas Hyde in his 1892 pamphlet *On the Necessity for De-Anglicising Ireland*, in which Hyde warned that if the Irish did not stop importing English customs and manners they were in danger of becoming 'the Japanese of Western Europe'. 75 BNL, *Hon*, 29.1.16, p. 4. 76 BNL, *Nat*, 4.5.18, p. 2. 77 BNL, *SF*, 24.10.14, p. 2.

catholic, although the Flemish-speaking Belgians are the only catholics the majority of whom go to Mass; the Servians, who will not permit a catholic Bishop in their territory; the Montenegrins, who tolerate Catholicity, but no more; the Russians, who impose civil disabilities on Roman catholics; and the Japanese, the one great non-Christian Power.[78]

Propagandists underlined Russian atrocities in East Prussia, especially against religious figures. Russian troops did behave abominably in the eastern reaches of the German empire. According to the contemporary American journalist Will Irwin, the worst atrocities of war occurred in Serbia, closely followed by the Russians in East Prussia, while the Germans in Belgium came a distant third.[79] The catholic archbishop of the Galician city of Lemberg, in the Austro-Hungarian Empire, was imprisoned and then sent to Siberia after he urged his flock to remain loyal to Emperor Franz-Josef following the Russian capture of the city. This incident raised a storm of protest in the nationalist press in Ireland as well as the catholic press in Great Britain. MacNeill urged his readers to remember the case of the archbishop of Lemberg when recruiters presented them with Belgian Cardinal Mercier's famous anti-German pastoral letter, and urged Parliament to take up the Archbishop's case and force Foreign Secretary Sir Edward Grey to intercede with the Russians.[80]

Lawrence Ginnell MP, the only consistent supporter of Sinn Féin in the House of Commons, raised the issue in early May 1915 to no avail. The *Spark* railed against the brutal ignorance of the English, and excoriated the '80 Catholic members ... 70 of them from Ireland' for all keeping silent on the matter except for Ginnell. Even worse, the more than one hundred 'catholic' newspapers in Ireland had all refused to publish a report of Ginnell's questions on this subject.[81] Griffith questioned what the banished archbishop would think of 'Catholic Ireland' if he learned that the catholic Lord Mayor of Dublin had participated in a recent 'Russian Flag Day'.[82]

The hypocrisy of the sudden sea-change in Britain's attitude to Russia following the outbreak of war was noted derisively by Edward Dwyer, who marked the 'great decrease in the number of books annually published dealing with the Russia of pre-war days'.[83] Many favourite anecdotes about Russia no longer appeared: 'we no longer hear of the knout, of the thousands of miles' tramp of convicts to frozen Siberia; that the virtuous heroine resisting the Governor is no longer bound to the stake, stripped, and lashed unmercifully'. The reason for this change was simple, he concluded. 'There are nowhere, now, atrocities, cruelty, evil, sin, save in Germany, Austria, and Turkey'.[84]

78 Ibid.   79 Cit. in Read, 1941, p. 24.   80 See *IV*, 16 January, 20 February, and 20 March 1915.   81 BNL, *Spark*, 2.5.15, p. 4.   82 BNL, *Nat*, 25.9.15, p. 1.   83 BNL, *Gael*, 5.2.16, p. 14.   84 Ibid.

The Russian Revolution and subsequent execution of the Tsar ameliorated Russia's harsh imperialism. Nationalist propagandists, in the main, ignored the revolution itself, but Griffith remarked in September 1917 'now that Russia is free of Tsardom, there is hope for the Small Nations whom the Tsar crushed'.[85] Griffith was especially sympathetic to the Ukrainians, whose national poet, Shevchenko, had been banished fifty years earlier for astonishingly 'Irish' reasons:

> He was exiled to the Caucasus by the Tsar's officials for the crime of – no, not carrying a hurley or singing 'Easter Week' – but of making patriotic verses. The beauty of the poem reflects the same sentiments as are found in Irish poetry, and thus show how close is the kindred of the oppressed peoples.[86]

The execution of Tsar Nicholas II and his family provided a convenient excuse for Griffith to insult Lloyd George. 'Now that the Tsar of Russia has, as reported, been executed', Griffith remarked in August 1918, 'Mr Lloyd George must hold the record for autocracy. Certainly, we know of no dictator in Western Europe who can match him in acts of repression'.[87]

Racist atrocity propaganda was in part a product of its time. Remarks about blacks, Japanese, etc, which to-day would be criminal, were widely accepted and believed eighty years ago. Nevertheless, Irish nationalist ideology was xenophobic and moralistically insular. Racism, anti-Semitism, and xenophobia all played a part in propaganda long before the war began, but the outbreak of the Great War caused this sort of propaganda to take on a new dimension. Germany was challenging the armed might of England, and in response England and her allies were forced to draw on the resources of their far-flung empires. England's use of native troops, and the perceived hypocrisy of alliance with other imperialist or irreligious powers was perfect fodder for anti-British propaganda. To the propagandists of advanced nationalism, Germany, not England, was the champion of Christianity, the pure white bulwark against the invading hordes of pagan, immoral barbarians. By praising Germany, propagandists further highlighted differences between Britain and Ireland, drawing on prevalent racist attitudes to encourage anti-British sentiment. Griffith had always likened Ireland's cause to Germany more than any other nation,[88] and its resistance to the armed attacks of England and her allies during the war further paralleled Ireland's resistance to the immorality and brutality of English culture. As he wrote in *The Influence of Fenianism*:

---

85 BNL, *Og*, 29.9.17, p. 6.   86 Ibid.   87 BNL, *Nat*, 3.8.18, p. 1.   88 James E. Combs, 'The Language of Nationalist Ideology: A Content Analysis of Irish Nationalist Publications, 1906–1914' (University of Houston, M.A., 1969), p. 91.

When Fenianism attempted armed and open war with the British Empire, the British Empire was able to defeat it without calling the French, the Russians, the Japanese, the Servians, the Belgians, the Italians, the Ghoorkhas [*sic*], the Senegalese, and the Fiji Islanders to its aid, but the spirit of Fenianism, which was the spirit of Young Ireland, which was the spirit of Ancient Ireland, it could not defeat. Fenianism had recalled Irishmen to their manhood.[89]

The 'Spirit of Ireland' might have been able to resist the mental depredations of the British, but the physical oppression by the British was unstoppable. To defeat the armed might of the British Empire, something more would be needed. In the early years of the Great War, before the Easter Rising proved to some that violence might be a feasible response to British rule, advanced nationalists increasingly turned to Germany, and the idea of German rule in Ireland, as the magical solution to their situation. The next section will examine the British attempt to horrify the Irish population with tales of German invasions, and, in turn, the fantasy of German rescue created by Irish nationalists.

III

The spectre of Germans invading the sacred soil of Ireland appeared frequently in pro-war recruiting propaganda, especially in recruiting posters created by the three official organisations responsible for army recruiting in Ireland.[90] The horrific moment of domestic invasion by German soldiers was vividly rendered in the graphic poster (figure 3.2) created for the CCORI by the same artist who painted *Will You Go or Must I?* Asking '*Is Your Home Worth Fighting For?*', the poster implied that the same terrors visited on other occupied countries would happen to Ireland unless men joined up before the Germans invade. The viewer is placed in an odd, covert position, seeing the events from within the lighted stove. The firelight, which is the only source of illumination for the poster, highlights the pointing baby, who makes the shape of a gun with its hand, and the face of the woman, wakening echoes of the popular wartime song *Keep the Home Fires Burning*. Similarities in colour connect the red, brown, and green suit of the young husband with the plants on the windowsill and the dishes on the table. The central figure of the man is completely impotent, helpless to resist the depredations about to be visited on the old, the young, and the woman in his

---

89 UCD, Terence MacSwiney Papers: Arthur Griffith, *The Influence of Fenianism*, fols. 9–10.
90 Respectively the Central Council for the Organisation of Recruiting in Ireland (CCORI), 1914–15; the Department of Recruiting for Ireland (DRI), 1915–18; and the Irish Recruiting Council (IRC), 1918.

3.2 *Is Your Home Worth Fighting For?* (CCORI recruiting poster, 1915, TCD)

care. His wife, dressed in a loose-fitting housedress and apron, is deliberately desexualized, accentuating her role as a mother rather than an object of sexual desire. The German soldiers, however, dressed incongruously in parade-ground *pickelhaubes* that would never be worn in combat, are embodiments of lust and cruelty. One, turning his face to the viewer, has a face like a pig.[91]

The advanced nationalist reaction to this type of propaganda falls roughly into two broad categories: practical responses that served to counter-act the horror stories of pro-war scare-propaganda, and the creation of 'rescue fantasies' involving the intervention of Germany. The most basic form of practical response in the nationalist press was an allaying of actual fear about the German army, whipped up early in the war by the English and daily press in Ireland. In the first November of the Great War, Griffith's *Eire Ireland* took it as a duty to 'try and avert the panic which would follow a German invasion of these shores if the Press-schemes have borne fruit'.[92] 'Tell your mothers, tell your daughters, tell your children, tell everybody', continued the article, 'that they have nothing to fear from the Germans'. The Germans would treat the Irish well unless people foolishly took the advice of novelist H.G. Wells, whose suggestions for a home militia to defend Great Britain were being widely disseminated at the time.[93]

German propaganda also tried to reassure Irish audiences about their good intentions. The Germans were aided in spreading their message by the advanced nationalist press, which used reports from Germany to bolster their own arguments for supporting Germany. Two weeks after promising to stop the panic created by the pro-British press, *Eire Ireland* reported on a column in the German government organ, the *Norddeutsche Allgemeine Zeitung*, in which the author claimed that Germany would never invade Ireland with a view to conquest.[94] Eighteen months later, the brief-lived *Gael* gave a good review to a German propaganda leaflet *Great Britain and Europe*. The author of this pamphlet maintained that Ireland had to be made free in order to preserve European free trade and the freedom of the seas.[95] German propaganda was also directed specifically at Irish Catholics, especially in light of the German invasion of Belgium. Irish propagandists reprinted an article from a Milwaukee, Wisconsin, newspaper, the *Catholic Citizen*, which reported a Reichstag speech by Herr Mathias Erzberger, the leader of the Catholic Centre Party. Erzberger demanded the freedom of Ireland, 'this truest and purest of small nations', and maintained that independence would be won by the 'sword of Germany'.[96]

Nationalist propagandists, especially before the Easter Rising, continued to encourage the idea that Germany would aid Ireland in her struggle for freedom. Casement's Irish Brigade was the embodiment of this idea, and, understandably,

91 TCD, Irish Recruiting Posters, Case 55d/109. 92 BNL, *EI*, 10.11.14, p. 3. 93 Ibid. 94 BNL, Ibid., 24.11.14, p. 3. The author was almost certainly Roger Casement. 95 BNL, *Gael*, 19.2.16, p. 13. 96 TCD, Samuels 3/36.

advanced nationalist journalists were reluctant to admit the failure of his recruiting efforts inside Lemberg Prisoner of War Camp. In March 1916, Eoin MacNeill, who as president of the Irish Volunteers was in a position to know the truth about Casement, still claimed bravely that stories about Casement's reception that had been gleefully reported in the pro-war press were completely false. MacNeill believed that a German offer of complete Home Rule was still better than paying £8 million a year to the British treasury, and scoffed at the idea that Casement was 'mauled' by Irish POWs when he made this announcement.[97] MacNeill was certain that the British press would improve upon this story, false though he might claim it to be.[98] 'Next time the story appears', he wrote, 'it will tell us that the Germans have promised to let us off with Eight Millions of an annual tribute, and that Sir Roger Casement, when he told this to the Irish prisoners, was immediately asphyxiated'.[99]

Cultural phobia about the Germans could also be dispelled in more subtle ways. Griffith and other advanced nationalist leaders were, in the main, Teutonophiles. Even before England and Germany began to creep towards confrontation, Griffith frequently held Germany to be a paragon of morals, cultural values, and learning.[100] Germany was the world leader in Celtic studies and philology, a fact that greatly impressed Eoin MacNeill, Douglas Hyde, and other leaders of the Gaelic cultural revival which marched in step with the growth of Irish nationalism in the first decades of the twentieth century. MacNeill reacted angrily to the actions of the Cork and Dublin Corporations in stripping the great German linguist Kuno Meyer of the freedom of those cities,[101] and accounts of Meyer's work featured prominently in Griffith's short-lived but highly irritating (to the British) newspaper, *Scissors and Paste*.

German culture was celebrated at a Sinn Féin sponsored lecture at Sinn Féin's Dublin headquarters in November 1914, where Seosamh Ua Croifte (James Crofts) spoke on 'Some Aspects of German, Austrian, and Hungarian Music'. Mr Ua Croifte also played the 'Libestrainne' [*sic*] No. 3, and the 'March' from *Tannhäuser*. His brother, the enormously popular singer Gerard Ua Croifte (Gerald Crofts), joined him, and performed the German military songs 'Die Wacht am Rhein' and 'Gott Erhalte Franz der Kaiser'. The evening ended with a quartet, composed of the two Ua Croiftes, Mr J. Rawl, and Mr Mac Giolla Ruadh, who sang the 'Benedictus' from Schubert's Mass (No. 1).[102] Advanced nationalists who did not attend concerts or lecture series on the music of the Central Powers could occupy their time learning Eamonn Ceannt's popular song,

---

97 BNL, *IV*, 4.3.16, p. 1.   98 In fact, as MacNeill well knew, Casement's visits to Lemberg had been met with some degree of physical violence, necessitating Casement's ignominious rescue by camp guards.   99 BNL, *IV*, 4.3.16, p. 1.   100 Combs, 1969, p. 91, et fl.   101 BNL, *IV*, 16.1.15, p. 1. Meyer was stripped of this honour following the publication of an American speech he gave supporting the formation of an Irish Brigade in Germany.   102 BNL, *SF*, 21.11.14, p. 4.

Ireland Over All, set to the tune of the German national anthem, *Deutschland Über Alles*. The song was widespread before the Easter Rebellion, and Ceannt's execution afterwards boosted sales enormously.[103]

A final form of practical response, and the most important, was the strict neutrality line espoused by many of the nationalist leaders. Jim Larkin and James Connolly's newspaper, the *Irish Worker*, carried the slogan 'We Serve Neither King nor Kaiser' on its masthead, and a banner with the same saying bedecked Liberty Hall, headquarters of the Irish Citizen Army, until its destruction in the Easter Rising. Connolly was also president of the Irish Neutrality League, founded in October 1914 by himself, Griffith, Sean Milroy, Constance Markievicz, Francis Sheehy-Skeffington, William O'Brien, and other nationalist, labour and pacifist leaders to promote Ireland's strict neutrality in the 'Anglo-German war', and to devise means of protecting the young men of Ireland from any form of conscription.[104] To the more militant wing of the nationalist movement, neutrality in the war was an act of empowerment. *Irish Freedom* headlined its first wartime issue with the line 'Germany is Not Ireland's Enemy', and specified in an article 'Neutral – for the Present'[105] what the Irish strategy in this war would be:

> Ireland is not at war with Germany ... For the present, Ireland is neutral. She must stand aside, though ready and quick to take action ... The time will quickly come, perhaps in a month, when Ireland's honour and Ireland's cause will demand action. In that event the world will know we are not a cowardly rabble, but a people striving to re-establish the freedom of their country.[106]

Eoin MacNeill responded angrily when John Redmond called him a 'pro-German'. He maintained in the *Irish Volunteer* that men who were servile to Britain, including unionists, would become just as slavish to Germany if Ireland were conquered by that European power. Paraphrasing Geoffrey Keating, MacNeill gave his proud opinion of Ireland's position in the war. 'I do not accept it as the destiny of Ireland, my mother country', he cried, 'to play the harlot to any alien Power, and I do not envy the son of Ireland who takes upon himself the office of procurer'.[107] In the first war-time issue of *Sinn Féin*, Griffith lashed out against the 'base attempt ... made by our slavish Press to evoke in Ireland, not a pro-Irish, but an anti-German sentiment'. 'Germany is nothing to us in herself', he reminded his readers, 'but she is not our enemy. Our blood and our miseries

---

103 Cf. TCD, Samuels 5/56. 104 NLI MS 13954: William O'Brien Papers, Correspondence on Irish Neutrality League, 1914-15, Letter of Introduction, 5 October 1914. 105 Reprinted as a widely circulated poster (see Public Record Office, CO 904 161/3, Distribution of Anti-Recruiting Leaflets, 1915-16 [*sic*], November 1914). 106 BNL, *IF*, September 1914, p. 1. 107 BNL, *IV*, 8.4.15, p. 1.

are not upon her head'. While maintaining a technically neutral stance towards the European conflict, Griffith was greatly impressed by the strong and virile example that Germany set for the men of Ireland:

> Who can forbear admiration at the spectacle of the German people, whom England has ringed round with enemies, standing alone undaunted and defiant against a world in arms. If they fall, they will fall as nobly as ever a people fell, and we the Celts may not forbear to honour a race that knew how to live and how to die as men.[108]

Pro-war propagandists attempted to reasonably show what a German occupation of Ireland would be like. A large textual poster created early in the war, entitled 'Germany Wants Ireland!' clarified why Germany would invade Ireland. According to this piece of propaganda, a successful German invasion would do more than simply introduce the 'horrors and frightfulness' of occupation to Ireland. Germany would turn Ireland into a naval fortress, the 'Heligoland of the Atlantic', and introduce conscription. Even worse, the Irish countryside, with its rich farmland, would be turned into a 'place in the sun' for German colonists. Ireland would be planted by foreigners, just as Poland had been.[109]

In response to this sort of clear vision of post-invasion Ireland, anti-British propagandists had to create an alternate image of reality, using similar images and ideas to convince the Irish that in fact a German invasion would be beneficial to Ireland and Irish nationalism. Griffith, for the most part, did this by resorting to his tried and true method of 'spin' – twisting the phrases of pro-war propagandists to produce a message that supported his views. In September 1914 he did this with a recruiting message spread in England, which had pointed out the realities for England if Germany successfully conquered them. The English were warned that they would become colonists of Prussia, their children would be forced to speak German, they would be taxed to support the oppressive German army, and their streets would be filled with German troops. Griffith drew the obvious parallel. Mimicking exactly the language of the recruiting appeal, he wrote 'since Britain beat us, we are colonists of England, our children are taught English, and compelled to speak it. We are taxed to keep up the English army, which keeps us down. Our streets are filled with English troops'.[110] Roger Casement pointed out to readers that any sort of occupation would be better than the English occupation of Ireland. If it invaded, Germany was more likely to treat Ireland well, since German culture was more advanced than its English counterpart. *Irish Freedom* also made the dubious claim that Ireland

---

108 BNL, *SF*, 8.8.14, p. 4.   109 TCD, Irish Recruiting Posters, Case 55c/95.   110 BNL, *SF*, 12.9.14, p. 2.

under German rule would in fact be in keeping with the teachings of Wolfe Tone, who had encouraged the idea of a 'European Ireland'.[111]

Practical responses to propaganda about the dangerous potential of a German invasion of Ireland could allay civilian fears, and give propagandists a further chance to ridicule British war aims and rhetoric. But this form of response made little attempt to examine what Ireland would be like if Germany *did* succeed in landing. Readers were assured that the occupation would be better than England's rule, but this was hardly enough to make people actually desire a German victory in the war, or more specifically, a German victory that included the occupation of Ireland. Advanced nationalist leaders were themselves unsure about how to react if the Germans actually landed in Ireland. It was simple for British officials and journalists to tar all advanced nationalists with the same 'pro-German' brush, but in fact Irish support for German activities in Ireland was far more equivocal. The IRB and Clan-na-Gael actively worked with German officials in the United States and Germany, trying to get the support of Germany for an armed uprising, but an Irish rebellion was different from a German invasion through the back door of the United Kingdom. At a meeting of the IRB on 4 September 1914, at which plans for what would become the Easter Rising were first mooted, Sean T. O'Kelly recalled that the men present (which included Griffith but not MacNeill) decided to accept an offer of German help if it was forthcoming according to their own desires, but to fight German troops if they landed in Ireland without invitation.[112]

Propaganda, however, deals with the imagination of reality rather than the unvarnished truth of political action. While advanced nationalists of all stripes might be reluctant actually to aid a German invasion, and, if militant, even go so far as to threaten war against Germany if it occurred, in their propaganda a complex and fascinating series of stories, poems, and editorials explored what Germany would do for the Irish when they landed. This construction of an imagined future, developing in chronological parallel and in many of the same newspapers as the more reasoned reactions to threats of German invasion, created the idea of an omnipotent Germany which would save Ireland from her oppressor, and force the creation of an Irish state.[113] An examination of this propaganda reveals a construction of Ireland as either completely helpless or virtually powerless, of Germany as an external, uncontrollable force, which would descend from beyond and smash the English, and of a nationalist

111 BNL, *IF*, September 1914, p. 1. 112 NLI MS 20763: William O'Brien Papers: News-clippings on Easter Rising, etc. 113 Invasion tales and stories were a popular genre in the years preceding the Great War. These books, often serialized from newspaper articles (most famously in the 1908 *Battle of Dorking*) also appeared in specifically Irish versions, often revolving around the Home Rule crisis of 1911–14. For more information, see Eileen Reilly's 'Beyond gilt shamrock: symbolism and realism in the cover art of Irish historical and political fiction, 1880–1914', in McBride (ed.), 1999, pp. 95–112.

discourse which, at times, especially before the Easter Rising, focused far more on the fantasy of salvation rather than the competent, realistic work which must be done to produce success in real life.[114]

Stories created by advanced nationalist propagandists were many and complex. Such fantasies appeared in most of the newspapers, crossing boundaries of militancy and politics within the nationalist movement. Within this system, however, details of the fantasies fit an intriguing psychological pattern. In all these fantasies, Ireland was a junior partner of the German army. Vague references to 'fights for freedom' occur here and there, and at times the Irish Volunteers help the Germans directly, but it is always the might of the Germans that saves Ireland. When the Germans do invade, they remain in Ireland as benevolent protectors. This occupation would do more than just make Ireland 'better'. It would enable the Irish to live their revenge vicariously, as the Germans would beat the English, imprison them and treat them the way the English had historically treated the Irish. What the Irish could not do on their own, Germany, the christian champion, would do instead.

The most explicit and detailed versions of these fantasies appeared in the *Irish Volunteer* in 1914 and the *Spark* in 1916. Both stories are crafted in a similar fashion, stringing together a series of reports from the near future in which the first days of the German occupation of Ireland are discussed. In 'An Clairin Dubh's' 'The Coming of the Hun', published in the *Irish Volunteer*, when the Germans occupy Dublin, under the command of the Emperor, City Hall, rather than Dublin Castle, becomes their headquarters. From the rooftops fly the flags of the Irish Republic and the city of Dublin, by express order of the German Emperor. When the flags were raised, all German troops in the vicinity came to attention, and the Emperor's 'pet regiment' fired a Royal Salute. The Germans immediately arrest any English soldiers they find about Dublin. The day following the occupation a Royal Proclamation is issued in Irish, German, and English. Kaiser Wilhelm claimed he had 'watched with interest your splendid fight for national freedom', and that while many Irishmen had fought against Germany in the 'late, lamentable war', Ireland's 'popular army' – the Irish Volunteers – had refused to join their enemies to fight the Germans. It was because of this that the Irish flag was permitted to fly, and that the German flag would never be raised without the 'sanction of the Irish nation'. Ireland would be permitted 'the completest [sic] measure of freedom any country could desire. We are not treating you as a conquered nation – we have not conquered you –

---

114 This closely parallels the central elements of a Freudian beating fantasy. Margaret Ann Fitzpatrick Hanly's 1995 book, *Essential Papers on Masochism* (New York, 1995) draws together many of the most important works on this subject. For central theorists after Freud, see especially R.M. Loewenstein (1957), 'A contribution to the psychoanalytic theory of masochism'; S.L. Olinick (1964), 'The negative therapeutic alliance'; D.L. Rubinfine (1965), 'On beating fantasies'; and K.K. & J. Novick (1987), 'The essence of masochism'.

therefore, we have no right to assume any semblance of conquerors'.[115] At the end of the proclamation, the Kaiser called upon public representatives to meet with him at noon on the next day so that he might hand over the government of the country to them and assist them in setting up a new form of rule on the island. Ireland quickly adjusted to the presence of German soldiers. While their 'guttural accents' sounded odd in Grafton Street, the Germans were orderly, and moved about the town in a quiet fashion. Many of the officers and men spoke good English, and one of the officers even went to the National University and spoke to the 'professors' there in Irish. Interviewed by the newspaper, he said that he 'cannot understand our ignorance of Irish. We are, he says, living in ignorance of a great heritage'.[116]

In the *Irish Volunteer*, the extent of Irish causal action in the 'fight for freedom' was left to the reader's imagination. The passive action of the Irish Volunteers, standing by and bearing their suffering rather than listening to the blandishments of recruiting sergeants, was the deciding factor in Germany's generous occupation of Ireland. The *Spark*'s prescient 1916 St Patrick's Day story, 'The Dawning of the Day', told the story of a German invasion of Ireland in the spring of 1916.[117] German troops pour ashore in the west and the south, and immediately after they achieve a beachhead and begin to inflict heavy casualties on the British forces, the Irish Volunteers lead a co-ordinated rising across the entire island. The story ends six months later, when Volunteer leaders come out of the Wicklow Mountains and found the Irish Republic in the ruins of Dublin.[118] Here, Irish patriots have taken a far more active part in overthrowing the English than in the *Irish Volunteer*'s tale, but Germany still must take the initiative, invade, and bear the brunt of the fighting before the Irish can do their part.

These elements of fantasy, either that Germany alone would wreak Ireland's vengeance on Britain, or that together the two countries would crush the British spider, saw poetic expression as well. In the autumn of 1914, an Irish-American woman responded to the American publication of Germany's anti-English 'Song of Hate', and printed a poem entitled *England* in the *New York Times*. Griffith saw the poem and reprinted it in *Eire Ireland*. The poem perfectly sums up the relationship between the downtrodden figure of Ireland, and the superhuman, spiritually driven symbol of Germany. The past heroes of Irish history could not alone save Ireland, so God turns to a new, more powerful force:

> They have stood at the Judgment-Place,
> The Saints, the Heroes of our race,

---

115 BNL, *IV*, 7.11.14, p. 7.　116 Ibid.　117 BNL, *Spark*, 19.3.16, pp. 2–4.　118 Patrick Maume makes the astute observation that this fantasy was very similar to the actual plan for an invasion of Ireland suggested to German officials by Joseph Plunkett during his 1915 visit to Germany (Maume, 1999, p. 176).

> Through the long Night of the Tyrant's sin
> Ireland has trusted her cause to Him.
> 'Vengeance is Mine, I will repay',
> And God fulfills [*sic*] his word to-day
> Through GERMANY!¹¹⁹

The Germans would do more than just help the Irish found a new republic. They would also act as the new law, bringing vengeance down upon the erstwhile British oppressor. The Reverend Michael O'Flanagan, who would become President Pro-Tem of Sinn Féin when de Valera and Griffith were both jailed in the summer of 1918 following the 'German Plot' arrests, wrote a dialogue for the *Spark* in January 1916 entitled 'Wrong Bait'.[120] In it, two men debate over what would happen if Germany invaded Ireland. One states that Germany would destroy all of Ireland's churches, as they had in Belgium. O'Flanagan's alter-ego responds sarcastically that Germany never would invade Ireland, because Britain was 'Mistress of the Seas' – but if they did, there would be no outrages. 'Ireland, if it was a part of the German Empire, would be one of the far parts', wrote O'Flanagan, 'and Germany would have to treat us well'. Most importantly, 'She would have enough to do building jails and packing juries to keep the English down. She would be very glad to make friends of the Irish'.[121] Griffith presented a similar fantasy in a *Nationality* editorial from the previous November. In 'Aids to English Recruiting',[122] Griffith imagined that the Germans would immediately suppress British maritime commerce, and prohibit industrial competition, thus reducing England to a state of 'economic slavery'. They would incorporate England into a 'Reichsland', and rule it from Berlin, with a mockery of self-representation. Taxes would be raised, and the money used to 'bribe and corrupt those who might champion it [England], if God had been stronger than Mammon in their souls'.[123] Armed men and spies would fill the countryside, the educational system would be corrupted, and in the end, the Germans would 'take the manhood from them and leave them as ghastly caricatures of man moulded in the image of God, as the Ape is of Plato'.[124] In other words, the Germans would do to the English exactly what Griffith and other leading propagandists maintained the English had done to the Irish for 700 years. A day of reckoning was at hand, and it would be a reckoning created by the might of the German Empire.

Writers less certain of the rectitude of the advanced nationalist cause twisted these fantasies, producing satirical works which mocked both sides in this propaganda war and their seeming obsession with debating the merits or demerits of the Germans. A savage chaffing of nationalist fantasies about

---

119 BNL, *EI*, 10.11.14, p. 2. **120** BNL, *Spark*, 23.1.16, pp. 1–2. **121** Ibid. **122** BNL, *Nat*, 20.11.15, p. 4. **123** Ibid. **124** Ibid.

German support appeared in 1918. Published simultaneously in Dublin and London, and written by the unionist author of *The Farm at Lough Gur*, Lady Mary Carbery,[125] the spoof novel *The Germans in Cork* claimed to be the collected letters of 'Baron Von Kartoffel', the German military governor of Cork, to his wife. Kartoffel was a hard-nosed Prussian with very little sympathy for the Sinn Féiners. While he did decorate a few men and women who had supplied U-Boats with petrol and food during the war, or spied in Big Houses, or generally incited the populace to rebellion,[126] he had little patience with most advanced nationalists. When a large delegation of Sinn Féiners appeared outside his residence carrying banners, thinking they would be invited to form 'a sort of council or governing body – a medium, in short, for the lavish expenditure of German gold',[127] Kartoffel heard them out, and then announced to the stunned crowd that they were to be deported to the Baltic coast of Germany, where the young men would be conscripted into the army, and the rest would farm small plots of land.[128] Kartoffel cleaned up Cork with a macabre vigour, gassing the inhabitants of the asylum and converting it into a forced place of residence for the Cork slum-dwellers.[129] When he showed signs of mercy, his elder brother admonished him to:

> Remember that the sole reason of England's failure in governing Ireland was her weak sentimentality. Be stern, be severe, be frightful even, but never be sentimental.[130]

In the last eighteen months of the war, rescue fantasies about Germany appeared with far less frequency in the advanced nationalist press. In part this was because after the United States' entry into the war, there was a much slighter chance for Germany to be in a position to invade either Great Britain or Ireland. Utopian fantasies in nationalist propaganda instead began to focus on the promise of the post-war peace conference, at which the Americans would force the British to recognize the inherent right of Ireland to exist as an independent nation. In many ways, despite earlier fantasies not depending on a Rising, it was the reality of the Easter Rebellion that killed the fantasy of German rescue. Then, for a brief week, propaganda of word suddenly became propaganda of deed. German aid was forthcoming for this Rising, but on a scale far smaller than constructed in the stories of propagandists. The Rising can be seen as a combination of mentalities, a week of destructive mayhem and suicidal splendour, which mixed the wish for independent action and the need to depend on the help of other powers. Irish rebels rose alone, in the end, but their leaders

---

[125] My thanks to Dr Patrick Maume (Queen's University, Belfast) for this information. [126] Lady Mary Carbery, *The Germans in Cork*, (Dublin, 1918), pp. 80–1. [127] Ibid., p. 3. [128] Ibid., p. 4. [129] Ibid., p. 8. [130] Ibid., pp. 54–5.

Liars, savages, and the champion of Christianity

believed that German help was on the way. At his court-martial, Patrick Pearse claimed that 'Germany is no more to me than England is ... My aim was to win Irish freedom: we struck the first blow ourselves'.[131] But in a farewell letter to his mother written after his capture, he closed with the postscript 'I understand that the German expedition which I was counting on actually set sail but was defeated by the British'.[132] Here was a result unimagined by all propagandists. On the one hand, Irish rebels had held the centre of their capital city for six days. On the other, the German 'expeditionary force', the force that would have swamped the British and sparked a national revolt, had consisted of one ship, a ship that had been scuttled before the eyes of two British gunboats. Reality, as it tends to do, had defeated fantasy. But in ridding nationalist discourse of this form of fantasy, it allowed propagandists to find other, more effective ways of defeating British rule in Ireland.

---

131 Cit. in Ruth Dudley Edwards, *Patrick Pearse, the Triumph of Failure* (London, 1977), p. 318. **132** Cit. in Ibid., p. 314

4

Youth, sex, and Charlie Chaplin: 'moral tone' and the Irish revolution

The importance of 'moral tone' to Irish revolutionary discourse did not come about due to the war, but the socio-cultural dislocations of war, and the support of the Irish Parliamentary Party for the British war effort gave advanced nationalist moral crusaders new impetus in their campaigns. The highlighting of moral dichotomies between Britain and Ireland was central to the construction of a new Irish identity. In constructing a model for a new Ireland, propagandists of the advanced nationalist movements during the Great War had to also develop an image for an ideal revolutionary, both male and female. Propaganda that encouraged moral development was aimed particularly at a youthful market. In propagandists' opinions, 'youth' could be as old as seventeen[1] and thus propaganda addressing moral issues had to find a way to cater to the needs and tastes of a very diverse audience, ranging in age and interests from the youngest children through grown adults. Of the newspapers and magazines surveyed in this study, three, *Fianna*, *Young Ireland*, and *St Enda's*, were intended specifically for children, while children's columns also appeared in *Irish Freedom*, *Sinn Féin*, the *Irish Volunteer*, the *Spark*, the *Gael*, *Honesty*, and the *Catholic Bulletin*. Children were considered a crucial future resource for the Irish state. In seeking to educate children, propagandists sought the *tabula rasa* of nationalism – a clean field upon which to sow new ideas of the meaning of Irishness.[2] Editors of children's papers were especially worried about the atmosphere of English immorality perceived to permeate Ireland during the war. *Young Ireland (Eire Og)* was dedicated by Aodh de Blacam to doing 'a large part in ending the sale of bad Cross-Channel papers and their shoneen Irish imitators'.[3]

Propagandists also turned to attack old enemies of catholicism – drink, immoral literature, and Freemasonry, in an effort to build clerical support and draw in supporters who agreed with the moral stance of advanced nationalism without necessarily being aware of the political implications. These implications, however, were never far from the surface. The constant comparison drawn in this

---

[1] Cf. BNL, *Fianna*, August 1915, p. 12. [2] The pre-dominance of youth within the IRA has been the subject of excellent recent research from Peter Hart, *The IRA and Its Enemies* (1998) and Joost Augusteijn, *From Public Defiance to Guerrilla Warfare* (1996), as well as Marie Coleman's unpublished Ph.D. dissertation (UCD) on County Longford during the Irish Revolution (1998). David Fitzpatrick first mooted the role of youth in the Irish revolution in his *Politics and Irish Life* (1977). [3] BNL, *Og*, 21.4.17, p. 1.

propaganda was between the noble Gael and the debased Saxon – all evil and filth flowed from East to West, and propagandists reiterated time and time again the necessity to rid Ireland of the English garrison before it could become pure and wholesome again. British newspapers that propagated immorality were singled out for special condemnation. Propagandists often complained about unfair censorship practices. 'The grossest, most brutal, and most insane immorality may be, and has been, propagated by British newspapers', wrote Sean Doyle, 'and the British Censor "winks the other eye"'.[4]

The image of Great Britain as an unclean and impure sink of perversion reached its apogee in scare propaganda about venereal disease and the immoral sexual threat of English troops in Ireland. Discourse in this area was directed solely at adults, and functioned as much to control women as it did to demonize the British and make pariahs of them. Moralistic propaganda, therefore, must be examined on three levels – first, as a system of educating the young and constructing a new form of national identity, second, as a way of gaining clerical and popular support through attacking threats to Catholicism, and third, as a way of controlling women's sexuality and demonizing the British.

The Great War, in the opinion of advanced nationalist propagandists, changed the rules of the fight against immorality: it damaged the Irish Parliamentary Party's ability to support anti-British moral crusades. Thus, by taking a leading role in these old battles, advanced nationalists gained clerical support for their moral stance long before the traditional date of 1918.[5] This clerical support encouraged popular support, which propagandists helped exploit by focusing on encouraging Irish youth to join nationalist movements. Even though constitutionalists actually continued to fight against immorality throughout the war, clerical support for advanced nationalism was given as soon as advanced nationalists began to assume a leading role – an action which appears to have occurred because propagandists believed the Irish Parliamentary Party could no longer combat immorality.

I

Propagandists encouraged their readers to emulate an idealized Irish revolutionary. Readers could become nationalists at any age, but the greatest effort was made to convert Irishmen while young, and to hold exemplars, both fictional and real, up to the youth of Ireland. What traits made up the ideal male Irish revolutionary according to propagandists? On a basic level, the speaking of Irish was considered important, if not essential, to patriotism.[6] *An Claidheamh*

---

4 BNL, *Spark*, 7.2.15, p. 1.   5 For this more traditional view, cf. Lyons, 1971, Tom Garvin, *Nationalist Revolutionaries in Ireland, 1858–1923* (Dublin, 1987).   6 It is paradoxical that Arthur Griffith, the most prolific and important propagandist of the war, barely spoke Irish.

Soluis believed that the best fighters came from Irish-speaking districts, and hinted to pro-war recruiters that it would not 'increase the desire of an Irish speaker to enter the army if he be told that his Irish name of Seaghan Mac Gabhann is not good enough and must be translated as John Smith'.[7] The failure of the British government to adequately provide for bilingual education in Irish-speaking districts was roundly condemned. Griffith reported in 1915 that only 217 out of 8,229 primary schools in Ireland permitted bi-lingual education, and that 'no Irishman who does not speak and write English will be admitted as a lawyer, a clergyman, a doctor, an engineer, an accountant, or even a civil servant'.[8] With normal middle-class avenues of advancement closed to the monolingual Irish-speaker, he could concentrate on being a pure nationalist. Teaching children Irish was especially encouraged. George Monks produced a set of cartoons on Irish education in 1917 for *Young Ireland* that directly satirized English recruiting posters. In one, a parody of the famous 'What did you do in the Great War, Daddy?', a small child carrying a hurley is shown speaking to his tweed-suited father. 'What will you say to your son in 20 years', asks the caption, 'when he says 'd-tuigeann tu Gaedilg [*sic*]?'[9] Another frequently reprinted Monks cartoon showed a man wearing a Tara brooch pointing directly at the viewer and asking 'Are You Learning Irish?' – a copy of the Kitchener recruiting poster.[10] The recruiting poster imitations not only mocked British practices – they stood as a manifestation of a discourse that turned learning Irish into a battle for the survival of Ireland's soul:

> The battle for Irish Nationality proceeds with undiminished reality. It is a spiritual combat. The battle is being fought not in the trenches but in the Gaelic classrooms, in the school, and in the home. The number of lives lost in the fight may be small, but none the less is this fight of Irish Nationalism of vast import.[11]

Racial pride in the uniqueness of the 'Irish Mind' soon elided into fantastical claims and racist remarks. *Nationality* reported with a straight face in 1915 that Herbert Pim ('A. Newman') was about to publish a work that claimed that 'contemporary with Plato, the most famous doctrines of the great philosopher were independently developed and elaborately set forth by the Druids in Ireland'.[12] The superiority of the Celtic mind was beyond doubt for propagandists across the spectrum of advanced nationalism. Speaking at the Catholic Truth Conference in 1914, Professor Arthur Clery reminded his listeners 'that [the Irish] mind is provided with a filter which excludes what is worthless and false in foreign matter'.[13] Since the minds of the Irish apparently

---

7 BNL, *ACS*, 10.10.14, p. 9.   8 BNL, *Nat*, 24.7.15, p. 1.   9 'Do you speak Irish?'   10 BNL, *Og*, 13.10.17, pp. 1 and 3.   11 BNL, *Spark*, 31.10.15, pp. 1–2.   12 BNL, *Nat*, 18.12.15, p. 2.   13 BNL, *ACS*, 24.10.14, p. 6.

refused to accept foreign matter, the recent governing practices of the British made no sense at all. 'Asquith has such little appreciation of the Irish mind', continued Clery, 'that he sends us for chief Castle official an English Jew, the most despised of all men-on-the-make, because the least understanding'.[14]

For the Irish revolution to succeed, patriots were required to take their unique minds and turn them towards unity and away from the party politics that characterized the 'degenerate' constitutional form of nationalism.[15] Unity was urged especially for the members of Na Fianna Eireann. In *Fianna*, Putnam McCabe reminded readers that:

> It is love and self-sacrifice that binds us together for one great cause – the cause of Ireland's Freedom. In this cause we must lose ourselves as units … We are but insignificant and harmless little atoms taken each by himself.[16]

Stressing the importance of youthful loyalty and unity was hardly unique to an Irish nationalist youth organisation. The Fianna, however, strove to differentiate themselves from other youth movements, especially Baden-Powell's Boy Scouts.[17] In March 1915 *Fianna* urged its readers to emulate the Boy Scouts in doing a good deed a day, but to make a more productive choice of deed. 'Anyone can lead a blind man across the road and say to himself 'Now I have done a good turn', but would it not be better to help a fellow-member in the Fianna to get on; for everyone is not blessed with an over abundance of brains'.[18] Lest one think that the Fianna were composed of heartless muscular Catholics, the boys were also instructed on how to deal with common situations such as a fire in a crowded theatre. If this happened, the Fianna were to stay in their places, try to arrange for the performance to continue, and if this did not work, to 'start the singing of some popular national song, and induce as many others to join in the singing. This, as a rule, reassures the people somewhat'.[19]

At the heart of the Fianna's attraction (as well as that of the Irish Volunteers) was the link between volunteering and manliness. Young men and boys who

---

14 Ibid. For more on Clery, see Patrick Maume, 'Nationalism and Partition: the political thought of Arthur Clery', *IHS*, vol. 31, no. 122 (Nov. 1998), pp. 222–41, and Maume, 1999, p. 224.   15 In so encouraging their readers, propagandists were engaging in an especially specious hypocrisy. The advanced nationalist movements in Ireland, as this book has emphasized, were themselves rived with ideological differences.   16 BNL, *Fianna*, March 1915, p. 3.   17 Although both organizations appear to have struggled slightly with adolescent homo-eroticism. Willie Nelson's off-hand 1915 remark that 'the first qualification' for being an officer in the Fianna was 'Love for Boys' should probably be disregarded; however Nelson did advise poets in the movement that 'I have no objection to the usual run of verse, but I must protest when the burthen of a page and a half of verse happens to be the colour of a fellow's hair' (*IV*, 23 January 1915).   18 BNL, *Fianna*, March 1915, p. 3.   19 BNL, *IV*, 24.10.14, p. 16.

joined the Fianna entered a world in which strong friendships between males was the key to success. As with the Boy Scouts in England, the Fianna were compared to battalions of grown soldiers.[20] War for the boys was seen as a great adventure, in which they would be able to play a 'man's part'. Willie Nelson frequently recalled the exploits of young Boer scouts during the South African War, as well as the exciting stories leaking back from the front of French and German messenger boys in the trenches.[21]

Once the boys grew up, they took their place in the Irish Volunteers, a body of manly men. Propagandists dwelt on the physicality of the Volunteers. Commenting on a St Patrick's Day 1915 parade of Volunteers in Dublin, the *Spark* recalled the Volunteers' 'manly, alert bearing ... fine physique', which 'won the admiration of all who saw them'.[22] Sinn Féin contrasted the conduct of its leaders after the Rising with the begging and whining Irish Parliamentary Party,[23] calling on men and women to 'vote for the manly, independent policy – Sinn Féin'.[24]

Irish propaganda generally considered England to be a den for cowards and capitalists. Respect was felt for the British who enlisted, but only scorn was reserved for the un-manly millions who did not. Englishmen were savagely mocked for keeping theatres open, attending football games, and encouraging the enlistment of 'subject races' of the Empire while refusing to serve themselves.[25] Specific attacks upon the cowardice of Irish Parliamentary Party volunteers, who at first seemed to reserve staff jobs for themselves,[26] vanished only with the deaths in action of Tom Kettle and Willie Redmond. The government's attempts to impose conscription in Ireland in the spring of 1918 were partly greeted with fury by propagandists because they claimed that the 'West End is full of eligible young men ... shirking under the Government Umbrella'.[27]

John Bull was depicted (figure 4.1) as a corpulent capitalist, happy to sacrifice the working man but completely unaware of the possibility that Germany might

---

20 The best analysis of the links in male bonding between the Scouts and the army is Joanna Bourke, *Dismembering the Male: Men's Bodies, Britain, and the Great War* (London, 1996), esp. chapter 3, 'Bonding'. 21 BNL, *IV*, 12.12.14, p. 8. 22 BNL, *Spark*, 25.4.15, p. 4. 23 NLI, ILB 300 Series, ILB 300 P1, fol. 30. 24 NLI MS 18388: Sinn Féin Propaganda, 1918–1929, C.2, 1918. 25 Cf. BNL, *EI*, 13, 17, 18 & 28 November 1914; *Nat*, 23 October 1915. The *Irish Weekly Independent* agreed, running a front-page Gordon Brewster cartoon in September 1916 that mocked English shirkers at football matches, contrasting 'The Capture of Guillemont and Ginchy by the Connaughts, Leinsters, and Munsters' with the 'Capture of English shirkers by the Military'. (BNL, *IWI*, 16.9.16, p. 1). The *Sunday Freeman's Journal* had a different view. In 1914, it complimented the Football Association in its decision to continue playing matches, claiming that 'it is no bad testimony to the nerves of a nation' for hundreds of thousands to watch football with the enemy only twenty miles across the channel. (BNL, *SFJ*, 1.11.14, p. 4). The Football Association gave in to mounting public pressure in 1916, and cancelled any further professional matches until the end of the war (Arthur Marwick, *Britain in the Century of Total War* [London, 1968], p. 69). 26 Cf. BNL, *Nat*, 25 September, 23 October, 25 December 1915. 27 Ibid., 13.4.18, p. 1.

THE COMING OF THE HUN.

4.1 *The Coming of the Hun* (*Irish Worker*, 21 November 1914)

actually invade the home island.[28] The idea that the war was being fought in order to preserve English industry and capture German trade infuriated propagandists. The editor of the *Cork Celt* complained in 1914 that 'English industries must be protected by the sacrifice of the lives of the sons of Irish mothers'.[29]

Capitalist pressure for war allowed certain propagandists to air their anti-Semitic beliefs. Griffith was happy to point out in 1915 that it was 'an English Jew' – the Home Secretary Herbert Samuel – who broke a commandment by organizing the British War Loan for that year in such a way that he had 'served both God and Mammon'.[30] The presence in Ireland of 'Fly-Boys', men of military age who had fled Great Britain to avoid conscription, was roundly criticized in the advanced nationalist press. Only M.S. O'Lonnain in *Young Ireland*, however, realized what was supposedly behind the presence of so many 'fat, well-fed, sensual looking animals'.[31] He claimed that most were English Jews, who had been able to flee to Ireland ahead of the law because 'Jewish influence is so extremely powerful in Masonic circles that British Ministers have been ordered by their competent Masonic superiors to sing dumb'.[32]

28 BNL, *IW*, 21.11.14, p. 1.   29 KSRL, OH G26: *CC*, 31.10.14, pp. 2–3.   30 BNL, *Nat*, 24.7.15, p. 2.   31 BNL, *Og*, 30.3.18, p. 3.   32 Ibid.

In contrast to these 'Jewish' cowards, who took sensual pleasures in drink, horse-racing, and even more immoral pursuits,[33] purity and chastity were held as crucial components of the Irish revolutionary. The National Council of Sinn Féin's 1917 pamphlet *The Ethics of Sinn Féin*, distributed around Ireland in direct violation of British censorship laws, urged the policy of 'Me Féin' on its readers. 'Each of us is the Irish nation in miniature', read the pamphlet. 'Therefore, we ought each to make ourselves as like as possible to what we think the Irish Nation ought to be'.[34] Readers were urged to consider whether the ideal Ireland would be 'chaste or impure, ill-mannered or courteous, self-sacrificing or selfish?' and warned that 'a drunken or bad-tempered Sinn Féiner will be used by our critics as an argument against Sinn Féin'.[35]

Purity, both of mind and body, was instilled in nationalists from the youngest age. *St Enda's*, a brief-lived children's supplement to *Irish Fun* edited by Brian O'Higgins, included 'A body to keep clean and healthy, as a dwelling for his mind and a temple for his soul' in a list of 'What God Gives a Boy'.[36] Current and future members of the 'Army of Ireland' – the Irish Volunteers – 'should realize the responsibility of belonging to ... an army of stainless record and unblemished honour'.[37] The Irish Volunteers were the most active of revolutionary organizations during and after the Great War, and the youth being groomed for membership in their ranks were encouraged as well to be activists for the Irish revolution. As early as September 1914 in its 'Grianan na n-Og' column for children, *Irish Freedom* urged its young readers to 'chant from end to end the litany of English crimes in Ireland and re-awaken the hearts that have grown heedless ... they can train and drill and learn the use of arms'.[38] *Young Ireland (Eire Og)* reminded its readers that commitment to nationalism did not end when the British were finally ejected from Irish shores. '*Young Ireland*, when Corruption is dead', wrote Aodh de Blacam, 'will only be at the beginning of its work. That work will absorb the life-efforts of a generation'.[39]

This sort of activism was sustained, and in some instances possibly created, by a purposeful linkage of Catholic faith to the struggle for Irish nationhood. De Blacam wrote that 'so long as Ireland is Gaelic she will be true to God and to S. Patrick. Those who are enemies of the Gael will always be found at heart to be insincere Catholics, if not outright enemies of the Church'.[40] The *Catholic Bulletin*, the most influential of religious publications in Ireland during the war, went so far as to remind its readers that 'waving a flag, or wearing a badge is no

---

33 Ibid., 13.4.18, p. 1.   34 NLI, *The Ethics of Sinn Féin* (1917), p. 2. This is very close to the beliefs espoused by John Mitchel in his *Jail Journal* – an idea, as Roy Foster has written, of 'the personal identification on the part of a long line of Irish activists of their country's history with their own identity' (R.F. Foster, 'History and the Irish Question', in *Paddy & Mr Punch: Connections in Irish and English History* [London, 1993], pp. 1–2).   35 Ibid., pp. 2–3.   36 NLI, *St Enda's*, July 1918, p. 67.   37 NLI, *An t-Oglach*, 15.8.18, p. 1.   38 BNL, *IF*, September 1914, p. 8.   39 BNL, *Og*, 12.5.17, p. 1.   40 Ibid., 28.4.17, p. 1.

longer the sum total of young aspirations. You can serve your country best, first by praying, and getting others to pray'.[41]

Once Sinn Féin began to challenge the Irish Parliamentary Party in by-elections, faith was cleverly linked to this campaign propaganda. An event (probably fictitious) of de Valera's 1917 campaign in East Clare was captured in the poem *The Angelus*.[42] Following a speech by de Valera, MacNeill rose to address the crowd when 'sweet came the tones of the Angelus bell':

> A moment passed as the sound reached his ear,
> Then he called out aloud to a priest standing near,
> 'The Angelus, Father', and bowed was each head,
> As the message of God in the old tongue was said.[43]

Faith was closely linked to sacrifice. Mary Butler reminded her readers of Father Dineen's Famine story about a 'little Kerry boy' who declared '*B'fhearr liom an bas* (I would rather die)' than go to the 'soupers'. 'Die he did that night', wrote Butler. 'That heroic child typified the Gaelic Nation. It is a nation of martyrs and confessors'.[44] The series of obituaries for young men who fought during Easter Week published in the *Catholic Bulletin* from July 1916 accentuated their membership in organisations such as the Boys' Sodality,[45] or the St Patrick's Total Abstinence League,[46] and made sure to mention that the youngest recorded combatant, the twelve-year-old younger brother of the late Sean Howard, defended the Convent in Brunswick Street.[47]

The ultimate paragon of faith and sacrifice after the Easter Rising was Patrick Pearse. Pearse as a boy was held up as the perfect combination of manliness, faith, courage, and purity:

> Some of the less far-seeing boys were inclined to think that Paddy was 'no good' because he did not play with them or join in all their pranks. Those who knew him better were aware that he was no weakling or molly-coddle ... He joined our boxing club, too, and I often saw him take a beating like a man and a sport. He loved fun and his laugh was loud and healthy. He never smoked on the sly, except perhaps the experimental brown paper we all indulge in when young. In a large school there were many boys who were fond of telling ugly stories. Never, on any occasion, did an improper

---

41 Bod., *Catholic Bulletin*, August 1917, p. 504.   42 This poem appears in two sources: NLI MS 18464, in which it is credited to a Revd P. Barr, and in the November 1918 *Catholic Bulletin*, p. 552, credited this time to an 'M.A. Fottrell'. S.B. Ferrario (Princeton University) has pointed out that this poem could be sung to the tune of the Marian hymn 'Immaculate Mary'.   43 NLI MS 18464: *The Angelus*, and Bod., *Catholic Bulletin*, November 1918, p. 552.   44 Bod., *Catholic Bulletin*, February 1916, p. 103.   45 Ibid., September 1916, 'Charles D'Arcy', p. 524.   46 Ibid., October 1916, 'John Healy', p. 580.   47 Ibid., July 1916, p. 393.

or even a violent word pass his lips. He was good in every sense, but there was not a scrap of the 'goody-good' about him. I think that, from the first day he realized he had a country, he loved Ireland ... No person that I ever met had such a love for the Boyhood of Jesus. He felt that, for true and noble boys, Jesus is a veritable joyous companion, and that He, who as a Boy ran round and played in Nazareth, loved little boys especially and was with them in all their troubles.[48]

Pearse's last hours were thought to have been passed in silent communion with the Virgin Mary (figure 4.2).[49] Pearse himself urged youthful sacrifice, most famously in his 1915 pamphlet *Ghosts* when he declared that the 'old heart of the Earth needed to be warmed with the red wine of the battlefields',[50] but also in some of his Irish-language writing, translations of which were published in

The Last Hours of Padric Pearse
BEFORE HIS EXECUTION MAY THE 3rd 1916.

4.2 *The Last Hours of Padric Pearse* (propaganda poster, 1916, KSRL)

48 NLI, *St Enda's*, April 1918, p. 19.   49 KSRL, E813: Pamphlets on the Easter Rising, E813:1, 'The Last Hours of Padric [sic] Pearse'.   50 Patrick Pearse, 'Ghosts', in *Political Writings and Speeches* (Dublin, 1952), p. 92.

advanced nationalist newspapers during his lifetime. His 1913 play, *Owen*, has as its hero a young boy who is shot by the police in 1867 while covering the escape of his Fenian schoolmaster. This uncomfortably realistic fantasy was published in *Fianna* in December 1915.

Other future leaders of the Rising weighed in. In the *Fianna Handbook*, printed in 1914 by Patrick Mahon, Roger Casement produced a chapter on 'Chivalry' that upheld the Fenian prisoners of 1867, especially John Boyle O'Reilly, as 'perfect models of chivalrous behaviour'. According to Sir Roger Casement, 'chivalry dies when Imperialism begins'.[51] Terence MacSwiney added his voice to the fray:

> We must realise that this is a trial of our youth and fresh manhood. The sacrifice to be worthy of the name must be paid by our best of blood. Our old men will not suffice: they have filled out their lives, and in the ordinary course of nature must soon surrender everything. It is to the young we must look, because they have life before them.[52]

Those Fianna who took the advice of MacSwiney and others, and immolated themselves upon the altar of nationalist sacrifice at the Easter Rising, were variously commemorated. *The Fianna Heroes of 1916*, published in early 1917 by Cumann na mBan, marked the deaths of eight members of the Fianna who were executed or died in the fighting. 'There is but one life worth living – an Irish life;' began the pamphlet, 'and one death worth dying – a hero's death'.[53] Con Colbert and Sean Heuston, executed leaders of the Rising, were pictured, and Sean Healy, who was killed aged fifteen (the youngest combatant to fall in the Rising), also had a photo on the back cover. If his baby face (figure 4.3) was not enough to remind readers of the youthful sacrifice at Easter, the authors reiterated that 'it was not only grown-up men and women who answered the call to arms. Young boys, little more than children, cheerfully offered their services and their lives in the sacred cause'.[54]

Sacrifice was the final proper act in a young nationalist's life. In dying for Ireland, nationalists at whatever age achieved their ultimate goal. Even after death, these ideal revolutionaries could continue to serve their cause. Following the Rising, both Markievicz and Hobson consciously used the figures of Colbert and Heuston to recruit more youth for the Fianna. 'Join the Fianna' reads a handbill from 1917. 'Learn to be Irishmen, learn how boys can work for Ireland, learn how boys have fought for Ireland, learn how boys have died for Ireland. In the name of our Boy Martyrs, Con Colbert and Sean Heuston, we call on you to join their Organization'.[55]

51 KSRL, OH B3731: *Fianna Handbook* (Dublin, 1914). 52 BNL, *IV*, 31.7.15, pp. 4–5. 53 KSRL, OH Q42: Sinn Féin Pamphlets, Q42:72, *The Fianna Heroes of 1916*. 54 Ibid. 55 Ibid., D1248: 'Freedom' Scrapbook, 'Join the Fianna' (1917).

4.3 *Sean Healy*
(propaganda leaflet, 1917, KSRL)

The course of development for an ideal male revolutionary was clearly mapped out and understood by propagandists. From earliest youth, especially by joining Na Fianna Eireann, boys trained for the day when they would reach manhood and join the Irish Volunteers. Along the way, their lives should reflect the idealized purity of this fictional nation – exercising body and mind through healthy and chaste activities, learning Irish, and being active in the cause of Irish freedom. Supported by a faith in Christ and encouraged to sacrifice by propagandists, a few actually completed this pattern and died, like Sean Healy, with the words 'God Bless the Volunteers' on their lips,[56] thus hoping to ensure a moral and free future for the land they loved.

II

Despite the presence of feminists such as Helena Moloney and Hanna Sheehy-Skeffington, the formation of the female nationalist groups Inginidhe na hEireann (Daughters of Ireland), and Cumann na mBan, and the participation of women in the Easter Rising itself,[57] propagandists nevertheless struggled

56 Ibid., OH Q42:72, 'The Fianna Heroes of 1916'.   57 For information on Irish feminism,

throughout the Great War to construct the model for a female revolutionary. In a time of revolutionary change, women and girls were placed in a difficult position. On the one hand, inequality and prejudice towards women were seen as products of British imperialism, and the Proclamation of the Irish Republic issued at Easter 1916 made certain to call equally on both Irishmen and Irishwomen.[58] At the same time, propagandists articulating the ideals of the Irish revolution balked at promoting full equality for women, and maintained a moralistic and particularly conservative Catholic approach to the role of women in society and the home.

Just as male revolutionaries were supposed to be pure and chaste, women of the Irish revolution showed their nationalism in part through their modest dress and demeanour. M.K. Connery was an isolated voice against the growing tide of complaint against modern fashion, complaints encouraged by important members of the Catholic hierarchy. Writing in 1917, Connery felt that the amount of attention paid to women's fashions in the midst of a world war was ridiculous. Cardinal Logue had recently informed a group of men that short skirts and thin stockings on women were 'an outward and visible sign of the decadence of their morals'.[59] Connery sarcastically responded that while the attention of His Eminence to such a mundane problem was emblematic of his 'essential humanity', that nevertheless 'the length of the European war (with all the multiplied horror and tragedy it connotes) would present itself as a more urgent human problem to set before Irish Catholics than the length of women's skirts'.[60]

This reasoned attitude was rare, if not unique, in advanced nationalist publications. Decadent and immoral fashions were seen as a British innovation – thus to attack modern clothes and modern style was to attack England. True Irishwomen were traditionally modest, and the decent glories of pre-lapsarian times were frequently recalled in the advanced nationalist press. 'A Northern Priest' asked his readers rhetorically what they 'think of the tendencies of modern female fashions? Are they in keeping with our traditional female modesty, that forms such a glorious part of our Gaelic inheritance',[61] and urged nationalist women to 'instead of adopting meekly every silly and indecent fashion from abroad, set about devising their own costumes'.[62] Propagandists did have to

see Margaret Ward, *Unmanageable Revolutionaries* (London, 1983). For a pioneering albeit inadequate study of female participation in the Easter Rising, see Ruth Taillon, *When History Was Made: The Women of 1916* (Belfast, 1996). **58** The best analysis of the proclamation itself is Liam de Paor's *On the Easter Proclamation and Other Declarations* (Dublin, 1997), in which he explores the historical and artistic roots of every line of this important document. He gives credit for the inclusion of 'Irishwomen' in this peroration to the influence of James Connolly, arguing that Connolly alone among the Easter leaders involved in the creation of this document saw women as comrades and equals. (de Paor, 1997, pp. 44–5). **59** NLI, *IC*, October 1917, p. 386. **60** Ibid. **61** BNL, *Og*, 6.7.18, p. 3. **62** Ibid. Such rants against foreign fashion were not new to the wartime press – more than 25 years before, in his lecture 'On the Necessity for De-Anglicizing Ireland', Douglas Hyde had complained bitterly about

fight against a socio-cultural bias towards English fashions. Ireland during the Great War, especially urban Ireland, despite the protestations of cultural revivalists, was in tastes and style firmly part of the United Kingdom, and thus took its cues from London.

Young women were encouraged to emulate the fashions of the past. Such encouragement easily led to exaggerated claims about Gaelic fashion sense that bordered on the lunatic. The regular 'Cailin's Column' in *Young Ireland* published a picture by the Irish artist Sadhbh Trinseach showing the wife of Cuchulain and her maidens doing embroidery on a hill-fort (figure 4.4). The column's author remarked 'It will be agreed that the fashions of two thousand years ago compare favourably with what we copy from London to-day'.

This hearkening back to the Gaelic past operated on more levels than that of female modesty. For feminists such as Maire Nic Chearbhaill, Gaelic Ireland was also a time of absolute equality between sexes. Despite pictures of Emer and her maidens embroidering while their men-folk fought, Gaelic culture was held up as a model of gender advancement. In Nic Chearbhaill's opinion, 'the fineness and nobility of a country's civilization is always indicated by the position that women hold in it'.[64] Since 'Irish women were granted every privilege' while Irishmen controlled Ireland, it naturally showed 'how much higher the Irish civilization was then that which was imposed upon us'.

In order to live up to their Gaelic ancestors, women were placed in the difficult position of being simultaneously encouraged to be modest and demure, and lionized for activist conduct against the English.[66] Constance Markievicz was the only propagandist, however, who actually encouraged women to arm themselves with spiritual and physical weapons for battle:

> Arm yourselves with weapons to fight your nation's cause. Arm your souls with noble and free ideas. Arm your minds with the histories and memories of your country and her martyrs, her language, and a knowledge of her arts, and her industries. And if in your day the call should come for your body to arm, do not shirk that either.[67]

In encouraging such behaviour, Markievicz was in a tiny minority among propagandists. Indeed, many propagandists took a direct anti-feminist line in their writing. Nellie Carey, a fifteen-year-old prize winner in the *Catholic Bulletin* for her essay 'Are Boys or Girls the More National?' remarked 'of course, a girl cannot shoulder a gun or wield a sword',[68] while Maeve Cavanagh admonished her readers 'I am not a girl, not a man, so do not write "dear sir" to me again. I'm

the tendency of city-dwellers in Ireland to purchase and wear cheap cast-off suits from London clerks, rather than cloaking themselves in the more traditional coats and breeches.
63 BNL, *Og*, 2.6.17, p. 8. 64 Ibid., 21.4.17, p. 6. 65 Ibid. 66 BNL, *EI*, 19.11.14, p. 1.
67 TCD, Samuels 2/44a. 68 Bod., *Catholic Bulletin*, February 1916, p. 103.

LIFE AMONG THE GAELS OF OLD :
Emer Instructing Her Maidens in Embroidery.

4.4 *Life among the Gaels of Old* (*Young Ireland (Eire Og)*, 2 June 1917)

not a suffragist, so I do not claim a man's privileges'.[69] Even such nationalist champions of women's rights as the Sheehy-Skeffingtons found themselves attacked in the advanced nationalist press for being anti-Catholic. Francis Sheehy-Skeffington's 1915 play, *The Prodigal Daughter*, was panned in the *Spark*, the reviewer especially condemning a line of the suffragette heroine in which she tells her father 'that week-day Mass is just an excuse for idleness with the most of us'.[70] The author of the review believed that one could work in advanced social and political movements while remaining a Catholic, and was irritated that 'Mr Skeffington's heroine lends colour to the contention' that this was impossible.[71]

Francis and Hanna Sheehy-Skeffington both struggled to co-ordinate their nationalist, feminist, and pacifist points of view. Writing to Mrs G.B. Shaw in 1914, Francis Sheehy-Skeffington excused the absence of a consistent advanced nationalist tone in the *Irish Citizen* by maintaining that the paper approached the European war 'solely from the feminist standpoint'.[72] A central problem with equating anti-war and feminist/suffragist positions was that the British

69 BNL, *Gael*, 19.2.16, p. 12.   70 BNL, *Spark*, 25.7.15, p. 4.   71 Ibid.   72 NLI MS 22259 (iii): Sheehy-Skeffington Papers, Letters from FSS, October to December 1914, FSS to Mrs G.B. Shaw, 14 December 1914.

suffragette movement had called an unofficial truce with the British government upon the outbreak of war. Although Hanna Sheehy-Skeffington and other Irish feminists repudiated this alliance, the taint nevertheless stuck.[73] Suffrage was associated with pro-war recruiting conferences, such as a Dublin meeting in January 1915 addressed by Mrs Pankhurst, a meeting suggested to a reluctant Sir Matthew Nathan by Mrs Dacre Fox and Miss Grace Roe.[74] The refusal of the British government to permit a separate Irish delegation to travel to the International Women's Conference at the Hague in May 1915 (Louie Bennett, a Protestant, was allowed to travel as part of the British delegation, a decision which heightened accusations of religious discrimination) resulted in protests being organized by Hanna Sheehy-Skeffington and the staff of the *Irish Citizen*.[75] These protests were encouraged by Pearse and MacDonagh, who both sent messages of support,[76] but the lack of publicity for these events in newspapers other than the *Irish Citizen* leads one to conclude that male advanced nationalists rarely supported direct feminist action.[77]

This double standard, in which nationalist women were encouraged to be both passive and active, was further encouraged by propagandistic praise of feminine suffering. The Virgin Mary's conduct at Golgotha was held as the ultimate example, perfectly summarized by Estlinn O'Ruairc: 'The women of Ireland know a Queen beloved of Christ', she wrote, 'whose crown was one of sorrow ... and who with a sad smile of sympathy encourages them to be brave and cheerful, for there is no grander privilege on earth than for a woman to suffer and be strong'.[78] The conduct of Cumann na mBan volunteers during the Easter Rising, especially the women who rescued and nursed wounded men under fire, went some way towards erasing the kind of stereotypical woman's role praised by O'Ruairc. Poetry after the Rising commemorated the courage of these 'girls of Ireland', the 'colleens tried and true/Who shared in all the perils/Of the brave and gallant few'.[79]

If nothing else, the Easter Rising provided young male nationalists with a slew of active role models. Did the Rising do the same for young women? Maud Gonne, an older champion of the cause, had not participated in the Rising, and indeed rarely if ever appears in First World War propaganda.[80] The case of

---

73 Despite the anti-British comments by such leading suffragists as Sylvia Pankhurst, who issued a public statement condemning the British conduct at Bachelor's Walk (see NLI MS 24135: Sheehy-Skeffington Papers, Letters from Irish Women's Franchise League, 1912–15). 74 Bod., Sir Matthew Nathan Papers, Nathan MS 467: Memoranda of Interviews: Ireland, vol. I: October 1914 to March 1915, Mrs Dacre Fox and Miss Grace Roe, 6 January 1915, fols. 88–90. 75 Cf. Ward, 1997, pp. 66–9. 76 Ibid. 77 Nor indeed did constitutionalists of the Irish Parliamentary Party – yet another example of unconscious similarities between these branches of nationalism. 78 BNL, *IV*, 21.8.15, pp. 6–7. 79 UCD, P102: The O'Rahilly Papers, P102/495, '1916'. See also 'A Song of the Cumann na mBan' (UCD, The O'Rahilly Papers, P102/495) and Terence MacSwiney's 'The Women of Ireland', published in his collection *Battle Cries* (KSRL, OH B4573). 80 One important reason for this omission is the heroicisation of her ex-husband, Major John MacBride.

Youth, sex, and Charlie Chaplin: 'moral tone' and the Irish revolution 147

Constance Markievicz is more complex. Having taken a commanding role in the Rising, and been sentenced to death, she would seem an ideal role model. However, this conduct, combined with her Protestant antecedents and unusual married life, caused adulation for her to be absent from the advanced nationalist press. In 1917, *Nationality* complimented the cities of Kilkenny and Sligo for making Markievicz an honorary citizen, remarking on 'Madame Markievicz's transparent sincerity and devotion to her country',[81] but this was rare praise. Markievicz only received great attention from the advanced nationalist propaganda machine while she was in prison. In part, this was because her enforced captivity placed her in a more traditional and passive role – thus empowering men who helped her. Propagandists who agitated for her could therefore be seen as the saviours of an unfortunate woman, rather than as co-conspirators with a woman who did not adhere to traditional gender roles. Colonel Maurice Moore helped lead a campaign for restoring prison privileges to the Countess. Writing in December 1916, he lamented her imprisonment among 'the dregs of the population. She has has [*sic*] no one to speak to except prostitutes [*sic*] who have been convicted for murder or violence, and the atmosphere and conversation in which she has lived all this time has been "the atmosphere and conversation of a brothel"'.[82] Markievicz, a woman of the Anglo-Irish aristocracy who had fallen from political grace through her actions, was kept purposely with other 'fallen women'.

Indeed, while some propagandists admired Markievicz's actions the woman of 1916 who was considered a best role model for the young women of Ireland was Grace Gifford Plunkett.[83] Gifford almost literally wed herself to the cause of Irish freedom, marrying Joseph Plunkett the night before he was executed. This sacrificial courage on her part was commemorated in floods of poetry and ballads. Gifford was a better role model than Markievicz because she followed the more traditional female path, bringing glory upon herself through noble suffering and chastity.

If Grace Gifford was the ultimate exemplar of revolutionary womanhood, then her brief-lived relationship with Joseph Mary Plunkett was the *ne plus ultra* of nationalist relationships. The issue of social and sexual relations between men and women was a fraught one, all the more so because of the conservative Catholic background of many propagandists. Since nationalists were supposed to dedicate their lives to the love of country, and since this love was at times vocalized in propaganda through the idea of blood sacrifice, nationalist couples were given the highest praise when the man chose to destroy himself on the altar

---

81 BNL, *Nat*, 28.7.17, p. 1. 82 NLI MS 10580: Maurice Moore Papers, Documents Pertaining to trial of Constance Markievicz. 83 Kathleen Clarke and Hanna Sheehy-Skeffington also came to prominence as widows, as did Mrs Pearse as the mother of Patrick and William, but these women were all older, and less suitable as models for the young.

of Irish freedom. Subtitled 'A Romance of Easter, 1916', a ballad entitled *The Irish Green*, written by an anonymous author in 1917 and sung to the tune *The Jackets Green*, told the story of a young couple parted by the Easter Rising. The woman remembers 'One April day my true love came/To say farewell to me;/And I knew full well but I would not tell/Why the parting was to be'.[84] Her young man, her 'true love', dies while holding the breach in a building. The woman refuses to cry – instead 'I think with pride/Of him who last I seen,/When he said good-bye and left my side –/All dressed in his Irish Green'.[85] As can be seen with other forms of post-Rising sacrificial propaganda, the young woman is not granted the right to mourn the loss of her future husband. Rather, as with Markievicz in prison, or Gifford in the chapel at Kilmainham, she is placed by propagandists in the traditional position of a passive sufferer.

Complete corporeal sacrifice was an ideal that only a few couples could reach. All nationalist couples, however, were encouraged to sacrifice slothful pleasures by propagandists, and told to work hard for a new nation. Early in 1914, Terence MacSwiney[86] warned readers of the *Irish Volunteer* that 'we have allowed a standard to gain recognition that is a danger alike to the dignity of our womanhood and the virility of our manhood'.[87] What was this dangerous standard? According to MacSwiney, a man who preferred his 'ease to any troubling duty' easily became the slave of a house rather than its lord, and found his mate only 'in the woman who prefers to be wooed with trinkets, chocolates, and theatre to a more beautiful way of life that would give her a nobler place but more strenuous conditions'.[88] MacSwiney's point is clear – not only does he compare a woman's dignity with a man's virility, dividing the central characteristics of gender into a passive and an active form, but he insists that the only way for women and men to be equal, for a woman to not degrade herself, and for a man not to lose his masculinity through some form of degenerate sexual enthralment, was for couples to suffer together for the sake of the Irish nation. It seemed that for a relationship to work, two main components had to be present. First, the relationship had to be virtually, if not completely chaste; second, the relationship had to occur for patriotic reasons.

Relationships were often crudely sketched in propaganda. When the young Fianna narrator of 'A Day in Clare' meets the virginal Nora, 'a fine type of country girl, with all the charms of her maidenhood',[89] he patronizingly informs the readers 'she is trying to understand things'.[90] Nora already understands the central issues involved in becoming the lover of a Fianna scout. She tells the

---

84 TCD, Samuels 5/122. 85 Ibid. 86 MacSwiney's early death in 1920 from the effects of a 74-day hunger strike would bring fame to his widow and a greater role in the Dail for his equally extreme sister, Mary. 87 KSRL, OH G27: *FF*, 31.10.14, pp. 6–8. 88 Ibid. 89 BNL, *Nat*, 25.8.17, p. 3. 90 Ibid.

narrator that 'she has seen soldiers clicking their heels in her village, and did not like them – but they were not Fianna Fail'.[91] Most importantly, she insists in a 'quiet, convincing way' that 'she will not go as far as Mars with you'.[92]

Propagandists easily exploited patriotic women's attitudes to soldiers in the British army. A handbill from 1917 addressed to Inginidhe na hEireann attacked women who walked out with soldiers, insisting that those who did were 'walking with traitors'.[93] Women could use their influence to encourage army recruiting, and Irish nationalist women could use this same sexual and romantic influence 'for the glory of God and for the honour and freedom of Ireland'.[94] Indeed, the role of women in recruiting was another of the few areas of propaganda during the Great War in which advanced nationalists directly parodied British recruiting tactics. A recruiting poster warning women that 'if your young man neglects his duty to Ireland the time may come when he will *neglect you*' was twisted in the *Spark* into a message urging Irishwomen to scorn the 'man who fails his country'[95] – the man who failed to work for a free Ireland.

So long as relationships were conducted along patriotic and chaste lines, propagandists would approve. For younger nationalists, especially in the Fianna, propagandists had to find a way to cater for social needs while still controlling youthful impulse. Social evenings gave members of Na Fianna Eireann a chance to mix with young women in a safe environment that was not directly religious, and parents could rest easy that the entertainments and interactions would be appropriate and supervised.[96] Sinn Féin leaflets published in 1917 encouraged the social side of nationalism, an attraction highlighted by Peter Hart and David Fitzpatrick in their research into motivations for joining the Irish Volunteers. Copying the more successful Gaelic League, Sinn Féin's National Committee decided that social re-unions 'keep alive those countless personal friendships which cement indissolubly the bonds of comradeship'.[97]

Relationships between men and women were seen as a way of advancing the national cause. Propagandists did not ignore the attraction of joining the Fianna or Sinn Féin in order to meet members of the opposite sex, and in fact, such behaviour was encouraged. Only one kind of relationship beyond basic friendship existed for proper nationalists, however, and this was a pure and chaste relationship in which love for one's country and God far outweighed the personal affection between individuals. Relationships like these were encouraged for the

---

91 Ibid. 92 Ibid. 93 Calling troops resident in Ireland 'traitors' does not discredit the arguments advanced in chapter one. Volunteers or regular troops in Ireland were viewed differently from those Irish troops facing danger on the front line. 94 NLI MS 5637: Robert Barton Papers, Scrapbook, vol. I, fol. 49 95 BNL, *Spark*, 28.3.15, p. 2. 96 A typical Fianna Ceilidhe for St Patrick's Day 1915 featured Eamonn Ceannt on the Irish pipes, Eoghan O'Brien appeared along with the Celtic Glee Singers, a Captain Martin was to premiere a new dance step entitled the 'Cor na bhFiann', and Miss Mollie O'Byrne was set 'to charm all and sundry – with her singing of course' (*IV*, 20.3.15, p. 8). 97 TCD, Samuels 2/9.

future, a future that would, it was hoped, contrast greatly with the immoral present of Ireland at war.

III

The presence of British troops in Ireland affected the morals of Irishmen, and, along with the opportunity given to women to work in wartime industries in Great Britain, presented a metaphorical and genuine danger to safety and purity of Irish women. On a metaphorical level, the identification of Ireland itself with the figure of a woman almost inevitably led to comparisons between English occupation and rape. Maeve Cavanagh's Erin, asleep on the waves, was brutally assaulted by an England with 'lust in his eyes', and blood-soiled, grasping hands.[98] On a more practical level, writers in the *Irish Citizen* fought a difficult battle to shift the blame for the social evil of prostitution and the danger of assault from women to men. Women's innocence was greatly promoted in advanced nationalist journals throughout the war, yet this was done in an effort to attack the depravities of the English garrison. Indeed, by attempting to control the discourse of sexuality during the war, propagandists sought to control the sexual desires and impulses of women, even more than men. Spontaneous sexuality was ignored, or condemned, and writers focused on the dangers inherent in sexual attraction. The British garrison in Ireland was evil for succumbing to such immoral desires and harming women. The women themselves were given an unenviable choice of roles in advanced nationalist propaganda. Either they could be condemned for being sexually aggressive, or they could be depicted as passive and fragile vessels, constantly in danger of being crushed by rampant male desires. As will be seen throughout the following examples, sexual discourse during the war can, at a basic level, be divided into these two categories. Women were both threatening and threatened, and the discourse of morality, produced putatively for the sake of national decency, must also be seen as being produced as an absolute means of control.

Patriotic Irishmen, naturally, did not harm Irish women in any way. Lawrence Ginnell was even cheered for suggesting that Irishmen were 'incapable' of ruining women.[99] Homosexual Irish patriots were dealt with very obliquely. Reports of Roger Casement's predilections were rarely discussed in the advanced nationalist press. Only Herbert Pim in the *Irishman* dared to address this topic in any detail. Writing after Casement's death, he claimed that it was difficult to understand the sort of mind that would believe the 'recital of distorted details concerning the private character of a man'. He blamed German-American Jews for encouraging the spread of this story, which circulated mainly through the Jewish neighbourhoods of Whitechapel and Maida Vale in the *Daily Express*.[100]

98 BNL, *Nat*, 17.7.15, p. 5.   99 BNL, *IV*, 24.10.14, p. 2.   100 BNL, *Irishman*, 15.8.16, p. 2.

Pim also claimed to have received written proof of a plan in the autumn of 1915 to arrest Casement for a 'foul criminal offence'. Eoin MacNeill was shown this proof, and said only 'so they are at their old game again!'[101] Propagandists preferred in the main to ignore his rumoured homosexuality, blaming these rumours on the British, and focused instead on his kindness to old women and the courage with which he faced death.[102]

The only way in which Irishmen could be brought to immoral sexual behaviour was to join the army. One of the central worries about conscription was that it would shatter the morality of the countryside. Once young men were removed from the constraints of life at home, argued the *Hibernian* in 1915, they too easily turned to drink and 'keeping company with the unfortunate women' who surrounded barracks.[103] Proper Irishmen were shocked by the lewdness of English society.[104] In Dora Sigerson Shorter's 1918 story, 'Women and Children', an Irish recruit spends his last day in London before shipping to France visiting the syphilis ward of a children's hospital ('This is sin') and being accosted by poor women offering him their virgin daughters. In the dawn, he leaves bitterly 'to fight for the safety of the women and children'.[105]

The British garrison in Ireland, especially in Dublin, and its female hangers-on, was widely criticized for its lewd behaviour. The Reverend F.S. Pollard in the *Hibernian* considered the garrison's conduct to be 'a glaring scandal', and angrily complained that 'unsexed young girls and foul-mouthed soldiers startle the ears of passers-by with their horrifying cross-talk'.[106] Note here that the companions of the soldiers are described as 'unsexed' – in part because they probably wore their hair stylishly short, but also because by breaking traditional roles – by engaging in dirty 'cross-talk' with Ireland's hereditary enemy, these women lost any privileges of their gender. The *Hibernian* was not particularly concerned with these women's virtue, only that the garrison was insulting the morals of decent citizens.[107]

The British garrison was also violent, and advanced nationalist journals made sure to report on cases in which soldiers were accused of assaulting women. The conduct of troops who beat women's faces 'out of recognition',[108] or who took a

---

101 Ibid., 16.9.16, p. 4.   102 Bod., *Catholic Bulletin*, May 1918, pp. 230–34, and September 1916, p. 466.   103 BNL, *Hib*, 18.12.15, pp. 2–3.   104 This lewdness was considered one reason for Parnell's fall from grace in 1890–1.   105 BNL, *Og*, 13.4.18, pp. 5–6.   106 BNL, *Hib*, 13.11.15, p. 5.   107 Reverend Pollard would continue his attacks two months later, condemning the 'scenes beyond description' he witnessed at the departure of the LNWR boat for Holyhead. Again, 'sexless' women make their appearance as they say good-bye to the soldiers leaving for service (*Hib*, 8.1.16). In response to the writings of Pollard and the publicity given the situation on the Quays by nationalist city councillor P.T. Daly, DMP Commissioner Walter Edgeworth-Johnstone investigated the matter, reporting to Nathan that the women seen behaving in such a manner were 'hysterical' from seeing soldiers off to England, and were 'not women of a disreputable class' (Nathan MS 455, fol. 14v). 108 BNL, *Nat*, 26.6.15, p. 1.

woman to the Tivoli, gave her five naggins of whiskey, and then left her in the street to die of alcohol poisoning,[109] were contrasted with recruiting campaigns that advertised the British army as protectors of women and children against the rapacious Hun. James Connolly quickly came up with a solution to help Irish women feel safe at night. 'If you would make Dublin clean in its moral standards', he wrote, 'REMOVE YOUR GARRISON'.[110] Connolly, a practical propagandist, desired to change the focus of his condemnation from the morality of women to the direct conduct of the British garrison, thus making a political rather than a moral point.

When it came to the idea of protecting women, Connolly was opposed to the creation of women police or women patrols, an idea suggested and supported by Louisa Connery in the *Irish Citizen*. Connery, and later such Ascendancy luminaries as Ishbel, Lady Aberdeen, the wife of the Viceroy, felt that the 'Enthusiasm' displayed by women in the neighbourhood of military camps at the outbreak of the war had led to 'grave moral disorders'.[111] The creation of a force of female police to control these women, or short of that, the creation of a voluntary body of women who would patrol the camp area, was thought by Connery and Aberdeen to be the best solution. Despite the support of Lady Aberdeen and the official gazette of the DMP and RIC, Sir Matthew Nathan in Dublin Castle was extremely reluctant to approve such a creation. Meeting with feminists Mary Hayden and Mrs Anna Haslam[112] in October 1915,[113] he agreed to investigate whether or not Ha'Penny Bridge was being used for 'immoral purposes', but informed the women that their arguments in favour of women police served only to discredit the British soldiers. They agreed, promising that in fact they blamed the women and not the soldiers for such lewd conduct.[114]

It was precisely this sort of middle-class condemnation of female activities that Connolly hated, and so opposed the imposition of women's patrols. Women police officers, or women volunteers, would not interfere with the 'johnnies of the suburbs', the 'swanks', or the officers of the garrison conveying women about in motor cars, 'but the poor working class girl will have a new terror added to her life'.[115] In the end, women volunteer patrols appeared in Dublin by 1917, and the

109 BNL, *Spark*, 16.5.15, p. 3.   110 NLI, *WR*, 23.10.15, p. 4.   111 NLI, *IC*, 13.2.15, p. 299. The Catholic Truth Society enraged some advanced nationalists in 1915 by forming an alliance with Ascendancy Protestants over this issue, permitting Lady Fingall to speak in favour of women's patrols at its annual meeting (cf. BNL, *WIT*, 23.10.15, p. 5).   112 A Quaker leader, Mrs Haslam was one of the founders of the Dublin Women's Suffrage Federation in 1873, and became one of the first Irishwomen to vote in 1918, at the age of 86. My thanks to Dr Senia Paseta (St Hugh's College, Oxford) for this information.   113 He had met with Mrs Norris Goddard and Miss Redington Roche for the same reason in November 1914 (Nathan MS 467, fols. 18–19).   114 Bod., Sir Matthew Nathan Papers, Nathan MS 469: Memoranda of Interviews: Ireland: Volume III, October 1915 to May 1916, Interview with Mary Hayden and Anna Haslam, 23 October 1915.   115 BNL, *Worker*, 9.1.15, p. 2.

Irish Citizen switched its pressure to urging the government to pay the two volunteers an adequate salary, and not treat them as 'sweated workers'.[116]

Propagandists maintained that Irish 'girls' placed themselves in the greatest danger when they went to England to work in military industries.[117] Members of the Catholic hierarchy urged nationalists to protect Irish women, who in their naturally innocent state were considered easy prey for 'white slavers'[118] or Englishmen who spent time in 'disreputable coffee-houses'.[119] Resistance to the corruption of newly socially mobile women's morals was used as part of Joseph McGuinness' by-election campaign in South Longford in 1917. Referring to the case of one Mary Gorman, a munitions worker from Ireland, who had been recently fined 20 shillings for 'committing an offence' on Hampstead Heath with an English soldier, a poster for McGuinness urged the fathers and mothers of Longford to consider 'Redmond, Dillon, and Co'.s "free gift" of Irish Manhood's Blood and Woman's Virtue to John Bull'.[120] This poster reveals more than a canny use of propaganda – a woman's virtue, in the eyes of Sinn Féin propagandists, was equal to a man's life. Redmond *et al.* killed men by taking their blood, and destroyed women by taking their virtue. The clergy echoed this attitude. Without virtue and honour, wrote the Reverend Dr Gilmartin in 1918, there was nothing left for a woman 'but the Dead Sea fruit of illicit enjoyment'.[121]

Propagandists had trouble understanding how many clerics could actively support recruitment when the War Office debated opening official military brothels in France,[122] or the *Daily Sketch*, supported by 'Redmond the Prevert [*sic*]', published a photograph of British Red Cross nurses in pyjamas and pierrot hats entertaining troops.[123] At least, if soldiers were going to be encouraged to visit brothels, they could do so across the water in France. However, propagandists knew that prostitution thrived in military areas, and in Edwardian times, prostitution always brought with it the dread scourge of that 'loathsome and unmentionable disease',[124] syphilis.

116 NLI, *IC*, April 1917, p. 253. 117 The *Irish Weekly Independent* partially agreed, encouraging a closer monitoring of British labour exchanges that brought over girls aged 15 to work in munitions' factories. However, the *Independent* supported women working for the war effort (BNL, *IWI*, 24.3.17, p. 4). An exception to this kind of attitude were propagandists in the *Irish Citizen*, who warned readers that Irish women were at danger in Ireland as well as abroad, and called on parents to 'stop living in the age of Brian Boru' (*IC*, October 1918, p. 625). Nationalist writers in the *Freeman's Journal* also supported a clerical campaign to help Irish women in Great Britain. This support was hampered, however, by the *Freeman* acknowledging that men and women were needed in British munitions factories (Cf. BNL, *WFJ*, November 1918 ff). 118 NLI, *IC*, April 1917, p. 253. 119 BNL, *Og*, 21.9.18, p. 3. 120 NLI, ILB 300 Series: ILB 300 P4 fol. 50. 121 BNL, *Og*, 21.9.18, p. 3. 122 Ibid., 9.3.18, p. 1. 123 From the *Daily Sketch*, 26 January 1916: 'Cheering up their Patients: This is how the nurses of the Southern Military Hospital, Liverpool, amuse their patients. A threat to banish him from the entertainment is sufficient to keep a wounded Tommy in order' (British Newspaper Library). Above reference in BNL, *Spark*, 13.2.16, pp. 3–4. 124 NLI, *An t-Óglach*, 14.9.18, p. 4.

By threatening men, women, and even unborn children at the most basic level, through the act of procreation, syphilis and the fear of this disease created an absolute 'other' in opposition to the pure Irish person – a moral and physical pariah who brought ruin to morality and literal degeneracy to the body. Syphilis was not an Irish disease, insisted propagandists.[125] Instead, it had been brought to Ireland by England, a nation 'fighting for Christianity and civilization'.[126] If all moralistic propaganda had as one of its goals a demonisation of the British 'other', then the branding of the garrison soldier as a syphilitic was the ultimate form of rejection and condemnation of British rule in Ireland.[127]

What exactly was the rate of venereal disease in the British army at the time of the First World War? Statistics, unfortunately, are unreliable, and vary widely. A pre-war Sinn Féin poster (figure 4.5) used War Office returns to show that the rate of venereal infection in the British army was almost ten times that of Germany, with more than one fifth of the soldiers and sailors infected.[128] Richard Davenport-Hines cites the far lower figures of 5.1% for soldiers in 1913, and 7.3% for sailors in 1914.[129] Joanna Bourke's statistics are probably the most reliable – showing a drop in hospital admissions for venereal disease from 6.1% in 1911 to less than 3.7% in 1916. Bourke uses these figures to buttress her argument that the 'conscript armies were less prone to sensualism', and 'a majority of British servicemen never had casual sex with any woman during their active military service'.[130] The debate over the exact figures continued to concern British authorities in Ireland during the war. Following publicity over the general immorality of the Dublin garrison in the autumn of 1915, Sir Matthew Nathan ordered Major-General L.B. Friend[131] to send him official returns for the number of soldiers receiving treatment for venereal diseases. Friend replied that out of approximately 35,000 troops in Ireland, only 236, or less than 1%, were in Portobello Hospital at the time suffering from VD. This compared favourably to the July 1914 rate of 2.14% hospitalised for VD.[132] This finding satisfied Nathan, but advanced nationalists refused to believe these low figures. In June 1918, the

125 Although W.B. Yeats in 1910 recalled J.M. Synge's remarks about the *Playboy* rioters: 'A young doctor has just told me that he can hardly keep himself from jumping on to a seat, and pointing out in that howling mob those whom he is treating for venereal disease'. (W.B. Yeats, 'J.M. Synge and the Ireland of his Time', in *Essays and Introductions* [London, 1961], p. 312). 126 BNL, *Nat*, 9.3.18, p. 1. 127 Indeed the power of using venereal disease as a mechanism for the control and casting out of minorities can be seen throughout history. In Nazi propaganda, syphilis was alleged to be caused by Jews (cf. Sander Gilman, *The Jew's Body* [New York, 1991]). In more recent times in the UK, tabloids have openly debated the possibility of HIV being passed on to heterosexuals by bi-sexual revenge squads (cf. Richard Davenport-Hines, *Sex, Death, and Punishment: Attitudes to Sex and Sexuality in Britain since the Renaissance* [London, 1990]). 128 KSRL, Q38: Irish Political Leaflets, Q38:2, 'Irishmen – Why Don't You Join the Army?' (1913?). 129 Davenport-Hines, 1990, p. 179. 130 Bourke, 1996, p. 156. 131 General Officer Commanding the Troops in Ireland, August 1914 to Easter 1916. 132 Bod., Sir Matthew Nathan Papers, Nathan MS 452–3: Ireland Correspondence Do-G, Friend to Nathan, 6 and 7 November 1915, fols. 301–3.

THE BRITISH ARMY in which Irishmen are asked to enlist is the **MOST IMMORAL** Army **IN THE WORLD.** According to figures published by their own War Office, the number of men in the different **ARMIES OF EUROPE** treated annually for **LOATHSOME DISEASES** brought on by **PERSONAL IMMORALITY** is as follows:—

GERMAN.	RUSSIAN.	FRENCH.	AUSTRIAN.	ITALIAN.	BRITISH.
27 Per 1,000 Men.	34 Per 1,000 Men.	51 Per 1,000 Men.	65 Per 1,000 Men.	94 Per 1,000 Men.	212 Per 1,000 Men.

In 1895, **522** men per **1,000** in the **BRITISH ARMY IN INDIA** were admitted to **HOSPITAL** for **LOATHSOME DISEASES.** **THE ENGLISH GOVERNMENT PAYS** annually **£490** to Cork, **£250** to Dublin, **£100** to Naas, for accommodation **FOR PROSTITUTES FOR** their **SOLDIERS.**

IRISHMEN---WHY DON'T YOU JOIN THE ARMY?

4.5 *Irishmen – Why Don't You Join the Army?* (Sinn Féin leaflet, 1913 (?), KSRL)

military intelligence officer for County Roscommon reported the arrest of a man who stated at a meeting of a Town Council that 'over 90% of the British army were suffering from syphilis'.[133]

Despite the empirical evidence which shows a general decrease in the cases of venereal disease during the war, the concentration of young male volunteers in army camps around the UK led to a fear that prostitutes would spread disabling disease among them. Debate began again over whether to reinstate the Contagious Diseases Act (CDA). In Ireland, the *Irish Citizen* led the resistance to this plan. Dr Kathleen Lynn, who would later become head of Sinn Féin's Public Health Department, argued that state regulation of vice increased the rate of venereal disease, as men believed it was quite safe to visit prostitutes, and thus placed 'no control on their sexual appetites'.[134] While the CDA was never re-established, the emendation of the Defence of the Realm Act in March 1918

---

133 PRO, Colonial Office Papers, PRO CO 904/157/1: Military Intelligence Reports, 1916–18, County Roscommon, June 1918. 134 NLI, *IC*, 14.11.14, p. 204. See also *IC*, 28.11.14.

to include Regulation 40D, making it an offence for women who carried a venereal disease to have intercourse with a member of the armed forces,[135] was greeted with protests by the Irish Women's Franchise League.[136] These protests were mainly ignored, even by the advanced nationalist press, in part because syphilis and other venereal diseases were seen not as the province of Irish women, but rather as the problem of the British garrison. Again and again throughout the war this point was hammered home in propaganda. Kathleen Lynn linked immorality and venereal disease, claiming that parts of Ireland far from garrison towns were completely free of such diseases;[137] four years later, *An t-Oglach* urged its Volunteer readers to pass along the news that 'leprosy, smallpox, and a loathsome and unmentionable disease are rampant' among troops stationed at Athlone and Phoenix Park.[138] *Irish Freedom* was more subtle, claiming to be sympathetic that 'Tommy' had to go to Belgium to get shot, yet at the same time remarking that 'Ireland is as relieved by his departure as a clean person would be by escaping the proximity of some diseased creature'.[139] The British soldier in Ireland, often a regular rather than a new volunteer, was seen as a filthy and diseased creature, a sub-human threat to the cleanliness and virtue of women and children. The Catholic hierarchy joined in the scaremongering about the British threat of horrible diseases. In the midst of the Conscription Crisis a Father Rafferty cried 'God help the Catholic women and girls of Ireland if English soldiers were let loose among them, as they would be ruined, as those soldiers were suffering from the vilest diseases known ... he prayed that they might never know anything of these diseases'.[140]

The prospect of demobilized Irish soldiers returning to their homes after the war filled some propagandists with dread. In March 1918, Local Government Boards in Ireland began to encourage workhouse officials to establish venereal wards in their poor hospitals. Arthur Griffith took this to imply that syphilis-ridden veterans would be loosed on the countryside after the war, and suggested the construction of 'internment hospitals'.[141] Joanna Bourke's research into the effects of the Great War on masculinity has shown that men who were crippled or mutilated in the war were treated with a good deal of compassion afterwards, and yet those who had been ill were treated shabbily and accused of malingering or worse.[142] These same attitudes seem to have appeared in Ireland among advanced nationalists. Wounded Irish soldiers, as has been discussed elsewhere, were treated with kindness and a pitying sympathy. Irish veterans who had acquired syphilis, however, lost their right to an Irish nationality by behaving in

---

135 Davenport-Hines, 1990, p. 228.   136 BNL, *Og*, 31.8.18, p. 2.   137 NLI, *IC*, 14.11.14, p. 204.   138 NLI, *An t-Oglach*, 14.9.18, p. 4.   139 BNL, *IF*, September 1914, p. 1.   140 UCD, Denis McCullough Papers, P120/7: copy of Cardinal Gasparri's letter and accompanying extracts from speeches, etc. on Conscription, sent by Government to Rome (May 1918).   141 BNL, *Nat*, 9.3.18, p. 1.   142 Bourke, 1996, esp. chapters one, two, and five.

this immoral fashion. Medical specialists within Sinn Féin, such as Kathleen Lynn[143] and Richard Hayes, urged that every one of the estimated 100,000 returning Irish soldiers be given blood tests, and those who were found to be infectious should be detained in institutions until cured.[144] Lynn and Hayes estimated that 15,000 of the returning veterans would have syphilis, and that it would be a 'hideous national sin' if the Irish people allowed these men to infect 'thousands of yet unborn Irish children ... with the stigma of this foulest and most shameful of diseases'.[145]

IV

The moral probity and purity of Irish nationalists stood as a bulwark against the dangers of British culture. In the opinion of wartime propagandists, four British *bêtes-noirs* in particular threatened Irish culture: drink, music halls, salacious literature, and Freemasonry. None of these issues was created by the war, but the war in both practical and emotional ways, heightened concern. Practically, the war brought an increase in Irish enlistment, leading more men into the temptations offered by barrack life. The war also increased the mobility of women, exposing them to salacious entertainment far removed from parental or clerical supervision. More importantly, the war increased fears of alien cultures. Just as Germans were demonized in pro-war propaganda, so too the immoral figures of British music hall artists and writers became symbols of foreign interference in the new Ireland. Freemasonry, long allegedly part of an international anti-Catholic plot, became more threatening when propagandists linked the war to Masonic cabals.

Concern over the morals of Irishmen and women was an old issue among Irish nationalists. Temperance movements had the longest gestation in Ireland, dating back to the mass movement led by Father Theobald Mathew in the 1840s. Strong links between distillers and the Irish Parliamentary Party were mocked and exploited by advanced nationalists, some of who were teetotallers.[146] Dublin-based 'Vigilance Committees', including representatives of the Irish Parliamentary Party as well as future advanced nationalist leaders, galvanized into action by the vitriol of D.P. Moran's *Leader*, and encouraged by Catholic priests and hierarchy, had led efforts in the first decade of the twentieth century to ban salacious literature and discourage the appearance of music hall acts in Dublin. A crusade against Freemasonry was, in turn, part and parcel of Catholic culture

---

143 Lynn's younger brother was one of the approximately *c.*100,000 Irish soldiers who returned from service in the British army. My thanks to Jane Leonard for this point. **144** NLI, ILB 300 Series, ILB 300 P5 fol. 45. See also Maume, 1999, p. 209. **145** Ibid. **146** Tom Garvin, 'Priests and Patriots: Irish Separatism and the Fear of the Modern, 1890–1914', *IHS*, vol. 25, no. 97 (May 1986), pp. 76–7. See also FitzGerald, 1968, p. 35.

at the turn of the century, and had been encouraged in Ireland by organisations such as the Catholic Defence Association, which sought to convince Catholics that Protestants in secret organisations were out to deny Roman Catholics their political and socio-economic rights.[147]

When the Irish Parliamentary Party came out in support of the British war effort, anti-British diatribes in their press were toned down, thus giving advanced nationalists the chance to become the main proponents of moral reform in Ireland. This assumption of the lead is in some ways the most important effect of the Great War on this form of propaganda, for by linking a moral crusade to a political stance, propagandists attained clerical support. In Roman Catholic Ireland, clerical support equalled popular support, and thus followers began to flock to the banners of advanced nationalism.

Drink and drunkenness were linked directly to the Irish Parliamentary Party, considered a main route by which English customs and manners entered Ireland.[148] Patriotic Irishmen did not drink, or if they did, drinking simply led to the enunciation of anti-British sentiments.[149] The English were depicted as a nation of beer-swilling cowards. Griffith mocked the *Daily Mail* in 1917 for insisting that England needed both 'more men' and 'more beer' to win the war,[150] while Brian O'Higgins linked moral cowardice with drunkenness in his 1915 poem 'A Nail in the Kaiser's Coffin', written in response to an English brewery advertisement which asked people to 'Order a pint of beer and drive a nail into the Kaiser's coffin'.[151] 'When the war is over O', sang the British drunkards of O'Higgins' poem, 'We'll load a train with British beer/And meet the boys at Dover O'.[152]

The threat of drunkenness also permitted propagandists to attack the morals of the wives of Irish soldiers in the British army. Since most of the enlisted volunteers in Ireland during the First World War were urban and working class,[153] their wives, known as 'Separation Women', supported themselves on the

147 Cf. Senia Paseta, *Before the Revolution: Nationalism, Social Change, and Ireland's Catholic Elite, 1879–1922* (Cork, 1999). 148 Cf. BNL, *Spark*, 11.4.15, p. 2; NLI, *Irish Fun*, August 1917, p. 43. Nevertheless, both the *Freeman's Journal* and the *Irish Weekly Independent* supported the work of the Ulster Temperance Council and the Father Matthew Temperance Union during the war (cf. *WFJ*, 7.2.15, 4.3.16, p.4; *IWI*, 1915 fl., 4.3.16, p. 3). 149 Cf. BNL, *EI*, 28.11.14, p. 1. 150 BNL, *Nat*, 28.7.17, p. 6. 151 This was in response to the recent tax imposed on breweries, a tax which whiskey distillers avoided in part due to political pressure from the Irish Parliamentary Party. The Parliamentarians were a thorn in the side of temperance reformers throughout the war. Lloyd George, who declared in March 1915 that drink was the deadliest enemy England faced in the war, pushed through licensing law restrictions against the protests of the IPP, which felt that Irish industry would suffer if pubs' opening hours were restricted. (cf. Marwick, 1968, pp. 83–84). Beer prices in fact went up three-fold in Ireland during the war, and this is one possible reason why drunkenness actually decreased in some areas of Ireland between 1914 and 1918 (cf. Laffan, 1999, p. 268). 152 BNL, *Spark*, 28.3.15, p. 3. 153 Cf. Staunton, 1986; Dooley, 1995.

Youth, sex, and Charlie Chaplin: 'moral tone' and the Irish revolution 159

THE
IRISH PARTY'S
Only Props
IN LONGFORD

4.6 *The Irish Party's Only Props in Longford* (by-election poster, 1917, KSRL)

separation allowances provided by the British government. This class of women was a frequent target for advanced nationalist (although not labour) vituperation. Priests claimed that women who drank this 'blood money' committed the ultimate act of depravity, and would have an awful reckoning on judgement day.[154] A poster for Joseph McGuinness' 1917 by-election contest in County Longford (figure 4.6) combined the idea of alcoholic and moral/sexual depravity.[155] The ragged hoydens shown swilling porter and bearing both Union Jacks and banners for the Irish Parliamentary Party candidate are marked as libertines by their ragged yet gaudy clothes. Yet, while these women are held as figures of opprobrium, their actions in invading the male sphere of the public

154 BNL, *Hib*, 30.10.15, p. 1.   155 KSRL, DK17, Sinn Féin Leaflets, DK17:8:30, 'The Irish Party's Only Props in Longford' (1917).

house, and socialising rowdily with each other, are all signs of a freedom that was denied the 'purer' female supporters of Sinn Féin.[156]

The enormously popular music hall was also something which would be denied to both male and female nationalists. Certain propagandists active during the Great War, especially Arthur Griffith, had been instrumental in leading opposition to the production of Synge's *Playboy of the Western World* at the Abbey in 1907. Thus, opposition to 'immoral' entertainment did not appear overnight. However, most advanced nationalists stopped supporting vigilance committees and truth societies during the war.[157] The main reason for this was because the Parliamentary Party's support for the British war effort was thought to compromise their moral stance. The Dublin Vigilance Committee, supposedly influenced by leading member J.D. Nugent's friendship with the French Premier and Freemason René Viviani, was accused of refusing to help nationalist campaigns against smut.[158] In fact, the Dublin Vigilance Committee retained the powerful support of the *Freeman's Journal* throughout the war. The newspaper sponsored a float at the annual Vigilance Demonstration in November 1915,[159] and featured reports on the annual vigilance convention and meetings of the Catholic Truth Society.[160]

In their own eyes, however, advanced nationalists' uncompromising anti-British attitude gave them an advantage in the war against immorality. Propagandists insisted that 'smutty papers ... the dirty song, the suggestive film, the indecent revue'[161] were all made in England for exportation to Ireland, and considered Redmondism to be synonymous with vulgarity and immorality.[162] Advanced nationalists contrasted music halls with the more wholesome forms of entertainment to be found in Germany (or at the very least, the lack of such degraded amusements imported from Germany).

Protest as they might, advanced nationalists could not deny the popularity of music halls in Dublin.[163] An awareness of popularity is most visible in the subject matter of some anti-recruiting jokes published during the war. An old lady, stopped with her son in the street by an officer and told that 'The Empire now needs every man', replied 'that she cared nothing about the Empire – her son worked in the Tivoli!'[164] The *Spark* in its turn mocked all the current foibles and

---

156 For an excellent study of the political and socio-cultural background to the Longford by-election, see Coleman, 1998. 157 With the exception of Herbert Pim's *Irishman*. While Pim was imprisoned immediately after the Easter Rising, the newspaper implicitly supported the Dublin Vigilance Committee campaign against immoral literature (BNL, *Irishman*, 15.5.16). Once Pim was released, he became more extreme than the Vigilance Committee. 158 Cf. *Og*, 18.8.17, p. 4. 159 BNL, *SFJ*, 11.9.15, p. 6. 160 Ibid. 161 BNL, *Gael*, 5.2.16, p. 6. 162 BNL, *Spark*, 7.3.15, pp. 2–3. 163 A similar problem dogged the *Freeman's Journal*. Despite giving positive coverage to the efforts of vigilance committees and truth societies, the very popularity of the music hall ensured ample and regular reports in the newspaper about the entertainments on offer in Dublin (cf. BNL, *FJ*, 3.8.14; 11.8.14; 23.8.14, etc). 164 BNL, *Hib*, 14.8.15, p. 4. The four largest music halls in 1914 Dublin were the Royal, the Empire, the Tivoli, and the C.Y.M. Pantomime.

activities of the Irish Parliamentary Party in an August 1915 issue, yet chose to do so (figure 4.7) by pretending that the parliamentary and English leaders were all appearing in the 'Imperial Theatre of Varieties'.[165]

Advanced nationalists attempted to present alternative forms of entertainment. This could be the Irish Theatre of Edward Martyn, a theatre which *An Claidheamh Soluis*, forgetting its bitter dispute with Martyn in 1903, told its readers would 'show them that there is dignity in their Irish nationality'.[166] Readers who wanted to know more about Martyn were encouraged to attend his theatre. There they would learn the truth far better than by reading the 'sultry pages' of the 'godless hedonist' George Moore's *Hail and Farewell*.[167] Aware that Martyn's mixture of Irish translations and repertory theatre[168] might be too high class for some nationalists, propagandists also promoted concerts at which 'Irish-Ireland Artistes' could appear. A typical programme for one of these concerts in 1917, in which 'all artistes appearing on stage [had] participated in the 1916 Rising', is reproduced in figure 4.8.[169] Joseph Mulkearns, 'the Rajah of Frongoch', honed his performance in Frongoch, and returned to grace patriotic stages in Ireland throughout the rest of the war. Nationalist concert parties were even formed, touring Ireland in the best tradition of the music hall act. The best known of these was the 'P & C's', led by Jack O'Sheehan until he was sentenced to two years' hard labour in 1918 for singing 'Felons of Our Land' and 'A Soldier's Song'.[170] Mass entertainments could be even more bizarre. The farewell 'carnival' held for Jim Larkin at Croydon Park in October 1914 before he left for America included speeches, a display by the Irish Citizen Army, and, recalling Buffalo Bill's Wild West Show,[171] an 'Attack on an Irish Emigrant Cavern. Rescue by American Army'.[172]

In the *Spark*, Sean Doyle was careful to differentiate between music halls and 'West British' music halls. A central place for entertainment was a 'potent instrument of reform, culture, and progress', but the sort of music halls seen in Dublin had become instead 'a blot on civilization'.[173] The *Hibernian* felt that music halls, and in particular their lurid hoardings, existed only to whet the immoral desires of young men and even young women.[174] But while propagandists blustered about these working-class arenas of amusement,[175] they reserved their wrath for immoral and perverted plays that catered to more middle-class tastes. Herbert Pim blamed the distractions of the war for the

165 BNL, *Spark*, 21.8.15, p. 4.   166 BNL, *ACS*, 14.11.14, p. 5.   167 Ibid., 9.1.15, p. 4.
168 A typical bill in January 1915 consisted of Eimar O'Duffy's 'The Phoenix on the Roof', Villiers de l'Isle Adam's 'The Revolt', and 'Fe Brigh na Mionn', an Irish translation of Rutherford Mayne's 'Troth' (Cf. *ACS*, 9.1.15).   169 KSRL, C3196: Sinn Féin Leaflets (uncatalogued).   170 Cf. BNL, *Og*, 14.9.18, p. 3.   171 Ironically, Queen Victoria greatly enjoyed Buffalo Bill's show.   172 BNL, *IW*, 17.10.14, p. 2.   173 BNL, *Spark*, 28.3.15, p. 4.
174 BNL, *Hib*, 7.7.15, p. 1.   175 Although Sean Doyle made sure to insist that he himself was 'not a molly-coddle', and enjoyed 'a man's story' as much as anyone else (BNL, *Spark*, 28.3.15).

========= IMPERIAL =========
THEATRE OF VARIETIES,
LOWER CASTLE YARD, DUBLIN.

Resident Manager	MATTHEW NATHAN
Advertising Manager	W. M. MURPHY
Chucker-Out	STEPHEN HAND

MONDAY, AUGUST 23, 1915
6.45 ——— TWICE NIGHTLY ——— 9.0

VIVIANI QUARTETTE
in a Rousing Revue—
PARLEZ VOUS FRANCAISE,
specially adapted from Fred Karno's Latest by
JIMMY GALLAGHER, Ireland's Own Gom-Actor,
introducing a Special Scena,
"PUTTING OUT THE LIGHTS,"
A Parisian game, produced for the First Time
on any Stage.
J. D. NUGENT as Viviani. JOE DEVLIN as Clemenceau.
T. P. O'CONNOR as Grand Master.
JIMMY GALLAGHER "HIMSELF" as Buffoon.

WEE JOEY, THE MIDGET WONDER,
in his Marvellous Transformation Act,
"ANCIENT ORDERS UP-TO-DATE."

MAX GREEN, The Fly Boy,
presents a Grand Scenario, "THE JAIL BIRD,"
featuring John Saturnus Kelly as "The Sparrow"

SPECIAL EXTRA.
HUSH MONEY,
By the Freeman's Journal Staff,
Under Distinguished Patronage.
W. H. Brayden as The Telephone Call Boy.
J. P. Gaynor as The MUCK-RAKER

GUSSIE BIRRELL, Humorist, in his latest song success A "Friend" in Need	TOMMY KETTLE, The One-and-Eightpenny Gent, The Outcast of the Family

JOHNNY DILLON, the "Melancholy Humbug,"
in a fresh outburst of Political Imbecility.
THE "IMPERIAL" BIOSCOPE. Always Up-to-Date
and Interesting. The Perfection of Faking.

MR. JOHN REDMOND'S Brilliant Company,
in the Famous One-Act Tragedy,
"ON THE STATUTE BOOK."
——— 72 Silent Performers. ———
The Great No-Action-Play that has attracted the attention
of the Whole World.
The Greatest Achievement in the History of Mummery.
Preceded by the Famous Curtain Raiser,
"THE SUSPENSARY ACT."
"The unfortunate man who cannot see the merits of this
piece, or who is so debased as not to join in the applause of the
Peoples of the Earth, who have set themselves so ener-
getically and successfully to maintain the rights of Small

4.7 *Imperial Theatre of Varieties* (*Spark*, 21 August 1915)

―――EASTER WEEK―――
Commemoration Concert

THEATRE ROYAL
TO-NIGHT AT 8

THE "EASTER WEEK PLAYERS"
will present
"THE SINGER"
By P. H. Pearse.

Cast—Miss L. O'Brennan, Miss A. Taaffe, Oscar Traynor, Sean McEntee, P. Houlihan, Maurice Brennan, M. Smith.
Produced under the personal direction of OSCAR TRAYNOR.

THE "FRONGOCH OLD BRIGADE"
will present a Song Scena—
"FRONGOCH 1916"
Being a Reproduction of Camp Life in Frongoch.
Produced under the personal direction of SIMON DONNELLY.

The above will be supported by a high-class IRISH-IRELAND CONCERT by the following EASTER WEEK Artistes:

SEAN NEESON	THOS. J. BEVAN
(Baritone)	Late O'Mara and Flintoff Moore Opera Cos.
Municipal School of Music, Cork	
ERNIE NUNAN	COUNTESS MARKIEVICZ
Ireland's Premier Step-Dancer	Recitation

ALL ARTISTES APPEARING ON THE STAGE HAVE PARTICIPATED IN THE 1916 RISING

PRICES:
Gallery, 1/-; Upper Circle, 2/-; Parterre, 2/6; Dress Circle, 3/6; Seat in Box, 5/-
All Seats in the Theatre can be Booked at Theatre Box Office.

Tickets may be had at O'Hanrahans, 384 N. C. Rd.; Messrs. Brennan & Walsh, O'Connell St.; Hoban's, Parnell St.; Mrs. T. Clarke, D'Olier St.; Moore's, Redmond's Hill; or at Sinn Fein H. Q., 23 Suffolk Street.

Corrigan & Wilson, Printers, Dublin.

4.8 *Easter Week Commemoration Concert*
(Sinn Féin advertisement, 1917, KSRL)

production in September 1916 of the musical *My Lady Frayle*,[176] a play that 'abounded in jokes and suggestions of the most immoral character'.[177]

Pim's protest against this play can be seen on two levels. First, and most simply, he objected to the somewhat daring lyrics of the author, Arthur Wimperis, and the plot, a modern re-telling of *Faustus*. However, a closer examination of his screed against this play reveals that in fact he was sarcastically attacking British policy in Ireland. By insisting that this sort of play would not have been permitted in Dublin before the war, he argued that the focus of coercion and control in Ireland had shifted from moral control to political control. Propagandists differentiated between the two forms of censorship, going so far as to request the British censor to 'put its foot down on the moral assassins who flood Ireland with filth from the English printing presses ... chain up or smother the authors of the indecent songs and 'jokes' which you are permitted to *cheer* at the Hippodrome'.[178] Pim asked rhetorically 'whether the theatrical censor and his staff have given up the business and are employed in political censorship?'[179] Pim also protested against the cultural hegemony of Britain. *My Lady Frayle* reached Dublin shortly after its premiere in London, and it was precisely this sort of importation which propagandists both before and during the war fought so hard against.

Leaving the sub-Wodehouseian world of musical comedy, nationalists also complained about non-musical comedies. 'George Birmingham's' play, *General John Regan*, revived by the Abbey Theatre in 1917, was marked in *Nationality* as 'the foulest play ever staged in Dublin'.[180] What in particular did Griffith find so perverse in Birmingham's comedy about the fictional liberator of Bolivia?[181] Originally written in 1913, Birmingham's play is completely devoid of any salacious or sexually immoral implications. Most likely, Griffith objected to the author, as Birmingham (Canon James Hannay) was considered a 'great hater of Sinn Féin',[182] and had resigned under a cloud from the Gaelic League when it emerged in 1907 that he and Birmingham were the same man. Second, the play depicts Irish life in a small rural town as stultifying, and the main heroes of the play are the men who trick Dublin Castle into providing them with a chunk of money for the purported statue of General Regan. Rather than being 'Sinn Féin' and self-reliant, the characters in this play scheme away and easily find ways to take advantage of the benevolent Union. Griffith would also probably have taken

---

176 Book by Arthur Wimperis and Max Pemberton, Lyrics by Arthur Wimperis, Music by Howard Talbot and Herman Fink. First produced at the Shaftesbury Theatre, London, by Robert Courtneidge, 1916.   177 BNL, *Irishman*, 23.9.16, p. 1.   178 BNL, *Spark*, 7.2.15, p. 1.   179 BNL, *Irishman*, 23.9.16, p. 1.   180 BNL, *Nat*, 1.9.17, p. 4.   181 This revival received a good review in the *Irish Times*, which remarked that this was 'Irish drama of the best type'. The audience seemed to enjoy it as well, responding quickly to 'the rapid witticisms in which the comedy abounds' (*Irish Times*, 28.8.17, p. 4).   182 BNL, *Nat*, 1.9.17, p. 4.

offence to scenes in which the local brass band revealed its ignorance of such patriotic standards as 'A Nation Once Again', and 'Who Fears to Speak of '98'.

Just as specific authors were attacked, so too were specific artists. Sarah Bernhardt was called blasphemous for twisting scripture in her play *Les Cathedrales*, crying 'Father, forgive them not, for they know what they do'.[183] Charlie Chaplin[184] was accused of cowardice and greed,[185] while the Polish Madame Yavorska was condemned for misplaced patriotism after she sang the Russian National Anthem, 'Rule Britannia', and 'God Save the King' to a Dublin audience.[186]

The only specific song that one can find attacked consistently in the advanced nationalist press is *It's a Long Way to Tipperary*.[187] The popularity of this song in the British army, and the idea that *Tipperary* was a proper Irish song, enraged nationalist propagandists around the world. Irish-American writers were especially vituperative about *Tipperary*, and their articles were eagerly reprinted in advanced nationalist journals in Ireland proper. Writing in the *San Francisco Leader*, Father Yorke summarized the problem of *Tipperary*, stating that it 'is not a song, and it is not Irish. It is a cockney music hall jingle, and its words are a libel even on the stage Irishman'.[188] Propagandists protested especially against the fourth verse, in which 'Paddy' apologized to his 'Molly O' for his atrocious spelling, claiming 'Remember it's the pen that's bad – don't lay the blame on me'. *Tipperary* furthered anti-Irish prejudice, leading Englishmen to think of the Irish as 'grinning baboons',[189] whose lips dripped 'with obscenity and Birmingham-filth'.[190] For Griffith, the song highlighted the immorality of British culture – Piccadilly and Leicester Square, the London highlights of the song, made Griffith think of 'Babylon and Belshazzar'.[191]

The protests against *Tipperary* formed a foundation upon which a form of resistance to music hall entertainment could be built. Pro-Germanism was encouraged by writers who detested *Tipperary*, and the 'martial vigour' of the German race was linked to songs such as 'The Watch on the Rhine',[192] and the

183 BNL, *Hon*, 29.1.16, p. 3. 184 It is rare to see accusations hurled at the cinema in advanced nationalist propaganda, most likely because the medium had yet to make great inroads in Ireland. The *Gael* in February 1916 did however list the cinematograph as a 'diabolical invention', and a 'mental atrocity', a form of entertainment only patronised by 'shoneens', and responsible along with music halls and newspapers for harming the innocent public (cf. *Gael*, 12.2.16). In 1916, the *Irish Weekly Independent* supported Home Secretary John Simon's contention that the cinema was partly responsible for the rise of juvenile crime, and must be censored and controlled (cf. *IWI*, 28.10.16, p. 4). For more on British cinema during the First World War, see Rachael Low, *The History of the British Film, 1914–1918* (London, 1950). 185 BNL, *Hon*, 1.4.16, p. 4. 186 BNL, *EI*, 4.11.14, p. 2. 187 *Tipperary* was also disliked by the *Sunday Freeman's Journal*, although with less intensity. It editorialised: 'As a song it is the poorest stuff in the world ... we are glad it is not as universally popular with the soldiers as we had been led to believe' (BNL, *Sunday Freeman's Journal*, 24.1.15, p. 4). 188 BNL, *EI*, 23.11.14, p. 2. 189 Ibid. 190 BNL, *Hon*, 18.12.15, pp. 1–2. 191 BNL, *Nat*, 14.8.15, p. 4. 192 BNL, *EI*, 23.11.14, p. 2.

choral training given to conscripts in the German army.[193] Native composers were also encouraged to either write new melodies or resurrect old Irish tunes to replace the current 'music-hall rubbish'.[194] Proper martial tunes inspired volunteers to defy the British crown. Terence MacSwiney reported the actions of Cork volunteers when they escorted J.J. Walsh to the train station[195] in words that linked songs to violence. The Volunteers, he wrote, had specifically refused to sing 'A Long Way to Tipperary', instead, 'they swung on their heels like one man, and in one voice sang "Let Erin Remember the Days of Old". The fire of it! No – we are not terrorized'.[196] Children especially were encouraged to discard 'meaningless jingles depending on the "rattle of the bones"'[197] and to learn instead the 'exquisite national melodies' of Ireland.[198]

More direct forms of resistance to music hall songs were also suggested. The *Hibernian* encouraged a boycott of all such entertainments, crying 'In the name of God, let us end it or mend it!'[199] The *Gael* recalled the *Playboy* riots, urging its readers to inaugurate a campaign of 'fierce, organized rioting against vile productions'.[200] Nationalists were told to gather outside music halls, and at a given signal from inside the hall, force their way in and physically clear the house. Thus an 'Era of Decency' would appear in music halls and cinemas.[201]

Boycotting was also urged against the popular English literature and newspapers that contributed to the growing immorality of Irish youth. Herbert Pim managed to gain the support of Cardinal Logue in his campaign against 'grossly improper literature' and newspapers such as the *Umpire*, the *Sunday Chronicle*, *News of the World*, *Reynold's Newspaper*, and *John Bull*, the majority of which were 'discharged from cross-channel steamers to the sound of church bells on Sunday morning'.[202] Novels and popular children's papers were considered responsible for the presence of 'neurotic children',[203] and writers went so far as to condemn Alfred, Lord Tennyson for having a 'gross mind', and urged school authorities to burn the 'debasing writings' of Tennyson and Macaulay.[204] Mass-circulation papers in Ireland were unable to support such a crusade in good conscience, as their columns were often filled with salacious accounts of divorce, breach of promise, and murder cases, both in Ireland and England.[205] This gave

193 BNL, *Hon*, 18.12.15, pp. 1–2. 194 KSRL, OH G27: *FF*, 26.9.14, p. 4. 195 An employee of the Post Office, Walsh had been ordered to take up employ in England after his volunteer activities came to the attention of authorities. 196 KSRL, OH G27: *FF* 17.10.14, p. 2. 197 Bod., *Catholic Bulletin*, August 1918, p. 399. 198 Ibid., February 1917, pp. 115–120. Singing these melodies became a wide-spread form of resistance after the Easter Rising. Prisoners in the dock often sang the *Soldier's Song* and *The Wearing of the Green* (cf. *WFJ*, 17.11.17). 199 BNL, *Hib*, 7.7.15, p. 7. 200 BNL, *Gael*, 12.2.16, pp. 7–8. 201 Ibid. 202 Cf. BNL, *Irishman*, 15.5.16; 21.10.16. 203 BNL, *Gael*, 12.2.16, pp. 7–8. 204 BNL, *Og*, 14.7.17, p. 3. 205 The *Irish Weekly Independent*, with the largest circulation of weekly papers in Ireland (an average of 50–72,000 copies/week in 1914–15; 50–69,000 copies/week in 1915–16 [*IWI*, 30.9.16, p. 4].), was a particular offender (cf. *IWI*, 25.3.16, 22.4.16, 10.6.16, etc).

advanced nationalists yet another opportunity to assume a greater leadership role in the fight against immorality.

While some of the resentment felt by propagandists for the immorality of British youth papers may be cynically attributed to professional jealousy (*Fianna* and *Young Ireland (Eire Og)* had to convert to adult papers to survive, while *St Enda's*, the children's supplement to *Irish Fun*, lasted only a year), the central fury of propagandists was reserved for one man alone: Alfred Harmsworth (Lord Northcliffe), the Irish press baron who controlled *The Times* and the *Daily Mail*, as well as producing vast amounts of popular and children's newspapers.[206]

Most propagandists conveniently forgot Harmsworth's Irish background,[207] focusing instead on the wickedness wrought by his newspapers. Harmsworth was 'the Cromwell of journaleese [*sic*]',[208] an 'evil genius' who existed only to feed human weaknesses and fill reading hours with 'triviality or gross idiocy'.[209] When Harmsworth wasn't corrupting morals, he was busy encouraging a 'healthy Imperial outlook'[210] among young readers. If this wasn't enough to condemn him in advanced nationalist eyes, by January 1916 he had grown blasphemous, printing an article in *Answers* that claimed the Kaiser was the Devil incarnate.[211]

Blasphemy, however, was only what one could expect from a man such as Lord Northcliffe, who among his other faults had joined the Freemasons. Anti-Masonic agitation by advanced nationalists dated far back before the Great War. Encouraged by the support of anti-Masons in the Catholic hierarchy (for indeed Freemasonry had often been condemned by papal authority), propagandists such as D.P. Moran and Arthur Griffith led the campaign against Masons in public life. The threat of Freemasonry was in part due to its secret nature,[212] in part due to the pre-war scare propaganda of the Catholic Truth Association and other such organisations, and in part due to the anti-Semitic xenophobia felt by many propagandists. Griffith had linked Freemasons with Jewish supporters of the British war effort in South Africa, claiming that inhabitants of 'Jew-Burg' (Johannesburg) wanted nothing more than a Boer defeat in the South African War of 1899–1902.[213] Popular Catholic (and anti-Semitic) publications such as the *Irish Rosary* and D.P. Moran's the *Leader* campaigned for committees of Catholics in business to be set up in order to counter-act the influence of Freemasons among the Protestant business community in Dublin.[214]

This paranoia of anti-Catholic plotting continued during the Great War. W.J. Brennan-Whitemore flogged an old horse, accusing the 'Jew-cum-Mason'

206 The most important of these papers were *Answers*, the *Magnet*, the *Boy's Friend* and the *Girl's Friend*, and *Home Notes*. Other comic papers for boys included *Chips* and *Comic-Cuts*. 207 The exception being Sean Doyle in the *Spark*, who sarcastically described Lord Northcliffe as 'The "Successful" Irishman' in December 1915 (cf. *Spark*, 5.12.15). 208 BNL, *Nat*, 24.7.15, p. 5. 209 BNL, *Irishman*, 8.12.17, p. 4. 210 BNL, *Spark*, 5.12.15, p. 2. 211 BNL, *Nat*, 5.2.16, p. 1; *Answers*, 29.1.16, p. 211. 212 One could replace the word 'Freemason' with 'Jesuit' and match Catholic and Protestant propaganda. 213 Cf. Novick, 1997b, for more on Griffith's anti-Semitic roots. 214 Garvin, 1986, p. 78.

journalistic agencies, naturally headquartered in London, of circulating 'malicious and abhorrent calumnies upon the Catholics of Ireland'.[215] Thomas H. Burbage, an anti-Semitic columnist for J.J. O'Kelly's *Catholic Bulletin*, laid off the Jews briefly in February 1917 to explain to his readers that Masonic ritual made a mockery of Christian morals, consisting mainly of a 'degenerate and revolting form of phallic worship ... symbolism that fills the mind with impure and obscene imagery'.[216] Such perversions were clearly popular in countries outside Ireland, and Arthur Griffith especially used this as a way of blaming the Freemasons for the suffering of the Great War. After the United States entered the war in April 1917, he turned away from his pro-American stance[217] to prove that Masonry was 'solidly ranged' on the side of the Allies. According to Griffith's calculations, 84% of the known Masons in the world fought on the side of the Allies, as opposed to only 7% with the Central Powers. Since the war was therefore created by Freemasons, and more specifically by the Grand Orient chapter of Freemasons, it should be seen as 'a gratuitous insult to Catholics'.[218] By connecting Freemasonry so directly with the Allied war effort, Griffith clearly defined his anti-war stance as synonymous with his Catholic beliefs, and challenged the overwhelmingly Catholic population of Ireland to go against their own religion by joining the British army.

According to nationalist propaganda, Ireland had better resisted the inroads of Masonry than other European countries, but she was still under threat. Freemasons had infiltrated the educational system, leading to a decline in Irish being taught in the schools.[219] The appointment of the Jewish Sir Matthew Nathan to the position of Under-Secretary helped the Masons achieve a further foothold in Dublin Castle, as it was widely suspected that 'Signor' Nathan was a member of the Grand Orient Lodge.[220] The Reverend F.S. Pollard in the *Hibernian*, a strong crusader against Freemasons and Jews, reacted strongly when Dublin Alderman Alfred Byrne lost a by-election in 1915. Byrne's defeat was seen by Pollard as being caused by a conspiracy between Jews, Orangemen, and Freemasons. Pollard blustered away, threatening the 'hell-hounds' who had been let loose 'to down a Catholic', and insisting that 'someone has got to sup sorrow with a long spoon', before he would let the matter lie.[221]

The Irish Parliamentary Party was seen as a primary conduit through which Godlessness and Freemasonry entered Ireland. Joseph Devlin was accused of entering into a secret alliance with the Grand Orient via Sir Matthew Nathan,[222]

215 BNL, *Gael*, 26.2.16, p. 5.   216 Bod., *Catholic Bulletin*, February 1917, p. 97.   217 Although this was a brief conversion. Griffith would quickly re-focus on influencing American votes at a post-war peace conference, at which he and other Sinn Féin leaders hoped to get Ireland recognised as a free nation.   218 BNL, *Nat*, 9.6.17, p. 1.   219 BNL, *Og*, 16.3.18, p. 1.   220 BNL, *SF*, 28.11.14, p. 1.   221 BNL, *Hib*, 2.10.15, p. 8.   222 BNL, *SF*, 28.11.14, p. 1.

and the advanced nationalist press was outraged in May 1915 when T.P. O'Connor, Joe Devlin, Stephen Gwynn, W.A. Redmond, the Lord Mayor of Dublin (Lorcan Sherlock) and J.D. Nugent met with the socialist French Premier and Masonic leader René Viviani[223] and presented him with the 'sympathy of the Irish people'.[224]

The unholy foursome of threats to the morals of the Irish people did not originate with the Great War, but the events of the war sharpened their danger, and heightened the importance of counteracting them. By blaming the British for the presence of drink and immoral entertainment, and the Freemasons for the slaughter of the war, advanced nationalist propagandists were able to turn the decision to support their views from a political to a moral ground. Devout Catholics saw propagandists such as Griffith, Doyle, and Pim take on the mantle of the pre-war vigilance and truth societies, and gain the support of the hierarchy. By so doing, propagandists, whatever their personal views of music halls and drink, presented themselves as champions of decency and morality.

VI

At its most basic level, propaganda directed at people's morals sought to both create an idealized (and fictive) revolutionary and highlight as a sharp contrast the degenerate and debased nature of British and pro-British people. The construction of idealized imagery helped propagandists exert control over their audiences. Men could be influenced while boys, and women's impulses and desires could be contained through a strictly controlled discourse of sexuality and danger. Clerical support for advanced nationalism came forward first through an alliance forged upon moral grounds, through the crusade against improper literature and entertainments headed by Herbert Pim. By attacking the evils of intemperance and the threat of Freemasons and music halls, advanced nationalists inherited a long tradition of moralistic propaganda. However, the Great War, by increasing the mobility of the population (thus exposing more young men and women to moral danger) and by heightening the awareness and hatred of the 'other', contributed to the transition from moral propaganda to political propaganda. When the lines between the two styles blurred, support grew for a set of movements that sought to create in Ireland a revolutionary and yet conservative new nation.

223 Viviani was a great enemy of the Catholic press in Ireland. In 1906 he had championed the secularization of state education, and in a speech to the French Parliament, boasted that his party had 'extinguished in heaven those lights that never will be relit'. For more on Viviani, see Maume, 1999, p. 165. 224 Cf. BNL, *Spark* 2 and 9 May 1915; *Nat* 24 November 1917, 2 February 1918. The *Freeman's Journal* applauded the meeting (cf. *WFJ*, 2.5.15, p. 4).

5

Land agitation, famine, and the Great War, 1914–18

Chapter Four demonstrated how the Great War gave new opportunities to advanced nationalists in their long campaign for a moral Ireland. This chapter will examine how the Great War influenced another lengthy battle – the approach of Sinn Féin and other advanced nationalist groups to land agitation, and issues of putative famine. Through this examination, a new aspect of the Irish revolution will be analysed. How did the propaganda of advanced nationalism, created for the most part by men and women who had lived their lives in an urban setting, both reflect realities of the revolution, and construct a fictional, imagined landscape of its own in which to base a romantic movement for national independence? The chapter is divided into three parts, exploring first how an idealized view of Ireland was constructed by pro-war propagandists, and how advanced nationalists responded to this. Following this exploration of fantasy, practical efforts to persuade farmers are examined, the efforts made either to build support for the war effort or 'Sinn Féin', and finally, how these efforts were perceived in propaganda.

This chapter argues that while Sinn Féin and other advanced nationalist groups had difficulty finding a way to practically address issues of food distribution and pricing at a time when Great Britain controlled markets and courts, the opportunity offered by the Great War to move from fantastic images of the countryside to realistic approaches to agrarian issues was quickly exploited.

I

Ironically, pro-war propaganda used ancient symbols of the Irish landscape more frequently than anti-war propaganda. With larger budgets, and without the fear of confiscation by the police or military, pro-war propagandists could afford to produce large, visually splendid posters, with enormous print runs. One example of a visual poster using landscape symbolism dates from June 1915. Produced by the Dublin firm of James Walker for the CCORI, the poster shows the figure of Queen Maeve dressed in flowing ancient robes and a golden crown. A blue shawl is wrapped around her, and she stands in bare feet on a green hill, her long red hair falling loose to her waist. The figure is far more ethereal than sexual. Her right hand is raised aloft in benediction, and her left hand steadies an Irish harp that reaches her shoulder. All around her is an Irish landscape drawn in soft shades of green, purple, and yellow, the colours blurring into the shape of a town with church steeples in the distant background. The peaceful landscape and the pseudo-religious figure of Queen Maeve are contrasted with the scene visible through her harp. Like a lens or window into another world, the harp frames the figure of a Sergeant-Major in the British army blowing 'Charge' on his bugle. Behind him, in a landscape of war, two soldiers fire an artillery piece, while shells burst overhead. The landscape of Ireland, represented both by the figure of the Queen and by the colours of the hills, stands for peace, and a place, it is hoped, worth leaving to save.[1]

The British use of other important 'Irish' symbols was hampered by the fact that many of the images used in recruiting posters were either forbidden to Irish troops at the front, or actually illegal to display in Ireland. An ironic illustration of this problem is offered by the poster 'The Call to Arms', 20,000 copies of which were produced in July 1916.[2] The poster shows an Irish piper decked out in green regimentals with a khaki kilt and a green bonnet playing the Uileann Pipes. Crouched beside him is a large Irish wolfhound, while in the background an Irish regiment[3] marches up a country road, led by a less traditional (albeit more realistic) fife and drum band, past a large green flag bearing an uncrowned harp. With the exception of the Irish wolfhound, two of whose breed joined the Sixteenth (Irish) Division as mascots, and the band, nothing shown in the picture was actually permitted by the British government. Two regiments of the Sixteenth Division were piping regiments, and thus allowed to employ regimental pipe players, but they were forbidden to dress them in any traditional costumes, as was the custom in the Highland Scots regiments. John Redmond bitterly complained about this rule shortly after the division was formed,[4] but as photographic evidence clearly shows, the Division was unable to modify pipers' uniforms even after they went to the Western Front.[5] As for the Irish flag with an uncrowned harp, this was actually considered an illegal device, and displaying one was worthy of prosecution under the Defence of the Realm Act.[6]

Pro-war propaganda created a similar divide to anti-war material between the city and the country. Obviously, propaganda that supported the British war effort did not associate the town with the colonizing perversions of the Sassenach, but both forms of propaganda did look to the countryside as the site of 'Irish Spirit',

1 TCD, Irish Recruiting Posters Collection, Case 55A: 11. 2 Ibid., Case 55A: 21. 3 Possibly the Inniskilling Fusiliers, as a device in the upper right corner of the poster is similar to their regimental badge. 4 NLI MS 15259: John Redmond Papers, Memoranda on Recruiting, 1914–15. 5 Imperial War Museum, London (IWM), Department of Photographs, Q.4198: 'Battle of Guillemont. Men of the 16th (Irish) Division in a lorry going back for a rest after taking Guillemont. 3 September 1916. Passing 'Minden Post', Fricout-Maricout Road, Minden Post, W.S.W. of Carnoy'. 6 Anon. *Two Years of English Atrocities in Ireland* (Dublin, 1919), p. 9. This crime was rarely prosecuted – in 1915, the *Irish Weekly Independent* ran a recruiting cartoon displaying an uncrowned flag without any penalty (BNL, *IWI*, 20.3.15, p. 1).

5.1 *Farmers of Ireland* (DRI recruiting poster, 1916 (?), TCD)

which manifested itself in volunteering, either for the army or the Irish Volunteers. An early recruiting poster entitled 'The REAL Irish Spirit' showed a young man wearing breeches and gaiters, with a city hat holding a sprig of shamrock in the band.[7] He gestures to a private ahead of him, and cries 'I'll go Too!' The young man has left his natural habitat (the city), and gone into the Irish countryside, which is depicted in varying shades of green wash, and consists of a body of still water, green hills, and an old town with the remnants of a church and round tower. Once in the countryside, the man discovers his 'Irish Spirit', and is immediately motivated to fight in the British army.

Pro-war propagandists also closely linked Catholicism to farming. Farmers themselves were held up as paragons of religious faith and virtue. Two intriguing posters from early 1916, using the same artwork, show a farmer stopped in the middle of plowing his potato field, staring in awe at an apparition of St Patrick who is gesturing to a ruined cathedral in the sky, which floats amidst a heavenly sunburst.[8] In one of the posters, St Patrick asks 'Can You Any Longer Resist the Call?' In the other, the poster states simply 'Ireland: Land of Saints and

7 TCD, Irish Recruiting Posters Collection, Case 55c:98.

Soldiers'. The latter example was so melodramatic that it warranted a sarcastic column by Maeve Cavanagh in a February 1916 issue of the *Gael*, in which she attacked the British corruption of the putative saying of St Patrick, 'Ireland: Land of Saints and Scholars'.[9]

The posters of farmers undergoing religious rapture were virtually unique in that they actually showed a farmer in action. Direct visual appeals to farmers were rare in pro-war propaganda, and the landscape featured much more in fantastical imagery than in practical recruiting attempts. 'Farmers of Ireland' (figure 5.1) is an interesting combination of the practical and the fantastic in a recruiting appeal. The title applies directly to farmers, stating 'Join Up & Defend your possessions'.[10] The artwork, however, borders on the unrealistic. The poster shows a column of soldiers dressed in marching order striding around a curve in a wide and well-tended country road. On either side of the road, a substantial farm stretches across the hills to the horizon. On the right, a grain field with four well-tended haystacks borders on a substantial farmstead, while on the left, behind a smaller cottage, a herd of sheep, cows and horses cover hilly grassland. The farm is obviously that of a prosperous grazier, rather than a small tillage farmer or even tenant. In the right rear distance, behind a well-dressed mother and child waving farewell, the sun is setting. Everything in the picture – the rich farm, the animals, the land itself, even the women and children, number as the 'possessions' worth fighting for.

One practical advantage that the outbreak, and more importantly, the lengthy continuation of the war offered Irish farmers was the dramatic rise in prices for staple crop exports. Ireland had long been the 'granary of England',[11] growing all the more so as Britain fell into an agrarian depression during the last quarter of the nineteenth century.[12] As the war dragged on, and U-boat sinkings cut into imports from the United States, Irish crops and livestock became all the more essential to the hungry millions across the Irish Sea. Small farmers also enjoyed the passage of compulsory tillage acts in the winter of 1917–18, which forced all farmers to set aside ten percent of their land for tillage, and, if they did not wish to farm the land themselves, to rent it to small-holders or agricultural labourers. This act was rarely enforced, which caused much complaint,[13] but the intent at least was there. When the British were in need of food for import, farmers could indeed support the war effort more by staying on the land than by enlisting. Thus, the unusually low levels of voluntary enlistment by farmers and their sons, a trend seen across the United Kingdom, does not necessarily relate at all to the

---

8 Ibid, 55c:87 and 55c:110.   9 BNL, *Gael*, 26.2.16, p. 2.   10 TCD, Irish Recruiting Posters Collection, Case 55c: 93.   11 Cf. BNL, *Nat*, 29.12.17, p. 3.   12 Avner Offer, *The First World War: An Agrarian Interpretation* (Oxford, 1989), pp. 82–103, et fl.   13 Erhard Rumpf and A.C. Hepburn, *Nationalism and Socialism in Twentieth Century Ireland*, (Liverpool, 1977), p. 21.

revolutionary fervor (or lack of it) among farmers.[14] Pro-war propagandists were naturally reluctant to publicize the economic advantages of the Great War, feeling that farmers should support the war effort out of patriotism, not out of mercenary desire.[15]

To counter the practical advantage of higher prices gained by supporting the British war effort, anti-war propaganda focused on a series of economic arguments, highlighting the inefficiency of British agricultural officials, and emphasizing the increase in taxes necessitated by the war. These arguments stood advanced nationalists in good stead for two major reasons. First, it gave anti-war propagandists an argument with national, rather than solely local appeal. Second, during the by-elections fought by Sinn Féin in 1917 and 1918, leading up to the General Election of December 1918, election propaganda could attack the co-operation of the Irish Parliamentary Party candidates with the government that was taxing farmers, and even occasionally threatening to give land to supporters of the war effort.

In the spring of 1918, the Treasury responded to wartime exigencies by placing a further tax on farmers in the United Kingdom. Having recently led his men out of the House to protest the passage of a conscription bill for Ireland, John Dillon complained ineffectually that 'the outrageous tax on farmers would never have been proposed had the Irish Party remained in Parliament with undiminished power'.[16] Sinn Féin propagandists disputed this point, noting that tax had been assessed only on entire valuations from 1915, a time at which members of the Irish Party had supposedly claimed to have 'the Government in the hollow of their hands'.[17] In the first three years of the war, tax on Ireland was increased by more than 100%, a sum of £12,632,000. The Irish Party 'might as well have been in Timbuctoo'.[18] Sinn Féin, especially Arthur Griffith, was held up as the honest answer to the hapless Home Rulers, the policy that 'will defeat the designs of the robber'.[19]

Resistance to special income taxes for farmers, based on the value of their farms, was a central component of post-Rising Sinn Féin publicity. In the summer of 1917, seven Sinn Féin leaflets were issued from National Headquarters in Dublin, and distributed at Cummain (branches) around the country. The second, *Farmers! Your turn now*,[20] warned its readers about the dangers of remaining 'under the power of the English Exchequer'. Irish farmers, whom the author of the pamphlet complimented as 'a very shrewd folk, very quick to know their interests and the interests of their country',[21] were informed that a Home Rule Parliament could raise this tax, but not relieve the farmers of

14 See David Fitzpatrick, 'The Logic of Collective Sacrifice', *The Historical Journal*, vol. 38, no. 4 (Dec. 1995), pp. 1017–31. 15 KSRL, OH C1627: Sir Horace Plunkett, *Agricultural Co-Operation and the Present War: An Appeal to the Department and Societies* (Irish Agricultural Organization Society Pamphlet no. 1), pp. 4–5. 16 NLI, ILB 300 Series, ILB 300 P1, fo. 45. 17 Ibid. 18 Ibid. 19 Ibid. 20 TCD, Samuels 2/8. 21 Ibid.

a single penny. 'This may seem', the author concluded, 'like a very bad joke; a joke bordering almost on tragedy; but it is there in the Home Rule Act'.[22] The only chance the Irish had was 'to cut clear of the English Exchequer altogether'. A man deaf to patriotic appeals might nevertheless support Sinn Féin 'for his own interests or the health and prosperity of the country'.[23]

The possibility that land might be given to English soldiers after the war awakened deep historical fears that were easily exploited by Sinn Féin. Stephen Gwynn made a proposal in June 1918 that some Irish land could be offered to veterans after the war as a gesture of goodwill. The plan fell flat, but Dillon and other leaders of the Irish Parliamentary Party said nothing against it, and Sinn Féin propagandists quickly interpreted their silence as tacit approval. 'Save Your Land', cried a handbill printed in response: 'Every Vote against Sinn Féin is a Vote for the Planters'. Sinn Féin members were jailed solely because they were 'an obstacle to the new plantation'.[24]

Pro-war propagandists also tried to frighten farmers into volunteering with the notion of post-war plantations in Ireland, plantations designed and manned by German citizens. The Rapid Printing Company in Dublin printed 15,000 copies of a poster in August 1916 that asked 'Can You Irish Farmers Afford ... to have your LAND calmly confiscated to German farmers?'[25] A more detailed poster agreed with advanced nationalist propagandists, stating 'Germany Wants Ireland'[26] – but for very different reasons. Germany wanted 'to use Ireland's rich and thinly-populated soil as a "place in the sun" for some of surplus agricultural population'. 'German Agricultural economists' had worked on plans for this colonization for years. Lest Irish farmers think Germans too benign for such actions, the poster reminded them that 'Ireland would be colonised by German "Planters" as Prussian Poland has been colonized under the "Ansiedlungs Kommission" during the past forty years. There would be intense agricultural development in Prussianised Ireland; but it would not be for the Irish farmers and their sons'.[27] Sean Doyle countered these arguments, assuring 'the farmers of Ireland that not even an Irish haystack is in danger from the Germans'.[28]

Advanced nationalists had a better time demolishing a more specific German scare story that began late in 1915. The Department of Recruiting for Ireland (DRI) produced a pamphlet that told 'Irish Farmers: Every one of your farms is carefully mapped and recorded in Berlin'.[29] The text reported a speech by Mr T.P. Gill of the Department of Agriculture, in which Gill warned his Tipperary audience that their farms were marked for future German colonists.[30]

---

22 Ibid.   23 Ibid., Cf. also KSRL, DK 17: Sinn Féin Leaflets, DK17:8:60 'Farmers and Income Tax' (1917) for an example of agrarian election propaganda used in the East Clare by-election of 1917.   24 NLI MS 18388: Sinn Féin Election Propaganda, 1918–20, 11.   25 TCD, Irish Recruiting Posters Collection, Case 55a:24.   26 Ibid, Case 55c:95.   27 Ibid.   28 BNL, *Spark*, 13.2.16, pp. 3–4.   29 NLI, ILB 300 Series, ILB 300 P4 fo. 96.   30 Ibid.

This story, very possibly true, was then exaggerated by newspapers, and confused with a report about a German officer who was found on the Western Front carrying a map of Ireland. John Redmond declared that this map was 'so minute that not only every parish, but practically every farm in every parish was marked on it'.[31] It did not take a genius to punch some holes in this story. The *Hibernian* reminded its readers that a map of Ireland showing every farm would have to be drawn on a scale of at least six inches to every mile, and that in law cases about farms, maps three times larger than this had to be produced to provide clear enough detail. This would make the entire map measure 'over one hundred and fifty feet in length and about eighty feet in width'.[32] The author thought it 'strange we never hard [sic] tell of his [sic] stupendous German giant that gadded about Flanders, France, and all along the Rhine, with a map of Ireland rolled up as big as Nelson's Pillar'.[33] The *Spark* guessed that the map would be even bigger. Its 'chief cartographer' said that the map would be 'sufficiently big to allow the marking out of a 100 yards race course on which sprinters could train', and that the Germans had probably cleverly disguised the map as a ground sheet upon which '200 men could find sleeping accommodation'.[34] Comparisons abounded to the 'German Giant' who had dragged this map about. The *Gael* reached back into the past, and remarked that:

> If the terrible 'Huns' bring him to Ireland, Hempenstall [sic], the Walking Gallows of Ninety-Eight, will be in the twopenny place with him. Why, he could take up Redmond himself, Wee Joe,[35] William Martin Murphy, and half-a-dozen others, and by merely essaying himself to yawn, with his giant arms holding them against his back, break their necks in a jiffey. Glory be to God![36]

The *Hibernian* chose more modern figures of nationalist contempt, declaring that the German would be larger than Max Green, John Redmond, William Redmond, William Archer Redmond, and Mike O'Leary, V.C., all put together.[37]

By constructing a fictional Irish landscape, and populating it with mythical figures of Irish history and legend, pro-war propagandists attempted to link their cause with Ireland itself, to parallel joining the British army with defending the land and culture of Ireland. Pro-war propagandists also went beyond fantasies of green fields, using the concrete advantages of wartime pricing to encourage farmers to support the war effort. This line of attack was used somewhat reluctantly, as it was considered mercenary, and advanced nationalist groups, especially Sinn Féin, were easily able to counter economic arguments with appeals that emphasized the rise in land and income taxes during the war, rises

31 BNL, *Spark*, 5.3.16, pp. 2–3.   32 BNL, *Hib*, 26.2.16, p. 8.   33 Ibid.   34 BNL, *Spark*, 5.3.16, pp. 2–3.   35 Joseph Devlin.   36 BNL, *Gael*, 11.3.16, p. 6.   37 BNL, *Hib*, 26.2.16, p. 8.

which naturally had ill effects on most farmers. The contentious issue of land seizure was used by both sides, pro-war propagandists claiming, occasionally to the point of impossibility, that the Germans would seize all Irish lands, and the anti-war advanced nationalists exaggerating occasional proposals about land distribution after the war into a new plantation.

II

Advanced nationalist propagandists had to find a way to appeal to men and women who would not be swayed by flights of fancy. Realistic propaganda, propaganda that dealt with the socio-economic realities of farming as opposed to the fictional construction of an imaginary landscape, encouraged people to view advanced nationalism as a viable alternative to constitutional nationalism or British colonial administration.[38] How did advanced nationalist propagandists depict the practical agrarian actions of Sinn Féin and others? Other scholars, especially Paul Bew[39] and Patrick Maume,[40] have explored the relationship between Sinn Féin and agrarian radicalism. This section will explore how some of the radical agrarian activities of Sinn Féin were perceived in propaganda, and how what was reported reflects the difficulties advanced nationalists had with Ireland's traditional linkage between agrarian unrest and nationalism.

Paul Bew has shown that by the outbreak of the Great War there were two major problems with this link. First, by 1914, two-thirds to three-quarters of farmers in Ireland owned their own land.[41] Second, many nationalists were also graziers, and therefore the old divide between a land-hungry majority and the rich landlords who grazed their cattle across vast grasslands was no longer tenable.[42] Advanced nationalist propagandists attempted to reproduce this dichotomy, setting themselves up as champions of the poor tenant farmer against the greedy Home Rule graziers who supported the war effort. As with the general combination of agrarian radicalism and nationalism at the time, there were two central problems with this propaganda technique. When war began, the vast majority of Ireland's populace and leaders supported the war effort. Two leading agrarian agitators, John Dillon and William O'Brien, threw themselves into recruiting for the British army. Advanced nationalism enjoyed the constant support of Lawrence Ginnell, MP for Westmeath, who had played a leading role

---

38 This was even reluctantly admitted by the *Weekly Freeman* in 1917, which remarked that 'If Sinn Féin can either force the amendment of the Order [the Meat Order attacking the free export of Irish cattle] or discover a method of moderating its evil effects the result will be more impressive than a thousand "sword speeches"'. (BNL, *WFJ*, 8.9.17, p. 5). 39 See his chapter 'Sinn Féin, Agrarian Radicalism and the Irish War of Independence, 1919–1921', in D.G. Boyce (ed.), *The Revolution in Ireland, 1879–1923* (London, 1988), pp. 217–35. 40 Cf. Maume, 1999, pp. 167, 179, 202. 41 Bew, 1988, p. 221. 42 Ibid.

in the recent 'Ranch War' of 1906–8, but his presence alone was not enough to always outweigh the opposition of Dillon, and even more, O'Brien. With the absence of the land as a national issue, propaganda that emphasized this question was by necessity extremely localized. Such parochialism was a double-edged sword for advanced nationalists. On the one hand, local propaganda showed their greater connection to the people, and emphasized the disconnection of many Irish Parliamentary Party MPs from their constituents.[43] Robert Brennan, Sinn Féin Director of Publicity in 1918, and his assistant, Frank Gallagher, both supported a localized style of propaganda. Gallagher recalled sending draft handbills to small towns and rural areas showing how Sinn Féin doctrine applied to local situations. He felt that local points of policy were far more effective than national arguments.[44] However, this localism also forced much of the propaganda to be reactive rather than proactive, appearing only in response to recruiting meetings at which Redmondites spoke about the land, or to public remarks made by pro-war graziers. Advanced nationalists searched in vain for a national hook on which to hang their arguments about land ownership.

MacNeill in the *Irish Volunteer* angrily attacked graziers in Navan after they claimed that the land in Meath, 'the most fertile valley in Europe', was 'too rich for tillage'.[45] Navan was a decaying town because of the graziers, MacNeill felt, and the only way these 'big prairie men' could justify their existence was 'to take refuge in a complaint never before spoken of any soil on God's earth'.[46] Appeals to localized areas often played up class differences between graziers and small farmers.[47] Anticipating later forced tillage orders, *Fianna* encouraged the British government to clear broad ranches, arguing sarcastically that 'in those pressing times … it should be a good, loyal, Imperialistic move to clear off the bullocks from those ranches and put the plough to work thereon'.[48]

Advanced nationalist propagandists also used mockery to a large extent in agrarian propaganda. At times, humour was completely disconnected from reactive propaganda. In October 1917, with the Irish Parliamentary Party beginning to lose by-elections,[49] and Sinn Féin meeting in its first Ard-Fheis since the Rising, *Irish Fun* published the following inane joke: 'Any sign of the blight on the potatoes yet, Seamus?' 'No, father, not a sign, thank God. It's on the Parliamentary Party it fell this year'.[50] A doubtful exchange was reported in the *Irish Volunteer* from a recruiting meeting. Having told the farmers in the

---

43 Cf. *Glancing Back: 70 years' experience and reminiscences of pressman, sportsman, and member of Parliament* (London, 1933), the memoirs of Irish Parliamentary Party MP for West Galway William O'Malley, in which he admitted to having visited Ireland only three times during the Great War. Patrick Maume disagrees, claiming that 'all Irish Party candidates in by-elections after the rising appealed to localism; of Sinn Féin candidates only McGuinness and Dr Vincent White (defeated in Waterford City) had local ties' (Maume, 1999, p. 198). 44 Gallagher, 1953, p. 46. 45 BNL, *IV*, 30.1.15, p. 1. 46 Ibid. 47 BNL, *Fianna*, 29.1.16, p. 15; *Spark*, 5.3.16. 48 BNL, *Fianna*, 29.1.16, p. 15. 49 The Irish Parliamentary Party had lost by-elections in February, May, July, and August 1917. 50 NLI, *Irish Fun*, October 1917,

audience that the Germans would occupy their farms, an orator went into the crowd to gauge their reactions. According to the *Irish Volunteer*, 'he spoke to a local farmer about the horrors and dangers of the war, and drew the reply, "It's the blessing of God we are a neutral country, anyhow"'.[51] Actual recruiting meetings were often reported in advanced nationalist newspapers, always making it seem as if the meetings were complete failures. When local people actually disrupted meetings, newspapers could make the recruiters look ridiculous without actually contravening any censorship regulations. Arthur Griffith excelled at this style of mockery, and used it to a great extent early in the war to attack the Home Rule MPs who were busy recruiting for the British army. Griffith published an agrarian example of this kind of mockery in November 1914 following an unsuccessful recruiting meeting at Dundrum at which John Hackett, MP spoke. Locals, led by members of the Knockaville Labour League, derided Hackett's attempts to call on the names of old Tipperary land war heroes (such as Father Matt Ryan) to support his cause. According to Griffith, the following 'is a fair sample of the eloquence displayed on both sides':

> **Hackett**: 'Tis grand to see all this one-time ranch divided up. (Chorus of voices: 'We needn't thank you'. 'What about Hugh Ryan and the Inch boys?' 'Why don't you divide up your own grass land?' 'You always helped the grazier, Jack'. 'Up Dwyer', etc). Hackett: Father Matt called me a wolf. (A voice: You're more like an ape).
>
> **Hackett**: Father Matt was never in anything National. (Storms. Voices: 'You're a liar'. 'Remember the Land League'. 'Up, Father Matt'. Great cheering).
>
> **Hackett**: I'd sooner follow Monsignor O'Ryan – (Voices: 'Down to the officer's mess, is it?' 'Father Matt's no landlord's priest', etc).[52]

While the vision of the hapless Hackett might raise a few chuckles, and Sinn Féiners who were at the meeting in Dundrum might have their nationalist convictions reinforced through publicity, the truth remains that such accounts did not form a national level of appeal for the advanced nationalist cause. The relative lack of anti-grazier propaganda in the newspapers with national circulation bears this contention out, and reinforces Rumpf's idea about the politically and socially divisive nature of agrarian agitation.[53]

Although Charles Townshend maintains that land agitation (and seizure) was a central element of the 'dynamism' of the nationalist movement from 1916 to 1921,[54] the reluctance of propagandists to publicise land seizures, and indeed the declaration by both Sinn Féin Headquarters and the command of the Irish

---

p. 70.   **51** BNL, *IV*, 28.2.16, p. 1.   **52** BNL, *EI*, 20.11.14, p. 2.   **53** Rumpf & Hepburn, 1977, p. 21.   **54** Charles Townshend, *Political Violence in Ireland* (Oxford, 1983), p. 339, cited

Volunteers forbidding district Sinn Féin councils from promoting and Irish Volunteer officers from participating in cattle drives,[55] demonstrates both the complex nature of agrarian action in the earliest part of the Irish revolution, and a stark dichotomy between the depiction and reality of agitation during the Great War. As this chapter is concerned with depictions and perceptions more than action and reality, such research does not contradict Townshend. Rather, it shows the possibility that the activities of agrarian agitators, men and women in the country who formed such important elements of the independence struggle were a source both of pride and embarrassment to the relatively moderate (and almost entirely urban) propagandists of the revolution.

Propagandists needed to find a kind of agrarian propaganda that could appeal to rural inhabitants on a national level. This could not be a fantasy about the nationalist appeal of the countryside, nor was it, despite some attempts, to be the struggle for land ownership between tenant farmers and graziers. Indeed, it was not until the fourth year of war that propagandists were given the perfect national argument: the spectre of that most feared of Irish calamities, famine.

As a member of the United Kingdom, Irish food exports and imports were governed in time of war by directives from the British government. This policy, which took advantage of Ireland's fertile agrarian production, admittedly took the line of the 'greatest good for the greatest number', and thus controlled Irish exports in order to feed the population of Great Britain. While the government was obviously not going to leave Ireland to starve, advanced nationalist propagandists were able to seize on the control of export trade as an example of policies that would lead to famine if left alone.[56]

A good example of how advanced nationalists twisted a relatively beneficial British policy is the drama that surrounded cattle trade in 1917. In August 1917, in an attempt to decrease the cost of beef, the British government forbade the practice of stall-feeding animals.[57] Griffith and Sinn Féin called this 'War on the Cattle Trade', and produced a special Sinn Féin leaflet on this topic, intended for national distribution. For Sinn Féin, this was a perfect example of how an uncaring Britain destroyed an Irish rural industry.[58] The same month, the British government set controls on the cattle trade with its Cattle Prices Order. This was

in Bew, 1988, p. 225. **55** Fitzpatrick, 1977, p. 132. **56** The Irish Parliamentary Party was also very concerned about agrarian issues, and editorials that attacked British governmental policy appeared in the *Weekly Freeman's Journal* throughout the war. These editorials reached a climax in 1917 and 1918, appearing in more than 1/3 of the issues from those years. As with moral issues, however, the *Freeman's* attacks on the British control of food exports were blunted by its support for the status-quo in time of war. **57** Stall-feeding is a practice whereby livestock are fed in their stalls rather than grazed. This raises the cost of feed, but has two distinct advantages for farmers: 1. It allows them to grow crops as well, and 2. The livestock produce ample manure for fertilisation the following spring. In times of peace, under a free market, the higher cost of feed is amply offset by a rise in market prices for beef. **58** It is ironic that Sinn Féin should so quickly defend the grazing industry. However, I believe that

'the most ruinous restriction and the most deadly yet imposed',[59] wrote Griffith. The passage of the act resulted in a glutted market and an enormous slump in prices, and, if this wasn't bad enough, the British Food Controller had passed the act without consulting a single 'Irish agricultural interest'. Griffith puzzled over this enigma. 'As a rule in most business transactions', he wrote, 'the seller is supposed to have something to say over the price'.[60]

A revelation in September 1917 by the President of the Board of Agriculture that the government was considering lifting an embargo on Canadian cattle gave Griffith the chance to turn the cattle trade issue into a direct call for independence. In March 1917, the President had said publicly that he would not consult the Irish Department of the Board of Agriculture about this issue. 'It is coolly assumed that Ireland has no voice at all', wrote Griffith, 'in a matter that vitally concerns her largest export trade'.[61] This neither surprised nor bothered Griffith:

> For trade purposes we are always regarded as a foreign country by English Ministers. We are only united for the purpose of taxation. What is required is that our relations should be put on a regular footing as a foreign country.[62]

While the cattle trade was a large and important rural industry, it alone did not determine whether or not Ireland or Great Britain starved.[63] Famine was an ultimate terror for the men and women of nationalist Ireland, men and women whose own parents or grandparents had lived during the Great Famine itself. Long before the drawn-out struggle of the Great War caused a genuine fear of starvation to permeate the United Kingdom, advanced nationalist propagandists were warning their readers of the dangers of wartime famine.

The general formulation for famine scares was simple. Roughly, a European war would bring about great restrictions in trade.[64] With its population almost entirely dependent on agrarian imports for their food, Britain would begin to starve. If willing to continue the war, the British government would immediately strip Ireland of her food, surplus or otherwise, and this in turn, as it supposedly had in the 1840s, would lead to an Irish famine. In its first wartime issue, Arthur Griffith's *Sinn Féin* published a note on its front-page predicting famine if

this was a situation of adversity creating strange bedfellows. Hence Griffith in *Nationality* publishing a paean of praise to Ireland's cattle trade, based in 'the bosom of the green valleys of Kerry and the rich table lands of Limerick' (*Nat*, 27.10.17).   59 BNL, *Nat*, 18.8.17, p. 2.   60 Ibid.   61 BNL, *Nat*, 29.9.17, p. 1.   62 Ibid.   63 The cattle trade issue was not supported by every advanced nationalist group in Ireland. The *Irish Citizen* praised the British government in December 1917 after it forbade the export of milch cows, milk, and butter from Ireland – a ban that harmed Irish dairy farmers, but salved some fears of an Irish famine (cf. *IC*, December 1917, p. 389).   64 An idea shared by many war planners in Great Britain and Germany (see Offer, 1989, esp. pp. 217–33 and 321–54).

foodstuffs were exported during the war.[65] The Reverend Michael O'Flanagan, later to become President pro-tem of Sinn Féin, issued another early warning about famine. Speaking at a meeting in Sligo in front of Mr T.W. Russell, the Minister for Agriculture, O'Flanagan declared that 'when it comes to England and Ireland starving, Ireland will have to starve first. Even though a famine appears in Ireland, England will go with the war and allow Ireland to starve'.[66]

All things left as they were, England would starve before Ireland, and this did not escape the notice of bragging nationalists. Arthur Griffith in 1915 compared what would happen if England and Ireland were 'ringed around with a wall of steel'. Faced with such a situation, he made the ridiculous claim that:

> England would be able to provide food for her population for just two months – using up dogs, cats, and horses, she might hold out for a further ten days ...
> But an Ireland ringed around with a wall of steel could not be starved. A besieged Ireland at the present time could feed a population of 7,000,000 people indefinitely.[67]

Eighteen months later, with some talk of famine in Ireland beginning, he warned his readers that 'the people of Ireland cannot be starved without their own consent'.[68] While blaming Ireland's 'enforced connection with England' on the threat of Germany's 'submarine blockade', Griffith maintained nevertheless that 'there can be no famine in a country raising more food than its inhabitants consume ... the only means whereby famine can be produced in 1917 are the means by which famine was produced in Ireland in 1847 – the unrestricted export of food to England'.[69]

The *Hibernian* managed to turn some of the early efforts by the Department of Agriculture to promote the growth of food crops into an anti-recruiting editorial. In March 1916, the editor pointed out that one cannot grow food on grass lands without labour, and yet the same government which encouraged the breaking up of grass lands was also trying to 'have the labour reduced to almost vanishing point'[70] by recruiting. 'In the words of the homely proverb', wrote the editor, 'you cannot have your loaf and eat it'.[71]

Real worries about a famine throughout the United Kingdom began in the winter of 1917. Prices for foodstuffs in Great Britain and Ireland began to rise dramatically in January 1917, and certain staples, such as potatoes, began to run short in Great Britain following a bad potato harvest in the winter of 1917. This shortage was offset by good harvests in the final six months of the year, but as another war winter arrived, it became obvious that serious food shortages were

---

65 BNL, *SF*, 8.8.14, p. 1. 66 BNL, *IV*, 23.10.15, p. 1. 67 BNL, *Nat*, 4.9.15, pp. 4–5. 68 BNL, *Nat*, 24.2.17, p. 4. 69 Ibid. 70 BNL, *Hib*, 18.3.16, p. 4. 71 Ibid.

the norm all across Great Britain.[72] In Ireland, there was less immediate danger of food shortages, as the island was still predominantly an agrarian economy. However, the shortages in Great Britain had drastically raised food prices across the United Kingdom. The *Irish Citizen* warned that these prices alone would cause a famine, even though Ireland produced most staple foods.[73]

Famine seemed a real threat to others outside of advanced nationalist movements. Leading Home Rulers Lionel Smith-Gordon and Cruise O'Brien wrote *Starvation in Dublin* in 1917, examining in a scholarly manner what they perceived to be the genuine threat of starvation facing the working class in Dublin during the war. They called on Irishmen to help solve this problem themselves, warning that 'revolutionary spirits' are brewed by a lack of food.[74] They blamed the threat of starvation on the rise in food prices and a breakdown in distribution to the cities before sending the food either to England or to the front.[75]

With Great Britain teetering on the brink of starvation, and food shortages and out-of-control prices appearing in Ireland, something clearly had to be done. Practical responses to famine had been mooted as early as October 1914. In the *Irish Volunteer*, John Brennan called on Irishmen to 'give Asquith an Irish answer. Hold the food and send no recruits'.[76] The same newspaper a year later reported on Michael O'Flanagan's Mitchelesque speech at Sligo, in which he advised:

> Let each farmer keep at least enough oats on hand to carry himself and his family through in case of necessity until next year's crop. And if any Government dares to commandeer your oats, remember that it is better to die like men fighting for your rights than to starve like our poor misguided grandfathers seventy years ago (loud applause).[77]

By keeping controls on food prices and exports through 1917, the British government had attempted to help keep Ireland from starving, but these new regulations, especially regarding enforced tillage, were proving difficult to enforce.[78] Sinn Féin and other advanced nationalist groups saw their chance, and requested local committees (as well as clergymen) to supervise local food distribution. The National Committee of Sinn Féin, having already begun to publish charts of annual Irish food consumption,[79] also asked local clubs to conduct a census of the food and resources available to each locality.[80] More here was at stake than saving Ireland from a famine. Proper control of food

---

[72] Wilson, 1986, pp. 513–14.   [73] NLI, *IC*, September 1917, p. 377.   [74] A fear shared by the 'Irishwomen's Association', which wrote the British Food Controller in early 1917 that discontent among the poor was growing rapidly owing to the difficulties in acquiring basic necessities of life such as sugar, milk, and bread (Cf. *IC*, March 1917, p. 250).   [75] TCD, Samuels 2/70.   [76] BNL, *IV*, 31.10.14, p. 13.   [77] BNL, *IV*, 23.10.15, p. 1.   [78] Fitzpatrick, 1977, p. 140.   [79] BNL, *Nat*, 17.11.17, p. 3.   [80] BNL, *Nat*, 1.12.17, p. 1.

distribution would give Sinn Féiners invaluable local government experience, and might prove a breakthrough moment for the national acceptance of advanced nationalism. David Fitzpatrick puts it well: 'Sinn Féin saw its chance both to humiliate the government and to bring its own activities out of mere politics into the everyday concerns of the people'.[81]

Early publicity for the efforts of Sinn Féin came from the *Irish Citizen*, which welcomed 'the movement which the Sinn Féin party have put on foot to induce the farmers to give preference first to Irish buyers'.[82] The writer acknowledged the difficulties faced by anyone in business 'asked to refuse a good offer, a thing which the Irish producer is being asked to do now for the sake of his compatriots', but warned that such measures were necessary, as famine to-day 'is almost at our doors. To-morrow it will be here'.[83] *Nationality* went so far as to congratulate an Orange Lodge in County Down for acting 'in the spirit of Sinn Féin'.[84] Needing funds, the Lodge hired a piece of land, grew some flax, and sold the crop for £155. Acknowledging that Sinn Féin was 'in grave need of money', the article suggested that every club in rural districts should do the same, thus providing food for its constituents and money for the Sinn Féin cause. *Nationality*'s relatively large circulation was utilized by the Sinn Féin Food Committee to spread their message of self-reliance far and wide. Reprinting a poster from the South Tipperary Comhairle Ceanntair, the paper urged farmers 'in the interests of the entire community as well as for their own sakes'[85] to keep sufficient potatoes and grains to supply people's food and seed for the next year. The populace was cautioned that they would have to depend on home produce for the next six to eight months, and that a shortage of corn and potatoes might cause an Irish famine. Merchants were warned not to export food (thereby keeping the country from 'the horrors of another '47').[86]

Despite national level appeals in *Nationality* and other newspapers, roughly co-ordinated by the Sinn Féin Food Committee, responses to the threat still differed around the country. *Young Ireland (Eire Og)* lamented that despite the good showings of some districts, such as Oldcastle, in taking steps to 'safeguard the lives of their people', 'many localities do not yet seem to realise the impending danger ... What shall future historians write of the wisdom and foresight of the Ireland of 1918?'[87] This particular historian would maintain that despite the good intentions of advanced nationalists, their efforts to stop a famine were riddled with problems. The British government controlled the sale of goods, and was able to set the price for export sale higher than the price for the internal sale of grains and livestock.

More importantly, the British government also controlled the courts, and by 1917, selling to non-approved buyers was a criminal offence. Farmers and

---

81 Fitzpatrick, 1977, p. 140. 82 NLI, *IC*, January 1918, p. 593. 83 Ibid. 84 BNL, *Nat*, 19.1.18, p. 1. 85 BNL, *Nat*, 26.1.18, p. 1. 86 Ibid. 87 BNL, *Og*, 16.2.18, p. 5.

tradesmen all across the United Kingdom were arrested and fined for exercising their attenuated rights to a free market.[88] In February 1918, John Fleming of Tooremore briefly became an advanced nationalist celebrity after he was fined 10/6 for refusing to sell his crop to the English, and going instead to a Sinn Féin Market in Killarney. *Young Ireland (Eire Og)* heralded him proudly, agreeing that 'the food he had raised was for the Irish people', and praising him in Irish 'Maith a fear, a Sheain'.[89] *Nationality* went further, reprinting part of the transcript from Fleming's court hearing. After he was fined 10 shillings, Fleming gave this patriotic speech, linking his small contribution to the nationalist cause with the courage of men who faced guns in Dublin:

> I will not pay any fine. My potatoes are my own and will only be given to the Sinn Féin Club or the Irish people. What I grow on my land I will keep for home consumption. Mr Wynne [the Resident Magistrate for Tooremore], you can't frighten me, even if you put me up against the wall and riddled me with bullets. I ignore any policeman coming inside my boundary. The Irish people want their own food, and we must keep it for them.[90]

The 'Sinn Féin Market' at which Mr Fleming sold his potatoes was part of Sinn Féin's general effort to take control over the distribution of food. These markets, created to help the poor from starving, met with mixed results. While propagandists in Dublin enthused about their advantages, rural districts often found the markets causing unexpected problems. David Fitzpatrick's research in County Clare showed evidence of other organizations already distributing food to the poor, and in Ennis, the low prices at the Sinn Féin market lowered prices in all the stores, and actually bankrupted several merchants who supported Sinn Féin, as they had depended on the sale of farm produce for their livelihood.[91]

The urban-rural dichotomy that much of this agrarian propaganda has demonstrated is nowhere clearer than in the suggestions made by the Sinn Féin Food Committee for the preservation and creation of food in the countryside. Composed mainly of urban dwellers (the chair was Lawrence Ginnell), the Sinn Féin Food Committee never quite managed to have the impact its members so desired. Occasional successes, such as when Food Controller Diarmuid Lynch managed to stop a shipment of pigs from being exported out of Dublin, were celebrated in song. Catal Mac Dubgaill's 'The Pig Push', dedicated to Lynch, honoured the great adventure of the day on which Lynch made his move:

---

88 Wilson, 1986, pp. 515–16. 89 BNL, *Og*, 9.2.18, p. 2. 90 BNL, *Nat*, 23.2.18, p. 1.
91 Fitzpatrick, 1977, pp. 140–1. J.P. Farrell, MP, condemned Sinn Féin's efforts in 1918, stating that 'there was no need for setting up artificial barriers to prevent the fairs and markets of the country being held, and prevent the farmers disposing of their surplus stock' (BNL, *WFJ*, 19.1.18, p. 5).

> The boys they commandeered the pigs and drove them down the street,
> Says they 'The common Irish should have something nice to eat'.
> And though all the pigs they kicked and squealed and struggled very hard,
> They slaughtered all the thirty-four in the Corporation Yard.
> ...
>
> CHORUS
> We'll have pig's cheek and pork chops enough for you and me;
> There'll be rashers for our breakfast and some sausages for tea.[92]

Lynch's success in slaughtering pigs for the Irish republic was rare. For the most part, the men and women of the Sinn Féin Food Committee, with little knowledge about the realities of rural life and food production, produced earnest yet useless advice for dealing with the threat of famine.

When the Conscription Crisis of April and May 1918 raised the further possibility of having to supply bands of fugitives with provisions, the Food Committee issued a leaflet detailing how rural and town committees could become self-sufficient in food production and provision. The difference in advice between the rural and urban suggestions highlights the alienation of Sinn Féin propagandists from rural life. For the towns, the Committee advised its constituents to discourage panic buying, and, showing an awareness of urban poverty, made sure to include an *apologia* to the urban poor, promising that they were not mocking their needs in suggesting that everyone keep a full larder. Wealthy neighbours were encouraged to help the poor from starving. Shopkeepers and merchants were encouraged to stock large quantities of imperishable foods, and townsmen were advised to learn about substitutes for standard foods (for example, oatmeal for wheaten flour), and to grow vegetables and keep poultry if they could.[93]

In contrast to this type of sound theory, countrymen were vaguely advised to 'have pigs cured locally', 'make as much cheese as possible', and, most importantly, to 'remember that the National life is of more value than immediate personal gain'.[94] Another Sinn Féin poster solemnly warned farmers that 'we cannot exist as a people – we cannot exist as a Nation – without food'.[95] Country folk were advised that 'Salmon is a food as well as a luxury. It loses nothing by salting or smoking', and were exhorted to 'Make War on the Rabbit'.[96]

When it came time to actually attract farmers to their cause, advanced nationalist propagandists were unable to find a realistic appeal that could work on a national level. Economic arguments on the disadvantages of the Union for

---

92 KSRL, DK 17, Sinn Féin Leaflets, DK 17:9:8, 'The Pig Push' (1918). 93 NLI MS 15653: William O'Brien Papers, Folder 2 (Mansion House Conference, 1918–19), 'Notes on Food Supplies' (1918). 94 Ibid. 95 NLI, ILB 300 Series, ILB 300 P5, fo. 2. 96 Ibid.

farmers were legion, but the comfortable living and rise in land ownership under British rule enjoyed by most farmers was also manifest. Mockery of British propaganda perhaps amused, but was not able to transcend the local level. Despite a number of serious and quite well-meaning attempts to avert famine, advanced nationalists were unable to compete with a government system that already controlled markets and market prices, as well as a legal system that enforced the sale of goods during time of war. At the same time, members of Sinn Féin local committees gained valuable experience in the difficulties of local government, and showed, to some degree, their imaginative capabilities in running an agrarian market economy. These men and women, extolled in propaganda, may have been disconnected from the rural supporters of Sinn Féin, but the publicity for their genuine efforts did far more than fantasy images of the Irish countryside in bringing about the victory of Sinn Féin in December 1918.

6

Humour in advanced nationalist propaganda

Earlier sections of this book have examined the links drawn between advanced nationalism's anti-British message and anti-war propaganda. Specific aspects of life that the war created (Irish casualties in the army, atrocity propaganda), as well as older concerns of propagandists (morals and the land) were intertwined with the war itself in order to exploit growing anti-war sentiment in the population. A thematic study of the chronological development of this propaganda shows the importance of the war to Irish political discourse. But how much did the war, and the Easter Rising, influence the language of propaganda itself? In this chapter, and in the final one of the book, more generalized styles of propaganda are studied: humorous propaganda and propaganda which encouraged differing forms of aggression. As with earlier themes, these styles of propaganda carried a specific purpose: the incitement of anti-British feeling. And as with earlier material, these two styles encouraged these feelings by focusing on the war. Unlike more specific themes, however, the Easter Rising also played a large role in the intensification of this propaganda. By simultaneously bringing home the reality of conflict, and creating the possibility of political success, the Easter Rising and its immediate aftermath contributed greatly to a brutalization of discourse in propaganda – a pattern by which the language and form of propaganda became more and more aggressive as the war years passed, changing from irony and mockery in humour to cruel satire, and from fantastic calls for sacrifice to stark threats of physical violence in its aggressive form.

This chapter undertakes a thematic study of humorous propaganda, permitting an examination of ideas which resound throughout this book – depictions of gender and gender identity, the general growth of aggression during the war, and images of sacrifice. Previous studies of sacrificial imagery have concentrated on non-humorous propaganda,[1] neglecting a type of propagandistic imagery and imagination that forms a substantial corpus within the propaganda of First World War Ireland.

The use of humour in propaganda, and especially the use of humour as a defensive weapon of ridicule both in peace[2] and in wartime propaganda, has long

---

1 Cf. Richard Kearney, *Myth and Motherland* (Belfast, 1984) and *Transitions: Narratives in Modern Irish Culture* (Manchester, 1988); Mary Condren, 'Sacrifice and Political Legitimation: The Product of a Gendered Social Order', *Journal of Women's History*, vol. 6, no. 4/vol. 7, no. 1 (double issue) (Winter/Spring 1995), pp. 160–89; Ellis, 1997.   2 Cf. Sigmund Freud, *Jokes and their relation to the unconscious* (1905), tr. James Strachey (London, 1960); Daniel Gerould,

been recognized by historians.[3] However, when scholars of First World War Ireland have chosen to use visual or textual advanced nationalist propaganda in their work, this propaganda has almost always consisted of serious depictions of the struggle for nationhood between the Irish and the British. Using only this sort of propaganda distorts our image of what these propagandists produced, as well as their rationale for propaganda production. This chapter will demonstrate that humour was an important element in advanced nationalist propaganda,[4] and that it was also an extremely mutable element as the war progressed.

A clear trend can be seen in the style and content of humorous advanced nationalist propaganda. In the early months of the war in 1914, the humour in Irish propaganda was mainly ironic,[5] mocking the general war effort with absurd stories that parodied early British propaganda styles. As the war dragged on and became bloodier, flippant joking about the actions of the war itself stopped for some time, the humour directed at the events of the front becoming morbid. Mockery of British domestic policies in Ireland continued, especially the participation of the Irish Parliamentary Party in recruiting for the British army. After the Easter Rising brought home to Ireland the realities of war, a more sarcastic form of humour appeared, attacking arbitrary actions by the British in Ireland, and gleefully revelling in British casualties suffered around the world. Finally, the appearance of a renascent Sinn Féin Party as a genuine electoral challenger to the Irish Parliamentary Party in late 1917, followed by the Conscription Crisis of 1918, coalesced humour directed against the war and humour directed towards the Home Front in a brutal and violent attack on the war and the Redmondites who had involved the Irish.

I

When war came, the editorial position of advanced nationalist newspapers was clear. 'Germany is not Ireland's enemy', cried a bold headline on the front page

'Tyranny and Comedy', in Maurice Charney (ed.), *Comedy: New Perspectives*, *New York Literary Forum*, vol. 1 (Spring 1978), pp. 3–30; Benedict R. O'G. Anderson, 'Cartoons and Monuments: The Evolution of Political Communication Under the New Order', in D. Jackson and Lucien Pye (eds.), *Political Power and Communication in Indonesia* (Berkeley, 1978), pp. 282–321; James C. Scott, *Weapons of the Weak* (New Haven, 1985) and *Domination and the Arts of Resistance: Hidden Transcripts* (New Haven, 1990). 3 Cf. Harold Lasswell, *Propaganda Technique in the Great War* (New York, 1922); and for a good analysis of attitudes in Germany during the First World War, Eberhard Demm, 'Propaganda and Caricature in the First World War', *JCH*, vol. 28, no. 1(Jan. 1993), pp. 163–92. 4 Unsurprizingly, constitutional nationalists also used humour against the advanced nationalists before 1916. The *Freeman*, the *Irish Independent* and the *Irish Times* all ridiculed and mocked the 'mosquito press' until the Easter Rising, and only stopped joking about advanced nationalism when Sinn Féin had begun to win a significant number of by-elections in 1917. 5 I take my definitions for these somewhat nebulous terms of humour from the *Concise Oxford English Dictionary* (1995).

of the September 1914 *Irish Freedom*.[6] While advanced nationalists were united in their opposition to the war, they displayed a great diversity in their presentation of anti-war propaganda. Of the six Dublin-based[7] advanced nationalist and labour newspapers with national circulation in 1914, only one, the extremist IRB *Irish Freedom*, presented a consistently absurd view of the war. Arthur Griffith's two papers, *Sinn Féin* and *Eire Ireland*, occasionally produced jokes about the war and recruiting, but Griffith's bitterness about the war and general intellectual tone precluded much humour. The same tenor was evident in the *Irish Volunteer*. Edited first by Laurence de Lacey and then later by Bulmer Hobson and Eoin MacNeill, the newspaper prided itself on being the official voice of 'Ireland's Army', and thus took itself and its journalism very seriously. As the *Irish Citizen* focused mainly on feminist issues within the war, this left only Jim Larkin's labour paper the *Irish Worker*. Here again we see the appearance of humour about the war, but humour in a predominantly visual form.

Japes, jokes, and snide poems about the British were common in the pre-war *Irish Freedom*. The immediate equation of the war with British imperialism quickly exposed the war effort to humorous denigration. The support of the Irish Parliamentary Party for recruiting, and the heavily censored and constantly cheerful news about the war carried by English and conservative Irish papers became obvious targets for the mocking irony of nationalist comic writers. The most wide-ranging piece of ironic humour produced by *Irish Freedom* in these early days of the war was their two issue series 'War Notes', which were claimed to have been produced from a special arrangement with the 'Associated London Press'. Very little was sacred to the author[8] who wrote these mocking parodies of official news digests from the front. O'Higgins made ludicrous remarks that echoed the optimistic tone of official reports, claiming that the BEF destroyed a German army of 60,000 men while losing only their commander-in-chief's brandy flask,[9] and giving the Royal Navy credit for destroying the German navy twice-over with the loss of only one cruiser to the floating carcass of a seahorse.[10]

Any opportunity to ridicule the recruiting efforts of the Irish Parliamentary Party was seized with great alacrity by advanced nationalists. The apparent hypocrisy of the Parliamentarians was excoriated. Advanced nationalists especially disliked Thomas Kettle, who volunteered for the army in October 1914,

'Irony': an expression of meaning, often humorous or sarcastic, by the use of language of a different or opposite tendency; 'absurd': wildly unreasonable, illogical, or inappropriate; 'mockery': derision or ridicule; 'sarcasm': the use of bitter or wounding remarks. 6 BNL, *IF*, September 1914, p. 1. 7 While the *Irish Volunteer* was initially edited in Enniscorthy, I count it here as a Dublin newspaper, as editorial control soon passed to Bulmer Hobson and Eoin MacNeill in Dublin. 8 These notes were published anonymously, but in *War Humour and Other Atrocities*, published in 1915, they are re-printed and credited to 'Brian na Banban' (Brian O'Higgins). 9 BNL, *IF*, September 1914, p. 6. 10 Ibid., September and October 1914.

When the " T Kettle " Sings ;
OR,
The Professor on the War Spout.

6.1 *When the 'T' Kettle Sings* (*Quiz*, October 1915)

considering him an alcoholic and a savage foe of separatism.[11] K. O'Doherty called him 'Tommy Atkins Kettle' in *Eire Ireland*,[12] and the obvious pun on his last name was mocked further by Gordon Brewster (regular editorial cartoonist for the *Irish Weekly Independent*) in the monthly humour magazine the *Quiz* (figure 6.1).[13] Even Kettle's volunteering did not excuse him from the pens of advanced nationalist propagandists. Griffith pointed out that both Kettle's commission and Stephen Gwynn's enlistment as a private were something of a sham. Gwynn was used first as an ambulance man and Kettle as an interpreter, thus avoiding any possibility of their being exposed to enemy fire.[14]

11 Maume, 1999, p. 163.   12 BNL, *EI*, 24.11.14, p. 2.   13 NLI, *Quiz*, October 1915, p. 5.
14 BNL, *EI*, 23.11.14, p. 2, and 30.11.14, p. 2.

In keeping with their more serious tone, *Sinn Féin* and *Eire-Ireland* rarely used direct humour to attack the recruiting efforts of the Redmondites. Not so *Irish Freedom*, which made the recruiting campaign a central part of their parody 'War Notes'. In September, readers learned that Redmond, T.P. O'Connor and John Dillon had all volunteered for active service. A month later, Dillon was already a Field Marshal. A custom-made uniform was being made for him, complete with a capacious haversack slung from his hip to hold his recruiting speeches.[15] Dillon's patriotism clearly inspired his fellow Irish MPs, as twenty-five promptly volunteered, so long as they were allowed to serve at Westminster, be regularly supplied with tea on the terraces, and wear their silk hats in action.[16]

The en-masse volunteering of Irish MPs had a few disadvantages. The Home Rule Bill was placed on the Statute Book, which remained in London, but the bill 'seemed to like its new position', and visitors from Ireland who applied to Redmond could view the bill from 10–5 Monday to Friday.[17] Indeed, despite the troubles caused by the war, the war notes in *Irish Freedom* remained supremely ironic, seemingly always optimistic and unfazed by anything. The Empire was to be kept safe, not by the men volunteering throughout Ireland for the BEF, but rather because 100,000 commanders of the Irish Volunteers[18] had been assigned, most of who were captains or colonels.[19] The Ballyraimeis (or 'Nonsense Town')[20] Board of Guardians, a fearsome body, unanimously passed a resolution warning the German army not to come near its town at the 'peril of its existence'. Allying with the local district council, they sent a final ultimatum to Germany notifying them that the town was now at its full war strength.[21] A month later, these brave men were joined by the Ballycrawler Old Age Pension's Bureau, which pledged, following a meeting attended by the clerk and two other members, to support fully John Redmond's recruiting campaign.[22]

Jim Larkin's socialist labour paper, the *Irish Worker*, gives one another interesting perspective on the use of humour against the early recruiting campaign. No friend of the more right-wing advanced nationalist groups, Larkin nevertheless detested the war and wished for Ireland to remain neutral, in

---

15 BNL, *IF*, September 1914, p. 6, and October 1914, p. 6.   16 BNL, Ibid., October 1914, p. 6.
17 BNL, Ibid.   18 Pre-Split Irish Volunteers, so therefore equivalent to the National Volunteers (post 24 September, 1914). The tendency of the National Volunteers to exaggerate their numbers following this split was gleefully marked by Francis Sheehy-Skeffington in the November issue of *Irish Freedom*, in which he pointed out in a letter to the editor that the latest lists released of National Volunteer members were incorrect. 'In this list, no fewer than sixty-four names appear twice, and three names no less than four times each ... it is easy to compile long lists on this principle' (BNL, *IF*, November 1914, p. 8).   19 BNL, *IF*, September 1914, p. 6.   20 This echoes other 'fool' towns in folk traditions around the world. The most famous perhaps is Chelm, although a better example would be the Russian-Jewish town 'Glupsk', or 'Nonsense', about which many Yiddish stories are written. My thanks to Dr Jeremy Dauber (Columbia University) for this point.   21 BNL, *IF*, September 1914, p. 6.   22 BNL, *IF*, October 1914, p. 6.

alliance with working men around the world. The *Irish Worker* published regular political cartoons on its front page, all by Ernest Kavanagh,[23] and from August to December 1914, these cartoons presented a caricatured chronology of Redmond's recruiting efforts.

Redmond and United Irish League leader William O'Brien appear in late September 1914 in the cartoon 'The Redmond-O'Brien Press Gang'. Dressed as Napoleonic sailors, they drag an unwilling Irish Volunteer towards Lord Kitchener, who stands outside the War Office, saying 'This way to the European Shambles'. The implications of this cartoon are clear, especially when viewed alongside the title of Maeve Cavanagh's poem, 'The Coming of the Irish Judas and his Paymaster', which appears underneath the cartoon. The men who were loyal to Ireland, who were to split off from the National Volunteers two days after this cartoon appeared, would not listen to the blandishments and bribes of the British. To fulfil the promise of recruits he made in return for his payment of Home Rule, Redmond is forced to press men into service.[24] The alignment of Redmond with the ur-traitor Judas is ubiquitous in early nationalist propaganda. Every major advanced nationalist paper at this time ran an editorial about Redmond's recruiting efforts, (originally printed in *Sinn Féin*) entitled 'The Irish Judas', and 'Judas' was used in art as well to signify the Parliamentary leader.

The climax of the Irish autumn recruiting campaign came on 25 September 1914, when Prime Minister Asquith spoke with Redmond at a great recruiting meeting in Dublin's Mansion House. Unfortunately for the Redmondites, this meeting was somewhat of a failure. Asquith attended under heavy guard, and very few recruits volunteered following the meeting.[25] D.P. Moran, whose paper the *Leader* was under close surveillance by the British government, was forbidden entry, despite claiming that he was opposed to Sinn Féin. In retaliation, he published a list of all the Orangemen and Freemasons in attendance at the meeting.[26] Kavanagh slipped into the meeting, and managed to produce caricatures of some of the famous personages involved. Writing three years later in the *Catholic Bulletin*, J.J. O'Kelly claimed that these 'racy cartoons of the different speakers not only aroused the liveliest interest at the time but, in the face of denials subsequently attempted, contributed to stereotype the parts played by Irish politicians in the recruitment campaign then seriously initiated'.[27] Kavanagh's caricatures mocked all the prominent men at the meeting. 'Judas Empire' Redmond appears, as does the 'Melancholy Humbug', John Dillon.

23 Ernest Kavanagh ('EK'), a leading nationalist and labour cartoonist in Dublin from 1911 to 1916. Much of his work was published in *Irish Freedom*, *Irish Worker*, and *Worker's Republic*. Brother of Maeve Kavanagh [or Cavanagh], the 'poetess of the Revolution', he joined the Irish Citizen Army when it went out during Easter Week, and was killed on the steps of Liberty Hall aged 32 (information from the *Catholic Bulletin*, December 1917, pp. 780–1).   24 BNL, *IW*, 26.9.14, p. 1.   25 BNL, *SF*, 3.10.14, p. 3.   26 Ibid.   27 Bod., *The Catholic Bulletin*, December 1917, p. 781.

British government officials too are on the scene, Asquith, Birrell, and the doddering Viceroy, Lord Aberdeen.[28]

The mocking images of Redmond were even crueller in the later cartoon 'Judas' March on Wexford!'[29] Redmond, dressed like a little child in ludicrous soldier's uniform and sword that drags on the ground, leads on his hobby horse. Behind swarm a motley crowd of his supporters, including 'Stephen the Stuffer' or Stephen Gwynn, accused by advanced nationalists of stuffing ballot boxes, Lorcan G. Sherlock, the pro-British Lord Mayor of Dublin, who had recently accused advanced nationalist propagandists of taking German gold for their services, and members of the 'All for William League' that supported Redmond's sometime ally William O'Brien of the United Irish League.

When not actively recruiting men, Redmond and his followers encouraged civilians to participate in fund-raising drives and other charity events to benefit the soldiers at the front. The actual charitable efforts were undertaken mainly by Anglo-Irish and 'Castle Catholic' families,[30] and were brutally attacked throughout advanced nationalist newspapers. Redmond's patriotic speeches had quick effect, *Irish Freedom* claimed, for the Dowager Lady Duffer immediately began to collect cigarette cards to send soldiers at the front, while Queen Mary and Lady Londonderry formed a volunteer ambulance corps dedicated to patching up the differences between Liberals and Tories.[31] Lady Aberdeen, wife of the Viceroy, was completing her collection of Irish microbes,[32] which were to be launched among the Germans at the soonest possible moment.[33] An anonymous letter to the editor entitled 'Gather 'em Up!' asked *Irish Freedom*'s 'patriotic', 'large-hearted', and 'imperial minded' readers to give to charities supporting 'brave defenders of the Empire' who were going to join the ranks of the missing at the front. Desired items, which should be thoroughly disinfected before leaving Ireland, included:

> Dress shirts, pianos, boiled potatoes (mashed, if possible), champagne, packs of playing cards, gold or silver coins, boxes of cigars or cigarettes, soap for the sore feet of the soldiers, portraits of Messrs. John Redmond and John Dillon, motor-cycles, chocolates, lucky bags, notepaper (scented), Eau de Cologne, socks (with flowered clocks on ankles), words of music of the song 'It's a long, long way to Berlin', war maps to guide the missing

---

28 BNL, *IW*, 3.10.14, p. 1. 29 BNL, *IW*, 10.10.14, p. 1. 30 Sir Matthew Nathan met frequently with people involved in such work, including Mrs Foran of Listowel, who reported regularly to him on the state of Sinn Féin in County Kerry and was wont to assure him that she could take care of the Sinn Féiners herself. Nathan also was a regular attendee at Red Cross concerts in Dublin, most of which he considered to be '2nd rate' (cf. Nathan MS 467–69, Interviews, Ireland, Vols. 1–3, & Nathan MS 50, Diary 1915). 31 BNL, *IF*, September 1914, p. 6. 32 Ishbel Aberdeen was known as 'Queen T.B'. for her charitable efforts to combat this disease in Ireland. 33 BNL, *IF* October 1914, p. 6.

soldiers back to their regiments, prayer books (with or without prayers), vaseline, bottled stout, ham sandwiches, and miniature Union Jacks.[34]

Lady Aberdeen's actual efforts to form sock donation and knitting clubs for soldiers on the front line were mocked in the ballad 'Song of the Socks' by leading writer Brian O'Higgins ('Brian na Banban'). Sung to the tune of 'God Save Ireland', it ran in part:

> God save the King and God save Ireland!
> Get a sack and start the work to-day;
> Pick up all the socks you meet,
> For the English Tommies' feet,
> When they're running from the Germans far away![35]

British censorship of the Dublin advanced nationalist press forced the advanced nationalist propagandists into more subtle means and methods of propaganda production and dissemination.[36] Supporters of the republican cause in America had less to worry about. Memoranda were circulated to intelligence staff in Dublin Castle after the New York *Times* and *Herald Tribune* both reported in October 1915 that a Mr Dixie Hines, manager of the 'Irish Actors', 'admits that he has been offered German money to produce an Irish Home Rule play written specially to rouse feeling against Great Britain'. In the same month, Mr Denis Spillesey, head of the 'United Irish American Societies' boasted that he had sent large quantities of arms to Ireland in a private yacht with the help of Sir Roger Casement. When asked by reporters whether the 'German expedition would sail over the British Fleet or dive under it, ... he, with a wave of the hand, brushed away that difficulty as too trifling to discuss'.[37]

Until the Easter Rising, *ad hoc* censorship by the British, organized mainly through the military intelligence office of Major I.H. Price, or through Dublin's G Division of the DMP, remained quite effective, although humorous propaganda still managed to reach the streets. Maeve Cavanagh published her second poetry collection, *Sheaves of Revolt*, in 1914. The book avoided the notice of Castle authorities for a year, despite including such intensely phrased anti-recruiting jingles as *Colonel Downing's 7th Pals Battalion*. 'Colonel Downing' attacked the recruitment of a Dublin 'Pals' Brigade with vicious humour, echoing the old Irish lament *Johnny I Hardly Knew Ye*:

34 BNL, Ibid., November 1914, p. 6.   35 BNL, Ibid., November 1914, p. 7.   36 Cf. Novick, 1997a and 1999.   37 NLI MS 26159: Brennan Papers, Official Memoranda, 1915, re Suppression of seditious newspapers, German intrigues among Irish-Americans, and Irish-American groups. No evidence can be found for Dixie Hines' claim. However, the New York *Tribune* reported the plan of 'General Spellisy' [*sic*] on 13 September 1915 to invade Ireland with 400 thousand men in order to resist conscription. A friend of Spillesey's denied this report on 12 October 1915.

> So hurry up and take the 'bob',
> The 'Butcher' cannot wait;
> The German guns are talking
> At a most terrific rate.
> And if you should crawl back
> Minus arm or minus leg,
> You'll get leave to roam your city
> To sell matches – or to beg.[38]

Despite Cavanagh's efforts to stem recruiting, and the humorous and ironic accounts of the war produced with such profusion in these early months of the war, men still joined Col. Downing's 'Brigade', just as they did the rest of the Tenth and Sixteenth Irish Divisions, and the 36th Ulster Division. In August 1915, following hard on the heels of the men of the Dublin and Munster Fusiliers who had been cut to shreds in the sea off Gallipoli in April 1915, men of Col. Downing's Brigade landed at Suvla Bay just north of the Gallipoli peninsula in an effort to draw Turkish defenders away from the beaches at the southernmost tip of the peninsula. The landings were initially successful but, as the new troops sat roasting in the hot sun, Turkish defenders returned and re-fortified their positions along ridges above the beach-head. When the attack was finally launched off the beaches on 8 August, massacre resulted for the Irish and ANZAC troops who had come so many thousands of miles. These losses, coupled with the destruction and wastage of the war in general, which had dragged bloodily into its twelfth month with casualty lists the only thing that grew inexorably, harmed recruiting far more than propaganda alone ever could.

II

When the reality of slaughter on the battlefield began to sink in in Ireland through the summer and autumn of 1915, recruiting figures began to drop away. As has been discussed elsewhere, propagandists harnessed a growing popular frustration with the war, changing their own attitude towards Irish soldiers from denigration to sympathy and respect. The violent events of 1915 helped change not only general attitudes to the war, but also how the war was depicted in humorous propaganda.

1915 was the apogee of humorous propaganda during the war. The first wave of advanced nationalist newspapers with national circulation had mostly disappeared after the British seizures of *Irish Freedom* and the *Irish Worker*, but propagandists quickly launched new newspapers. By the spring of 1915 the *Irish*

---

38 Maeve Cavanagh, *Sheaves of Revolt* (Dublin, 1914), pp. 36–7.

Volunteer and the *Spark* were publishing regularly,[39] and the summer saw the beginnings of Griffith's *Nationality* and the radical AOH journal the *Hibernian*. Seamus Upton's *Honesty*, 'an outspoken scrap of paper', would follow in the autumn of 1915. In other media, nationalist humorists discovered new outlets for their work. Recently published comedic poems and war notes by Brian O'Higgins, 'Myles Malone', and 'Willie Wagtail' were published in the anthology *War Humour and Other Atrocities*. The monthly comic journals the *Quiz* and its descendant *Irish Fun*, edited by Brian O'Higgins, appeared on the scene, created as a 'tonic in type' for the 'millions of readers' whose nerves were shattered by the war and political events in Ireland.[40] Under O'Higgins' direction the magazine would produce the best work of renowned political cartoonists such as J.J. O'Hea ('Spex') and Michael Reidy ('Miceal') for the rest of the war, and put forward a consistently anti-war and anti-Irish Parliamentary Party line.

The linkage in *Irish Fun* between the war and the Irish Parliamentary Party forms the keynote for the change seen in the style of humour during 1915. As volunteer Irish casualties mounted in Gallipoli, Mesopotamia, and the Western Front, fewer and fewer jokes were found about the war, and the irony and absurdity which characterized the humour of 1914 became far more bitter.

Most importantly, jokes about the Irish troops ceased. An important distinction was drawn, both in comedic and serious propaganda, between the activities of the Irish troops at the front, which were both admired and pitied, and their efforts in recruiting, which continued to be mocked. Lieutenant Michael O'Leary, V.C., was widely insulted in the advanced nationalist press for his efforts in aiding recruiting.[41] *Honesty* mocked him with the fictional character of Private Pat McGinty, V.C., who joined the British army fresh out of jail, won the Victoria Cross for being wounded, and then proceeded to travel around the United Kingdom completely drunk, insulting Englishmen at recruiting meetings.[42]

The continued recruiting activities of Redmondites came in for ceaseless mockery. John Redmond himself travelled to visit Irish troops on the Western Front in the late autumn of 1915. While there he addressed various regiments, toured a model trench, and even fired a howitzer at the German lines. Advanced nationalists greeted his actions with disgust. Comedic propagandists delighted in mocking his incongruous behaviour, both in poems and cartoons. 'Namesake' wrote a ballad 'General John Redmond' in which Redmond boasts of his part in winning the war, claiming 'I fired the big shot that blew thim [*sic*] all to

39 As discussed in the introduction, the *Irish Volunteer* had never ceased publication.
40 NLI, *Irish Fun*, October 1915, p. 2.   41 BNL, *Spark*, 18 July 1915, 12 December 1915; 23 January 1916.   42 BNL, *Hon*, 6, 13, 27 November, 4, 18 December 1915, and also in Maume, 1999, p. 163. It is interesting to note that by insulting British civilians, Pat McGinty gains back a measure of his nationalist spirit (or pride) – or perhaps, he never quite lost all of this ethos. The name 'Pat McGinty' is also likely to be a reference to the older ballad *Paddy McGinty's Goat*.

Timbuctoo!/Get ready a big goold [sic] V.C. to hang upon me chest/For wipin' out the Huns that held the trinches [sic] in the West!'[43] Michael Reidy's cartoon in *Irish Fun* (figure 6.2) showed Redmond anxiously firing a pop-gun at a tin German soldier while Irish troops roared with laughter.[44]

While recruiting continued to be widely mocked, the war itself lost much of its humour in 1915. Jokes about the actions of the war turned very grim, and the humour became a mix of anger and despair. James Connolly declared in June that the latest reports showed the Allies had captured 3 yards 2 feet and 7 inches of German territory, and the Germans then recaptured 3 yards, 1 foot and 11 inches of ground. 'Thus', he wrote, 'it is easy to calculate how long it will take to get to Berlin'.[45] Arthur Griffith mocked the tendency of pro-war newspapers to report only allied success. In November 1915, he wondered how the editors who published such consistently false news 'do not go insane'.[46] A Gordon Brewster cartoon (figure 6.3) from the October 1915 issue of the *Quiz* showed that nationalist propagandists were already depicting conscription as certain death.[47] The ultimate manifestation of anti-war humour in 1915 appeared in J.J. Burke's direct and bitter satire of Irish recruiting posters, published in the *Worker's Republic*. Burke changed one or two words in each poster title[48] to show what he thought would be the certain result of enlistment:

Irishmen! Join an Irish Regiment *to die*!

Is your best boy in the *Casuality* [sic] *Lists*?

What will you say to your children when they ask you what you did *with your arms and legs* in the Great War? *If you are not there, what will your Wife say*?

Will you go or must *the poor English*?

An Appeal to gallant Irishmen could be put SOFT SOAP FOR THE DIRTY IRISH!

England's threat *to Ireland* – the Amending Bill! – *the division of Ulster!* – or *the Ulster Division*!

Step inside could be changed into *Commit Suicide*, and *Recruiting Office* SHOULD be turned into *Lunatic Asylum*![49]

1915 can be seen as a year of great change in humorous attitudes to the war itself. Following the mounting casualties of Irish volunteers in Gallipoli and elsewhere, propagandists grew more reluctant to joke about the war, and turned their comedic attentions mainly to the recruiting efforts of the Irish Parliamentary Party. Irish troops, and the actions in which they were involved,

---

43 BNL, *Spark*, 20.2.16, pp. 3–4.   44 NLI, *Irish Fun*, Christmas and New Year's 1916, p. 55.
45 NLI, *WR*, 26.6.15, p. 1.   46 BNL, *Nat*, 27.11.15, pp. 5–6.   47 NLI, *Quiz*, October 1915, p. 7.   48 The originals can be found in Trinity College Dublin's collection of Irish Recruiting Posters.   49 NLI, *WR*, 23.10.15, p. 2.

Humour in advanced nationalist propaganda 199

"DON'T LARF, CHUMMIES! THE BLOKE'S DOIN' 'IS LITTLE BIT.
(The Leader of the Irish race says that during his recent visit to Flanders he fired a 9-inch gun.)

6.2 *'Don't Larf, Chummies!'* (*Irish Fun*, Christmas and New Year, 1916)

were no longer mocked. But if the actions of the war away from Ireland changed the attitude to Irish troops, and to the war itself, what effect did the Easter Rising, a moment in which the horrors of war were directly brought home to the domestic population of Ireland, have on humorous depictions of soldiers and the war?

Not surprisingly, following a Rising in which regular British troops had fought Irish rebels in the streets of Dublin, far less pity was wasted on the mounting casualties of the British troops. Brutally, humorous propaganda began to revel in the destruction of those who had fought the Irish. Perhaps the most extreme example of this is Seamus O'Sullivan's ('Do Capa') ballad *The Rats Came Out*, from the summer of 1916. It tells the story of the battle of Jutland, the Pyrrhic victory won by the British Grand Fleet against the German High Seas Fleet in the North Sea on 31 May 1916. The battle left the British with dominance of the North Sea, but at a high cost. The Royal Navy lost 6,000 men to the German's 2,500 casualties, and more British than German ships were sunk. While later histories would change opinion, the battle was greeted in 1916 as a British defeat. O'Sullivan drew an explicit link between some of the ships which sank at Jutland and the gunboats which had shelled Dublin a month earlier during the Easter Rising:[50]

50 Although he was in fact incorrect. The gunboat HMS *Helga*, which shelled Liberty Hall

The Quiz

"ON THE ROAD."

HARVESTER: "Any work to-day, Pat?"
PAT: "No, Con; go back and tell Northcliffe and Company they sent you here on a fool's errand."

[At numerous public meetings throughout the country resolutions have been carried unanimously denouncing any attempt to introduce Conscription into Ireland.]

6.3 'On the Road'. (*Quiz*, October 1915)

Queen Mary had a thousand men their like we'll never see again
Because they're food for fishes now and cods dislike saur-kruat [*sic*]
They got bowled out in a jiffey twas quite different from the Liffey
and not at all like Liberty Hall the time the rats came out.[51]

The Germans had not been able to help the Irish rebels properly at Easter, but they helped the Irish victims of the Rising to have to their revenge from beyond the grave a month later:

And then they gave 'What For' to Black Prince and Warrior[52]
And our claims to rule the waves these German beggars flout
Between ourselves I'm free to say, Twere better far we stayed away
From Jutland's Shore that day in May the German rats came out

MORAL

The blood of murdered Irishmen appeals to Heaven once again
The Fleet that shelled old Dublin Town have got a clean knock-out
True Irish hearts will ever pray that God will speed the coming day
When Britain's fleet is swept away when next the rats come out.
May it be soon and sudden.[53]

Other propagandists combined this attitude to the British with a general anti-war message. By the winter of 1917, with no end to the war in sight and the slaughterhouse of the Somme, on whose chopping block two Irish divisions were destroyed, behind them, propagandists cried out against the futility and waste of King George's war. *A Ballad of European History*, which was to be 'Prescribed instead of Irish, 1916–17, for Teachers under the National Board',[54] contained an A-Z of Current Affairs for teachers to use in the classroom. The entire alphabet was slanted against the British and allied war effort, including:

A is for Asquith, not easily caught. Shook hands with Sinn Feiners and said he forgot.[55]

Actions involving the British and Commonwealth forces were mocked, though the author made sure to exclude any mention of Irish troops' involvement. British actions at Easter were especially excoriated:

T stands for Turk – the unspeakable One. From Gallipoli sands made the Anzacs all run.

and other sections of the Liffey Quays at Easter was not part of the Grand Fleet. 51 TCD, Samuels 5/1b. 52 Two of the British ships sunk with great loss of life by the German fleet. 53 TCD, Samuels 5/1b. 54 NLI MS 5637: Robert Barton Papers, Scrapbook, vol. I, fols. 50–1. 55 Ibid.

> Y for New Ypres, which stands on the Liffey, By British Huns shelled to the ground in a jiffy.[56]

In the midst of this humorous piece, a very different tone appeared when the fighting realities of war were discussed:

> M stands for munitions, and murder, and mud, Manure pits of men, and muck marshes of blood.[57]

Here was the fact of war, the 'face of battle', as experienced not just by Englishmen who had allegedly murdered women and children in Dublin, but by Irishmen who had volunteered to join the British Army. Mocking the Irishmen who served in the war appears to have been a taboo subject with all Irish propagandists. Ironically, as Jane Leonard and Peter Hart have pointed out, a service record made one a pariah in post-revolutionary Ireland, and could lead to beatings or execution by the IRA.[58] But mocking these men and the sacrifices they made was implicitly forbidden during the war itself. Indeed, any form of self-abnegation, whether that meant insulting Irishmen who joined up, or in any way caricaturising the nationalist argument, is for the most part absent from this propaganda. The bitter anger of later humorous propaganda is reserved for those who encouraged the men to join.

The reluctance to write about Irish casualties did not stop the Irish propagandists from sardonically ridiculing British war aims. Sean O'Casey, whose first major publication was a collection of propagandistic ballads entitled *Songs of the Wren* (Feb./March 1918), published his song *We've Captured the Cave of Machpelah* in *Songs of the Wren no. 2* (April – June [?] 1918).[59] Written between December 1917 and the spring of 1918, *Machpelah* jeers at the sort of 'triumphs' lauded by the British penny press:

> Hurrah! For John Bull and for Uncle Sam –
> We're losin' the War, but we don't care a damn.
> For we've taken the tomb of poor Abraham,
> An' we captur'd the Cave of Machpelah![60]

---

56 Ibid. 57 Ibid. 58 Leonard, 1997; Peter Hart, 'How to Inform on the IRA and Get Away With It (in Cork, 1919–1923)', paper to Seminar in Irish History, Prof. R.F. Foster, Convenor, Hertford College, Oxford, 21 October 1997. 59 Dating for these publications is taken from theories found in Ronald Ayling and Michael J. Durkan, *Sean O'Casey: A Bibliography* (London, 1978). O'Casey had published labour pamphlets before the war, but only became well-known with the publication of *Songs of the Wren*. For more on O'Casey's early years, see Robert Hogan (ed.), *Feathers from the Green Crow: Sean O'Casey, 1905–1925* (London, 1963). 60 TCD, Samuels 5/50.

Unlike the earlier anti-war absurdist propaganda of 1914, *Machpelah* directly attacked a particular action of the British Army. Taking the good news of a minor British victory, O'Casey is quick to point out that nevertheless the war is being lost, and that thousands of guns (and by extension thousands of men) have been lost to the more efficient German war machine. This is a far cry from joking that a sea horse sunk a British ship, or that the Commander-in-Chief had had his brandy flask snatched by an Austrian.[61]

III

How did the Easter Rising influence humorous depictions of British domestic policy in Ireland? The 'sacrificial' deaths of rebel leaders in Dublin during and after the Easter Rising spawned a veritable micro-industry of serious propagandistic commemorative kitsch. By Christmas 1916, a free-spending nationalist could buy colour prints of 'Inside the GPO' and 'His Easter Offering' ('A remarkable picture, depicting a dead Volunteer, having given his life to the cause of Irish Independence, lying at the feet of Kathleen Ni Houlihan. The tricolour flag is delicately and artistically introduced, and this picture ranks as one of the triumphs of Irish Republican artistry'). 'Dublin After the Bombardment', which was considered to be especially suitable for framing, incongruously featured a tank in front of the blazing ruins of the GPO.[62] Wealthier nationalists could do their Christmas shopping with J.J. Walsh of Dublin, who offered badges, beads, tricolour rosaries, jewellery, stationery, and rosettes of nationalist symbols.[63]

Humorous propaganda for the most part avoided the subject of Easter Week itself, for mocking an episode already sanctified was even more taboo than mocking Irish soldiers on the Western Front. However, the imposition of martial law during the Easter Rising, the en-masse deportations of Sinn Féin members following the Rising, and the general perception of increased brutality by the British government in Ireland provided ample fodder for the satirists of British policy. Under more stringent and arbitrary law humorous responses increased, reacting to the coalition of the 'ridiculous and terrifying'.[64]

Curiously, what we have in Ireland after 1916 is more the *perception* of increased arbitrariness, rather than the reality of such. While martial law was imposed in the middle of the Rising, and over 1,000 people were detained or deported immediately following, British authorities actually relaxed their attitude to the production of propaganda. A hint of this can be seen from the advertisements from reputable publishers cited above, who touted their wares

61 BNL, *IF*, September and October 1914. 62 TCD, Samuels 5/52. 63 TCD, Samuels 5/54. 64 Gerould, 1978, p. 4.

openly in Dublin. Occasionally, these publishing houses would be raided. Fergus O'Connor's establishment on Eccles Street was raided in December 1917, and sixteen seditious publications were seized, including songs by Sean O'Casey, copies of Roger Casement's speech from the dock, and commemorative postcards of Easter Week. Most of the items were destroyed two weeks later on order of the military authorities.[65] Such direct action was rare following the Rising. Disputes arose in June 1916 between General Sir John Maxwell, Dublin Castle, and the Home Office in England, when Maxwell wanted to clamp down on the sale of seditious literature and photographs, which he felt kept alive 'the feelings of disloyalty and unrest which culminated in the late Rising'.[66] Action was discouraged by Walter Edgeworth-Johnstone of the Dublin Metropolitan Police, who thought that it would be impossible to enforce any Defence of the Realm Regulation with regards to the photos, and that he could only try to discourage the sale of published items. This would have been enough for Maxwell, but then Home Secretary Herbert Samuel got wind of the controversy, and wrote to the Prime Minister and Maxwell strongly condemning any new promulgation of the original order. He felt that any action would cause so much unrest in the country that it would outweigh any benefit of seizing some seditious literature. Supported by the Prime Minister in this, the matter rested there, and propagandists were virtually free[67] to carry on their activities.[68]

Regardless of the laxer reality, what mattered to the propagandists was the perceived harshness of British policy. Propaganda in itself, like advertising, plays to the group psychology of its target audience. If the general attitude in the nation leaned towards a belief that the British were oppressive,[69] then this would be exploited in propaganda. 'Sliabh Ruadh' took the lyrical old tune 'The Mountains of Mourne', and waxed satiric about the British policy of detention at Mountjoy Prison in Dublin:

> In Dublin's big town, there are first-class hotels,
> Where they give board and lodging to all the big swells,
> There's blinds on the windows and bells on the door,
> And a beautiful carpet laid down on the floor;
> But the grandest of all, and 'tis now in full swing,
> I was there once myself, and I am able to tell
> That there's no 'digs' in Dublin like Mountjoy Hotel![70]

65 TCD, Samuels 1/5.   66 NLI MS 26154: Joseph Brennan Papers, Memos etc. re Seditious Leaflets and Photographs, June 1916.   67 British officials did investigate news-agents for selling seditious publications in 1916 (NA, CSORP 1916 7145); warned manufacturers of 'Sinn Féin' badges (NA CSORP 1916 10205, *Nat*, 13.10.17); and seized copies of Thomas MacDonagh's 'Last Address', prosecuting the printers and newsagents through which it was disseminated. (NA CSORP 1916 10768, 10965, 11263).   68 NLI MS 26154: Joseph Brennan Papers, Memos etc. re Seditious Leaflets and Photographs, June 1916.   69 Cf. PRO, Colonial Office Papers, CO 904/157: Intelligence Notes, Ireland, 1916–18, for monthly support of this contention from counties around Ireland.   70 TCD, Samuels 5/104.

Sliabh Ruadh produced a doubly ironic message. First, in his sarcastic comparison of a prison with a hotel, and then, more subtly, poking fun at the necessary 'rite of passage' which a spell in Mountjoy or another prison provided for the new leaders of nationalist Ireland. Peadar O Cearnaigh [or Kearney] took similar imagery a step further in his popular song *Dora*, published by The Art Depot in 1918. This is one of few ballads written at the time that was set to a new tune, and luckily, an edition survives which contains words and music. The melody is a lyrical waltz, with a range easily sung by an untrained voice. O Cearnaigh made explicit the genderization and personification of the Defence of the Realm Act (DORA), and with bitter sarcasm wrote about the identity of Ireland's new love and how she must be treated:

> It's Dora, Dora
> Oh, how we worship our Dora
> She came here to teach our young men how to live.
> How to forget, aye, and how to forgive,
> And should we Dora
> Ever displease or annoy,
> She'll treat us quite well in a first-class hotel
> With the beautiful name of Mountjoy.[71]

The irresistible pun of 'Defence of the Realm Act' with the common female name Dora highlights some of the gender issues raised by this propaganda. The cover sheet to the first edition of *Dora*, subtitled 'A Love Ditty on True Blue West British Lines', shows an artist's image of Dora. Dora (figure 6.4) is a pert, chic woman, dressed in the height of 1918 fashion, right down to the expensive hat with feathered plume, and showing a daring degree of slim leg. The breast piece of her dress is part of a Union Jack, around which she wears a chain, symbolizing chastity, enforced Union, and imprisonment. Her skirt is made of parchment declarations, reading 'Martial Law', 'Solitary Confinement', and 'Plank Beds'. Dora, holding keys, stands in front of the gate to Mountjoy Prison. The posters on the wall leave no doubt as to the source of this propaganda, and it is clear from the use of the phrase 'Hottentots' that the artist was familiar with the current nationalist slang term for a Sinn Féiner.[72] The image is placed in the

71 TCD, Samuels 5/145.   72 PRO, Colonial Office Papers, CO 904/164/4: Postal Censorship, Irish Internees, 1918, 'Code Words and Nicknames used in the Correspondence of Irish Internees'. Lord Salisbury infamously likened the Irish to Hottentots in the midst of the Home Rule debates in 1886. Speaking at St James' Hall, Lord Salisbury remarked, 'You would not confide free representative institutions to the Hottentots, for instance'. He later denied any implication of similarity (cited in L.P. Curtis, *Coercion and Conciliation in Ireland 1880–1892: A Study in Conservative Unionism* [Princeton, NJ, 1963], pp. 103–4). My thanks to Ian Sheehy and Dr Patrick Maume for their assistance in tracking down this reference. It is possible as well that the Sinn Féin nickname sprang from a more recent reference to Hottentots, which occurred when a Major Bowen, presiding at a 1917 Court Martial in Cork,

picture plane of the cover sheet as a central window or peep-hole to which the viewer's attention is immediately drawn. Surrounding this depiction of British oppression, however, the artist has placed swirling Celtic designs reminiscent of early Gaelic masterpieces like the Book of Kells. O Cearnaigh's name is in Gaelic script, and shamrocks and crosses litter the textual sections of the picture. The publication information is also presented in a mock Gaelic script, leaving only the price (in English money), the title, and the catch phrase in Romanic typeface.

The Defence of the Realm Act was perceived as having arbitrary power over the lives of nationalist Irish men. In an effort to combat this power, O Cearnaigh feminises the law, thus placing the act into a position of subordination to the men of Ireland. Despite this traditional role, however, enough of the power of the Act remains in its female personification to turn 'Dora' into a sexual predator:

> She came her among us to kiss us and hug us,
> And oh! how she cuddles us all.
> Her blue eyes are beaming, like two bay'nets gleaming,
> She brought us a supply of the same.[73]

In contemporary Sinn Féin slang, punishments incurred under the Defence of the Realm Act were referred to as 'Dora's caresses'.[74]

Other visual cartoons also showed female images of Ireland. These images were placed in traditional poses of submission and endangerment, threatened or imprisoned by the brutal British. In one such cartoon, from 1917, Ireland is a completely naked woman, with long black hair, who kneels with head lowered at the foot of steps. A harness is bound tightly to her breasts, attaching her to a pole marked 'British Imperialism'. Luckily for this helpless woman a man in pseudo-Celtic tribal garb has leapt to the top of the stairs and is swinging a sword marked 'Sinn Féin' at the rope that binds her.[75] Another sexualized Erin is also being tied up in a later cartoon entitled 'Conscription'[76] (figure 6.5). As can be seen, Erin is dressed in a more classical style, but the artist has still managed to drape her toga revealingly over her chest and leave very little of her leg to the imagination. This Erin is slightly more powerful, as she is struggling alone with John Bull, without the assistance of tribal warriors.

This cartoon is also fascinating for its depiction of John Bull. With his large flat feet and hooked nose, we have Bull the sexual predator as Jew,[77] an extremely unusual way of depicting England's national stereotype. Anti-Semitic imagery does appear in late nationalist humorous propaganda, with unusual targets.

---

replied to a prisoner's Irish statement by saying 'he did not understand the Hottentot language', and 'I don't care whether he is a Hottentot or a Sinn Féiner' (BNL, *WFJ*, 1.12.17, p. 1).   **73** TCD, Samuels 5/145.   **74** CO 904/164/4: Postal Censorship, Irish Internees, 1918, 'Code Words and Nicknames used in the Correspondence of Irish Internees'.   **75** TCD, Samuels 3/84.   **76** TCD, Samuels 4/8.   **77** Cf. Gilman, 1991, for analysis of how certain depictions of the body signify and symbolize caricatured Jews.

Humour in advanced nationalist propaganda 207

6.4 *Dora* (Ballad cover sheet, 1918, Samuels Collection, TCD)

'Following in Father's Footsteps'[78] (figure 6.6) shows a Semitic John Redmond,[79] clutching his parliamentary stipend of 400 pounds a year, trailing after a traditional view of John Bull. Racist imagery also appears in a 1918 cartoon[80] (figure 6.10) angrily denouncing the lack of self-government for Ireland when African colonies were being granted referendums on the subject. The cartoonist,[81] who is the same propagandist who drew the anti-Semitic cartoon in figure 6.7, shows two blacks adapting western paraphernalia and debating what form of government their 'nation' should have. The figures are ludicrous, and it is precisely their attempt to be western that is so ridiculous.

But cartoons and language that strike us today as patently offensive, and were certainly racist at the time, must still be viewed in context. A glimpse of pictorial depictions of Africans in early twentieth-century cartoon art shows that this black-faced caricature was commonplace. As the research of Patricia Anderson, Annie Coombes, and others has shown,[82] the combination of western cultural artefacts and the black African body was an area of both great intrigue and great amusement to Imperial audiences at the turn of the century. It is especially ironic that Sinn Féin would choose to use a set of images redolent of imperial jubilees to advance their republican cause.

Unravelling the meaning of anti-Semitic imagery linked to Redmond or 'John Bull' is slightly more difficult. While many Irish nationalists were personally anti-Semitic, a Jewish caricature remains an odd choice when attacking England. However, this choice helps increase both the sexualized threat and the money-loving character of England and its supporters. The anti-Semitic imagery reinforces an anti-bourgeois and specifically moral anti-British stance, and should be seen as an adjunct, rather than a central target, of propagandists.[83]

No aspect of British domestic policy was safe from the pens of propagandists. Sean O'Casey roundly denounced the delay of Home Rule even before the Rising. His famous *The Grand Oul' Dame Britannia* mocked Redmond:

> And Redmond now Home Rule has won,
> Ses the Grand Oul' Dame Britannia;
> And he's finished what Wolfe Tone begun,
> Ses the Grand Oul' Dame Britannia.[84]

---

78 TCD, Samuels 4/22. 79 Redmond was also nicknamed 'Judas' by advanced nationalists. 80 TCD, Samuels 4/22. 81 Possibly Gordon Brewster ('G.B'). 82 Cf. Patricia Anderson, *The Printed Image and the Transformation of Popular Culture* (Oxford, 1991); Annie Coombes, *Reinventing Africa* (New Haven, 1994); Patrick Brantlinger, *Rule of Darkness: British Literature and Imperialism* (Ithaca, NY, 1988); Sander Gilman, 'Black Bodies, White Bodies: Towards an iconography of female sexuality in late nineteenth century art', in H.L. Gates, Jr. (ed.), *'Race' Writing and Difference* (Chicago, 1991). For images of other cultures in literature, see Edward Said, *Orientalism* (London, 1978) and *Culture and Imperialism* (London, 1993). 83 For an expansion of this argument, see Novick, 1997b. 84 NLI MS 5637: Robert Barton Papers,

CONSCRIPTION

John Bull:— "I am on the Rocks, my dear, but let us DIE TOGETHER!"

6.5 *Conscription* (anti-conscription cartoon, 1918, Samuels Collection, TCD)

6.6 *'Following in Father's Footsteps'*
(Sinn Féin cartoon, 1918, Samuels Collection, TCD)

6.7 *'The Will of the People'* (Sinn Féin cartoon, 1918,
Samuels Collection, TCD)

Men who listened to Redmond's blandishments, and enlisted when he declared that Irishmen should join the British Army in return for Home Rule, were warned of their destiny:

> Each man that treads on a German's feet
> Will be given a parcel tied up neat —
> Of a Tombstone Cross and a Winding Sheet!
> Ses the Grand Oul' Dame Britannia.[85]

Two years later, after the Rising had marked a genuine blow for Irish independence, O'Casey returned to the subject of Home Rule in his sardonic *The Demi-Semi Home Rule Bill*:[86]

> The struggle now is over, oul' Ireland, sure, is free.
> An' if you don't believe it – well, just you wait and see!
> For the fruits of the Irish Party – tho' Sinn Feiners say they're nil –
> Is a demi-semi, semi-demi, demi-iiiiiiiii Home Rule Bill![87]

The Irish Convention, which met without success from 25 July 1917 to 5 April 1918 in an attempt to create a system of government for Ireland, was ridiculed in Patrick Hogan's *Lloyd George's Convention*. Hogan railed at the Convention, considering it nothing more than a DORA-managed publicity stunt for the Irish Parliamentary Party and British Government:

> I hear that each day they will pose 'fore the film,
> With John on the bridge and Wee Joe at the helm,
> Twice nightly, I'm told, but – 'Defence of the Realm' –
> The Picture's arranged by Mr Lloyd George.[88]

The encouragement of recruiting was quite possibly the most visible aspect of British domestic policy in Ireland before 1918, and this proved ideal fodder for humorous propaganda. Writers angrily mocked the 'lies' told by recruiters to get men into an army that was being slowly chewed to pieces in the charnel houses of France, Turkey, and Mesopotamia. The 'Rajah of Frongoch', Joseph Mulkearns, bearing the proud pseudonym of one who had been interned by the British in Wales following the Easter Rising, wrote both *Come Along and Join the British Army*, and the shorter ballad *A Recruiting Come-All-Ye*. Published by the Art Depot in early 1918, both of these ballads attacked the policy of recruiting and the future failure of the British to provide appropriately for veterans after the War. Parodying the 'Wearing Of the Green', *Come Along and Join the British*

Scrapbook, vol. I, fol. 27. 85 Ibid. 86 Sung to the tune of 'The Wearing of the Green'.
87 TCD, Samuels 5/49. 88 NLI MS 5637: Robert Barton Papers, Scrapbook, vol. I, fol. 14.

Army showed what could happen to those who listened Irish Parliamentary Party recruiters:

> Come along and join the British Army,
> Show that you're not afraid,
> Put your name upon the roll of honour
> In the Dublin Pals' Brigade.
> We send you out to die in France or Belgium
> 'Twill prove that you are true blue.
> When the war is o'er, if we want you any more,
> We'll find you in the S.D.U.[89]

Echoing pre-war anti-recruiting slogans, Mulkearns' *A Recruiting Come-All Ye* spoke straightforwardly about what the future held for veterans:

> You're sure of a share in the orphans' prayer
> While Britannia rules the wave,
> An Imperial kick when your day is done
> And an Irish pauper's grave.[90]

IV

So long as recruiting remained voluntary, domestic humorous propaganda remained relatively pacific. Irish Parliamentary Party recruiters were vilified, and the war was condemned, but it took events in 1918 for the propaganda opposed to the war, and the propaganda opposed to domestic policy to come together, and with one comedic voice, tie together support for the Redmondites with the war, and violently condemn the British war effort which these Redmondites supported. These events were the Conscription Crisis of April 1918, and subsequent electoral campaigns by Sinn Féin, and it is to the humorous propaganda produced during these troubled times that we turn in this final section.

The propaganda of early Sinn Féin campaigns contains a degree of humour, but of a non-violent sort. De Valera's campaign in the East Clare by-election of July 1917 was marked by an outpouring of pro-Sinn Féin propaganda. A pamphlet printed by his electoral committee combined a quote from the nationalist bishop of Limerick – 'Home Rule has been kept for many years dangling in front of Mr Redmond's nose like the carrot before the donkey' – with a picture of an idiotic ass and the slogan 'No Donkey MP for East Clare – Vote For De Valera!'[91] 'Mac Dubgaill' dedicated his new song, *The King of Ireland*, to

89 Ibid.   90 Ibid.   91 NLI MS 5637: Robert Barton Papers, Scrapbook, vol. I, fol. 62.

de Valera. Dubgaill combined his support for de Valera with remarks on the morbid nature of the Western Front, insulting Sir Douglas Haig, but remaining reluctant to insult the Irishmen who had joined the British Army:

> If De Valera took his place and tried to hate the Hun,
> With Irish Boys behind him, he could make the Germans run;
> But John Bull's our only enemy, and when he's dead and gone
> We will still have De Valera here in Ireland![92]

Cartoonists ignored the reality of de Valera's physique, and he was shown as the virile, manly embodiment of the new youthful Ireland, (figure 6.8) unmasking and destroying the evils of England.[93]

Patrick McCartan's unsuccessful campaign in South Armagh in January 1918 was also marked by relatively pacific humour. Cartoons in this campaign, between McCartan and T.P. O'Connor, such as Grace Plunkett's *Which do you Choose?*, focused mainly on class issues dividing the candidates. O'Connor is shown reclining on the deck of an English cruiser, his pockets stuffed with the 400 pounds a year he earned from the English King, and a bourgeois top hat tilted on his fat head. In contrast, McCartan, looking far more athletic than his surviving photos suggest, is shown shovelling coal in the stokehold,[94] thinking as he works that 'even if it's hard work and no pay, still it's for my country'. The contrast between O'Connor's outdated, complacent nationalism, and the virile, working-class radicalism offered by McCartan is made absolutely explicit in the drawings. Symbols echo back and forth between cartoons, reinforcing the centrality of several parliamentary attributes – top hats, 400 pound salaries, and corpulence (all middle class traits) are markers for Parliamentarians in both text and art.[95] Ironically, McCartan, a doctor and Fellow of the Royal College of the Surgeons, was both wealthier and better-educated than O'Connor.

Conscription, and its predicted result, is ridiculed in two cartoons (figures 6.9 & 6.10) from the winter of 1918. Both are done by George Monks, judging by both the stylistic similarity and the incongruous dog that is featured in the foreground of the picture plane in each cartoon. Figure 6.9, which reflects the genderized portrait of O'Cearnaigh's Dora in its title, shows the entire might of the British government in Ireland being brought to bear on a small group of little boys playing soldier in a farmyard. The ridiculous image of little boys drilling has a double resonance, mocking both the abolition of public drilling, and the efforts of the British to control the little children – all that are left after their brothers and fathers were forced to go to war. The special proclamations on the

---

92 Ibid., fol. 81.   93 NLI, *Irish Fun*, January 1918, p. 107.   94 A reference to a 1917 organising trip for Sinn Féin made by McCartan to America, during which he travelled disguised as a stoker aboard a tramp steamer.   95 NLI MS 5637: Robert Barton Papers, Scrapbook vol. I, fol. 84.

214 *Irish nationalist propaganda during the First World War*

DE VALERA'S HANDSHAKE

6.8 *De Valera's Handshake* (*Irish Fun*, January 1918)

wall were how changes in the regulations were publicized, and representatives of the British judicial apparatus are seen, including the army coming around the chicken house, a platoon of RIC men with batons, special branch men with their notebooks, and even two members of the DMP, standing in the centre foreground pointing to the action.[96]

While this cartoon comically represents Irish nationalist paranoia at the enforcement of DORA after conscription, figure 6.10, the first part of a Monks series on Irish conscription, represents British paranoia at the feared outcome of conscription.[97] While this image of a bound and gagged man being dragged along in front of the entire British army is absurd, archival research shows that contingency plans were being discussed as early as November 1915 for the enforcement of conscription in Ireland to include the use of an entire division of troops from England.[98]

[96] TCD, Samuels 4/14. [97] TCD, Samuels 4/9. [98] Bod., Sir Matthew Nathan Papers: Nathan MS 469, Memoranda of Interviews, Ireland, vol. III, Sept. 1915 to May 1916, Conference with Major-General Friend, Brigadier-General Greenfield, Neville Chamberlain, W.A. O'Connell, 17 Nov. 1915, fol. 93I.

Humour in advanced nationalist propaganda 215

GENTLE D. O. R. A.

6.9 *Gentle D.O.R.A.* (George Monks cartoon, 1918, Samuels Collection, TCD)

THE FIRST IRISH CONSCRIPT.

6.10 *The First Irish Conscript* (George Monks cartoon, 1918, Samuels Collection, TCD)

The attempted imposition of conscription in April 1918 following the German blitzkrieg of 21 March 1918 resulted in the brief unification of all nationalist parties in Ireland and the crystallization of Sinn Féin's electoral power and promise. Humorous propagandists denounced conscription, and metaphors and incitements to violence appeared in their work. Sean O'Casey raced *More Wren Songs* into print sometime between April and May. To the old air 'The Harp and the Lion', O'Casey put new words, re-titling it *England's Conscription Appeal to Ireland's Dead*. Passing through the long history of presumed Irish victims, from St Patrick to John Mitchel, O'Casey ended by having his British narrator address the recent martyrs of Easter Week:

> With confidence we beg to speak
> In words of friendship, smooth and fair,
> To shades of those in Easter Week,
> We shot within the Barrack Square;
> Brave, noble Spirits, whisper, hark ye,
> Make the Irish don the khaki
> And we promise that we'll grant ye
> Home Rule so full, 'twill sure enchant ye!
> Ha, Ha, Ha, Ha, Ha, Ha.
> The Spirits only said: We taunt ye!
> Ha! Ha! Ha![99]

O Cearnaigh's bloody *A Roving We Will Go* boasted of what Irish nationalists could do to the corpulent capitalist English (reprising the imagery of their Parliamentary supporters) with the guns and weapons to hand:

> We have a wee short rifle,
> We have a bayonet too,
> We have a big Howth Mauser –
> And you know what that can do.
> A ten-foot pike to buck him up
> When he is feeling low:
> We have them all for our friend John
> When a roving we will go.
> ...
> We'll slit his big fat belly
> And let his courage flow,
> And all the world shall praise us
> When a roving we will go.[100]

99 TCD, Samuels 5/51.   100 TCD, Samuels 5/93.

The reality of conscription, and of fighting on the Western Front three and half years into the war, was a terrifying prospect. Once conscription seemed a virtual certainty, this policy and the war in general began to be equated with the work of the Devil. *The Conscript's Chorus: An Execration of Lloyd George*[101] (figure 6.11) shows Lucifer as the 'Lawyer from Wales', beckoning with blood-drenched hand from the middle of Wales to an Irishman. This image provides an ironic counter-point to the image of the mud-soaked French charnel house of the Western Front as Hell on Earth.[102] If France was Hell to the British, then Britain, where the conscripts would be taken, was Hell for the Irish. A closer look at this cartoon shows another curious feature. If we look at the figure of the Irishman, we see that he is a curious amalgam of urban and rural types. His hat, rolled sleeves, and spade suggest a rural farmer, but the neatly trimmed moustache, trousers, waistcoat, and city shoes all point towards a city dweller. Staring defiantly at the Devil, he is all of Ireland combined into one man.

Although the Redmondites joined in the protest against conscription, many advanced nationalists considered this to be too little, too late, especially in light of their earlier support for the war and acknowledgment that conscription should happen if absolutely necessary. John Redmond himself, although dead by the time of the actual Conscription Crisis, was viewed in post-Rising humorous propaganda as a butcher of young Irishmen, who had outstayed his welcome after 1916. This gruesome imagery is well displayed in a 1917 cartoon from Belfast, printed by P. Quinn (figure 6.12).[103] The combination of the war and the Easter Rising, followed by the genuine threat of conscription, had brutalized the discourse of humorous propaganda, turning the absurd ridiculing of recruiting from the early years of the war into an angry and aggressive form of propaganda. Contrast the cartoon 'The One Bright Spot!' (figure 6.13), which appeared in the 7 November 1914 *Irish Worker*,[104] and the 1918 cartoon 'In his Own Juice'[105] (figure 6.14). In the one, we have Redmond being given a swift kick out of Ireland as Prime Minister Asquith looks on grumpily, in the other, three and a half bloody years later, he boils to death in a stew pot. Once the Conscription Crisis began, the anger felt by propagandists at the Irish Parliamentary Party leaders for having encouraged recruiting throughout the war boiled over, and direct equations between supporting the Redmondites and supporting the war were made. Violent metaphors imbue the late humorous propaganda of the war.

101 TCD, Samuels 5/82. The origin of this rhyme dates to an anti-Gladstone jingle written by Tories after the death of General Gordon at Khartoum. It was used in Ireland as early as the 1912 Insurance Act, when it was quoted by an O'Brienite local councillor in Cork. My thanks to Dr Patrick Maume (Queen's University, Belfast) for this information. 102 J.M. Winter, *Sites of Memory, Sites of Mourning* (Cambridge, 1997), p. 69. 103 KSRL, OH, Special Files (Uncatalogued), D1248: 'Freedom' Scrapbook. 104 BNL, *IW*, 7.11.14, p. 1. 105 TCD, Samuels 4/22.

The Conscripts' Chorus.

AN EXECRATION OF LLOYD GEORGE.

LLOYD GEORGE, no doubt, when his life ebbs out,
Will ride in a flaming chariot,
And will sit in state on a red-hot plate,
'Twixt the Devil and Judas Iscariot.
Ananias that day to Old Nick will say:
My precedence here now fails,
So move me up higher, away from the fire,
And make room for the Lawyer from Wales.

6.11 *The Conscripts' Chorus* (anti-conscription cartoon, 1918, Samuels Collection, TCD)

6.12 *Redmond & Co.* (cartoon, 1917, KSRL)

Joseph Mulkearns' ditty, *The Wreck of the 'No Far Distant Date'* used images of naval warfare to demonstrate the futility of the Irish Parliamentary Party's position in the autumn of 1918. John Dillon, on the bridge of this ship named after the date on which Home Rule was to be implemented, pilots the craft aimlessly about the Westminster Sea with the assistance of 'Skipper' Joe Devlin. Dillon suddenly spots a fleet of submarines, skippered by de Valera and flying the Irish tricolour. Devlin tells him about the crews: 'The crews upon his submarines, although it may seem queer/They work for Freedom, and they scorn four hundred pounds a year'. The first torpedo, marked 'North Roscommon', smashes into the ship. Lawrence Ginnell, from below, begs the leaders to abandon the ship – 'Sinn Féin on every side asails [*sic*]; its power grows day by day/Surrender to the people's call, from London stop away'. Dillon loses his nerve and begins to cry: 'Take to the boats, John Dillon sobs, and leave this doomed old craft,/The Irish Party's days must end a-clinging to a raft'. The Rajah rejoiced at their destruction: 'And here we leave them to their fate – this

6.13 *The One Bright Spot!* (*Irish Worker*, 7 November 1914)

band of British slaves, Soon! soon! the 'No Far Distant Date' will sink beneath the waves'.[106]

By December 1918, the Irish Parliamentary Party had sunk beneath the waves. World War had ended, and so had their political hegemony in nationalist Ireland. The reasons for the shift from the Irish Parliamentary Party to Sinn Féin are manifold, but a study of humour in propaganda demonstrates the historical, political, and cultural significance of even the smallest item, the most ridiculous joke. When the men and women who supported the cause of advanced nationalism used humorous propaganda during the war, they used it as both a defensive weapon against tyranny, turning the wielders of arbitrary power into laughingstocks, and as a means of stating their case in an appealing fashion. Far from being merely a curious facet of a marginal area of Irish history, humorous propaganda can stand for the methods and techniques of resistance in all the forms devized by advanced nationalism during the Great War. M.S. O'Lonnain,

106 TCD, Samuels 5/52.

6.14 *In His Own Juice* (Sinn Féin cartoon, 1918, Samuels Collection, TCD)

an editor of *Young Ireland (Eire Og)*, put it well. In the summer of 1918, he replied to critics with the remark 'If we occasionally make a joke it is just to drive home some truth. To quote George Bernard Shaw, "Our way of joking is to tell the truth – 'tis the funniest joke in the world"'.[107]

107 BNL, *Og*, 15.6.18, p. 3.

7

Aggression and the Irish revolution

The years of the First World War changed Ireland, and this change is both reflected. What is without doubt is that the war years saw Ireland 'changed, changed utterly' – and this change is both reflected ilected in, and caused by, the intensification of propagandistic discourse between 1914 and 1918. As shown in the previous chapter on humorous propaganda, one of the central intensifications which discourse underwent during the Great War involved brutalization and increasing aggression. This can be seen as clearly in serious propaganda as in comic. Aggressive propaganda had many different components – shifting opinions about the Great War, practical responses to violence within Ireland, symbolized by the 1916 Rising, and unrealistic commemorations of the leaders of the Rising, a form of martyrology that helped attract numerous recruits to the advanced nationalist cause. This chapter will chart the course of attitudes to aggression within Ireland, arguing that the differences in the use of aggression before and after the Rising highlight ideological differences within advanced nationalism, especially over the different concepts of what forms of aggression would be acceptable.

I

Much previous research on the rhetoric of the Irish revolution has focused on the notion of blood sacrifice, especially in the writings of Patrick Pearse and Joseph Plunkett.[1] While it is perhaps understandable that these men, as future leaders of the Easter Rising, should receive a good deal of attention by current scholars, a comprehensive study of the advanced nationalist press before the

---

1 Works in this area are many. For general discussions of rhetoric, see Richard Kearney, *Myth and Motherland* (Belfast, 1984), Peter Costello, *The Heart Grown Brutal* (Dublin, 1977), Seamus Deane, *Celtic Revivals* (London, 1985), O. Dudley Edwards and Fergus Pyle (eds)., *1916: The Easter Rising* (London, 1968), and Mairin Ni Donnchadha and Theo Dorgan (eds)., *Revising the Rising* (Derry, 1991). For Pearse, see R. Dudley Edwards, *Patrick Pearse: The Triumph of Failure* (Dublin, 1977), and Sean Farrell Moran, *Patrick Pearse and the Politics of Redemption* (Washington D.C., 1994). For other leaders of the Rising, F.X. Martin (ed)., *Leaders and Men of the Easter Rising* (Dublin, 1967) remains the best collection of essays on the subject. The writings of Pearse and Plunkett are contrasted at times with the more hard-headed practicality of James Connolly. Unbiased biographies of James Connolly are difficult to find, perhaps the best of a dull lot is Austen Morgan, *James Connolly: A Political Biography* (Dublin, 1988).

Rising reveals an aggressive discourse which spanned an entire spectrum of sacrifice. Aggressive discourse about Ireland in the twelve advanced nationalist newspapers with national circulation before the Rising[2] stretched from simple encouragement and praise of suffering to extreme demands for complete sacrifice, demands which expressed an extraordinary degree of masochism that went beyond even Pearse's promotion of sacrifice. These most extreme demands, however, were mostly limited to the writing and editorial output of one man, the Cork-based Terence MacSwiney. The lack of widespread extremism leads to the conclusion that the basic idea of blood sacrifice, an idea that has taken on great importance from the study of writings by Pearse and his cohort, was not central to advanced nationalist propagandists before the Rising.[3]

Newspapers that encouraged their readers to suffer for the cause of Ireland created a more complex and interesting set of writings than the newspapers that urged martyrdom. Readers could suffer for any patriotic Irish cause, and there were a fair number of these causes. The Gaelic Leaguers who bought *An Claidheamh Soluis* were enjoined to suffer for the sake of the Irish language. Douglas Hyde, far from a political extremist,[4] told listeners at the Mansion House in March 1915 that 'peoples to-day went to war for crude, modern tongues – Poles, Hungarians, Boers – and here was a language almost without a rival in ancient tongues. Was that not worth a struggle?'[5]

Those nationalists who chose to struggle and sacrifice for the cause were praised, especially, as with the Young Irelanders and the Fenians,[6] if they went to prison. 'Felony and honour blend',[7] wrote Herbert Pim ('A. Newman') after he, Denis McCullough, Ernest Blythe, and Liam Mellowes were sentenced to prison for refusing to obey deportation orders. The best men suffered anguish for their beliefs. After Sean MacDermott was sentenced to four months' imprisonment in June 1915, Brian O'Higgins contrasted the 'smiles for all who would

---

2 *Sinn Féin, Eire Ireland, Irish Volunteer, Irish Freedom, Gael, Spark, Honesty, Worker's Republic, Nationality, Cork Celt, Fianna Fail,* and *Fianna*. One should also mention *Irish Work* and the *Worker*, two short-lived replacements for the *Worker's Republic* after it was closed by the British in December 1914; as well as *An Claidheamh Soluis*, the newspaper of the Gaelic League, which had grown quite advanced by 1915.   3 There is a legitimate argument for taking the poetry and writings of Pearse, Plunkett, MacDonagh, et al. as propaganda, for the material was often consciously written to promote an ideology. However, even if one accepts this definition, these men were still in a minority. Patrick Maume adds the names of Pim and MacDermott to the list of men supporting blood-sacrifice, but this still leaves the men supporting blood sacrifice in a minority of activists (Maume, 1999, p. 198).   4 Indeed, Hyde resisted the politicization of the Gaelic League, and resigned as its director in mid-1915 when it became clear that advanced nationalists had taken over the League and were basically using it as a front for the IRB.   5 BNL, ACS, 20.3.15, p. 4.   6 The influence of John Mitchel's 1854 *Jail Journal*, a text that Arthur Griffith would later insist every local Sinn Féin club should own, can not be exaggerated.   7 BNL, *Nat*, 7.8.15, p. 3.

barter/Their souls in the devil's mart –/But torture and pain for the noble'.[8] Men could make their literary reputations from a stint in prison. Requested by the Reverend F.S. Pollard to give an account to the *Hibernian* of his imprisonment, Sean Milroy responded with a three month long serial 'Memories of Mountjoy', which ran from September to December 1915, and later became a book. 'Memories' is a jocular account of a bleak prison, with little hint of any suffering. Indeed, the physical consequences of imprisonment were rarely acknowledged.[9] A gleeful account of 'The Return of the Felons', telling *Nationality*'s readers about the festivities which greeted McCullough and Pim when they returned to Belfast upon their release, only mentioned in passing that 'the audience learned that Dinny [Denis McCullough] was still suffering from the effects of his incarceration'.[10]

Such manly posturing was merely a manifestation of an element central to all aggressive propagandistic discourse in Ireland (and indeed around the world) – the complete sublimation of the self before national interest. 'A Veteran' in the *Irish Volunteer* solemnly told his readers that Ireland 'needs our every thought and prayer. She needs now the warm love of her daughters and the courage and daring of her sons. Of her and her only we must think'.[11] Connolly was aware of the vengeful power which suffering could create. In a Lalorite editorial which he had excised from the final issue of his *Irish Worker*, only to publish it two weeks later in *Irish Work*, he warned the British that 'if you strike at, imprison, or kill us, out of our prisons and graves we will still evoke a spirit that will thwart you, and mayhap, raise a force that will destroy you'.[12] Connolly's words were prophetic, and from his awareness, and his ability to ignore the self, it was but a short step to the harsher demands of martyrdom.

Propagandists who asked their readers to be willing to die for Ireland were relatively unimaginative, following a well-trodden metaphorical path that highlighted the historical contribution of Ireland's past martyrs, and offered fresh sacrifice upon the stained altar of nationalism. The ways in which these authors suggested martyrdom did, however, vary quite greatly.

Herbert Pim wrote a 'national anthem' that was published in both Griffith's *Eire Ireland* and Connolly's *Irish Worker*. Set to the exact scansion of *God Save the King*, the anthem began 'Mother of martyrdom/See every true man comes/Offering his sword'.[13] Those who made this offering, who chose what Eileen ni Captaig felt was 'death with freedom's vision' rather than 'in slavery still to languish',[14] could help attain Constance Markievicz's 'crimson dream of

8 BNL, *Spark*, 20.6.15, p. 4. 9 With the exception of A. Newman's 1915 pamphlet *What it Feels Like*, which details the relatively benign treatment he received in a Belfast prison (*What it Feels Like*, Sinn Féin 'Tracts for the Times', no. 8, 1915. Held in Cambridge University Library). 10 BNL, *Nat*, 20.11.15, p. 6. 11 BNL, *IV*, 24.10.14, p. 12. 12 BNL, *Irish Work*, 19.12.14, p. 2. Cited also in part in Costello, 1977, p. 72. 13 BNL, *EI*, 5.11.14, p. 2 (also in *IW*, 14.11.14). 14 BNL, *Gael*, 29.1.16, p. 20.

martyred men' – Ireland's 'regal crown of state'.[15] The idea of martyrdom, and of the final battle in which heroes would fall, naturally formed a dramatic and attractive picture to many of these writers, even if the battle itself would be a defeat. John F. O'Donnell told a woman what she would see when the golden day dawned:

> You see our corpses strew the field;
> You see our standard in the dust;
> You see our legions backward reeled
> Before the foes' imperious thrust.
> We'll dare all that before we yield –
> The cause is good and God is just.[16]

One of the central attractions which martyrdom held for readers (apart from the religious aspect, which will be discussed later) was the knowledge that past nationalist martyrs were honoured above all, and that those who died would join a long list of heroes. For 'An Bruceallach' ['The Brook'], 'not even our lying foes dare deny' that 'Ireland's son's for their sireland dear/Have been ever ready to do and die'.[17] Not just history should drive potential martyrs, however. The advanced nationalist press gave its writers the opportunity to lecture readers on the appropriate motivation a patriot should feel. Addressing the question of martyrdom with a particularly muscular Christian approach, the *Spark* suggested that 'men do not immolate themselves for hatred; it is love, love of God, of country, or kindred that impels them to forego the pleasure and the spice of life'.[18]

Patriotism and devout national love alone might not be enough to inspire potential martyrs. Along with all other nationalist movements and governments, Irish revolutionaries used a set of symbols to influence their audience. These symbols were mainly ephemeral, and very similar to Fenian and Parnellite propaganda signs – the figure of Erin, the memory of past martyrs, images of the Irish landscape. Interestingly, the only physically concrete symbol used as an example of inspiration was the flag of the the Plough and the Stars used by James Connolly's Citizen Army.[19]

As with men and women who had been in prison, individual suffering did not matter to propagandists encouraging sacrifice. Cavanagh asked 'What matter then if in the gorge some few lie still and pale?' so long as 'thrice-purchased Freedom's haven' was reached.[20] Patriots were encouraged to reject all ties of

---

15 BNL, *Fianna*, December 1915, p. 12.   16 KSRL, OH G26: CC, 10.10.14, p. 4.   17 BNL, *Hib*, 28.8.15, p. 3.   18 BNL, *Spark*, 11.7.15, p. 3.   19 Cf. Maeve Cavanagh's 'The Flag of the Irish Republic' (*IW*, 31.10.14) and 'The Breaking of our Flag' (*WR*, 22.4.16).   20 NLI, *WR*, 11.9.15, p. 1.

family and marital love.[21] Margaret Gibbons' poem 'Fidelity' heroicized the figure of a man who rejected the entreaties of his mother, his sister and his sweetheart to stop his nationalist activities. Poised on the brink of giving in 'the vision of that fadeless land' rose to his eyes, and he proudly replied 'My life is hers – not yours'.[22]

The most extreme writer who published regularly in the advanced nationalist press before the Rising was Terence MacSwiney. His brand of religious self-immolation went beyond even a purposeful ignoring of human suffering. MacSwiney was the only contributor to the *Irish Volunteer* to express such dramatic views. In a long essay from May 1915, he reminded his readers to 'remember, your supreme triumph can only come in a moment of general despair'.[23] Sacrifice had to be made by the very best of Ireland. 'It is those who have everything to bind them to life', he wrote in July 1915, 'must be prepared to launch everything into the pit of death: from such a complete and ready surrender alone a regenerated people is born'.[24] By September, he was wishing poetically that his 'boys' could muster and march into certain death. He imagined that 'To-morrow they will march as one/Against the leaden hail', and called the loss of his fellow volunteers a 'sacred moment'.[25] MacSwiney was able to be even more masochistic in his own newspaper, the short-lived *Fianna Fail*, 'A Journal for Militant Ireland'. Without MacNeill or Hobson to moderate his more extreme impulses, MacSwiney published poems such as 'An Ode to a Bullet',[26] which begged the 'Swift Messenger of Death, your kiss of pain/Lay on my brow, before dishonour base/Shall once again drag low our ancient race'.[27]

MacSwiney's rhetoric also frequently introduced specifically Catholic themes into the idea of martyrological sacrifice. The Catholic faith professed by most of the nationalists active at this time naturally encouraged the importance of martyrdom in their outlooks. Pearse's brand of Catholicism, combined with the vibrant faith of propagandists such as Brian O'Higgins, created what John Newsinger has called a 'Catholic revolution'.[28] Catholicism was of central importance to these men and women, and nowhere was this more clearly expressed than in the writings which promoted Christian martyrdom.

MacSwiney asked God to 'teach us how to die',[29] and 'reckon up the price for

21 Demonstrated most famously in the concluding scene of W.B. Yeats' 1902 play, *Cathleen Ni Houlihan*. 22 BNL, *Hon*, 8.1.16, p. 2. 23 BNL, *IV*, 22.5.15, p. 6. 24 Ibid., 31.7.15, pp. 4–5. 25 Ibid., 4.9.15, p. 3. 26 It is intriguing to speculate on the similarities between this verse and both the 'decadent' homosexual poetry of the late 1890s as well as the homo-erotic underpinnings of First World War front-line verse, a theme explored by both Paul Fussell (*The Great War and Modern Memory*, Oxford, 1975) and Adrian Caesar (*Taking It Like a Man: Suffering, Sexuality, and the War Poets* [Manchester, 1993]), who advances the question of why 'homosexual or homoerotic love was predicated upon violence' (Caesar, 1993, p. 234). 27 KSRL, OH G27: FF, 17.10.14, p. 2. 28 John Newsinger, 'I Bring Not Peace But A Sword: The Religious Motif in the Irish War of Independence', *JCH*, vol. 13, no. 3 (June 1978), p. 609. 29 BNL, *IV*, 13.11.15, p. 6.

us, however great it be:/We'll pay it in our best blood for Ireland's liberty'.[30] Patriotism was seen as the absolute exercise of God's desire. 'If the upholders of the Union Jack choose to ... legally take my life for fighting against them', blustered Sean Doyle in his first editorial for the *Spark*, 'I shall go cheerfully before God and I shall say to Him: "I am come, my Father, before my time. Your enemies have sent me to prevent me doing your will on earth."'[31]

Pearse's Catholic rhetoric was complimented in the *Irish Volunteer*, Herbert Pim giving *From A Hermitage* a good review.[32] Maire de Buitleir's serial essay in *Nationality*, 'Sursum Corda'[33] marked the loss of so many fine nationalists in the fight for freedom, quoting Pearse's statement that 'many a delegate had been summoned to "the Ard Fheis of God"'.[34] Buitleir further agreed with Pearse that the Great War was a blessing. Not only were martyrs for Ireland being produced in the struggle against the English, but 'on all sides there is evidence that faith in God and love of country have been strengthened in those who have been through the fiery crucible of this war'.[35] If religious faith could begin to justify the slaughter of the battlefields, it is no strange thing to realise that Catholicism was being used to justify individual (and at times collective) sacrifice for the national good.

However, the concentration on the rhetoric of blood sacrifice, especially by Pearse, can cloud somewhat the picture of advanced nationalist discourse before the war. Writers other than Pearse and his fellow Easter leaders called for the ultimate sacrifice. Few, however, were as extreme, and the virtual absence of this style from the writings of such important propagandists as Griffith and MacNeill reveals ideological differences within the nationalist movement long before the Easter Rising, and highlights the dichotomy between the words and the actions of the Irish revolution.

II

Discussing the speech of Irish separatists, a recent study states 'most of the violence of their rhetoric was directed inwards'.[36] It is true that much propaganda written during the war presented the martyr as the ideal figure of emulation for advanced nationalists. However, from the very first days of the war, a form of aggression – utterly different from the internalized form expressed as a desire for martyrdom – made itself felt in the writings of more extreme propagandists. Even men like Griffith and MacNeill who believed the time was not ripe for violent revolution still allowed an aggressive tone to permeate their writings.

30 KSRL, OH G27: FF, 19.9.14, p. 3.   31 BNL, *Spark*, 7.2.15, p. 1.   32 BNL, *IV*, 3.7.15, p. 6.   33 A reference to a section of the Catholic Mass in which the congregation responds to a priest's command 'Lift up your hearts'.   34 BNL, *Nat*, 9.10.15, p. 3.   35 Ibid., 16.10.15, p. 2.   36 Ellis, 1997, p. 359.

Irish nationalists could attack the English by harming themselves, or they could attack the English directly.

If one general characteristic can be given to aggressive writing before the Rising, it is absolute impracticality. Rarely is any effort made to connect the fantasies driving the poetry, ballads, and articles written by propagandists with the reality of fighting a numerically and militarily superior foe. Only occasionally, as will be seen, did reality intrude on to the pages of the advanced nationalist press.

Writers threatened the British with escalating levels of violence. Occasionally, these threats came in response to actual British actions. When a mob at Liverpool turned back a shipload of emigrant young men from the west of Ireland in the autumn of 1915, forcing them off the ship which was to take them to America, the *Gael* declared 'some of those boys who were westward bound ... are anxious to meet some of those smug Englishmen in the Westland. 'Twill be a bad place for conscription shirkers from England to come for refuge'.[37] Three months later, the short-lived *Gael* was closed by the British after publishing an editorial which threatened to 'shock, demoralize, and rout' the English. Readers were reminded: 'if we want the revolution we must make it up, and we must realize that such cannot be accomplished without bloodshed ... We are at war with England, and must fight it to the bitter end'.[38]

Once Irishmen were armed, some propagandists encouraged the outbreak of warfare in Ireland. Ignoring the irony of praying for war one year into the Great War, Michael Scanlan wrote 'Let babblers cease/To prate of peace,/God bring us war, we say'.[39] Seamus Deane has made the point that this sort of rhetoric forms part of a pan-European 'cult of violence' which flourished in England and Germany[40] before the First World War.[41] However, in the rest of Europe such bloodthirsty language was fulfilled far earlier than in Ireland, in August 1914 rather than April 1916.

Armed violence was often promised in response to any threat. Following an incident in November 1915 in which a Dublin businessman asked people to boycott Irish firms that still employed young men, MacNeill lashed back, calling this a form of 'Hunger-Scription' which would force men into the army to avoid starvation.[42] Anticipating that this boycott could lead to genuine conscription, the *Spark* promised MacNeill to 'come with naked steel ... with bayonet, pike, and

---

37 BNL, *Gael*, 29.1.16, p. 15. *The Weekly Irish Times* congratulated the stokers on their patriotic action (BNL, *WIT*, 13.11.15, p. 6).   38 Ibid., 18.3.16, pp. 5–6.   39 BNL, *Hib*, 18.9.15, p. 4.   40 As well as France, though Deane fails to mention this country.   41 See Deane, 1985, pp. 63–74. Deane draws on the writings of F.S.L. Lyons (*Culture and Anarcchy in Ireland, 1890–1939*, Oxford, 1979), who shows the antecedent to Pearse's rhetoric lying with the popular novelist Canon Sheehan. The idea of a cult of violence is also explored at length by I.F. Clarke in his classic *Voices Prophesying War, 1763–1884* (Oxford, 1966) and in Oliver MacDonagh, *States of Mind: A Study of Anglo-Irish Conflict 1789–1980* (London, 1983).
42 Cf. BNL, *IV*, 25.12.15.

ball' and 'make a bloody Day'[43] if conscription arrived in Ireland. Peter Golden[44] revelled in the possibility of romantic mass slaughter:

> The stranger came into our land,
> Our countrymen to rob and kill,
> But our sword leaped forth like lightening [sic] darts,
> And their bones are bleaching many a hill,
> And while one Saxon skull is seen
> Our Irish blades with blood to wet,
> We'll still be true to Rosaleen
> And cling to Holy Ireland yet.[45]

Actual violent events before the Rising, frequently nothing more than donnybrooks surrounding election or recruiting meetings, were exaggerated from mob violence into chivalric combat. Writing to Griffith in November 1914, an anonymous volunteer reported what happened after 'Redmond set all the hooligans in Galway drunk' and 500 of them surrounded the Volunteers' HQ where 50 Volunteers were meeting. Since some children in the HQ were 'dying of fright', '[w]e gave most of our lads wooden drill-guns and decided to come out. Our appearance took their breath away. There was an ominous silence, a scamper, and when they saw we were so few they howled'.[46]

The *Irish Volunteer*, priding itself on being the official paper of the Volunteer movement, made more of an effort to be realistic in its use and encouragement of aggression. Almost every issue from 1914 to 1916 featured 'Headquarters Notes', which included sections that were supposed to serve as instructions in military tactics for eager Volunteer officers. Usually written by J.J. O'Connell and Eimar O'Duffy, with occasional contributions by Patrick Pearse,[47] these columns attempted to draw on the lessons of the European War. However, this was a mostly impossible task. The writers of these columns wrote as if the Volunteers were a fully formed and professional army, versed in British army training manuals, rather than the rag-tag collection of amateurs, courageous or otherwise, that they actually were.[48] Emblematic of this style is a 'Tactical Problem' published in January 1915. The author asked readers to outline the measures by which a blue force consisting of Volunteers from Clare, Limerick, Kerry, and

---

43 BNL., *Spark*, 21.11.15, p. 2.   44 Irish actor and second cousin of Terence MacSwiney. Golden emigrated from Ireland to the United States in 1901, and regularly toured giving recitals of poetry and prose promoting the Irish Republic. He befriended Ernie O'Malley after the war, and died in 1926 (cf. Richard English, *Ernie O'Malley: IRA Intellectual* [Oxford, 1998], p. 34).   45 BNL, *Hib*, 1.1.16, p. 6.   46 BNL, *EI*, 3.11.14, p. 3.   47 Hobson, 1968, pp. 68–9; Townshend, 1983, pp. 289–90.   48 British army manuals were regularly used in training the National Volunteers, and many of this constitutional organization's drill sergeants were ex-British army. Few of these ex-soldiers, however, joined the Irish Volunteers, forcing the more advanced volunteers to find a different way of training their men.

Cork could hold a defensive line below Lough Derg, stopping an invading force which had landed in Galway Bay and was marching inland toward Ballinasloe.[49] Readers were also urged to 'certainly use your men as cannon-fodder in war time; that's the way to win'.[50]

The Volunteers did not dream up technical military instruction via newspapers or books. Rather, as with so many other aspects of their organisation, they followed in the footsteps of the Fenian Brotherhood, who had helped make 'Charles Beggs'' equally unrealistic handbook *The Military Resources of Ireland* a best-seller in 1858.[51] Unlike the Fenians, the Volunteers were able to draw on the lessons of the Western Front and Gallipoli. Applying information from massive battles to the Irish arena met with mixed success. A special supplement in a January 1915 *Irish Volunteer* entitled 'Lessons of the Flanders Battles' taught its readers that hand grenades could burn hedges down just as easily as they were used to burn trenches on the Western Front.[52] Where, short of making crude bombs themselves, revolutionaries were supposed to acquire such advanced personal ordnance was left to the imagination.

Especially in the *Volunteer*, moderates quelled the excesses of propaganda. Despite having urged readers to use their men as cannon-fodder, Eimar O'Duffy ['E O'D'] nevertheless had begun his regular column 'A Military Causerie' by promising that his readers 'will be introduced to the battlefield gradually, as befits a nation of civilians'. Readers with illusions were warned: 'none of the manoeuvres you have yet been present at bears the faintest resemblance to a battle'.[53] One full year after publishing the supplement that encouraged actions with hand grenades, writers in the *Irish Volunteer* moderated their views far enough to urge readers to purchase a copy of the London *Times*, which included a supplement bearing Sir Ian Hamilton's full report on Gallipoli. 'Never again', opined the *Volunteer*, 'will any officer be able to get so valuable a textbook for a penny'.[54]

At isolated moments throughout the first two years of war, practical methods of using aggression and violence were encouraged by the press, especially in response to threatened acts of conscription by the British. When conscription was threatened, some newspapers advised resistance, but resistance in a measured, controlled, and thought-out way. This basic response can best be seen in an editorial from *An Claidheamh Soluis* in September 1915. 'The threat of conscription should lead to solidarity in Irish opinion against it', urged the author, encouraging men to heal the cracks within the movement, rather than exacerbate them through dramatic and divisive schemes. 'It will be the duty of every young Irishmen to resist any attempt that may be made to conscript himself or his fellows'.[55]

49 BNL, *IV*, 23.1.5, p. 6.   50 Ibid., 22.1.16, p. 2.   51 Townshend, 1983, pp. 33–34.   52 BNL, *IV*, 30.1.15, Supplement, 'Lessons of the Flanders Battles'.   53 Ibid., 9.10.15, p. 5.   54 Ibid., 15.1.16, p. 5.   55 BNL, *ACS*, 25.9.15, p. 4.

Actual threats quickly converted propagandists from fantasy to reality. The threat of 'Hunger-Conscription' in November 1915, and the knowledge that Great Britain would soon impose a full form of conscription, was first reacted to in the *Spark* by a mix of bluster and realism. While pleading to create 'A Bloody Day' on page two, journalists elsewhere in the same issue offered a reasoned argument for boycotting employers who dismissed young men.[56] One week later, in the same paper, Sean Doyle made the most explicit call for calm seen in pre-Rising propaganda. 'No rash act must precipitate a conflict', he wrote. 'To be conscripted, to be disarmed, are both unthinkable. To rush on the enemy's guns without cause and without hope may be magnificent, but it is not war. To the leaders we say, patience and boldness! To the rank and file, courage and discipline!'[57]

Two interesting points emerge from studying the incitement of realistic aggression before the Rising. First, examples of this type happened only in response to external events that impinged on domestic affairs, showing the way in which such factors influenced propagandistic writings. Second, the men and women who were writing in this style were mostly moderates, and most importantly, very few eventually participated in the Easter Rising. Indeed, the violence of the Easter Rising should not be predicted from reading the plethora of boasts and threats which emerged from propagandists before the Rising. A great gulf existed still in 1916 between those who spoke of revolution, and those who dared a revolt.

III

The rhetorical response to the Rising on the Home Front was far more complex, and in many ways more important than the simple divide which propagandists drew between British and Irish troops in the army, and between front line soldiers and the men who recruited them, reactions studied earlier in the book. The Rising further bifurcated the advanced nationalist attitude to aggression, and the way in which aggression was encouraged and channelled. Before the Rising, the vast majority of aggressive propaganda was based on fantasy, with a few isolated incidents in which realistic plans were mooted for possible response. The Rising showed propagandists the potential of literal resistance. Some used the opening provided by the swelling support for advanced nationalism following the Rising to introduce a practical campaign for election, equating votes for the new Sinn Féin party with the violence of the Rising. Others concentrated on commemorating the deaths of the men involved, encouraging further sacrifice in order to produce the romantic ideal of a free and independent Ireland.

56 BNL, *Spark*, 21.11.15, pp. 3–4.   57 Ibid., 28.11.15, pp. 3–4.

Historians who have studied the rhetoric of this period have often made the mistake of equating aggression with a desire for armed violence. Hence, they set up too sharp a dichotomy between the propagandists of Sinn Féin, especially Arthur Griffith and Herbert Moore Pim, and leaders of the Irish Volunteers, such as Éamon de Valera and Ernest Blythe.[58] While it is certainly true that Griffith and Pim were against armed rebellion, nevertheless the propaganda produced by both these men was aggressive, and, as this section will show, encouraged an active form of resistance via the ballot box. The poll and the by-election became the battlefields of the Irish revolution for Sinn Féin, the vote and the ballot paper the rifles and pikes with which to fight.[59] The renascent Sinn Féin party, especially after 1917 when de Valera assumed the presidency, should be seen not so much as a combination of active and passive resistance as a successful combination of forms of aggression;[60] de Valera, the romantic living martyr of Easter Week as a symbol for the physical force supporters, Griffith and Pim, experienced propagandists and organisers as the main voices of an intellectually aggressive and revolutionary party.

Once Sinn Féin began to contest by-elections with the run-off in Roscommon in February 1917, prior sacrifice became a practical help to election.[61] Men who had suffered from their activities in Easter week now saw real success grow from these times of hardship. The Sinn Féiners' lives in prison were often contrasted with the easy lives of parliamentarians. The South Longford by-election, contested by Joseph McGuinness while a prisoner in Lewes Jail, appeared to Griffith to be between 'the man who risks his life, sacrifices his liberty, and breaks his fortunes in an effort to restore his country to independence and prosperity, or ... the man who risks nothing, sacrifices nothing'.[62] A simple yet effective poster used for McGuinness, Cosgrave and Griffith showed a standing figure in convict garb with the slogan 'Put Him In to Get Him Out'.[63] Ernest Blythe's general election campaign in North Monaghan was aided by a pamphlet which listed his 'quota' – the number of times he had been warned under the Defence of the Realm Act, arrests, prisons, length of hunger strikes, length of time confined to

---

58 See especially Richard Davis, 'The Advocacy of Passive Resistance in Ireland, 1916–1922', *Anglo-Irish Studies*, vol. III (1977), pp. 35–5; and Keiko Inoue, 'Sinn Féin Propaganda and Nationality, 1916–1918' (UCD, M.A., 1989). 59 As D.G. Boyce points out, this sort of rhetoric was very similar to Parnellite Land War campaigns. (Boyce, 1982, pp. 315–19). 60 Contrary to the views of Pauric Travers, who maintains in his 1977 MA thesis that 'the post 1916 Sinn Féin party derived its impetus more from the tradition of 1916 than from Griffith. Dual monarchy and passive resistance were noticeably replaced at the Convention in 1917 by more radical and militaristic policies (Pauric Travers, 'The Irish Conscription Crisis, 1918' [UCD, M.A., 1977], pp. 118–19). 61 As with so much else, a forerunner can be seen with the election of the Fenian O'Donovan Rossa to parliament 1869 while he was a convicted felon. 62 BNL, *Nat*, 12.5.17, p. 4. 63 TCD, Samuels 4/117. Also cited in *Ellis*, 1997, p. 365.

areas, and length of imprisonment since the war began.[64] Blythe's 27 months in prison were quickly turned into strongly viable political capital.

The Sinn Féin electoral contests from 1917 were not an exercise in passive resistance, or organized pacifism. Rather, they took on the aspect of a military campaign. Discourse bristled with military metaphors. Even reserved English newspapers joined in. *The Manchester Guardian* declared that the Longford election result was 'equivalent to a serious defeat of the British army in the field'.[65] Griffith was gleeful at the seeming invincibility of Sinn Féin, and likened the movement to a tank. 'We hear of "Tanks" forging ahead over all obstructions, and accomplishing their object. Sinn Féin is an invulnerable political "Tank".'[66] A more classically-minded propagandist parodied Alfred, Lord Tennyson's famous *Charge of the Light Brigade*: 'Sinn Féin to right of them/Sinn Féin to left of them/Sinn Féin in front of them/Volley'd and thundr'd'.[67]

Every nationalist in Ireland was supposed to concentrate on practical efforts for independence. 'All our energies should be devoted to the preservation of our country', lectured *Nationality*, 'relying on ourselves and ourselves alone for the production of the necessities of life'.[68] Such efforts were to climax in the lead-up to the general election of December 1918. 'Work, work, work for the next three weeks as you have never worked before',[69] urged *Nationality* at the end of November 1918. Hard work was idolized as the highest form of sacrifice, above even the deaths of Easter leaders. The National Council of Sinn Féin issued a doctrine pamphlet in September 1917 that asked its readers to commit themselves to self-sacrifice. However, the author claimed 'I do not mean self-sacrifice in the narrow sense of the word – the willingness, for example, to die for one's country. That is a great thing – one of the greatest things in the world – but it is not everything'.[70]

Griffith and Pim did not ignore the symbolic value of the Easter deaths, rather this powerfully emotive symbol was used to demand greater practical labour from the survivors.[71] If Griffith and Pim were to concentrate on harnessing the political desires of the many new supporters for Sinn Féin around Ireland through a channelled and practical form of aggression, something first had to be done to draw these people into the nationalist fold. As Peter Hart has written, what propagandists successfully produced in Ireland after 1916 was a 'patriotic cult' centred on the images, written and pictorial, of the dead leaders of Easter. Hart, drawing on the memoirs of veterans, along with interviews conducted with ex-members of the IRA, believes that 'this new iconography was probably more influential than revolutionary ideas or texts'.[72] What we have after

64 UCD, Ernest Blythe Papers, P24/1017: Sinn Féin election propaganda for Blythe, N. Monaghan Election, December 1918. 1017 (1): 'Career of Ernest Blythe, Candidate for North Monaghan'. 65 BNL, *Nat*, 19.5.17, p. 4. 66 TCD, Samuels, 2/14. 67 BNL, *Nat*, 26.5.17, p. 3. 68 Ibid., 17.8.18, p. 1. 69 Ibid., 23.11.18, p. 1. 70 NLI, *The Ethics of Sinn Féin* (Dublin, 1917), 'Self-Sacrific', p. 6. 71 BNL, *Nat*, 7.12.18. 72 Hart, 1998, p. 207.

the Rising then, are groups of people who participated in the activities of the Volunteers and Sinn Féin because they were inspired by the example of Easter week, and influenced by the ephemera produced in commemoration, and who, once they were involved, were encouraged by Griffith to work for a new Ireland.

But what did the propaganda that influenced the initial decision to join actually say? Propaganda that commemorated the Easter Rising did more than simply memorialize the rebels. It encouraged further fantastical outbursts of masochistic violence. Sacrifice was praised, not in practical terms as in the election propaganda of Sinn Féin, but in a general vague sense that praised the act as much as the potential result. The suffering of survivors was ennobled, their grief ignored. The more one suffered, the more one grew as a nationalist. Even the pain of children whose fathers were dead or in prison was ignored. Children were encouraged not to weep.[73] 'God's Ways' in the Christmas 1916 issue of the *Irishman* asked children to reflect on the sorrows of a more immortal mother and child:

> Mother says to have no fear, that daddy's living still,
> And that You love him for his deeds, though men may bear him ill.
> Mary mother! your heart near broke when *your* Son went astray,
> So ask dear God to give me daddy back for Christmas day.[74]

Albinia Broderick raged against the way in which nationalist women were silenced and not allowed to properly mourn their dead. Her anger was directed both against the British government which had abused them so harshly and, though unspoken, against the further abuse of advanced nationalist propagandists, mostly male, who refused to acknowledge in writing their need to grieve:

> Silent we stand. The iron hand has smitten,
> rembling lips to peace again.
> Vein of our hearts, forgive our worthless weeping.
> We may not voice our pain.[75]

God, not men, would comfort the mourning women. Aodh Buidhe asked God to be a 'beacon light' and 'comfort her who sit to-night/Prayerful beside a lonely

---

[73] Peadar Kearney, author of the *Soldier's Song*, produced a truly reprehensible poem to his new-born son Pearse Kearney, in which he instructed the infant to try as Colbert tried/Or to die as Colbert died' and declared 'I would rather see you dead .../In your wee and narrow bed/Then to think that you should grow/And foregather with your foe,/They who laid your namesake low,/Daddy boy!' (Peadar Kearney, *The Soldier's Song and Other Poems* [Dublin, 1928], 'Daddy's Boy' [1917]). [74] BNL, *Irishman*, 23.12.16, p. 5. [75] NLI MS 12120: Roger Casement Papers, Poems on 1916: 'Ireland, 1916'.

fire'.[76] In contrast to the mothers of Irish soldiers who lamented their loss in France and Flanders, 'patriot mothers' were supposed to be proud of their sons' deaths. T.J. O'Connor's patriot mother told her son 'I'm glad, tho' sad my heart/You found a hero's grave'.[77] Sean MacEntee's prison poem on the same theme featured another 'Spartan mother' who declaimed 'Ah thank God you died for Ireland' as 'erect and unbewailing/She looked proudly on the dead'.[78] Grace Gifford Plunkett, ultimate heroine of the Rising for her touching yet bizarre marriage to Joseph Plunkett the night before his execution, was praised without stint:

> God bless thee, Grace Plunkett, thy faithful devotion
> Has won the great heart of a Nation to thee;
> And taught the cold Saxon how patriot 'Rebels'
> Must win out affection, till Erin be free.[79]

Ireland stood in alternately for Christ and the Virgin. Sibeal Tucaig declared 'I think that only Christ was ever loved/As Ireland is'.[80] Pearse's self-created similarity to Christ led Sean MacEntee to imagine a scene in which Eire held the infant Pearse 'fore-destined for the palm' on her lap and told him of the oppressions wrought by the English 'upon his house'.[81] Through the discourse of martyrdom, propagandists were easily able to ignore the harsh realities of the executions, and turn the deaths of nationalists into glorious sacrifices for a greater cause. 'Oh glory of crimson robe! Oh joy of martyr!' wrote an anonymous poet in 'The Martyrs'.[82] 'Sliabh Ruadh' [Red Mountain] felt that it would be a 'glorious death to stand before/The rifles at silvery dawn',[83] while 'Sist' made an explicit comparison to Christ in Piaras Beaslai's charity collection, *The Aftermath of Easter Week*, writing 'Red wine of joy stains every pierced side,/Sons of young Angus, princes of the morrow/Sunlight and wind acclaim the crucified'.[84] Even when living, the martyrs of Easter had been different from other men. 'A Year Ago To-Day', written by Hugh A. MacCartan supposedly from an anecdote related to him by 'the proprietress of a little County Wicklow Hotel', claimed that Plunkett, Pearse, and MacDonagh behaved 'with an old-world grace', and 'did not breathe the common air'.[85]

---

76 Bod., *Catholic Bulletin*, September 1917, p. 580.   77 Ibid., October 1917, p. 611   78 UCD, Sean MacEntee Papers, P67/3: Prison notebook in Lewes Prison, 27/12/16 – 1917. 'The Patriot's Mother' (Version I), fols. 79–79v.   79 UCD, The O'Rahilly Papers, P102/495: 'The Romance of Grace Gifford.'   80 KSRL, Special Collections B3615: Sibeal Tucaig, *After Easter* (Dublin, 1916), 'Love of Ireland', p. 2.   81 UCD, Sean MacEntee Papers, P67/3: Prison Notebook, 'P.H.P',. fol. 1.   82 UCD, The O'Rahilly Papers, P102/495: *Poems and Songs: The REBELS Who Died for IRELAND in Easter Week 1916*, 'The Martyrs'.   83 CUL HIB.916.9, *New Songs, Ballads, and Recitatives* (Dublin, 1916), ''Tis Noble to Die for Ireland'. 84 NLI, William O'Brien Papers, P75: *Aftermath of Easter Week* (Dublin, 1917), 'To Ireland, 1916', fol. 15.   85 NLI MS 5650: Robert Barton Papers, Scrapbook vol. II, 'A Year Ago To-Day'.

The dead were not to be mourned. Rather, they were to be envied. In a letter to one Mrs Malone, the mother of a man killed under his command during the 1916 Rising, Éamon de Valera tried to reconcile his beliefs with the reality of death. 'This Easter from his place in Paradise', he wrote, 'he sees us still struggling through this valley of tears, with the mists of future uncertainties before us. His fate is one for envy not for sorrow'.[86] De Valera acknowledged that this sentiment might seem 'callous',[87] but this did not stop Sinn Féin's Publicity Bureau from publishing this letter in 1917 and spreading copies of it around Ireland.

The apotheosis of sacrificial exultation was reached in September 1917 with the death of Thomas Ashe from the effects of force-feeding. The nationalist response to his death, both before, during, and after his funeral most clearly illustrates the combination of fantastical and practical aggression, and the way in which discourse had become brutalized since the summer of 1915.

A veteran of the Easter Rising, Ashe was re-arres veteran of the Easter Rising, Ashe was re-arrested in August 1917 in Dublin, and quickly went on hunger strike with his fellow prisoners to protest against their 'illegal' imprisonment. In mid-September, the Prison Board, directed by Max Green (son-in-law of John Redmond), decided to force-feed the striking prisoners. In conditions of great brutality, Ashe was twice force-fed, and then spent the night on his cell floor without bedding or shoes. By the morning of 25 September he was suffering from severe congestion of the lungs, and died that same night. Since the leaders of Easter 1916 had been buried in quick-lime to avoid any effort to make martyrs' funerals for them, Ashe's funeral was the first chance for advanced nationalists of Sinn Féin, the Irish Volunteers, the IRB, and the Citizen Army to stage a funeral since the death of O'Donovan Rossa in 1915. Ashe stood as both a symbol of his own courage, and as an emblem for the deaths of other nationalist leaders.

A comparison of the rhetoric surrounding the funerals of O'Donovan Rossa and Ashe illuminates some of the changes in discourse over the course of the war. Both funeral processions were planned and staged in the same way, consciously modelled on the Fenian funeral procession of Terence Bellew MacManus. For O'Donovan Rossa, rhetoric reigned supreme. A cross-nationalist committee was formed, with Pearse and Colonel Maurice Moore[88] sharing organizing duties, and a commemorative programme for the funeral was produced with essays by Moore, MacDonagh, Connolly, Griffith, and others on

86 TCD, Samuels 3/16. 87 Ibid. 88 Younger brother of George Moore, ex-Colonel of the Connaught Rangers and 'Military Director' of the National Volunteers. A constant thorn in Matthew Nathan's side, Moore became an advanced nationalist following the Rising, partly in support of the rebels, and partly because Irish Command had consistently refused him an active duty commission in the British army.

the legacy of Fenianism, the Irish Volunteers, the Fianna Eireann, and other topics of current nationalist interest. Funeral poetry was of similar bent for both men. Thomas MacDonagh instructed readers to 'Grieve not for him, speak not a word of sorrow/ ... The service of his day shall make our morrow/His name shall be a watchword in our story'.[89] Sean S. MacEvoy asked his readers in October 1917 to 'findeth comfort in the thought/That soon shall come the Happy Day/For which our latest martyr fought'.[90]

While the commemorative rhetoric surrounding the funerals was quite similar, the actual experience of the funerals was very different, as was the response in the advanced nationalist press following the interment of the two men. Sir Matthew Nathan's papers show that the British authorities in Dublin were not particularly concerned about the Rossa funeral. In late July, Nathan wrote to John Dillon asking him if there was any substance to the rumour spread by the *Daily Telegraph* that O'Donovan Rossa had renounced Fenianism on his death-bed, and proclaimed his support for the war effort. If so, Nathan hoped that this could be used to 'make the nature of the anticipated demonstration better attuned with the general feeling of the time'.[91] Having been told by railway authorities to expect around 14,500 extra people in Dublin, Nathan anticipated a demonstration, but did not expect trouble. Mainly, he appears to have been surprised that Colonel Maurice Moore planned to be in the procession.[92] Both Nathan and Birrell suspected that the demonstrations surrounding Rossa's funeral were emblematic of a growing discontent with the constitutional movement,[93] but their fellow officials thought nothing of the events. Colonel Walter Edgeworth-Johnstone, Chief Commissioner of the Dublin Metropolitan Police, did not even bother to send police note-takers to the funeral, claiming that 'it is not customary to send them to religious or semi-religious demonstrations'.[94]

Dublin Castle therefore missed the famous oration of Patrick Pearse. At Ashe's funeral two years later British note-takers were against absent, but this time absent in the face of far greater provocation. Michael Collins ordered a volley to be fired over Ashe's grave, and then spoke: 'Nothing additional needs to be said. The volley which we have just heard is the only speech which it is proper to make

---

89 UCD, Terence MacSwiney Papers, P48b/373: *In Memory of O'Donovan Rossa, Fenian* (Commemorative Programme, 1915), Untitled Poem by Thomas MacDonagh, fol. 6. 90 BNL, *Nat*, 20.10.17, p. 6. 91 Bod., Sir Matthew Nathan Papers, Nathan MS 464: Letter Book: Ireland, vol. III, July 1915 to September 1915, Nathan to Dillon, 22 July 1915, , fol. 142. 92 Ibid., Nathen to Birrell, fols. 193–195. 93 Ibid., and Nathan MS 449: Letters from A.B., 1914–1916, Birrell to Nathan, 3 August 1915, fols. 216–18. 94 Bod., Nathan MS 455: Ireland Correspondence J-L, Johnstone to Nathan, 29 July 1915, fols 3–4v. Funerals had long been a traditional way of evading Party Procession Acts, as the British usually did not send men to funerals out of respect for the religious aspect of the event.

above the grave of a dead Fenian'.[95] Collins, a physical-force man, had changed Pearse's dramatic words into action. In two years, the appropriate propaganda voice had been transformed from rhetoric to reality.

The theatre of Ashe's funeral also showed great changes in the support-base for the advanced nationalist movement. For the first time since 1861, when Archbishop Hughes of New York had spoken at a ceremony there for Terence Bellew Macmanus, an Irish Archbishop (Archbishop Walsh of Dublin) rode in the procession.[96] The very fact of a funeral procession was an act of active defiance on the part of the Volunteers, the Citizen Army, and Sinn Féin. Men carried rifles, wore uniforms, drilled publicly, and flew standards of the Republic and the Citizen Army, all in violation of more stringent Defence of the Realm regulations passed after the Easter Rising. Lacking the private papers of British officials at this late stage in the war, we can only guess at their rationale for allowing this to proceed. To contemporary observers, advanced and constitutional alike, Ashe's funeral was a demonstration of the viable strength of the advanced nationalist movement, a movement that the government had demonstrated it completely misjudged.

Foreshadowing alliances that bore fruit in the Conscription Crisis the following spring, constitutional and advanced nationalist newspapers supported the funeral procession. *New Ireland*, edited by Denis Gwynn and moving slowly over to a Sinn Féin line, trumpeted the 'tremendous potency of passive resistance' demonstrated by Ashe's death.[97] Even the *Freeman's Journal* called the funeral procession 'a warning which no Government, however blind, could misread', remarking that the 'challenge' of the procession was backed 'not just by Sinn Féiners alone, but by every Nationalist whose belief in Nationalism is a reality'.[98] Writing from experience, Hanna Sheehy-Skeffington in the *Irish Citizen* condemned the practice of force-feeding that had led to Ashe's death, asking 'all humane people in Dublin irrespective of politics, to join in a general campaign of protest against it, and to demand its immediate cessation and abolition'.[99]

The legacy of Ashe's death was completely different from the legacy of Rossa's. Although in retrospect one might argue that Pearse's inspiring performance at Rossa's graveside led to greater power for him among extremists in the advanced nationalist world, little practical result came of the high words spoken in memory of the old Fenian. Augustine Birrell considered the funeral to have been 'a melancholy spectacle the very height of unreality ... I don't suppose anybody in the whole Concorence [sic] cared for the Old Fellow – who never counted for anything at any time – but it was all done to annoy somebody'.[100] Once buried, once mourned, O'Donovan Rossa was forgotten.

95 Cit. in Townshend, 1983, p. 316, and Sean O Luing, *I Die in a Good Cause* (Tralee, 1970), p. 189. 96 O Luing, 1970, p. 187. 97 Cit. in Ibid., p. 191. 98 Cit. in Ibid., p. 191. 99 NLI, *IC*, October 1917, p. 381. 100 Bod., Sir Matthew Nathan Papers, Nathan MS 449: Letters from A.B., 1914–16, Birrell to Nathan, 3 August 1915, fols. 216–18.

With Ashe, the commemoration went far beyond an outpouring of ballads and laments.[101] Arthur Griffith asked readers of *Nationality* to 'vow that each one individually will raise to his memory the living monument of the Irish language'.[102] This idea did not remain words – within a week a 'Thomas Ashe Memorial Fund' had been inaugurated in *Nationality*, and the idea soon spread to all other advanced nationalist newspapers published at the time. Rather than simply mourn their lost leaders, readers and sympathisers could now convert their grief into a practical advance for the movement. *An Claidheamh Soluis* dedicated its entire 6 October 1917 issue to Ashe, bordering every column in black and adding its voice to those calling for a memorial to the young man. The *Catholic Bulletin* encouraged its young readers to 'speak Irish for five minutes every day in memory of Thomas Ashe ... you would thus bring a stone to the building of an Irish nation'.[103]

The British government was assailed on all sides. A coroner's jury in Dublin brought in a verdict of wilful murder against the prison authorities, and their findings were widely publicized in pamphlet form and in Sean O'Casey's *Lament for Thomas Ashe*, published in 1918. The 'overfed ruffians' who attacked Ashe and the Gaelic League were explicitly threatened in *Young Ireland*. In an editorial calling for revenge, the editor asked readers to imagine what the men responsible for Ashe's death must feel when 'they see a nation mourning for Thomas Aghas and looking threateningly at themselves in their aloof and selfish comfort'.[104]

With the commemoration of Thomas Ashe's death, the various strands of advanced nationalist aggression began to draw together. After the Easter Rising, more moderate propagandists channelled anger into practical work, urging their readers to aggressively pursue a victory for Sinn Féin at the polls. These same men, led as always by Griffith, now used Ashe's death to encourage the creation of more language schools and as a novel way of raising large sums for the Sinn Féin Party. Other propagandists in the aftermath of Easter Week had heroicized the sacrifice of the men involved, whitewashing the violence they had caused and turning dead men into martyrs. This romanticising of violence attracted people to the advanced nationalist movement, and with the death of Ashe, propagandists of this style began to shift from urging people to suffer and die for Ireland in emulation of the lost leaders to becoming violent for their cause. Aggression had been matched by aggression since the Rising – now violence had begun to increase. The attitude of the Irish Volunteers who marched through the streets of Dublin carrying loaded rifles in October 1917, led by men who considered rifle fire a requiem, would begin to assume greater importance within the rhetoric of the Irish Revolution.

---

101 Although as O Luing correctly points out, 'the ballads written about Ashe would fill a volume' (O Luing, 1970, p. 185). 102 BNL, *Nat*, 6.10.17, p. 2. 103 Bod., *Catholic Bulletin*, November 1917, p. 662. 104 BNL, *Og*, 6.10.17, p. 1.

IV

The Conscription Crisis of spring 1918, sparked by the necessity for increased recruitment after the successful German blitzkrieg of 21 March 1918, gave advanced nationalists a leading role in the fight against conscription. With the support of the Catholic hierarchy, they enjoyed an immeasurable advantage over Parliamentarians, who were viewed as hypocrites and johnny-come-latelys in the battle. The anti-nationalist *Daily Mail* reported that Sinn Féin delegates at an all-Ireland conference at the Mansion House on 18 April were 'greeted by a storm of cheering and cries of "Up, Sinn Féin!"' In contrast, the presence of Devlin and Dillon met with 'a quieter reception, mixed with some jeers'.[105] Rumours flooded Dublin. The diarist Alice Brunton reported rumours that Gurkhas were said to be arriving from India to garrison Ireland, and that Captain W.A. Redmond was in the Tower of London awaiting trial after he took off his uniform and used it to beat Lloyd George.[106]

Sparked by the development of an external event, the Conscription Crisis saw the simultaneous use of mass pressure and threatened violence. While men like de Valera, Griffith, Stack, and Figgis were writing the 'Anti-Conscription Pledge' and arranging with priests to distribute it on Sundays as part of the Mass, and William O'Brien was helping to organise a national labour stoppage on the 23 April, Irish Volunteers were reported to be collecting rifles all around Ireland. The *Irish Independent* reported 'in the Glen of Aherlow, Dundrum, and other districts, the farmers have handed over guns willingly'.[107]

Before the arrest of moderate Sinn Féiners in the trumped-up 'German Plot' of May 1918, mass pressure was the primary weapon used in the fight against conscription. Some devout nationalists turned to prayer for help. Brian O'Higgins' children's journal *St Enda's* reminded its readers that prayers were greater 'than guns, ships, or hosts of warring men',[108] while Alice Furlong's 'Conscription (To the Leaders)' gave credit to God, who 'showed the way by which our feet should run/In the high name of the redeeming Son'.[109] While some nationalists were content with prayer, it was their votes which were most encouraged by Sinn Féin. A vote for Sinn Féin was the only effective way to bar conscription short of armed violence, something that even Robert Brennan acknowledged in the propaganda he produced for the General Election after Griffith was arrested. A simple equation was created. A vote for Sinn Féin was a vote of resistance, while the reverse was equally clear. 'He who votes in Cavan to elect a man acknowledging the British Parliament votes for conscription'.[110] Only

---

105 NLI MS 7985: Alice Brunton Diary, 1918, *Daily Mail*, 19 April 1918.   106 Ibid., 19 & 27 April 1918.   107 Ibid., *Irish Independent*, 20 April 1918.   108 NLI, *St Enda's*, May 1918, p. 34.   109 BNL, *Nat*, 4.5.18, p. 3.   110 Ibid., p. 1.

Sinn Féin, 'The Uncompromising Obstacle to English Rule in Ireland', 'bars the way to CONSCRIPTION'.[111]

Passive resistance was encouraged, but even passive resistance was far more aggressive than before the Rising.[112] In January 1916 the old patriot John Sweetman had published a pamphlet entitled *Ireland and Conscription* in which he urged nationalists to refuse to march to barracks or camps if conscripted, and reminded readers that the British would not shoot many Irishmen, so the worst that could happen would be a term of imprisonment.[113] In contrast, the Mansion House Conference issued a leaflet to 'Local Defence Committees' urging them to stop railway traffic and work, hold the harvest indefinitely, to instruct the entire population of the parish on the necessity of warning young men about the approach of the police or military, and to help the young men, who were instructed to flee into the hills in groups of two or three.[114]

The arrest of Griffith and other leaders in May 1918 left advanced nationalist propaganda in the hands of more radical members. A combination of this enforced radicalisation with a genuine fear of being forced to serve on the Western Front and an anger at British aggression in Ireland all led to an increasing tension in advanced nationalist propaganda. Radicals dramatized the effects of voting against Sinn Féin. Rather than simply causing conscription, a vote for the supporters of the war would be an act of murder. 'They put the dagger into my grasp', cried a mother in 'The Blood Vote'.[115] 'It seemed but a pencil then;/I did not know it was a fiend a-gasp/For the priceless blood of men'.[116]

Anticipating victory in the General Election, Sinn Féin propagandists began to make ominous threats that hinted at the possibility of physical violence. 'Our Day Is Coming' responded a poster to reports of violence towards prisoners in Belfast.[117] Seamus O'Kelly warned readers in September 1918 that 'Sinn Féin in the future will have it still more in its power to pay back those who have not the courage or the manhood to meet it on open and fair political terms to-day'.[118]

Not only propagandists were growing more bloodthirsty in response to the threat of conscription. Although most priests were satisfied with the hierarchy's

---

111 NLI MS 18388: Sinn Féin Election Pamphlets, 1918–24, 18388/C1.   112 Indeed, the concept of passive resistance to militarism was older even than the Great War. These ideas originated with James Fintan Lalor, and after 1848 were resurrected by Bulmer Hobson in his 1909 book *Defensive Warfare: A Handbook for Irish Nationalists* (see Townshend, 1983, pp. 240–245 for an illuminating analysis of this work). During the Land War, Parnell formally wedded agitation to passive resistance.   113 CUL, HIB.7.918.14, *Ireland and Conscription* [erroneous dating at Cambridge – see BNL, *Nat*, 1 January 1916, p. 6 for an advertisement for this 'new pamphlet'. Also mark reception date of pamphlet at Cambridge, stamped March 1916.]   114 TCD, Samuels 2/132a.   115 This was originally an anti-conscription leaflet issued by the No Conscription Council of Sydney, Australia, and reprinted in *Young Ireland*.   116 BNL, *Og*, 5.10.18, p. 6.   117 NLI, ILB Series, ILB 300 P12, fol. 6.   118 BNL, *Nat*, 7.9.18, p. 2.

written support for the anti-conscription campaign,[119] some seized the opportunity to threaten armed violence against the British. The British government encouraged Cardinal Gasparri, the Vatican Secretary of State, to inform the Pope of what these priests were saying, and supplied him with a list of extracts from these sermons. According to Gasparri's letter, priests had no qualms about directly instructing their parishioners to resist arrest actively. Father Keane in Killina stated 'no man should have any doubt but to fire on the first man who will come to arrest him',[120] while the Reverend Fr O'Meehan reassured his parishioners that 'they were morally justified' if they took a life in self defence. Other priests urged their audiences to arm for the battle. Father Rahilly in Castleconnell 'told them to try and have something to defend themselves with; rifles, guns, machine guns, or cannon'.[121] In Silvermines, the Revd Culligan was more realistic, admitting that 'even a clasp-knife can be used'. Clergy volunteered to lead their flocks to the fray. At a public meeting in Cahirciveen, the parish priest shouted that 'when the hour of tribulation comes, the clergy will shed the last drop of their blood fighting with their flocks'.[122] A certain Father Prior was more direct, claiming simply 'if an English Tommy came to him and asked him to come along he would draw his revolver and put an ounce of lead in him'.[123]

The policemen were the real losers in these sermons.[124] Father O'Callaghan of Killyclougher reminded listeners that policemen who assisted in enforcing conscription were 'guilty of murder, and can never get absolution'.[125] *An Open Letter to an Irish Policemen*, written in the summer of 1918, urged policemen to co-operate against conscription all around Ireland. The British were intelligent enough, the author thought, to ensure that no policemen would have to seize his brother's gun by stationing policemen away from their families. This didn't matter, however, because 'Constable Burke down in Tipperary will do the same kind office for Sergeant Ryan's brother, while the Sergeant is busy looking up the guns in Galway, where Burke comes from'.[126]

Practical armed resistance was urged on men around Ireland. No longer would propagandists be content with fantasizing about wetting their swords in the blood of Saxon skulls. Now, in a realistic and measured way, they urged men to arm themselves with anything they could get. 'A pitch-fork is not as good as a machine-gun, but it's better than an idle surmise when you want to defend

---

119 Cf. Patrick Callan, 'Ambivalence Towards the Saxon Shilling: The Attitudes of the Catholic Church in Ireland Towards Enlistment During the First World War', *Archivium Hibernicum*, 1986 (vol. 41), pp. 99–111.   120 UCD, Denis McCullough Papers, P120/7: Copy of Cardinal Gasparri's Letter to Rome, 1918.   121 Ibid.   122 Ibid.   123 Ibid.   124 Supporting David Fitzpatrick's research showing the ill-effects of the Irish Revolution on police, especially the RIC (Fitzpatrick, 1977, pp. 3–39).   125 UCD, Denis McCullough Papers, P120/7: Copy of Cardinal Gasparri's Letter to Rome, 1918.   126 NLI MS 5637: Robert Barton Papers, Scrapbook vol. I, fol. 123.

yourself or capture a rifle'.[127] Men were encouraged to 'band [them]selves together to resist. Select in your districts suitable spots for entrenchments, objects suitable for barricades, lay in stores of provisions, choose men capable of leadership, and FIGHT FOR IRELAND IN IRELAND'.[128]

The appearance of *An t-Oglach* in mid-August 1918, edited by Piaras Beaslai, with contributors including J.J. O'Connell and Michael Collins, reinforced the idea that the Irish Volunteers were the central factor in the rise of an Irish revolutionary state. The Volunteers were ready, and their policy towards conscription was one of shedding English blood. 'The Irish Volunteers are the keynote of the situation', wrote Beaslai in October 1918. 'They are the reality, the grim reality that England cannot get rid of'.[129] A direct and reasoned response to British aggression was urged, echoing the suggestions made in the pre-Rising *Irish Volunteer*, save now these suggestions were the constant guide of the Volunteer movement, not simply occurring at isolated moments. The Easter Rising itself had proved that patriots in the right frame of mind could go out to battle without fearing death, and Beaslai exploited this unawareness of mortality. 'Every true Volunteer should know how to act for himself,' he wrote. 'It is his duty to resist to the death, to use every weapon in his power ... to make his death or capture dearly purchased by the lives of enemies'.[130]

Passive resistance to those who helped conscription was no longer enough. In a bloodthirsty article reprinted as a pamphlet, Ernest Blythe warned that:

> Any man who knowingly and willingly does anything to facilitate the working of the machinery of conscription, must be dealt with exactly as if he were an enemy soldier ... all these having assisted the enemy must be shot or otherwise destroyed ... we must show that it is not healthy to be against us.[131]

With words such as these inciting nationalists, the removal of any possible threat of conscription at war's end did little to change the bellicose atmosphere in Ireland. Advanced nationalists greeted the armistice celebrations with a mixture of disgust and violence. *Nationality* virtually ignored the end of the war, preferring to concentrate on the coming elections, while *Young Ireland* lamented the cowardice of various sections of Dublin's population that had refused to join the army and yet still waved Union Jacks.[132] Only *An t-Oglach* reported the violent events which surrounded the Armistice, and this report should certainly be doubted. According to *An t-Oglach*, a meeting of Irish nationalists at the Mansion House on 11 November caused 'the foreign garrison' to vow vengeance.

127 Ibid., fol. 122. 128 NLI ILB Series, ILB 300 P 12, fol. 37. 129 NLI, *An t-Oglach*, 29.10.18, p. 1. 130 Ibid., 14.9.18, p. 1. 131 Ibid., 14.10.18, p. 1, reprinted as leaflet 'Ruthless Warfare', preserved in TCD, Samuels 1/33, and cit. in Townshend, 1983, p. 320. 132 BNL, *Og*, 23.11.18, pp. 2–3.

This vengeance was wrought the following Wednesday, when a band of 700 soldiers, 'instigated and organized by their officers' attacked the Sinn Féin offices in Harcourt Street.[133] The offices were guarded by thirty Volunteers 'armed with sticks' who beat back the attack, landing 120 soldiers in the hospital and killing five of them, including an RAF officer.[134] This dubious incident is more important for what it symbolizes than the fact that it almost certainly did not occur.[135]

What this incident symbolizes is the central divide in advanced nationalist politics, one which lay dormant under the threat of conscription, but which would quickly re-emerge with peace. The moderates behind *Nationality*, technically the voice of the Sinn Féin Party, chose to virtually ignore the celebrations at Armistice, and concentrate on the practical work for the future. However, according to the organ of the Irish Volunteers, the only way in which this work could continue was through the armed and violent protection of the physical-force wing of the party.

Richard Davis has written that the election of 73 Sinn Féiners in December 1918 'did not give a mandate for a Republic to be torn from Britain by guerrilla warfare'.[136] However, the election of these representatives could not have come about if the war had not shown a way for the different discourses of revolution to succeed in influencing people. The attitude to the war, growing ever more brutal as the war itself grew more bloody, opened the door for an aggression towards recruiters which finally manifested itself in the violent discourse of the Conscription Crisis. Griffith, and before his return to unionism in summer 1918, Pim, formed a coherent electoral policy out of the violent legacy of the Easter Rising, rhetorically transforming resistance to the war into an aggressive act. This electoral policy was what voters in December 1918 chose, but many of the voters had been drawn into the movement through the commemorative propaganda produced after Easter 1916 which glorified the deaths of the Rising's leaders, and encouraged others to emulate them. The sheer violence of this 'self-cidal' rhetoric was easily re-directed towards the British, first with the death of Thomas Ashe, and then culminating with the final struggles against conscription.

---

133 Frank Gallagher recalls it slightly differently, claiming that mobs attacked Sinn Féin Headquarters on Armistice Day itself (Gallagher, 1953). **134** NLI, *An t-Oglach*, 30.11.18, pp. 3–4. **135** No other reference to this riot can be found. According to the *Weekly Irish Times*, Armistice passed noisily in Dublin, and the only trouble that night came from 'paraing of throughfares by organised bands of Sinn Féiners'. This trouble, however, took the form of singing party songs, breaking one window on Grafton Street, and getting in a tussle with a platoon of the DMP. Two constables were injured, and one had his helmet broken (BNL, *WIT*, 16.11.18, p. 1). Laffan (1999) cites a letter from Michael Collins to Austin Stack on 28 November 1918, in which Collins boasted that 120 officers and soldiers were injured and 5 killed in Armistice Day riots, and that only *An t-Oglach* had reported this because of political censorship (Laffan, 1999, p. 270). **136** Davis, 1977, p. 42.

How was this reflected in the pattern of support for advanced nationalism during and immediately after the war? Peter Hart's research shows that many men and women first joined the Volunteers because of the more radical post-Rising propaganda.[137] Many more voted because of the successful Sinn Féin electoral campaigns, both in by-elections and for the December 1918 General Election. Already this created a slight disparity between those who volunteered, and those who voted. Hart further makes clear that many of those who had volunteered for either Sinn Féin or the Irish Volunteers in the heady days following the Rising and most especially during the Conscription Crisis, dropped out of these movements after 1918.[138] This left advanced nationalism with two central groups, a group of hard-core volunteers influenced by actual experience in the Rising or in British prisons, faithful readers of *An t-Oglach*, and the men and women elected by the voters of Ireland in December 1918, men and women who seemed at first to be dedicated to a peaceful solution to Anglo-Irish difficulties. Here were the seeds of the Irish Civil War, seeds that were spread by the various forms of propaganda prevalent during the Great War.

The Great War brutalized the discourse of propagandists in Ireland. This was seen most clearly in their use of humour, but it can also be seen in their use of aggressive propaganda. Anti-war propaganda changed from passive to active as the war progressed, and fantasies of violence against the British government and its recruiters became realities, first at Easter 1916 and then in the columns of newspapers for the next thirty months. At its most effective, propaganda helps create a political transformation. Brutalized by the slaughter of the Great War, the discourse of aggressive propaganda forecast the rupture of the Irish Civil War; thereby influencing the greatest political change Ireland has seen this century.

137 Hart, 1998, p. 207. 138 Ibid., p. 243 et fl.

Conclusion

'Propaganda', wrote Jacques Ellul in 1969, 'will turn a normal feeling of patriotism into a raging nationalism. It not only reflects myths and pre-suppositions, it hardens them, sharpens them, invests them with the power of shock and action'.[1] Between 1914 and 1918, the patriotic ideals of advanced nationalists were turned into a true revolutionary nationalism, a nationalism that resulted in the democratic defeat of the Irish Party in December 1918. The chronology of these years is well known. Why the defeat happened can only be answered by an infinite and impossible study of individual motivation. We cannot explain why each individual who voted for Sinn Féin in December 1918 did so, but we can examine reflections of the general attitude of the revolutionary nationalists, and how these reflections changed as the war progressed. What happened in Ireland during the First World War was a political and social revolution, and like all revolutions, it was nourished by the propaganda of agitation.

The past ten years have seen a revolution in Irish historiography on the First World War. The pioneering works, of David Fitzpatrick and Terence Denman, followed now by illuminating local studies by Joost Augusteijn, Oliver Coogan,[2] Marie Coleman, and Peter Hart, have all shown once again the central importance of the Great War to Irish social and political life. This book, returning to the words, images, and ideas expressed in advanced nationalist discourse during the war itself, has attempted to show that the day-to-day events of the Great War shaped and moulded the thinking of advanced nationalists who went on to found a new state in the post-war years.

The Great War created manifold opportunities for advanced nationalist propagandists. In some areas, the war produced a situation that propagandists could easily exploit. The growing number of Irish casualties allowed propagandists to oppose the war while remaining sympathetic to the sacrifice of these men. British misuse of atrocity propaganda, and the truth-fogging effects of military censorship, combined to permit propagandists a depiction of Britain and the pro-war press as built on a framework of lies and immorality.

Irish society was changed as well by the war. The increase in social mobility, especially among young women, and the fear of outsiders stirred up by pro-war propaganda, were both linked by advanced nationalists to their old crusades

---

1 Ellul, 1969, pp. 40-1. 2 Oliver Coogan, *Politics and War in County Meath, 1913-1923* (Dublin, 1983).

against immorality and salacious literature. With the departure of parliamentary nationalists to the pro-war camp, advanced nationalists were left the field, and thus drew clerical and popular support for their efforts. The effects of the Great War upon farming and farmers, simultaneously increasing crop prices and raising the fear of famine, led Sinn Féin to create a series of local government initiatives that were given great publicity in propaganda and attempted to show voters that Sinn Féin was a viable alternative to the Irish Parliamentary Party or union with Great Britain.

While propagandists exploited specific issues by linking them to the war, the war itself, and its domestic manifestation in the Easter Rising, contributed to an intensification of propagandistic discourse. Words and images were brutalized in four violent years, and aggression became more and more central to the public face of the Irish Revolution. The Ireland that greeted a returning veteran in early 1919 would have been very different from the one he had left four years before. While, on the surface, the Irish supported the British war effort, at the same time another war raged between nationalists and pro-war supporters, a war fought on street corners and in the columns of the advanced nationalist press. By the act of linking the two war efforts, advanced nationalism leapt from the street corners, from the pages of small newspapers, all the way to the seat of power at Westminster. As Frank Gallagher would remember years later:

> Yet, despite it all the facts were got to the people, by secretly printed leaflet, by the Mosquito Press, by innocent-seeming letters to the daily papers and they led to the most spectacular victory in the history of Irish politics.[3]

We do not know exactly how effective propaganda was during the Great War – but it is clear from the victory of Sinn Féin in December 1918, and its victory in a majority of by-elections during the war, that propaganda aided the advanced nationalist campaign. Nicholas J. Cull has recently likened propaganda to lubricating oil: 'speeding processes when present, but bringing everything to a grinding halt if mismanaged'.[4] As this book has shown by linking support for advanced nationalism with halting the slaughter of war, propagandists helped to simultaneously shatter pro-war propaganda and smooth the way for the advent of a revolutionary government in Ireland.

---

[3] Gallagher, 1953, p. 43. [4] Nicholas J. Cull, review of Susan Brewer, *To Win the Peace: British Propaganda in the United States during World War II*, *History*, vol. 84, no. 275 (July 1999), p. 563.

Select bibliography

I. PRIMARY MANUSCRIPT SOURCES

London

Public Record Office, Kew
Colonial Office Papers, Ireland
Home Office Papers

Imperial War Museum
Recruiting Posters Collection
Department of Photographs

Oxford

Bodleian Library
Herbert Asquith Papers
Augustine Birrell Papers
Sir RCK Ensor Papers
Andrew Philip Magill Papers
Sir Matthew Nathan Papers

Cambridge

Cambridge University Library, Department of Special Collections
HIB Series

Dublin

Trinity College, Dublin
Department of Early Printed Books
Arthur Warren Samuels Collection
Irish Recruiting Posters Collection

University College, Dublin
Archives
Ernest Blythe Papers
Desmond Fitzgerald Papers
Thomas Kettle Papers
Denis McCullough Papers
Sean MacEntee Papers
Eoin MacNeill Papers
Michael J. O'Rahilly ['The O'Rahilly'] Papers

National Library of Ireland
Robert Barton Papers
Joseph Brennan Papers
Alice Brunton Papers
Roger Casement Papers
Maurice Moore Papers
William O'Brien Papers
F.W. Pennefather Letters
John Redmond Papers
Sheehy-Skeffington Papers
Clement Shorter Papers

General National Library Manuscripts:
ILB 300 Series Sinn Féin Election Pamphlets, 1918–1924
MS 984: Press Censorship Office, Circulars of Censored Material
MS 1428: 'The Slums and the Trenches', Essay by James Connolly
MS 8494: Correspondence on photo censorship, 1916
MS 10494: Précis of documents seized in raid on Sinn Féin Headquarters, 1918
MS 15317: Anonymous verses as if by an Irishman who fought against the Irish in Easter Week, 1916.
MS 18388: Manuscripts relating to Sinn Féin Election Propaganda, 1918–1924.
MS 18464: 'The Angelus': Song for de Valera's campaign in East Clare, 1917.

National Archives
Chief Secretary's Office Registered Papers, 1914–1918
Press Censorship Files, 1916–1918

Lawrence, Kansas

Kenneth Spencer Research Library, University of Kansas
P.S. O'Hegarty Collection
Paul Cusack Autograph Book (MS K18)
Sinn Féin Pamphlets (C3196: Uncatalogued)
Irish Political Postcards (C3385: Uncatalogued)
Leaflets on the Easter Rising (E813: Uncatalogued)

II. NEWSPAPERS/JOURNALS

An Claidheamh Soluis
Answers
An t-Oglach
Catholic Bulletin
Cork Celt
Daily Dispatch
Daily Mail
Daily Sketch

Dublin Gazette
Eire Ireland
Fianna
Fianna Fail
Freeman's Journal
Gael
Hibernian
Honesty

Irish Citizen
Irish Freedom
Irish Fun
Irish Independent
Irishman
Irish Review
Irish Times
Irish Volunteer
Irish Weekly Independent
Irish Work
Irish Worker
Leader
Nation
Nationality
New Statesman

New York Herald Tribune
New York Times
Nineteenth Century and After
Quiz
St Enda's
Scissors & Paste
Sinn Féin
Spark
Sunday Freeman's Journal
The Times
Weekly Freeman's Journal
Weekly Irish Times
Worker
Worker's Republic
Young Ireland (Eire Og)

III. PRIMARY PRINTED SOURCES

Anon., *Black Book of the War* (London, 1915).
Anon., *The Ethics of Sinn Féin* (Dublin, 1917).
Anon., *Two Years of English Atrocities in Ireland* (Cork, 1919).
Birrell, Augustine, *Et cetera* (London, 1930).
Blacam, Aodh de, *What Sinn Féin Stands For: The Irish Republican Movement in History, Aims and Ideals, Examined as to their Significance in the World* (Dublin, 1921).
Brennan, Robert, *Allegiance* (Dublin, 1950).
Brown, Mary J. and J.M. Stephen (eds)., *Poetry of Irish History* (Dublin, 1927).
Carbery, Lady Mary, *The Germans in Cork* (Dublin, 1918).
Cavanagh, Maeve, *Sheaves of Revolt* (Dublin, 1914).
——, *A Voice of Insurgency* (Dublin, 1916).
Choille, Breandan Mac Giolla (ed.), *Intelligence Notes of the Chief Secretary's Office, 1913–1916* (Dublin, 1966).
Committee on Alleged German Atrocities, *The Truth about German Atrocities* (London, 1916).
Cooper, Bryan, *The Tenth (Irish) Division in Gallipoli* (1918) (Dublin, 1998).
Davis, Edward (ed)., *Inside Asquith's Cabinet: From the Diaries of Sir Charles Hobhouse* (London, 1977).
Dickinson, Page, *The Dublin of Yesterday* (Dublin, 1929).
FitzGerald, Desmond, *Memoirs of Desmond FitzGerald, 1913–1916* (London, 1968).
Freud, Sigmund, *Jokes and their Relation to the Unconscious* (1905), tr. James Strachey (London, 1960).
Gallagher, Frank ['David Hogan'], *The Four Glorious Years* (Dublin, 1953).
Good, Joe, *Enchanted by Dreams: The Journal of a Revolutionary* (Edited by Maurice Good) (Dublin, 1999).
Great Britain, Royal Commission on the Rebellion in Ireland, *Report of Commission, Minutes of Evidence* (London, 1916).

Greaves, Charles Desmond, *The Easter Rising in Song and Ballad* (London, 1980).
Griffith, Arthur, *The Resurrection of Hungary* (Dublin, 1918 (3rd ed)).
Griffith, Kenneth, and Timothy O'Grady, *Curious Journey: An Oral History of Ireland's Unfinished Revolution* (Dublin, 1998 (2nd ed).).
Hanna, Henry, *The Pals at Suvla Bay* (Dublin, 1917).
Hannay, James, 'Ireland and the War', *The Nineteenth Century and After*, vol. 78, no. 462 (Aug. 1915), pp. 393–402.
——, 'Recruiting in Ireland To-Day', *The Nineteenth Century and After*, vol. 79, no. 467 (Jan. 1916), pp. 173–180.
—— ['George Birmingham'], *An Irishman Looks at his World* (London, 1919).
—— ['George Birmingham'], *General John Regan* (London, 1933).
Hansard, Parliamentary Debates, Commons, Fifth Series, vol. LXV – CX (London, 1914–18).
Henry, R.M., *The Evolution of Sinn Féin* (Dublin, 1920).
Hobson, Bulmer, *Ireland, Yesterday and Tomorrow* (Dublin, 1968).
Hopkinson, Michael (ed)., *Frank Henderson's Easter Rising: Recollections of a Dublin Volunteer* (Cork, 1998).
Hyde, Douglas, *On the Necessity for De-Anglicising Ireland* (Dublin, 1892).
Iarraidh, Gnathai Gan, *The Sacred Egoism of Sinn Féin* (Dublin, 1918).
Kearney, Peadar, *The Soldier's Song and Other Poems* (Dublin, 1928).
Lavery, Felix M., *Irish Heroes in the War* (London, 1917).
MacDonagh, Michael, *The Irish at the Front* (London, 1916).
——, *The Irish on the Somme* (London, 1917).
Mac Lochlainn, Piaras F., *Last Words* (Dublin, 1966).
MacSwiney, Terence, *Battle-Cries* (Cork, 1918).
Montefiore, Dora B. *From a Victorian to a Modern* (London, 1927).
Morgan, John Hartman, *German Atrocities: An Official Investigation* (London, 1916).
O'Doherty, Michael Patrick, *My Parents and Other Rebels* (Dublin, 1999).
O'Hegarty, P.S., *The Victory of Sinn Féin* (Dublin, 1924).
O'Higgins, Brian (ed)., *War Humour and Other Atrocities* (Dublin, 1915).
——, *Sentinel Songs* (Dublin, 1918).
O'Malley, Ernie, *On Another Man's Wound* (Dublin, 1936).
O'Malley, William, *Glancing Back: 70 years' experience and reminiscences of pressman, sportsman, and member of Parliament* (London, 1933).
Pearse, Patrick, *Political Writings and Speeches* (Dublin, 1952).
Pim, Herbert ['A. Newman'], *Sinn Féin* (Belfast, 1920).
Ponsonby, Viscount, *Truth and Falsehood in Wartime* (London, 1924).
Shaw, George Bernard, *O'Flaherty, V.C.* (Edinburgh, 1914).
Simplicissimus, *Gott Strafe England!* (Munchen, 1915).
Stacpoole, Henry de Vere, *Pools of Silence* (London, 1910).
Tucaig, Sibeal, *After Easter* (Dublin, 1916).
Tynan, Katharine, *The Years of the Shadow* (London, 1919).
Warwick-Haller, Adrian and Sally (eds)., *Letters from Dublin, Easter 1916: Alfred Fannin's Diary of the Rising* (Dublin, 1995).
Wimperis, Arthur, *My Lady Frayle* (London, 1916).
Yeats, William Butler, 'J.M. Synge and the Ireland of His Time', in *Essays and Introductions* (London, 1961), pp. 311–342.

Select bibliography 253

IV. SECONDARY PRINTED SOURCES

Allen, Kieran, *The Politics of James Connolly* (London, 1990).
Alter, Peter, 'Symbolism of Irish Nationalism', in Alan O'Day (ed)., *Reactions to Irish Nationalism* (London, 1987), pp. 1–20.
Anderson, Benedict R. O'G., 'Cartoons and Monuments: The Evolution of Political Communication under the New Order', in D. Jackson and Lucien Pye (eds)., *Political Power and Communication in Indonesia* (Berkeley, 1978), pp. 282–321.
Anderson, Patricia, *The Printed Image and the Transformation of Popular Culture* (Oxford, 1991).
Augusteijn, Joost, *From Public Defiance to Guerrilla Warfare: The Experience of Ordinary Volunteers in the Irish War of Independence, 1916–1921* (Dublin, 1996).
Ayling, Ronald, and Michael J. Durkan, *Sean O'Casey: A Bibliography* (London, 1978).
Barnett, L. Margaret, *British Food Policy during the First World War* (Boston, 1985).
Barthes, Roland, *Image-Music-Text*, tr. Stephen Heath (London, 1993 (2nd ed).).
Bartlett, Thomas, and Keith Jeffery (eds)., *A Military History of Ireland* (Cambridge, 1996).
Bew, Paul, 'Sinn Féin, Agrarian Radicalism, and the War of Independence', in D. George Boyce (ed)., *The Revolution in Ireland, 1879–1923* (London, 1988), pp. 217–35.
Bogacz, Ted, ' "A Tyranny of Words": Language, Poetry, and Antimodernism in England in the First World War', *JMH*, 58 (Sept. 1986), pp. 643–68.
Bourke, Joanna, *Dismembering the Male: Men's Bodies, Britain, and the Great War* (London, 1996).
Bowden, Tom, 'The Irish Underground and the War of Independence, 1919–1921', *JCH*, vol. 8, no. 2 (April 1973), pp. 3–24.
——, *The Breakdown of Public Security: The Case of Ireland 1916–1921 and Palestine 1936–1939* (London, 1977).
Bowman, Tim, 'The Irish Recruiting and Anti-Recruiting Campaigns, 1914–1918', in Bertrand Taithe and Tim Thornton (eds)., *Propaganda* (Stroud, 1999), pp. 223–39.
Boyce, D. George, *Nationalism in Ireland* (Baltimore, 1982).
——, 'The Marginal Britons: The Irish', in Robert Colls and Phillip Dodd (eds)., *Englishness: Politics and Culture, 1880–1920* (London, 1986), pp. 230–53.
——, *The Sure Confusing Drum: Ireland and the First World War* (Swansea, 1993).
——, '1916, Interpreting the Rising', in D. George Boyce and Alan O'Day (eds)., *The Making of Modern Irish History: Revisionism and the Revisionist Controversy* (New York, 1996), pp. 163–87.
Brantlinger, Patrick, *Rule of Darkness: British Literature and Imperialism* (Ithaca, NY, 1988).
Bracco, Rosa Maria, *Merchants of Hope: British Middlebrow Writers and the First World War, 1919–1939* (Oxford, 1993).
Buitenhuis, Peter, *The Great War of Words* (London, 1987).
Bull, Philip, *Land, Politics & Nationalism: A Study of the Irish Land Question* (Dublin, 1996).
Caesar, Adrian, *Taking it Like a Man: Suffering, Sexuality, and the War Poets* (Manchester, 1993).
Cahalan, James, *Great Hatred, Little Room: The Irish Historical Novel* (Syracuse, NY, 1983).

Callan, Patrick, 'Ambivalence Towards the Saxon Shilling: The Attitudes of the Catholic Church in Ireland Towards Enlistment During the First World War', *Archivium Hibernicum*, vol. 41 (1986), pp. 99–111.
Campbell, Colm, *Emergency Law in Ireland, 1918–1925* (Oxford, 1994).
Clark, Toby, *Art and Propaganda in the Twentieth Century: The Political Image in the Age of Mass Culture* (London, 1997).
Clarke, I.F., *Voices Prophesying War, 1763–1884* (Oxford, 1966).
Clarke, Samuel, and James Donnelly (eds)., *Irish Peasants: Violence and Political Unrest, 1780–1914* (Dublin, 1983).
Clifford, Brendan, *Ireland in the Great War* (Dublin, 1992).
Colum, Padraic, *Ourselves Alone! The Story of Arthur Griffith and the Origin of the Irish Free State* (New York, 1959).
Condren, Mary, 'Sacrifice and Political Legitimation: the Product of a Gendered Social Order', *Journal of Women's History*, vol. 6, no. 4/vol. 7, no. 1 (double issue) (Winter/Spring 1995), pp. 160–89.
Coogan, Oliver, *Politics and War in Meath, 1913–1923* (Dublin, 1983).
Coombes, Annie E., *Reinventing Africa* (New Haven, 1994).
Costello, Francis J., *Enduring the Most: The Life and Death of Terence MacSwiney* (Dingle, 1995).
Costello, Peter, *The Heart Grown Brutal: The Irish Revolution in Literature, from Parnell to the Death of Yeats, 1891–1939* (Dublin, 1977).
Curtis, L.P., *Coercion and Conciliation in Ireland 1880–1892: A Study in Conservative Unionism* (Princeton, NJ, 1963).
——, *Apes and Angels: Irishmen in Victorian Caricature* (London, 1997 (2nd ed).).
Darracott, Joseph, *The First World War in Posters* (New York, 1974).
Davenport-Hines, Richard, *Sex, Death, and Punishment: Attitudes to sex and sexuality in Britain since the Renaissance* (London, 1990).
Davis, Richard, *Arthur Griffith and non-violent Sinn Féin* (Dublin, 1974).
——, 'The Advocacy of Passive Resistance in Ireland, 1916–1922', *Anglo-Irish Studies*, vol. III (1977), pp. 19–34.
——, 'Ulster Protestants and the Sinn Féin Press, 1914–1922', *Eire Ireland*, vol. XV, no. 4 (Winter 1980), pp. 60–85.
Deane, Seamus, *Celtic Revivals* (London, 1985).
Demm, Eberhard, 'Propaganda and Caricature in the First World War', *JCH*, vol. 28, no. 1 (Jan. 1993), pp 163–92.
Denman, Terence, 'The catholic Irish soldier in the Great War: the racial environment', *IHS*, vol. 27, no. 108 (Nov. 1991), pp. 352–65.
——, *Ireland's Unknown Soldiers: The 16th (Irish) Division in the Great War* (Dublin, 1992).
——, 'The red livery of shame: the campaign against army recruitment in Ireland, 1899–1914', *IHS*, vol. 29, no. 114 (Nov. 1994), pp. 208–233.
Derez, Mark, 'The Flames of Louvain: The War Experience of an Academic Community', in Hugh Cecil and Peter H. Liddle (eds)., *Facing Armageddon: The First World War Experienced* (London, 1996), pp. 617–29.
Donnchadha, Mairin Ní, and Theo Dorgan (eds)., *Revising the Rising* (Derry, 1991).
Doob, Leonard W., 'Propaganda', in E. Barnouw *et al.* (eds)., *International Encyclopedia of Communications*, vol. 3 (New York, 1989), p. 375.

Dooley, Tom, 'Politics, bands and marketing: army recruitment in Waterford City, 1914–1915', *Irish Sword*, xviii, no. 72 (Winter 1991), pp. 205–19.
——, *Irishmen or English Soldiers?* (Liverpool, 1995).
Eby, Cecil D., *The Road to Armageddon: The Martial Spirit in English Popular Literature, 1870–1914* (Durham, NC, 1988).
Edelman, Murray, *Politics as Symbolic Action: Mass Arousal and Quiescence* (New York, 1971).
Edelstein, T.J. (ed.), *Imagining an Irish Past: The Celtic Revival, 1840–1940* (Chicago, 1992).
Edwards, Owen Dudley, and Fergus Pyle (eds)., *1916: The Easter Rising* (London, 1968).
Edwards, Ruth Dudley, *Patrick Pearse: The Triumph of Failure* (Dublin, 1977).
Ellis, John, *The Sharp End: The Fighting Man in World War II* (London, 1990 (2nd ed).).
Ellul, Jacques, *Propaganda*, tr. Konrad Keller & Jean Lerner (New York, 1969).
English, Richard, *Ernie O'Malley: IRA Intellectual* (Oxford, 1998).
Fish, Stanley, *Is there a Text in this Class?: The Authority of Interpretive Communities* (Cambridge, MA, 1980).
Fiske, John, *Introduction to Communication Studies* (London, 1990 (2nd ed).).
Fitzpatrick, David, 'The Geography of Irish Nationalism 1913–1921', *Past and Present*, no. 78 (Feb. 1978), pp. 113–44.
——, 'The Disappearance of the Irish Agricultural Labourer', *Irish Economic and Social History*, vol. VII (1980), pp. 66–92.
—— (ed)., *Ireland and the First World War* (Dublin, 1988).
—— (ed)., *Revolution? Ireland, 1917–1923* (Dublin, 1990).
——, 'The Logic of Collective Sacrifice: Ireland and the British Army, 1914–1918', *The Historical Journal*, vol. 38, no. 4 (Dec. 1995), pp. 1017–30.
——, 'Militarism in Ireland, 1900–1922', in Thomas Bartlett and Keith Jeffery (eds)., *A Military History of Ireland* (Cambridge, 1996), pp. 379–406.
——, *Politics and Irish Life 1913–1921: Provincial Experience of War and Revolution* (1977) (Cork, 1998 (2nd ed).).
Foster, R.F., *Modern Ireland, 1600–1972* (London, 1988).
——, *Paddy & Mr Punch: Connections in Irish and English History* (London, 1993).
——, *W.B. Yeats: A Life: Volume I: The Apprentice Mage* (Oxford, 1997).
Foucault, Michel, 'What is an author?', in J.V. Harari (ed)., *Textual Strategies* (London, 1980), pp. 141–60.
——, *Discipline and Punish: The Birth of the Prison*, tr. Alan Sheridan (New York, 1977).
——, *History of Sexuality* (3 vols). (New York, 1988–90).
Fussell, Paul, *The Great War and Modern Memory* (Oxford, 1975).
——, *Wartime: Understanding and Behavior in the Second World War* (Oxford, 1989).
Garvin, Tom, 'Priests and Patriots: Irish separatism and fear of the modern, 1890–1914', *IHS*, vol. 25, no. 97 (May 1986), pp 67–81.
——, *Nationalist Revolutionaries in Ireland, 1858–1923* (Dublin, 1987).
——, *1922: The Birth of Irish Democracy* (Dublin, 1997).
Gay, Peter, *The Cultivation of Hatred: The Bourgeois Experience, Victoria to Freud*, vol. 3 (London, 1995).
Gerould, Daniel, 'Tyranny and Comedy', in Maurice Charney (ed)., *Comedy: New Perspectives. New York Literary Forum*, vol. 1 (Spring 1978), pp. 3–30.
Gibbon, Luke, *Transformations in Irish Culture* (Cork, 1996).

Gildea, Robert, *The Past in French History* (New Haven, 1994).
Gilley, Sheridan, 'English Attitudes to the Irish in England, 1780–1900', in Colin Holmes (ed.), *Immigrants and Minorities in British Society* (London, 1978), pp. 81–110.
Gilman, Sander L., *The Jew's Body* (London, 1991).
——, 'Black Bodies, White Bodies: Towards an iconography of female sexuality in late nineteenth century art', in H.L. Gates, Jr. (ed.), *'Race' Writing and Difference* (Chicago, 1991), pp. 223–61.
Glandon, Virginia E., *Arthur Griffith and the Advanced Nationalist Press: Ireland, 1900–1922* (New York, 1985).
Greaves, Charles Desmond, *Liam Mellows and the Irish Revolution* (Dublin, 1971).
Haley, Bruce, *The Healthy Body and Victorian Culture* (Cambridge, MA, 1978).
Hanly, Margaret Ann Fitzpatrick (ed.), *Essential Papers on Masochism* (New York, 1995).
Harrison, Richard S., *Irish Anti-War Movements, 1824–1974* (Dublin, 1986).
Hart, Peter, 'The Geography of Revolution in Ireland, 1917–1923', *Past and Present*, no. 155 (May 1997), pp. 142–76.
——, *The IRA and its Enemies: Violence & Community in Cork, 1916–1923* (Oxford, 1998).
——, 'The Social Structure of the Irish Republican Army, 1916–1923', *The Historical Journal*, vol. 42, no. 1 (March 1999), pp. 207–31.
Hennessey, Thomas, *Dividing Ireland: World War I and Partition* (Dublin, 1998).
Herzstein, Robert, *The War that Hitler Won* (New York, 1978).
Hogan, Robert (ed.), *Feathers from the Green Crow: Sean O'Casey, 1905–1925* (London, 1963).
Hopkin, Deian, 'Domestic Censorship in World War I', *JCH*, vol. 5, no. 4 (1970), pp. 151–70.
Hutchinson, John, *The Dynamics of Cultural Nationalism The Gaelic Revival and the Making of the Irish Nation-State* (London, 1987).
Hyman, Louis, *The Jews of Ireland* (Dublin, 1972).
Hynes, Samuel, *A War Imagined: The First World War and English Culture* (New York, 1991).
Jackall, Robert (ed.), *Propaganda* (London, 1995).
James, Robert Rhodes, *Gallipoli* (London, 1965).
Jowett, Garth, and Victoria O'Donnell, *Propaganda and Persuasion*, 2nd Edition (London, 1992).
Jeffery, Keith, 'The Great War in Modern Irish Memory', in T.G. Fraser and Keith Jeffery (eds.), *Men, Women and War* (Dublin, 1993), pp. 136–57.
Karsten, Peter, 'Irish Soldiers in the British Army, 1792–1922: Suborned or Subordinate?', *Journal of Social History*, xvii (1983), pp. 31–64.
Kearney, Richard, *Myth and Motherland* (Belfast, 1984).
——, *Transitions: Narratives in modern Irish Culture* (Manchester, 1988).
Kee, Robert, *The Green Flag* (London, 1972).
Keogh, Dermot, *Jews in Twentieth-Century Ireland: Refugees, Anti-Semitism, and the Holocaust* (Cork, 1998).
Kris, Ernst, *Psychoanalytic Explorations in Art* (London, 1953).
Laffan, Michael, *The Partition of Ireland, 1911–1925* (Dublin, 1983).

———, *The Resurrection of Ireland: The Sinn Féin Party 1916–1923* (Cambridge, 1999).
Larkin, Emmet, *James Larkin: Irish Labour Leader 1876–1947* (London, 1965).
Lasswell, Harold, *Propaganda Technique in the Great War* (New York, 1927).
———, 'Propaganda', in Edwin Seligman (ed)., *Encyclopedia of the Social Sciences*, vol. XII (London, 1934)., p. 13.
Laurence, Dan H. (ed)., *Bernard Shaw Collected Letters: Volume 3, 1911–1925* (London, 1985).
Lawlor, Sheila, *Britain and Ireland, 1914–1923* (Dublin, 1983).
Le Bon, Gustave, *The Crowd: A Study of the Popular Mind* (London, 1947).
Lebow, Richard Ned, *White Britain and Black Ireland: The influence of stereotypes on colonial policy* (Philadelphia, 1977).
Leonard, Jane, 'The Reactions of Irish Officers in the British Army to the Easter Rising of 1916', in Hugh Cecil and Peter H. Liddle (eds)., *Facing Armageddon: The First World War Experienced* (London, 1996), pp. 256–68.
———, 'Facing 'the Finger of Scorn': Veterans' Memories of Ireland after the Great War', in Martin Evans and Ken Lunn (eds)., *War and Memory in the Twentieth Century* (Oxford, 1997), pp. 59–72.
Lloyd, David, *Anomalous States: Irish Writing and the Post-Colonial Movement* (Dublin, 1993).
Low, Rachael, *The History of the British Film, 1914–1918* (London, 1950).
Lyons, F.S.L., *Ireland Since the Famine* (London, 1971).
———, *Culture and Anarchy in Ireland 1890–1939* (Oxford, 1979).
McBride, Lawrence (ed)., *Images, Icons and the Irish Nationalist Imagination* (Dublin, 1999).
McCartney, Donal, 'The Political Use of History in the Work of Arthur Griffith', *JCH*, vol. 8, no. 1 (Jan. 1973), pp. 3–20.
MacDonagh, Oliver, *States of Mind: A Study of Anglo-Irish Conflict 1780–1980* (London, 1983).
McPherson, James M., *For Cause & Comrades: Why Men Fought in the Civil War* (Oxford, 1997).
Marquis, Alice Goldfarb, 'Words as Weapons: Propaganda in Britain and Germany during the First World War', *JCH*, vol. 13, no. 3 (July 1978), pp. 467–98.
Martin, F.X. (ed)., *The Irish Volunteers, 1913–1915* (Dublin, 1963).
—— (ed)., *Leaders and Men of the Easter Rising* (Dublin, 1967).
—— and F.J. Byrne (eds)., *The Scholar Revolutionary: Eoin MacNeill, 1867–1945, and the Making of a New Ireland* (Dublin, 1973).
Marwick, Arthur, *Britain in the Age of Total War* (London, 1968).
Maume, Patrick, *D.P. Moran* (Dundalk, 1995).
———, 'Nationalism and Partition: the political thought of Arthur Clery', *IHS*, vol. 31, no. 122 (Nov. 1998), pp. 222–41.
———, *The Long Gestation: Irish Nationalist Life, 1891–1918* (Dublin, 1999).
Maye, Brian, *Arthur Griffith* (Dublin, 1998).
Messinger, Gary S., *British Propaganda and the State in the First World War* (Manchester, 1992).
Mitchell, Malcolm, *Propaganda, polls, and public opinion: Are the people manipulated?* (Englewood Cliffs, New Jersey, 1970).
Moody, Theo, and F.X. Martin (eds)., *The Course of Irish History* (Dublin, 1984 (2nd ed).).

Moran, Sean Farrell, *Patrick Pearse and the Politics of Redemption: The Mind of the Easter Rising, 1916* (Washington D.C., 1994).
Morgan, Austen, *James Connolly: A Political Biography* (Dublin, 1988).
Muenger, Elizabeth A., *The British Military Dilemma in Ireland: Occupation Politics, 1886–1914* (Dublin, 1991).
Murray, Peter, 'Irish cultural nationalism in the United Kingdom state: politics and the Gaelic League 1900–18', *Irish Political Studies*, vol. 8 (1993), pp. 55–72.
Newsinger, John, 'I Bring Not Peace But A Sword: The Religious Motif in the Irish War of Independence', *JCH*, vol. 13, no. 3 (July 1978), pp. 609–628.
Novick, Ben, 'DORA, Suppression, and Nationalist Propaganda in Ireland, 1914–1915', *New Hibernia Review*, vol. 1, no. 4 (Winter 1997) [1997a], pp. 41–57.
——, 'No Anti-Semitism in Ireland? The Limerick 'Pogrom' and Radical Nationalist Stereotypes', *The Jewish Quarterly*, no. 168 (Winter 1997/98) [1997b], pp. 35–40.
——, 'Postal Censorship in Ireland, 1914–1916', *IHS*, vol. 31, no. 123 (May 1999), pp. 343–56.
O Broin, Leon, *The Chief Secretary: Augustine Birrell and Ireland, 1907–1916* (London, 1969).
——, *Dublin Castle and the 1916 Rising* (London, 1970).
O'Farrell, Padraic, *Who's who in the Irish war of independence and civil war, 1916–1923* (Dublin, 1997).
Offer, Avner, *The First World War: An Agrarian Interpretation* (Oxford, 1989)
O Grada, Cormac, *Ireland: An Economic History, 1780–1939* (Oxford, 1994).
O'Halpin, Eunan, 'British Intelligence in Ireland, 1914–1921', in Christopher Andrews and David Dilks (eds)., *The Missing Dimension: Governments and Intelligence Communities in the Twentieth Century* (London, 1984), pp. 54–77.
——, *The Decline of the Union: British Government and Ireland, 1892–1920* (Dublin, 1987).
O'Keefe, Timothy J., 'The 1898 Efforts to Celebrate the United Irishmen: The '98 Centennial', *Eire Ireland*, vol. XXIII, no. 2 (Summer 1988), pp. 51–73.
——, '"Who Fears to Speak of '98?" The Rhetoric and Rituals of the United Irishmen Centennial, 1898', *Eire Ireland*, vol. XXVII, no. 3 (Fall 1992), pp. 67–91.
O Luing, Sean, *I die in a good cause: A study of Thomas Ashe idealist and revolutionary* (Tralee, 1970).
O Mahony, Sean, *Frongoch University of Revolution* (Dublin, 1987).
Owens, Gary, 'Nationalist Monuments in Ireland c. 1870–1914: symbolism and ritual', in Raymond Gillespie and Brian Kennedy (eds)., *Ireland: Art into History* (Dublin, 1994), pp. 103–17.
Owens, Gary, 'Constructing the Martyrs: The Manchester executions and the nationalist imagination', in Lawrence McBride (ed)., *Images, Icons and the Irish Nationalist Imagination* (Dublin, 1999), pp. 18–36.
Paor, Liam de, *On the Easter Proclamation and Other Declarations* (Dublin, 1997).
Paseta, Senia, '1798 in 1898: The Politics of Commemoration', *Irish Review*, vol. 22 (1998), pp. 46–53.
Paseta, Senia, *Before the Revolution: Nationalism, Social Change, and Ireland's Catholic Elite, 1879–1922* (Cork, 1999).
Pearsall, Ronald, *The Worm in the Bud: The World of Victorian Sexuality* (London, 1993 (2nd ed).).

Philpin, C.H.E. (ed.), *Nationalism and Popular Protest in Ireland* (Cambridge, 1987).
Pick, Daniel, *War Machine: The Rationalisation of Slaughter in the Machine Age* (New Haven, 1993).
Pool, I.D., et al. (eds)., *Handbook of Communication* (Chicago, 1973). Qualter, Terence H., *Propaganda and Psychological Warfare* (New York, 1962).
Read, James Morgan, *Atrocity Propaganda 1914–1919* (New Haven, 1941).
Reeves, Nicholas, 'Through the Eye of the Camera: Contemporary Cinema Audiences and their 'Experience' of War in the film, *Battle of the Somme*', in Hugh Cecil and Peter H. Liddle (eds)., *Facing Armageddon: The First World War Experienced* (London, 1996), pp. 780–800.
Reilly, Eileen, 'Beyond gilt shamrock: symbolism and realism in the cover art of Irish historical and political fiction, 1880–1914', in Lawrence McBride (ed)., *Images, Icons and the Irish Nationalist Imagination* (Dublin, 1999), pp. 95–112.
Rickards, Maurice, *Posters of the First World War*. (London, 1968).
Roskies, David, *Against the Apocalypse: responses to catastrophe in modern Jewish culture* (Cambridge, MA, 1984).
Rudolph, G.A., *War Posters from 1914 through 1918 in the Archives of the University of Nebraska – Lincoln* (University of Nebraska, 1990).
Rumpf, Erhard and A.C. Hepburn, *Nationalism and Socialism in twentieth-century Ireland* (Liverpool, 1977).
Said, Edward, *Orientalism* (London, 1978).
——, *Culture and Imperialism* (London, 1993).
Sanders, Michael, and Philip M. Taylor, *British Propaganda during the First World War 1914–1918* (London, 1982).
Schama, Simon, *Landscape & Memory* (London, 1995).
Scott, James C., *Weapons of the Weak* (New Haven, 1985)
——, *Domination and the Arts of Resistance: Hidden Transcripts* (New Haven, 1990).
Scott, Peter T., *Home for Christmas: Cards, Messages and Legends of the Great War* (London, 1993).
Shields, Hugh, 'Printed Aids to Folk-Singing, 1700–1900', in Mary Daly and David Dickson (eds)., *The Origin of Popular Literacy in Ireland* (Dublin, 1990), pp. 139–52.
Stanley, Peter, *What Did You Do in the War Daddy?: A Visual History of Propaganda Posters* (Melbourne, 1983).
Stokes, Roy, *Death in the Irish Sea: The Sinking of the R.M.S. Leinster* (Dublin, 1998).
Taillon, Ruth, *When History Was Made: The Women of 1916* (Belfast, 1996).
Taithe, Bernard, and Tim Thornton (eds)., *Propaganda* (Stroud, 1999).
Taylor, Philip, *British Propaganda in the Twentieth Century* (Edinburgh, 1999).
Thompson, William Irwin, *The Imagination of an Insurrection* (Oxford, 1967).
Townshend, Charles, *The British Campaign in Ireland, 1919–1921* (Oxford, 1975).
——, 'The Irish Republican Army and the Development of Guerrilla Warfare, 1916–1921', *EHR*, vol. 94, no. 171 (April 1979), pp. 318–45.
—— *Political Violence in Ireland: Government and Resistance since 1848* (Oxford, 1983).
—— *Ireland: The Twentieth Century* (London, 1999).
Travers, Pauric, 'The Priest in Politics: the case of conscription', in Oliver MacDonagh, W.F. Mandle, and Pauric Travers (eds)., *Irish Culture and Nationalism, 1750–1950* (Dublin, 1983), pp. 161–81.

Vance, Norman, *The Sinews of the Spirit: The Ideal of Christian Manliness in Victorian Literature and Religious Thought* (Cambridge, 1985).
Ward, Margaret, *Unmanageable Revolutionaries: Women and Irish Nationalism* (London, 1983).
Ward, Margaret, 'Nationalism, Pacifism, Internationalism: Louie Bennett, Hanna Sheehy-Skeffington, and the Problems of "Defining Feminism"', in Anthony Bradley and Maryann Gialanella Valiulis (eds)., *Gender and Sexuality in Modern Ireland* (Amherst, 1997), pp. 60–84.
Williams, Gordon, 'Remember the *Llandovery Castle*: Cases of Atrocity Propaganda in the First World War', in Jeremy Hawthorn (ed)., *Propaganda, Persuasion, and Polemic* (London, 1987), pp. 19–36.
Wilson, Trevor, 'Lord Bryce's Investigation into Alleged German Atrocities in Belgium, 1914–15', *JCH*, vol. 14, no. 3 (July 1979), pp 369–83.
——, *The Myriad Faces of War* (Cambridge, 1986).
Winter, J.M., *The Great War and the British People* (London, 1985).
——, *Sites of Memory, Sites of Mourning* (Cambridge, 1997).
Zimmerman, G.D., *Irish Street Ballads and Rebel Songs, 1798–1900* (Geneva, 1966).

V. UNPUBLISHED DISSERTATIONS/THESES/PAPERS

Callan, Patrick, 'Voluntary Recruiting for the British Army in Ireland during the First World War' (UCD, Ph.D., 1984).
Coleman, Marie, 'County Longford, 1910–1923: A Regional Study of the Irish Revolution' (UCD, Ph.D., 1998).
Combs, James E., 'The Language of Nationalist Ideology: A Content Analysis of Irish Nationalist Publications, 1906–1914' (University of Houston, M.A., 1969).
Davis, Mary Elizabeth, 'Separate Imaginations: The Irelands of Patrick Pearse and Sean O'Casey' (UCD, M.Phil., 1968).
Ellis, John S., ' "Unity in Diversity": Ethnicity and British National Identity, 1899–1918' (Boston College, Ph.D., 1997).
Feeney, Vincent Edward, 'Sinn Féin, 1916–1918' (University of Vermont, M.A., 1968).
Goggin, Sheenah, 'The Easter Lilies: Cumann na mBan' (UCD, M.A., 1993).
Hannon, Charles, 'The Irish Volunteers and the Concept of Military Service and Defence, 1913–1924' (UCD, Ph.D., 1989).
Hart, Peter, 'The IRA and its Enemies: Violence and Community in Cork, 1916–1923' (TCD, Ph.D., 1996).
——, 'How to Inform on the IRA and Get Away with It (in Cork, 1919–1923)' (Presentation to Seminar in Irish History, Professor R.F. Foster, Convenor, Hertford College, Oxford, 21 October 1997).
Hurley, M.F., 'The Tone of Popular Nationalist Sentiment in Ireland as the setting for the policy of Armed Insurrection in 1916' (UCD, M.A., 1954).
Inoue, Keiko, 'Sinn Féin Propaganda and 'Nationality', 1916–1918' (UCD, M.A., 1989).
Lucey, Dermot. J., 'Cork Public Opinion and the First World War' (University College, Cork, M.A., 1972).

Moore, G., 'Anti-Semitism in Ireland' (Ulster Polytechnic, Ph.D., 1984).
Novick, Benjamin Zvi, 'No Ordinary War: Ireland during the First World War' (University of Michigan, A.B., 1996).
O'Flanagan, Neil, 'Dublin City in an Age of War and Revolution, 1914–1924' (UCD, M.A., 198).
Schneider, Eric F., 'What Britons Were Told about the War in the Trenches, 1914–1918' (Oxford, D.Phil, 1997).
Staunton, Martin, 'The Royal Munster Fusiliers in the Great War, 1914–1919' (UCD, M.A., 1986).
Travers, Pauric, 'The Irish Conscription Crisis, 1918' (UCD, M.A., 1977).

Index

Aberdeen, Lady 152, 194, 195
Aberdeen, Lord 194
Admiralty 77
An Claidheamh Soluis 30, 52, 110, 111, 133, 134, 161, 224, 231, 240
An t-Oglach 30, 48, 77, 78, 156, 244, 246
Ancient Order of the Hibernians 19, 84, 197
Anderson, Patricia 208
Ansiedlungs Kommission 175
Answers 167
Anti-Conscription Pledge (1918) 241
Antwerp, Belgium 106, 110
ANZAC Forces 62, 196
Ashe, Thomas 19, 50, 89, 237–40, 245
Asquith, Herbert 33, 44, 61, 84, 135, 183, 193, 194, 201, 217
Augusteijn, Joost 16, 247

Bachelor's Walk, Dublin 83–5
Baden-Powell, Lord 135
Balkans 51
Bank of Ireland 84
Barry, Tadg 61
Beaslai, Piaras 30, 34, 236, 244
Bennett, Louie 146
Bernhardt, Sarah 165
Bethlehem Steel 75
Bew, Paul 177
Birrell, Augustine 32, 33, 36, 44, 47, 81, 104, 194, 238, 239
Blythe, Ernest 224, 233, 234
Board of Agriculture 181
Boer War 19, 62, 91, 92, 98, 99, 136, 167
Book of Kells 206
Bottomley, Sir Horatio 88, 109
Bourke, Joanna 154, 156
Bowen, Paul 48

Boy Scouts 135, 136
Boys' Sodality (Dublin) 139
Brein, Oliver 47
Brennan, John 183
Brennan, Robert 27, 28, 30, 34, 178, 241
Brennan-Whitemore, W.J. 167
Brewster, Gordon 191, 198
British Expeditionary Force 83, 190, 192
British Grand Fleet 199
Broderick, Albinia 235
Brunton, Alice 241
Bryce Report 107, 109
Bryce, Sir James 107, 108
Buidhe, Aodh 235
Burbage, Thomas H. 168
Burke, J.J. 60, 92, 94, 100, 198
Butler, Mary 139, 228
Byrne, Alfred 168
Byrne, J. 66

Cahalan, James 28
Callan, Patrick 16, 20, 26, 43
Captaig, Eileen ni 225
Carbery, Lady Mary 130
Carey, Nellie 144
Carson, Sir Edward 20, 34, 45, 70, 75
Casement, Sir Roger 19, 69, 88, 94, 122, 123, 125, 141, 150, 151, 195, 204
Catholic Bulletin 30, 33, 67, 132, 138, 139, 144, 168, 193, 240
Catholic Citizen 122
Catholic Defence Association 158
Catholic Truth Association 167
Catholic Truth Conference (1914) 134
Catholic Truth Society 160
Cattle Prices Order (1917) 180
Cavanagh, Maeve 59, 63, 144, 150, 173, 193, 195, 226

Cavell, Edith 72, 79–81, 93, 98, 109, 110
CCORI 170
Ceannt, Eamonn 29, 123, 124
censorship:
  postal 26, 36
  press 26, 31, 36
Central Council for the Organization of Recruiting in Ireland [CCORI] 20, 73, 104, 120, 170
Chaplin, Charlie 165
Chearbhaill, Maire Nic 144
City of Dublin Hospital 80
Clan-na-Gael 32, 126
Clery, Prof. Arthur 134, 135
Codd, Pauline 25
Colbert, Con 141
Coleman, Marie 247
Collins, Michael 238, 239, 244
Compulsory Tillage Acts (1917–18) 173
Connaught Rangers 75
Connery, Louisa 152
Connery, M.K. 143
Connolly, James 20, 52, 58, 61, 83, 116, 198, 225, 226, 238
  attacks on wealth, 53
  editorship of papers, 30, 55, 124
  leadership of Easter Rising, 34
  nationalism, 29,
  suggestions for female safety, 152
Conscription Crisis (1918) 25, 50, 62, 156, 189, 212, 217, 239, 241, 245, 246
Constantinople 62
Contagious Diseases Act 155
Coogan, Oliver 247
Coombes, Annie 208
Cork Celt 30, 63, 137
Cork Corporation 123
Corriere de la Serra 110, 111
Cosgrave, W.T. 233
Crofts, Gerald 123
Crofts, James 123
Cromwell, Oliver 92, 167
Cull, Nicholas J. 248
Cumann na mBan 66, 141, 142, 146
Cumann na nGaedhael 19

Daily Dispatch 88
Daily Express 150
Daily Mail 88, 111, 158, 167, 241
Daily Sketch 88, 153
Daily Telegraph 238
Daly, P.T. 20
Dardanelles 61
Davenport-Hines, Richard 154
Davidson, Joseph 98
Davis, Richard 245
Davis, Thomas 35
de Blacam, Aodh [Hugh Blackham] 31, 30, 33, 70, 113, 132, 138
de Lacey, Laurence 30, 190
de Valera, Eamon:
  anti-Conscription pledge, 241
  as propagandist, 233
  commanding on Western Front, 213
  commanding submarine fleet, 219
  dislike of Arthur Griffith, 28, 33
  East Clare campaign (1917), 139, 212, 213
  jailed, 129
  reconciles with death, 237
Deane, Seamus 229
Decies, Lord 26, 37
Defence of the Realm Act (D.O.R.A.) 36, 52, 66, 155, 171, 204–6, 211, 214, 233, 239
Denman, Terence 16, 64, 247
Department of Agriculture 182
Department of Recruiting for Ireland (DRI) 21, 23–5, 175
Derby, Lord 23
Devlin, Joseph 54, 69, 70, 168, 169, 176, 219, 241
Dickinson, Page 17
Dillon, John 62, 67, 94, 96, 153, 174, 175, 177, 178, 192, 219, 238, 241
Dockrell, Maurice 25
Doob, Leonard W. 37, 38
Dooley, Thomas 24, 43, 48
Douglas, Lord Alfred 34

Doyle, Sean 30, 34, 44, 55, 75, 80, 100, 108–10, 133, 161, 169, 175, 228, 232

Dublin Castle 107, 204, 238
Dublin Corporation 53, 123
Dublin Metropolitan Police 47, 84, 152, 195, 204, 214, 238
Dungannon Clubs 19
Dwyer, Edward 30, 34, 54, 118

Easter Rising/Rebellion (1916) 16–19, 25, 36, 43, 50–3, 56, 59, 63–7, 69, 70, 83, 85, 86–9, 94, 122, 124, 127, 130, 136, 139, 141, 142, 146, 148, 161, 178, 188, 189, 199, 201, 203, 204, 211, 217, 223, 224, 227–30, 232, 234, 235, 237, 239, 240, 242, 244, 246, 248
Edgeworth-Johnstone, Walter 204, 238
Egan, Charles 98
Eire Ireland 29, 31–2, 36, 43, 97, 111, 122, 128, 190–2, 225
Ellul, Jacques 38, 40, 42, 247
Emperor Franz-Joseph 118
English Exchequer 174
Enniscorthy *Echo* 31
Erzberger, Mathias 122
Evening Telegraph 98

Fenians: 64, 238
  in Pearse's writings, 141
  military instruction, 231
  prisoners, 97, 141, 224
  propaganda symbols, 226
  propaganda writing of, 18
Ffrench, Alice 57
Fianna Fail (Newspaper) 29, 227
Fianna Fail (Political Party) 33
Fianna (Newspaper) 30, 85, 107, 132, 135, 141, 167, 178
Fianna (Organization) 19, 135, 142, 149, 238
Figgis, Darrell 241
Fitzgerald, Desmond 27, 42–4
Fitzpatrick, David 16, 48, 149, 184, 185, 247
Flanders 51, 64, 66, 231, 236
Fleming, John 185
Fogarty, Michael 89
Ford, J. 30

Foreign Office 81
Fox, Mrs. Dacre 146
Freeman's Journal 26, 47, 239
freemasonry 70, 117, 132, 137, 157, 160, 167, 168, 193
Friend, Major General L.B. 154
Furlong, Alice 241

Gael 30–1, 34, 36, 46, 59, 93, 110, 122, 132, 166, 173, 176, 229
Gaelic Athletic Association (GAA) 19
Gaelic League 19, 52, 149, 164, 224, 240
Gaelic Press 31, 36, 86
Gallagher, Frank ['David Hogan'] 27, 37, 178, 248
Gallipoli 17, 24, 50, 51, 54, 56, 61, 62, 196–8, 201, 231
Gaspari, Cardinal 243
General Election (1918) 51, 87, 89, 174, 187, 241, 246
General Post Office, Dublin 81, 203
German High Seas Fleet 199
German Plot (1918) 241
Gibbon, Margaret 227
Gill, T.P. 175
Gilmartin, Rev. Dr. 153
Ginnell, Lawrence 118, 150, 177, 185, 219
Goebbels, Joseph 38, 43
Golden, Peter 230
Gonne, Maud 19, 146
Good, Joe 45
Gorman, Mary 153
Graves, Robert 116
Great Famine 63, 91, 96–8
Green, Alice Stopford 19
Green, Max 176, 237
Grey, Sir Edward 118
Griffith, Arthur 20, 54, 57, 62, 66, 80, 83, 88, 91, 92, 96–9, 111, 114–17, 122, 125, 134, 164, 165, 167–9, 174, 179, 180–2, 190, 198, 230, 233–5, 238, 240
  anti-Conscription Pledge 241
  anti-Semitism 137
  arrested in German Plot 242

Griffith, Arthur (*contd*)
  at meeting to plan Easter Rising 126
  attitudes to John Redmond 67, 112
  circumvention of censorship 37
  demolishes 'Louvain Lie' 104–6
  editor of *Eire Ireland* 29, 128, 225
  editor of *Nationality* 29, 75, 76, 197
  editor of *Scissors and Paste* 36
  editor of *Sinn Fein* 29
  editorial style 30, 52
  forms electoral policy 245
  founds Irish Neutrality League 124
  hatred of daily press 103, 107, 124, 125, 158
  importance after Easter Rising 50
  influence as propagandist 28, 228
  influence of John Mitchel, 18
  insults Gwynn and Kettle 191
  Irish Transvaal Committee and *United Irishman*, 19
  jailed 129
  kinship with Boers 91
  kinship with Germany 119, 123
  newspapers 29, 32
  relationship with propagandists 31
  remarks on Russian Revolution 119
  responds to Bryce Report 109
  self-aggrandisement 34
  suggests internment hospitals 156
  supreme propagandist 32–4
Gwynn, Denis 62, 239
Gwynn, Stephen 25, 62, 169, 175, 191, 194

Hackett, John 179
Haig, Major 83
Haig, Sir Douglas 213
Hallinan, Dr. 89
Hamilton, Gen. Sir Ian 231
Hamilton, General Bruce 99
Hannay, James ['George Birmingham'] 23, 24, 62, 104, 164, 165
Hart, Peter 16, 46, 149, 202, 234, 246, 247
Hartmann, Cardinal 112
Harvey, Arthur 57

Haslam, Anna 152
Hayden, Mary 152
Hayes, Richard 157
Healy, Maurice 61
Healy, Sean 141, 142 (ill.)
Heligoland 125
Hennessey, Thomas 17
Henry, R.M. 43, 104
Heppenstall ['The Walking Gallows'] 94, 176
Hessian Regiments (1798) 93, 94
Heuston, Sean 141
Hibernian 30, 32, 63, 76, 94, 110, 151, 161, 166, 168, 176, 182, 197, 225
Hines, Dixie 195
Hitler, Adolf 38
Hobson, Bulmer 19, 20, 29, 30, 34, 85, 107, 141, 190, 227
Hogan, Patrick 211
Home Office 73, 204
Home Rule 60–1, 66, 123, 174, 175, 177, 179, 192, 193, 195, 208, 211, 219
Honesty 22, 30, 31, 34, 36, 54, 63, 80, 86, 93, 112, 132, 197
House of Commons 77, 118, 241
Howard, Sean 139
Hughes, Archbishop 239
Hulton, Sir William 88
Hyde, Douglas 123, 224

Imperial German Navy 190
Inginidhe na hEireann 142
International Women's Conference (1915) 53, 54, 146
Irish Republican Brotherhood 19, 29, 30, 32, 43, 75, 77, 126, 190, 237
Irish Recruiting Council 25, 77
Irish Actors 195
Irish Brigade (Boer War) 19, 92
Irish Brigade (World War I) 88, 122
Irish Bulletin 44
Irish Catholic 76
Irish Citizen Army 124, 161, 226, 237, 239
Irish Citizen 30, 53, 145, 146, 150, 152, 153, 155, 239
Irish Civil War 246

Irish Command 20
Irish Convention 211
Irish Creamery Managers' Association 66
Irish Freedom 29, 32, 36, 57, 98, 106, 124, 125, 132, 138, 156, 190, 192, 194, 196
Irish Fun 30, 138, 167, 178, 197, 198
Irish Independent 47, 75, 241
Irish National Foresters 19
Irish Neutrality League 53, 62, 124
Irish Parliamentary Party [IPP]: 90, 104, 133, 136, 158, 160, 174, 175, 178, 211, 212, 219, 248
  blamed for death of Irish recruits, 66, 67, 212, 217
  Boer War, 19
  candidates for 94
  challenged by Sinn Fein 87, 139
  conduit for Freemasonry 168
  defeated in December 1918 247
  degenerate elements within 67
  DRI, 21
  links to distillers 157
  Manchester Martyrs' Commemoration 98
  mocked in propaganda, 159, 161, 178, 197, 220
  Mosquito Press, 48
  support for recruiting propaganda, 26, 132, 189, 190
  use of *God Save Ireland* 91
Irish Republican Army 202
Irish Rosary 167
Irish Transvaal Committee 19
Irish Volunteer 30, 32, 36, 44, 48, 61, 98, 107, 124, 127, 128, 132, 148, 178, 179, 183, 190, 196, 197, 225, 227, 228, 230, 231, 244
Irish Volunteers 30–2, 47, 63, 66, 69, 77, 81, 84, 123, 127, 135, 136, 138, 149, 156, 166, 179, 180, 192, 193, 203, 230, 231, 233, 235, 237–41, 244–6
Irish Weekly Independent 48, 191
Irish Women's Franchise League 156
Irish Work 30, 225
Irish Worker 30, 36, 61, 84, 85, 92, 100, 107, 124, 190, 192, 193, 196, 217, 225
Irish World 52, 65
Irishman 29, 31, 32, 34, 36, 70, 235
Irwin, Will 118

John Bull 81–3, 110, 113, 136, 202, 206, 208
John Bull (Newspaper) 88, 166
Jowett, Garth 37, 38, 41
Judge, Michael 34
Jutland, Battle of 65, 199

Kaiser Wilhelm II 83, 92, 127, 128, 167
Kavanagh, Ernest 61, 193
Keating, Geoffrey 124
Kennedy, John B. 59
Kenny, Justice 45
Kesckemeti, Paul 38
Kettle, Thomas 26, 67, 69, 70, 136, 190, 191 (ill.)
King Albert of Belgium 83
King George V 201
King's Own Scottish Borderers 83
Kinsale Corporation 76
Kitchener, Lord 85, 134, 193
Knockaville Labour League 179
Knutsford Prison 65
Koelnische Zeitung 109, 110

Laffan, Michael 34, 47
Land War 91
Lane, Sir Hugh 73
Larkin, Jim 29, 30, 52, 53, 84, 124, 161, 190, 192
Lasswell, Harold 37, 39, 40
Le Bas, Hedley 23
Le Bon, Gustave 40
Le Matin 111
Leader 157, 167, 193
Leinster 76–9
Lemberg, Galicia 118
Lemberg Prisoner of War Camp 123
Leonard, Jane 64, 202
Lewes Jail 233
Liffey 202

Lloyd George, David 99, 119, 211, 216, 241
Lloyd, David 28
Logue, Cardinal 143, 166
Lonsdale, Sir John 21
Loos, Battle of 17, 63
Louvain, Belgium 104–6
Lusitania 72–6, 79, 109
Lynch, Arthur 92
Lynch, Diarmuid 185
Lynn, Dr. Kathleen 155–7
Lyons, F.S.L. 16, 46

Mac Dubgaill, Catal 185, 212, 213
Macaulay, Thomas B. 166
MacBride, John 92
MacCartan, Hugh A. 236
MacDermott, Sean 29, 34, 224
MacDonagh, Thomas 53, 146, 236, 238
MacEntee, Sean 236
MacEvoy, Sean 238
MacManus, Seamus 20
MacManus, Terence Bellew 19, 237, 239
MacNamara, Dr. 77
MacNeill, Eoin: 57, 60, 97, 106, 118
  accused of being pro-German, 124
  attempts to stop Easter Rising, 34
  East Clare campaign (1917), 139
  editor of *Irish Volunteer*, 36, 178, 190, 227
  German gold, 32
  influence as propagandists, 228
  Irish Volunteer movement, 47, 123
  reaction to Casement's alleged homosexuality, 151
  resists Dublin boycotts, 229, 230
MacSwiney, Terence 29, 30, 34, 141, 148, 166, 224, 227
Magill, A.P. 81, 104
Mahon, Patrick 31, 141
Manchester *Guardian* 234
Manchester Martyrs 18, 91, 97, 98
Mannix, Rev. Dr. 101
Mansion House Recruiting Conference 112
Mansion House, Dublin 84, 112
Markievicz, Constance 124, 141, 144, 147, 148, 225
Marne, Battle of (1914) 60
Marshall, Mrs. Leonard 87, 100
Martin, F.X. 16
Martyn, Edward 161
Mathew, Father Theobald 157
Maume, Patrick 34, 177
Mauretania 75
Maxwell, Gen. Sir John 204
McCabe, Putnam 135
McCartan, Dr Patrick 67, 68, 213
McCullough, Denis 20, 224, 225
McGuinness, Joseph 94, 153, 159, 233
McKenna, Patrick 94
McLaughlin, Henry 25
Mellowes, Liam 224
Mercier, Cardinal 104, 118
Mesopotamia 197, 211
Messines Ridge, Battle of 70
Meyer, Kuno 123
Milroy, Sean 124, 225
Mitchel, John 18, 216
Mitchell, Malcolm 40
Moloney, Helena 142
Monks, George 134, 213
Montefiore, Dora B. 52, 53
Moody, T.W. 16
Moore, George 161
Moore, Maurice 21, 26, 147, 237, 238
Moran, D.P. 29, 157, 167, 193
Morning Post 44
Mountjoy Prison 89, 204, 205, 225
Mulkearns, Joseph 35, 161, 211, 212, 219
Murphy, William Martin 176

Nathan, Sir Matthew 44, 73, 81, 146, 152, 154, 168, 238
Nation 44
National Gallery of Ireland 73
National University, Dublin 128
National Volunteers 24, 56, 57, 98, 193
Nationality 29, 31, 32, 36, 42, 44–6, 48, 63, 75, 76, 81, 88, 96, 110, 115, 129, 147, 164, 184, 185, 197, 225, 228, 240, 244, 245
New Ireland 55, 239

New Statesman 44, 45
New York *American* 87
New York Times 128
News of the World 166
Newsinger, John 227
Norddeutsche Allgemeine Zeitung 111, 122
Northcliffe, Lord 88, 108, 167
Nugent, J.D. 160, 169

O'Brien, Cruise 183
O'Brien, William 124, 177, 178, 193, 194, 241
O'Casey, Sean 28, 36, 202–4, 208, 211, 216, 240
O Cearnaigh, Peadar 28, 205, 206, 213, 216
O Concubair, Sean 57
O'Connell, J.J. 230, 244
O'Connor, Fergus 204
O'Connor, T.J. 236
O'Connor, T.P. 98, 169, 192, 213
O'Doherty, K. 191
O'Doherty, Michael Kevin 27
O'Donnell, John F. 226
O'Donnell, Manus 30
O'Donnell, Victoria 37, 38, 41
O'Duffy, Eimar 230
O'Flanagan, Michael 67, 129, 182, 183
O'Hea, J.J. 197
O'Hegarty, P.S. 29
O'Higgins, Brian ['Brian na Banban'] 30, 34, 58, 101, 138, 158, 190, 195, 197, 224, 227, 241,
O'Hourihan, Patrick 20
O'Kelly, J.J. 30, 168, 193
O'Kelly, Seamus 29, 242
O'Kelly, Sean T. 126
O'Leary, Michael, VC 111, 112, 176, 197
O'Lonnain, M.S. 34, 70, 113, 115, 137, 220
O'Malley, William 35
O'Rahilly, M.J. ['The O'Rahilly'] 30, 34, 88
O'Rahilly, Sergeant Major 75
O'Reilly, John Boyle 141
O'Ruairc, Estlinn 146

O'Sheehan, Jack 161
O'Sullivan, Seamus 66, 199
Ottoman Empire 107
Owens, Gary 28

Pankhurst, Mrs. Isabel 146
Pankhurst, Sylvia 84
Parliamentary Recruiting Committee [PRC] 20
Parnell, Charles Stewart 67
Partridge, William 53
Pearse, Patrick
  at O'Donovan Rossa's funeral (1915), 237–9
  claims at Court-Martial, 131
  compared to Christ, 236
  contributes to *Irish Volunteer*, 230
  holds off British army, 81
  idea of blood sacrifice, 223, 224
  religious faith, 227, 228
  supports feminist protests, 53, 146
  ultimate paragon of faith and sacrifice, 139, 140
  writes favorable review of 'Tracts for our Times', 98
Pennefather, F.W. 22
Pidgeon, Sylvester 84
Pim, Herbert ['A. Newman']
  apologizes for joking about Thomas Kettle, 70
  assumes mantle of Vigilance Committees, 169
  author of pamphlet on Manchester Martyrs 98
  author of *The Charmer* 57
  blames war for 'My Lady Frayle', 161, 164
  career, 32–4, 233
  claims Irish developed Plato's philosophy, 134
  Easter Rising, 34, 234
  editor of *Irishman*, 29
  forms electoral policy, 245
  gains support of Cardinal Logue, 166
  imprisoned, 225
  praises prisoners, 224

Pim, Herbert ['A. Newman'] (*contd*)
  pseudonym, 30
  reactions to Casement's alleged
    homosexuality, 150, 151
  relation to Griffith, 31
  reviews 'From a Hermitage', 228
Plunkett, Grace Gifford 147, 148, 213, 236
Plunkett, Joseph 147, 223, 236
Pollard, Rev. F.S. 30, 55, 92, 110, 151, 168, 225
Ponsonby, Lord 111
postal recruiting campaign (1915) 21, 22
Prendergast, Eileen 33
Press Bureau 100
Price, Major I.H. 46, 48, 195

Qualter, Terence 38
Quinn, John 15
Quinn, P. 217
Quiz 30, 191, 197, 198

Radio Telefis Eireann 16
Rafferty, Father 156
Ranch War (1906–1908) 178
Rapid Printing Company 175
Read, James Morgan 72, 79, 109, 111, 116
Redmond, John 21, 26, 46, 48, 54, 57, 61, 62, 66–8 (ill.), 84, 96, 98, 112, 113, 124, 153, 171, 176, 192, 194, 197–9 (ill.), 208, 211, 217, 230, 237
Redmond, William Archer 176, 241
Redmond, William 69, 70, 136, 169, 176
Reidy, Michael 197, 198
Reynold's Newspaper 166
Roberts, Lord 99
Robinson, Sir Henry 26, 104
Roe, Grace 146
Rossa, Jeremiah O'Donovan 19, 237–9
Roundwood Reservoir, Dublin 107
Royal Air Force 25, 245
Royal College of Surgeons 213
Royal Commission on the Easter Rebellion 46, 48
Royal Dublin Fusiliers 62, 63, 196

Royal Irish Constabulary [RIC] 22, 23, 26, 107, 152, 214
Royal Irish Regiment 54
Royal Munster Fusiliers 62, 196
Royal Navy 75, 77, 190, 199
Rumpf, Erhard 179
Russell, T.W. 182
Russian Revolution 119
Ryan, Fr. Matt 179

Salamanca, Spain 106
Samuel, Herbert 137, 204
Samuels, Arthur Warren 27
San Francisco *Leader* 165
Saxonia 22
Scanlan, Michael 229
Scissors & Paste 29, 31, 36, 123
Scollan, John J. 30, 112
Scott, James C. 15
Separation Women 158, 159
1798 Rebellion 91
Shaw, George Bernard 221
Shaw, Mrs. George Bernard 54, 145
Sheehy, Lieut. Eugene 93
Sheehy-Skeffington, Francis 30, 53, 54, 84, 88, 106, 124, 145
Sheehy-Skeffington, Hanna 30, 53, 84, 142, 145, 146, 239
Sherlock, Lorcan 31, 169, 194
Shevchenko 119
Shields, Hugh 35
Shorter, Dora Sigerson 151
Shortt, Edward 78
Sinn Fein (Newspaper) 29, 31, 32, 36, 117, 124, 132, 181, 190, 192, 193
Sinn Fein (Party) 49, 50, 76, 87, 129, 149, 154, 157, 160, 164, 170, 175–7, 180, 183, 184, 193, 205, 206, 220, 235, 237, 239, 248
  accused of supporting *Lusitania* sinking, 75
  advertised as party of peace, 69
  anti-recruiting, 19
  Ard-Fheis (1917), 178
  at Mansion House Conference, 241
  by-election campaigns, 51

December 1918 General Election, 15, 17, 242, 246, 247
Department of Publicity, 27, 237
deportation of members after Easter Rising, 203
Food Committee, 184–6
Food Markets, 185
ineffectiveness of propaganda, 47
offices stormed, 245
opposition to war/reading material in clubs, 18
Public Health Department, 155
publication of 'Sinn Fein Notes', 29
publishes 'Tracts for our Times', 98
resistance to DRI, 24
sponsors lectures on German culture, 123
support from Australian Irish, 101
supported by Laurence Ginnell, 118
use of headquarters by *Young Ireland*, 31
use of propaganda, 44, 67, 89, 136, 138, 208
wartime by-elections, 46, 139, 174, 189, 212, 213, 232, 234, 240, 246
women's virtue compared to men's life, 153
16th (Irish) Division 64, 171, 196
Smith, Sidney 54
Smith-Gordon, Lionel 183
Somme, Battle of 17, 65, 201
South Dublin Union 212
Spark 30, 31, 33, 34, 36, 44, 48, 55, 61, 73, 86, 111, 118, 127–9, 132, 136, 149, 160, 161, 176, 197, 226, 228, 229, 232
Spillesey, Denis 195
St. Enda's 30, 132, 138, 167, 241
St Patrick's Cathedral 66
St Patrick's Total Abstinence League 139
St Stephen's Green 64
Stack, Austin 241
Stacpoole, H. De Vere 108
Staunton, Martin 16
Sullivan, A.M. 25
Sunday Chronicle 166

Suvla Bay 196
Sweetman, John 242
Synge, J.M. 160

T. Fisher Unwin 109
Tank Corps 25
Tennyson, Alfred, Lord 166. 234
Tennyson, 2nd Lord 22
10th (Irish) Division 196
The Times 44, 110, 111, 167, 231
36th (Ulster) Division 196
Tierney, Mark 48
Tivoli Music Hall, Dublin 152, 160
Tone, Wolfe 126, 208
Townshend, Charles 179
Treasury Office 174
Trinseach, Sadhbh 144
Tsar Nicholas II 119
Tucaig, Sibeal 236
Tynan, Katharine 17, 55

Umpire 166
Unionist Party 21
United Irish American Societies 195
United Irish League (UIL) 91, 193, 194
United Irishman 19, 91
Upton, Seamus ['Gilbert Galbraith'] 22, 30, 34, 86, 110, 197

venereal disease 154–7
Ventersburg, South Africa 99
Verdun, Battle of 65
Vigilance Committees 157, 160
Viviani, Rene 117, 160, 169

Walcheren Expedition (1809) 54
Walker, James 170
Walsh, J.J. 166, 203
War Office 20, 61, 73, 193
Waterford *Standard* 43
Weekly Irish Times 22
Wells, H.G. 122
West Australian *Record* 93
Western Front 64, 69, 197, 203, 213, 216
Wimborne, Lord 21, 23
Wimperis, Arthur 164

Women Volunteer Patrols 152, 153
Wood, Sir Evelyn 92
Worker 30
Worker's Republic 30, 58, 60, 64, 198
Wounded Knee, Battle of 114, 115

Yavorska, Madame 165

Yeats, Lily 15
Yorke, Father 165
Young Ireland (Eire Og) 30–4, 66, 70, 113–15, 132, 134, 138, 144, 167, 184, 185, 221, 240, 244
Young Ireland Movement 224
Ypres 202

113 → interesting on propaganda re. polluting Christian & catholic races of Europe by bringing non-white barbarians into the war

124 → German

127 Ger. invasion, fictional futures — 1st Nov. 1914. Irish passivity reason for good treatment by Germany + tolerance of Irish nationhood — not a conquest.

134 Irish language 'Are you learning Irish?' parody Kitchener poster

135-6 Fianna manliness

137 anti-Semitism, NB. Home Sec. Herbert Samuel

138-9 Catholicity

139-40 Pearse as perfect child

148 MacS. on 'marriage'

149-50. nationalist relationships

150 → women, garrison, prostitution

165 - 'Long Way to Tipperary'

167-8 Freemasonry, anti-Sem — NB. Nathan a Jew + ... a Freemason